S0-AEM-534

THE IMAGE OF MAN

A *Review of Politics* READER

THE IMAGE

OF MAN

EDITED BY *M. A. Fitzsimons*

Thomas T. McAvoy, C.S.C.

Frank O'Malley

UNIVERSITY OF NOTRE DAME PRESS

1959

© 1959
University of Notre Dame Press
Notre Dame, Indiana

*The Library of Congress has cataloged
this book as follows:*

   The Review of politics.
      The image of man; a Review of politics reader. Edited by
   M. A. Fitzsimons, Thomas T. McAvoy [and] Frank O'Malley.
   [Notre Dame, Ind.] University of Notre Dame Press, 1959.

      451 p. 24 cm.

      1. Political science—Collections. 1. Fitzsimons, M. A., ed. II. Title.

   JA37.R4   320.82   59–9119 ‡

   Library of Congress

TABLE OF CONTENTS

THE IMAGE OF MAN

TWENTY YEARS OF

THE REVIEW OF POLITICS

For twenty years *The Review of Politics,* concerned with the philosophical and historical approach to the problems of the human community, has drawn for sources of value and illumination upon the classical and Christian heritage. This is the heritage that brings real and lasting form to our present civilization, that enables it amidst terrifying complexities to endure. To reveal and to implement the strength of this heritage, with all that it tells of the nature and meaning of man, his history and his institutions, is clearly a tremendous task which the editors have faced and undertaken in complete humility.

In this volume, there is to be found a selection of important and representative articles printed during these last two decades. Naturally, no ready-made unity is possible. But the editors and the various contributors have worked in an essential singleness of spirit which is expressed in the manifold ways here embodied. And the image of man that unfolds is an intellectual and spiritual rather than a merely rationalist figuration. *The Review* is anti-positivist and anti-behavioral, without scorning or neglecting the fruitful contributions of such approaches. Not at all indifferent to science or techniques, as the record shows, the journal has devoted itself to the *art* of politics (the sovereign conception of Aristotle), involving as it must every idea, matter, and action that deeply touch the life of man.

Although the development of *The Review* has been specifically affected by the tradition and thought of the Catholic Church, the journal altogether has provided a remarkable meeting-ground for scholars of various faiths and religious as well as intellectual connections from all over the world. Foreign authors have helped mightily to shape the character of *The Review.* Constantly and increasingly American writers have given excellent sustenance to the editors' intentions. It is most regrettable that many splendid essays have had to be omitted from this volume (actually some of the omitted have already been widely reprinted and the ones included seem more badly needed). At any rate, on this twentieth-anniversary occasion, the editors have only unlimited thanks to offer all those, present and absent, who have so greatly accommodated the spirit of *The Review of Politics,* so richly justified its foundation, maintained its progress, and warranted its future.

I

THE CHRISTIAN VIEW

OF MAN

AND SOCIETY

INTEGRAL HUMANISM

AND THE CRISIS

OF MODERN TIMES

Jacques Maritain

[1939]

I THE CRISIS OF MODERN TIMES

To AVOID misunderstanding, I should note at once that my point of view here is not that of the mere logic of ideas and doctrines, but that of the *concrete logic of the events of history.*

From the first point of view, that of the mere logic of ideas and doctrines, it is evident that there are many possible positions other than the "pure" positions which I shall examine. One might ask theoretically and in the abstract, what value these various positions have. That is not what I plan to do. In a word, my point of view is that of the philosophy of culture, and not that of metaphysics.

From this point of view, that of the concrete logic of the events of human history, I think that we may be satisfied with a rather general definition of humanism, such as the following:

To leave the discussion quite open, let us say that humanism (and such a definition may itself be developed along quite divergent lines) tends essentially to make man more truly human, and to manifest his original grandeur by enabling him to participate in everything which can enrich him in nature and history (by concentrating the world in man, almost in Max Scheler's words, and by making man as large as the world); it demands that man develop his powers, his creative energies and the life of reason, and at the same time labor to make the forces of the physical world instruments of his freedom. Certainly the great pagan wisdom, which, according to the author of the *Eudemian Ethics,* aimed to link itself to "that which is better than reason, being the source of reason," cannot be cut off from the humanistic tradition; and we are thus warned never to *define* humanism by excluding all

5

reference to the superhuman and by foreswearing all transcendence.

What is it that I call the concrete logic of the events of history? It is a concrete development determined on the one hand by the internal logic of ideas and doctrines, and on the other hand by the human milieu within which these ideas operate and by the contingencies of history as well as by the acts of liberty produced in history. Necessity and contingency are quite remarkably adjusted in this concrete logic, and to designate this logic we may use the word "dialectic" in the sense I have just expressed, a sense neither Hegelian nor Marxist.

And because we are here in the practical and existential order of human life, with the exigencies of the universe of desire and of its concrete ends, of passion and action, this dialectic involves a movement much swifter and much more violent than that of abstract logic. Positions theoretically tenable (rightly or not) are swept aside, because practically they appear at once *unlivable,* I do not say for such and such individual, but for the common consciousness.

Here we see the peculiar vice of classical humanism; this vice, in my judgment, concerns not so much what this humanism affirms, as what it negates, denies and divides; it is what we may call an *anthropocentric* conception of man and of culture. I am aware that this word is not too felicitous, but I have used it for want of a better. We might say that the error in question is the idea of nature as self-enclosed or self-sufficient.

Instead of an *open* human nature and an *open* reason, and these are real nature and real reason, people make out that there exist a nature and a reason isolated by themselves and *shut up* in themselves, excluding everything which is not themselves.

Instead of a development of man and reason in continuity with the Gospel, people demand such a development from pure reason apart from the Gospel.

And for human life, for the concrete movement of history, this means real and serious amputations.

Prayer, divine love, supra-rational truths, the idea of sin and of grace, the evangelical beatitudes, the necessity of asceticism, of contemplation, of the way of the Cross—all this is either put in parentheses or is once for all denied. In the concrete government of human life, reason is isolated from the supra-rational.

It is isolated also from all that is irrational in man, or it denies this—always in virtue of the very sophism that what is "non-rational," in the sense of not reducible to reason itself, would be "non-rational" in the sense of anti-rational or incompatible with reason. On the one hand, the life proper to the universe of will is ignored; and the non-rational in the very world of knowledge is equally ignored. On

6

the other hand, the whole world of the infra-rational, of instincts, of obscure tendencies, of the unconscious, along with that which it includes of malicious and indeed of demonic, but also of fecund reserves, is put in parentheses and modestly forgotten.

Thus, little by little, will spring up the man conformable to the pattern of *bourgeois pharisaism,* that respectable conventional man in whom the nineteenth century long believed, and in whose unmasking Marx, Nietzsche, and Freud will glory; and they really have unmasked him, while in the very act disfiguring man himself.

And at the same time, enormous promises have been made to man, ever since the days of Descartes. Wait but a while, they are told, and Progress will automatically bring about a complete felicity of release and repose, an earthly beatitude.

Very well, but *that will not do,* as the continuation of the story of history has shown. Having given up God so as to be self-sufficient, now man is losing track of his soul, he looks in vain for himself, he turns the universe upside-down, trying to find himself, he finds masks, and behind the masks death.

And then we witness the spectacle of a tidal wave of irrationality. Then comes the awakening of a tragic opposition between life and intelligence.

This opposition was begun by Luther, and carried on by Rousseau. But certain phenomena of symbiosis, which I have not time to analyze here, took place later.[1] Today this opposition appears sometimes in servile forms, for example in the form of the philosophy of Klages, or in the form of racism, or in the greatly simplified form of certain military men who shout: "Death to intelligence." I shall return to this point in a moment.

It appears also in noble and very noble forms—I am thinking of Nietzsche, of Kierkegaard, of Karl Barth, of Chestov. But even here, no matter with what intelligence they develop the theme that intelligence comes from the serpent, and no matter with what generosity they try to salvage human values, this position unmistakably gives way to what one may call a *counter-humanism.* I am not blind to the fact that one might raise objections here and ask whether a humanism defending man against reason is not conceivable. But my point is precisely that if we set out to defend man, not against a certain use of reason, but against reason itself, and against knowledge, the result—inevitably and in spite of everything—will be a counter-humanism.

Here it is evident that reason has been imperilled by rational-

---

[1] Notably in France, the Rousseauist current was swept away by the counter-current, the current of rationalistic humanism, which was later to be reinforced by the strong sentimental dynamism of Rousseauism.

ism, and humanism by anthropocentric humanism. Terrible voices rise up in man, crying out: We've had enough of lying optimism and illusory moralities, enough of hypocritical justice and hypocritical right, enough of the liberty which starves workmen and burns the stacks of grain, enough of the idealism which does us to death, which denies evil and unhappiness and robs us of the means of struggling against them; take us back to the great spiritual fruitfulness of the abyss, and the absurd, and the ethics of despair.

The lofty counter-humanism of a Kierkegaard or a Barth may be regarded as a mistaken Christian position. In Barth particularly it is a reactionary and archaic position, in as much as it signifies a will to absolute purification by a reversion to the past—in fact, a return to primitive Lutheranism. In Nietzsche it was rather a bewildered Christianity: no longer able to adore, he denied and blasphemed, and nevertheless he still sought and still loved. And all these lofty forms of counter-humanism—because in them is a spirit which protests against itself and destroys itself with a kind of Promethean generosity—still preserve admirable values of humanity and spirituality. But they are only of the passing moment, for they give way fatally to the servile forms of which I spoke a moment ago. Poor Nietzsche! The truly terrifying voice, the fatal voice is not the voice of Nietzsche, it is the voice of that mediocre and base multitude whose mediocrity and baseness themselves appear as apocalyptic signs, a voice which scatters to the four winds of humanity the gospel of the hatred of reason, in the form of the cult of the fecundity of war or in that of the cult of race and blood.

When love and holiness do not transform our human condition and change slaves into sons of God, the Law makes many victims. Nietzsche could not bear the sight of the lame and halt of Christianity; more even than Goethe, he rebelled against the Cross; he dreamed of a Dionysian superman, who was a fiction. Dionysius! The newspapers and radio give us news of him every morning and inform us as he leads his dance through the concentration camps, and the new ghettos where thousands of Jews are condemned to a slow death, through the cities of China and Spain eviscerated by bombs, through Europe maddened in an armament race and feverishly preparing for suicide. Nietzsche could not see that man must choose between two ways: the way of Calvary and the way of slaughter. The irrational tidal movement is in reality the tragic wheel of rationalistic humanism; it reacts against a humanism of reason closed up in itself, but it does so by leaving man open to the powers from below, shutting him off from higher communications and the spirit which liberates, and walling the creature up in the abyss of animal vitality.

We witness another spectacle, one quite the contrary, the spectacle of a continuation, aggravation, and exasperation of anthropocentric humanism in the direction which it had followed from its origin, in the direction of rationalistic hopes, now constituted no longer solely as philosophical religion, but as a lived religion. This development consists in the drawing out of all the consequences of the principle that *man alone and through himself alone, works out his salvation.*

The purest instance of this tendency is that of Marxism. No matter how strong some of the pessimistic aspects of Marxism may be, it remains attached to this postulate. Marx turned Hegelianism over— he put Hegelian dialectics (as Engels said) on its feet instead of on its head; but he remained rationalistic, so much so that for him the movement proper to matter is a *dialectical* movement. In Marxist materialism, it is not irrational instinct or biological mysticism, but reason which decapitates reason.

Man alone and through himself alone works out his salvation. Hence this salvation is purely and exclusively temporal; this salvation is accomplished naturally *without God,* since man is truly alone and acts truly alone only if God does not exist; and even *against God,* I mean against whatever in man and the human milieu is the image of God, that is to say, from this point of view, the image of heteronomy. This salvation demands the organization of humanity into one body whose supreme destiny is not to see God but to gain supreme dominion in history. It is a position which still declares itself humanistic, but it is radically atheistic and it thereby destroys in reality the humanism which it professes in theory. It is well known that dialectical materialism claims to be heir to classical humanism, and Engels used to write that the revolutionary proletariat was the heir to classical German philosophy. If it is true this is the most pure and therefore the most active form of the spiritual impulse which appeared earlier in the quite different form of rationalistic humanism, we understand that the god of rationalism does not count in the presence of this atheism, and that what remained of disaffected Christianity in classical rationalism is like a cake of starch in relation to such an alcohol. As for the humanism to which it invites us, the way in which revolutionary materialistic dialectic, as lived for twenty years in the country it conquered, has devoured its leaders, reduced their morality to that of the end justifying the means, and put to death or persecuted thousands of suspected men—this is sufficient to edify us on that subject.

There is finally a position removed as far from anthropocentric humanism as from anti-humanist irrationalism. This is the Christian humanistic position, according to which the misfortune of classical humanism was not to have been humanism but to have been anthropocentric; not to have hoped in reason, but to have isolated reason and to have left it to dry out; not to have sought liberty, but to have orientated itself toward the myth of the democracy of the individual, instead of toward the historical ideal of the democracy of the person.

In short, in this view the modern world has sought good things by bad ways; it has thus compromised the search for authentic human values, which men must save now by an intellectual grasp of a profounder truth, by a substantial recasting of humanism. In my opinion, we have today to deal with a considerable liquidation—a liquidation of five centuries of classical culture—the culture in question being a brilliant dissolution (in which new creative forces appear) of mediaeval civilization. It is the merit of Irving Babbitt and Paul Elmer More to have called attention to the historical necessity of a new humanism, and to the responsibilities of Rousseau in the tragedy of modern humanism. What I wanted to indicate in the preceding analysis is the breadth of this tragedy, the double responsibility of the rationalistic current and the irrationalistic current (the latter nevertheless depending on the former, as reaction on action), and the breadth with which we have as a consequence to conceive a new humanism. A new humanism ought then to be new in a singularly profound sense: it ought to evolve within the movement of history and create something new in relation to these five centuries that are behind us; if it has not such power to renew, it is nothing.

The new humanism must re-assume in a purified climate all the work of the classical age; it must re-make the science of man, find the rehabilitation and the "dignification" of the creature not in isolation, not in its being shut up in itself, but in its openness to the world of the divine and supra-rational; and this implies in practice a work of sanctification of the profane and temporal; it means, in the spiritual order, the discovery of the *ways of childhood* whereby the "humanity of God our Savior," as Saint Paul says, finds, with fewer human trappings, a readier way into man, and causes more souls to enter into His hidden task of suffering and vivifying; it involves, in the moral and social order, the discovery of a deeper and fuller sense of the dignity of the human person, so that man would re-find himself in God refound, and would direct social work toward an heroic ideal of brotherly love, itself conceived not as a spontaneous return of feeling to some illusory primitive condition, but as a difficult and painful conquest of the spirit, a work of grace and virtue.

Such a humanism, which considers man in the wholeness of his natural and supernatural being, and which sets no *a priori* limit to the descent of the divine into man, we may call the *humanism of the Incarnation.* It is an "integral" and "progressive" Christian position, which I believe conforms to representative principles of the genuine spirit of Thomism. And I am happy to find in agreement with it, not all theologians (that would be too much, and is never the case) but some theologians such as Père Chenu, Abbé Journet, and many others.

In the perspectives of this integral humanism, there is no occasion to choose, so as to sacrifice one or the other, between the vertical movement toward eternal life (present and actually begun here below) and the horizontal movement whereby the substance and creative forces of man are progressively revealed in history. These two movements should be pursued at the same time. To claim to sacrifice the second to the first is a sin of Manichaeism. But to claim to sacrifice the first to the second is materialistic nonsense. And the second, unless it is to turn to the destruction of man, is effected only when vitally joined to the first, because this second movement, while having its own proper and properly temporal finalities, and tending to better man's condition here below, also prepares in history the Kingdom of God, which, for each individual person and for the whole of humanity, is something meta-historical.

II SOME PROBLEMS

To examine all the problems raised by the preceding considerations would try the patience of the reader; these problems are in fact infinite. Let us eliminate first of all the problem of the *chances of realization,* near or remote, of an integral humanism such as I have tried to characterize. It is clear that the world's trend toward barbarism, now passing before our eyes at an accelerated speed, seems singularly unfavorable to such an occurrence. But the essential thing, if not for our dearest human interest, at least for our philosophy, is to know whether this true humanism answers to the tendencies of the creative forces which act in history simultaneously with the forces of degradation and disintegration, and which act more or less masked by them. If so, it will be necessary that the true humanism have its day, even though it be after a night of several centuries, comparable to the night of the early middle ages.

Next, it is proper to remark that the crisis of civilization, as it appears today in the concrete, is very far from being reduced to an opposition between the "pure" forms and tendencies of which I spoke in the first part of this essay.

Moreover, if we consider that complex ensemble of forces which we may call, in a general sense, totalitarian, we need to make a very neat distinction between their principle in the pure state and the realizations which it has or will produce in this or that place, and in which the contingency, resistance, and germination of life occasion all sorts of mixtures and, sometimes, attenuations.

Then, finally, it is just to say that in many aspects communist totalitarianism on the one hand (totalitarianism of the social community), and on the other hand, fascist totalitarianism (of the political State) or national socialism (of the racial community)—these two opposed species of totalitarianism present profound analogies and even phenomena of osmosis: not only in the order of political techniques, but in the order of principles themselves. Yet between these principles and these philosophical roots there are profound differences.

In spite of the combative pessimism imprinted on it by Marxism, communism has as metaphysical root an absolutely optimistic philosophy of man, that great optimistic mysticism which began with rationalism and was continued by the Encyclopedists, then by Jean-Jacques Rousseau, then by utopian socialism, on the one hand, and Hegelian philosophy, on the other. Practically, it denies that man is a creature of God, because it is unwilling to recognize in man that which comes from nothingness. Because of this optimistic basis, it does not profess to be totalitarian; the totalitarian principle is immanent in it as a vice and fatality, which one does not profess.

Fascism, on the contrary, has as metaphysical root an absolute pessimism of a rather voluntaristic and Machiavellian sort. Practically, it denies that man comes from the hand of God, and that he maintains within him, in spite of everything, the grandeur and dignity of such an origin. This pessimism, which invokes incontestable empiric truths, turns these truths into ontological lies, because the fact that man comes from God does not matter to it. Then it despairs of man —I mean of the human person, the individual person—in favor of the State. Not God but the State will create man; the State by its constraints will oblige man to come forth from the nothingness of the anarchy of the passions, and lead an upright and even a heroic life.

As for national socialism, it also makes the most fundamental mistake about the nature of man, since in practice it basically refuses to see in man the creature and image of God, and it uses man as zoological material: man must become the apotheosis of the telluric, primitive, and divine (demonic) element which is developed in him and by him, that is to say, in his blood and by his predestinated blood, in such a way that a quite apparently combative optimism, which is trust in force, is added to a fundamentally pessimistic conception of human nature.

Because of this pessimism, national socialism and fascism proclaim themselves totalitarian, and the totalitarian principle is raised up by them as a shield and standard.

In a word, looking at these two opposed totalitarian species, we might say that practically, existentially, we have on the one hand an atheism which declares that God does not exist and yet makes its own god of an idol; and on the other hand an atheism which declares indeed that God does exist, but makes of God himself an idol, because it denies in act if not in word the nature and transcendence of God: it invokes God, but as a spirit-protector attached to the glory of a people or a State, or as the demon of the race.

These remarks were made to avoid confusion. I would return now to the purely anti-Christian position of which I spoke at the outset, and which it would be better to call "anti-Christ," because it is less a question of doctrinal opposition to Christianity than of an existential opposition to the presence and action of Christ at the center of human history. To be brief, it is on the problems of the religious significance of racism and communism that I would say a few words. In this section I shall not speak of fascism, because, for various reasons on which I have not time to dwell, the religious or mystical dynamism of fascism is feeble (on the one hand, the resistance of the Catholic Church puts a considerable check on the pagan mysticism of Empire, on the other the idea of the State lends itself less readily to serve as substitute for the religious bond than does the idea of racial community); however, because of that, it is difficult for it not to submit, in this domain, to forms that are more virulent.

Let us consider first the racial principle in its pure state. From the point of view of the nexus of ideas, it appears that racism is, as we said, above all an irrational reaction. Think of the actual status of scholars in the country which seemed to have vowed forever to venerate them: racism is a protest of the man in the street against the scholar! More profoundly, it is a pathological protest, nourishing itself on the most absurd pedantry (but in such case, the more absurd the pedantry, the more efficacious it is), a pathological protest of nature with all its forces of vitality and ferocity rising out of the depths of mother-earth, with its needs of euphoria and power and physical beauty, with the implacable rage which can exalt instinct when the spirit betrays itself and becomes engulfed in animality, a protest against the messengers of the absolute and transcendent who had not sufficiently shared the miseries of human kind.

For we should recognize the chastisement exercised here against that primacy of the ideal unfaithful to itself, and, so far, artificial and hypocritical, which was the great vice of the Kantian nineteenth century and which we may call a clericalism of the reason. The world of elementary values in nature, of physical courage, of simplicity, no matter if brutal and gross; of that sort of natural, if cynical, candor by which the animal is not ashamed to exist nor has need to justify existence; the world of primitive feelings, of pacts such as exist even in the horde, of the instinct of physical solidarity such as exists among robbers, of the need of being together and feeling together such as exists even in the great herds on the prairies—this world can indeed be disciplined by true wisdom, which does not despise it and which turns it toward transformations of the spirit. But against false wisdom which humiliates and deceives it, some day or other it takes terrible revenge.

A mystic hatred of all intellectual or moral subtlety, of wisdom and all asceticism is thus developed; and at the same time a powerful religiosity, the natural religiosity inherent in the human substance down to its elementary physical fibers. God is invoked, but only in virtue of the testimony, if I may say so, of these elementary fibers and of the desire of nature written in the biological elements of the human being; and (because of the basic reactionary process which I indicated) He is invoked *against* the God of the spirit, of intelligence and love—excluding and hating this God. What an extraordinary spiritual phenomenon this is: people believe in God, and yet do not know God. The idea of God is affirmed, and at the same time disfigured and perverted. A God who will end by being identified with an invincible force at work in the blood is set up against the God of Sinai and against the God of Calvary, against transcendent Being, *He who is* and who dwells in inaccessible glory, against the Word who was at the beginning, against the God of whom it is said that He is Love. We are facing, not a pseudo-scientific atheism, but, if I may speak thus, a demonic para-theism which, while declining wisdom, is open to every kind of occultism, and which is not less anti-Christian than is atheism.

Of course, if it were not perverted thus, the testimony I just spoke of, that of the natural desire of God inherent in the elementary physical fibers of the human being, is in itself authenic and valid. Will it some day be able to free itself from the unregulated affective forces which set it against the testimony of the spirit? If so, on what conditions? And by what processes? Well, in any case, racism as it exists and acts in reality today and in the minds of today will have been evacuated.

This is because, if we take the point of view not only of the nexus of ideas but of society in the concrete, we see that racism is existentially bound to this demonic para-theism. For in its reaction against individualism and its thirst for a communion, it seeks this communion in human animality, which, separated from the spirit, is no more than a biological inferno. In the metaphysics of society in the concrete, the god of the community of the blood can only be the demon of the blood. Racial neo-paganism is thus lower than the paganism of classical antiquity, which was faithful to eternal laws and to the supreme Divinity. It brings into existence again the lowest elements of paganism.

The account of atheism and communism calls for a like discussion. From the point of view of the connection of ideas, one sees that the genesis of communism in Marx is of the philosophical order; it proceeds from impulses received from the Hegelian left and from Feuerbach; in Marx the theory of the alienation of work by private property presupposes *de facto,* before becoming first *de jure,* the Feuerbachian theory of the alienation of conscience by the idea of God.

And more profoundly, the discovery of historical materialism as Marx conceived it, implies an absolutely atheistic position; because it implies a universal process of substitution of the dialectic of history for all transcendent causality, and for the universe of Christianity in general; it implies consequently an absolute realist and naturalistic immanentism, by hypothesis exclusive of all divine transcendence.

For Marx, then, the historical and sociological action of religion works *necessarily* against the emancipation of the proletariat, because it is the action of a factor of the superstructure which is originally determined only by the need of justifying the economic exploitation of man by man.

If the master-idea of historical materialism can be purified, so as to designate henceforth only the essential (but not principal) importance of material causality in history, it is on condition that it break with Marxism, and replace the outlook of Hegelian dialectic by that of the fourfold causality of Aristotle.

This basic atheistic principle explains why the *existence* of class struggle (resulting from the capitalistic structure of economics) gave rise in Marx to a theoretic and practical *conceptualization* turning the class-struggle into a gesture of atheism, I mean a moral secession fully accepted by the dispossessed class, by the accursed of the earth, from the political community, which, no matter how oppressive and inhuman its economic structure might be, holds its natural value from God. This same basic atheistic principle explains also why, as the Webbs report, one of the deepest features of the new civilization worked out in the Soviet Republics is anti-godism; and why, as they also report, a formal pledge of atheism and of repudiation of every form of the supernatural is required in Russia of every adherent to the Communist Party, and even of every candidate for that party.

Are there yet other potentialities in Marxism? Because in Marx —as I have just tried to explain, by reason of a presupposed atheism —the social problem of the emancipation of the proletariat has in fact the priority over the metaphysical and religious problem, the class war over the anti-religious war, can we conceive within Marxism a development allowing a clearly affirmed dissociation between social theory and a materialistic conception of the world, and, on the other hand, a revision of the naive atheism which Marx held in the nineteenth century? If so, on what conditions? And by what processes? Well, in any case, communism as it exists and acts in reality today and in the minds of today would have to be evacuated.

This is because, if we take the point of view not only of the connection of ideas but of society in the concrete, we see that communism is existentially bound to atheism. For if it reacts against individualism, if it thirsts for communion, it does so without finding a principle superior to anthropocentric humanism; quite on the contrary, it aggravates the latter and seeks this communion in economic activity, in pure productivity, which, considered as the proper locus and homeland of human activity, is only a world of a beheaded reason, of reason without God. In the metaphysics of concrete social fact, the god of the industrial community can only be human reason as demiurgic manufacturer, the titanism of industry. Communism thus transforms Christian communion into another, a quite temporal communion, which is achieved by the abolition of private property.

Under this heading of communism and racism, we may make a concluding remark. If it is true that in the dialectic of culture, communism is the final state of anthropocentric rationalism, we see that in virtue of the universality inherent in reason, even in reason gone mad, communism is all-embracing, and sets itself against Christianity by pretending to substitute for the universalism of the Mystical Body of Christ its own earthly universalism; whereas racism, on its irrational and biological basis, sets itself against Christianity by rejecting all universalism, and by breaking even the natural unity of the human family, so as to impose the hegemony of a so-called higher racial essence.

We see also that communism tends, quite in the line of industrialistic rationalism and of capitalistic materialism, toward a transformation of economics by annihilating the ultimate cadres of bourgeois society, and that its directive elements are furnished it especially by a working population whose thought a century of socialistic tradition has disciplined in a revolutionary direction. Racism, on the contrary, and fascism do indeed exert on the energies of bourgeois society a high revolutionary pressure, and they do detest capitalism, but—being, above all, reactionary processes—they do not go on to a social transformation destructive of the ultimate machinery of capitalistic society. It is by another road, preferably by war, that they threaten its destruction. The masses on whom they depend belong especially to the middle classes on the path to proletarianism, classes whose affective mobility is very great. The personal magnetism of the leaders plays a major part; but the leaders could not make their enterprise succeed without the aid given them by strong privileged interests anxious to safeguard their own position.

III THE WORLD AND CHRISTIAN CONSCIENCE

A characteristic of the humanism which I call integral would be that, far from being limited to the élite, it would care for the masses, for their right to work and to a spiritual life, and for the movement which brings them, we may say, to an historically full age. On the social significance of such a humanism, I will simply say that in my opinion it should assume the task of radically transforming the temporal order, a task which would tend to substitute for bourgeois civilization, and for an economic system based on the fecundity of money, not a collectivist economy, but a "personalist" civilization and a "personalist" economy, through which would stream a temporal refraction of the truths of the Gospel.

This task is joined to a thorough awakening of the religious conscience, and I wish to insist on this point. One of the worst vices of the modern world is its dualism, the dissociation between the things of God and the things of the world. The latter, the things of the social, economic, and political life, have been abandoned to their own carnal law, removed from the exigencies of the Gospel. The result is that they have become more and more unlivable. At the same time, Christian ethics, not really carried out in the social life of peoples, became in this connection, I do not say in itself or in the Church, I say in the world, in the general cultural behavior, a universe of formulas and words; and this universe of formulas and words was in effect vassalized, in practical cultural behavior, by the real energies of this same temporal world existentially detached from Christ. Such a disorder can be remedied only by a renewal of the profoundest energies of religious conscience rising into temporal existence.

On the other hand, modern civilization, which pays dearly today for the past, seems as if it were pushed by the very contradictions and fatalities suffered by it, toward contrasting forms of misery and intensified materialism. To rise above these fatalities we need an awakening of liberty and of its creative forces, we need the energies of spiritual and social resurrection of which man does not become capable by favor of the State or any partisan pedagogy, but by a love which fixes the center of his life infinitely above the world and temporal history. In particular, the general paganization of our civilization has resulted in man's placing his hope in force alone and in the efficacy of hate, whereas in the eyes of an integral humanism, a political ideal of brotherly love alone can direct the work of authentic social regeneration: and it follows that to prepare a new age of the world, martyrs of love of neighbor may first be necessary. And this also shows how all depends here on a profound renewal of the interior energies of conscience.

Granted what I just said about the pathological process of vassalization, in the behavior of contemporary civilization, of religious formulas by worldly energies, we see that the renewal we speak of should be a kind of Copernican revolution, which would in no way affect doctrine, not even an iota of it, but would make a great change in the relative importance of the elements in the universe of action. It would consist in a general and bold acknowledgment of the primacy of the vital and the real (even the implicitly or virtually real) over matters of appearance and external formulation, let us say—for I am thinking primarily of the Christian conscience—of the primacy of the practically or vitally Christian over the nominally or decoratively Christian. Such a Copernican revolution would have notable consequences for the question of the ways and means of political action.

Truly speaking, it is the idea of the primacy of the spiritual which here dominates the debate. To say that Christianity will remake itself through Christian means or that it will unmake itself completely; to say that no good is to be expected from the enterprises of violence and constraint—with no compunction of heart and no interior reform or inner creative principle—enterprises animated by the same spirit which is at the elemental source of the evils actually suffered by civilization; to say that the witness and the patient and persevering action of the Christian spirit in the world is more important than the outer apparel of a Christian order, especially when those who pretend to save this order bind themselves, and also the order, either to established injustice or even to the immense pagan energies sweeping away one part of the actual world—this is simply to affirm that the principle of the primacy of the spiritual demands respect in the very mode in which men work to give it reality; it is simply to affirm that the primacy of the spiritual cannot be realized while denying itself.

I add that if it is true that the leaven of the Pharisees, against which Christ put us on our guard, represents—as Père Fessard, a Jesuit well known in Paris, has pointed out in one of his books— a standing temptation for the religious conscience, and if it is true that this leaven will not be totally expelled from the world till the end of time, then we must say that the renewal of the religious conscience of which I speak would be a step in the right direction, and a signal victory in the never-ending struggle of the religious conscience against Pharisaism.

At the same time, it seems clear to me that, in the temporal order, an attitude corresponding to what has always been called the liberty of the Christian before the world and the powers of the flesh, is the only one to safeguard—tomorrow and the day after, either as a favorable solution of the present crisis or as a dawn after a long night —the hope of men in the terrestrial efficacy of the Gospel, and of reason.

ON THE CHRISTIAN

IDEA OF MAN

Josef Pieper

[1949]

THE second part of the *Summa Theologica* of the "Universal Doctor," Thomas Aquinas, begins with the following sentence: *Because man has been created in God's image, now after having spoken of God, the archetype, we must still deal with His image which is man. (Summa Theologica I, II, Prologus.)* There is something peculiar about this sentence; its meaning must not be misunderstood. It is stated as a matter of fact but its meaning is not to be taken for granted. This first sentence of Moral Theology expresses a fact which has almost entirely disappeared from the knowledge of Christians of today; namely, the fact that moral doctrine is primarily and above all a doctrine about man; that moral doctrine must plainly reveal the conception of man, and that, therefore, the doctrine of Christian morals must concern the Christian model of man. This fact was a matter of course in the Christianity of the high Middle Ages. This fundamental conception—which, to be sure, was not definitely taken for granted as the polemical wording shows—compelled Eckhart to say two generations after St. Thomas: people should not think about what they ought to do, they should rather think about what they ought to be. But later on Moral Theology and above all moral preaching and exposition more or less lost this awareness. This is so true that textbooks of Moral Theology, which explicitly professed to be written "in the spirit of St. Thomas" differed with him on this main point. Here lies the root of the fact that the average Christian of today does not expect to find in moral doctrine anything about the true being of man or anything about the idea of man at all. On the contrary, the average Christian is wont to associate with the conception "moral doctrine" the idea of a doctrine about the deed and especially about the omission, about the permissible and especially about the impermissible, about what is bidden and especially about what is forbidden. But the first moral thesis of the "Universal Doctor" remains: moral doctrine must deal with the true conception of man. Naturally it must also treat of actions, of duties, of commandments, and of sins. But its primary subject is the right being of man, the idea of the good man.

The resolution of this problem of the Christian idea of man can be given in one sentence, even in one word: *Christ.* The Christian ought to be another Christ; he ought to be perfect like the Father of Jesus Christ. But this idea of the perfection of the Christian, all-comprehensive and, therefore, inexhaustible, needs to be analyzed, applied, and interpreted. Without such interpretation proceeding from the empirical nature of man and reality, this idea would always be exposed to the danger of abuse and misunderstanding, caused by short-circuiting. It is impossible to derive directly the concrete action in the concrete situation from the highest and ultimate idea of perfection. "Be perfect as your Father in heaven." It is precisely this formulation of the ultimate idea of a Christian to which the fourth Council referred in its famous sentence of the *analogia entis: inter Creatorem et creaturam non potest tanta similitudo notari, quin inter eos maior sit dissimilitudo notanda.* (Such a great similarity between Creator and creature cannot be mentioned without at the same time mentioning a still greater dissimilarity.) This sentence is directed against the possibility of a direct deification of man. Man, the Christian, albeit the perfect Christian, remains a creature, a finite being, even in eternal life. Now there certainly is more than one way of interpreting this ultimate Christian idea, not only "theoretically" but also historically. There are, for instance, an Eastern-Christian and a Western-Christian form of interpretation.

Thomas Aquinas, the great teacher of Western Christianity, decided to express the Christian idea of man in seven theses which may be summarized as follows:

1. The Christian is a man who—in faith—becomes aware of the Triune God.
2. The Christian—in hope—waits for the final fulfillment of his nature in Eternal Life.
3. The Christian—in the divine virtue of charity—inclines towards God and his fellowmen with an affirmation exceeding all natural power of love.
4. The Christian is prudent, that is, he does not permit the Yes and No of the will to disturb his view of reality; on the contrary, he makes the Yes or No of the will depend on the truth of actual things.
5. The Christian is just, that is, he is able to live in truth "with

the other"; he is conscious of being a member with others in the Church, in the nation, and in every community.

6. The Christian is brave, that is, he is ready to suffer wounds and, if need be, death for the sake of truth and the realization of justice.

7. The Christian is moderate, that is, he does not allow his will to have and his will to enjoy to destroy himself.

These seven theses suggest that the ethics of classical theology, as an explanation of the idea of man, is essentially a doctrine of virtues. More exactly they interpret the Biblical description of the perfection of the Christian by means of the sevenfold image of the three theological and the four cardinal virtues. It is, I think, most important to reveal once more to the general consciousness of our time this grand fresco of the idea of man as originally expressed in classical theology, a fresco which has faded to some extent and—even worse—which has been painted over many a time. This idea of man is significant not merely as a matter of "historical" interest, as a matter of showing "how it actually was." This interpretation of the ultimate human ideal is one that continues to hold good and it is, I think, truly essential for us to see clearly and to accept this idea of man. I shall now try to mark the contours of this image, above all in the realm of the four cardinal virtues, particularly at those points where the image has faded or has been painted over.

At the outset something must be said about the conception of virtue in itself. A few years ago, in a speech on virtue addressed to the Academie Française, Paul Valéry said: "Virtue, gentlemen, the word virtue is dead, or at least it is dying. It no longer presents itself as a direct expression of a conceivable reality of our time. Rather, I have heard it mentioned in social conversation only rarely and then in an ironical sense. This could mean that I mix with bad company only, unless I add that I don't remember ever having found virtue in today's books, in those most often read and most highly esteemed. Furthermore I do not know of any paper which prints it, nor, I am afraid, would risk printing this word without a humorous intention. So it has come about that the words 'virtue' and 'virtuous' can be found only in the catechism, in the Academy and in comic operas." This diagnosis of Paul Valéry is undoubtedly correct. But there is no reason to be too much surprised by it. On the one hand, it certainly indicates an entirely natural phenomenon, the natural fate of great words. On the other hand, it is quite possible that in a de-christianized era, demoniacal rules of language will effectively prevail. Accordingly, the good will appear as ridiculous in the "usage" of a language. Apart from this possibility we must not forget that Christian moral literature and moral preaching have not always made it very easy for the average man to perceive the true sense of the conception and the reality of virtue.

Virtue does not signify the mere correctness of an isolated action or omission. Rather virtue signifies that man *is* right in the supernatural and natural sense. Virtue means the enhancing of the being of man. Virtue is, as Thomas says, the *ultimum potentiae (Quaest. disp. de virtutibus in communi 17)*, the ultimate of what man is able to be. The virtuous man "is" the man who develops goodness through his deeds out of his innermost inclination and substance. No less important than the correct and true notion of virtue is a true insight into the hierarchy of the virtues. Today there is much talk about the "heroic" character of Christianity or about the "heroic" conception of life as the distinguishing characteristic of Christian life. Such expressions are only half-true and, therefore, half-false. The first and distinguishing virtue of the Christian is the supernatural love of God and neighbor. And all the divine virtues are superior to the cardinal virtues. And under the cardinal virtues bravery is not the first, but the third.

II

Among the cardinal virtues prudence ranks first. Prudence is not only the first among otherwise equivalent virtues; but it "gives birth" to all moral virtue. This thesis about the priority of prudence, the true meaning of which we are scarcely able to conceive, expresses more than a mere accidental sequence of the cardinal virtues. As it is, it expresses the fundamental constitution of reality in relation to the realm of ethics. Good presupposes truth and truth presupposes reality. For what does the priority of prudence mean? It means nothing but the realization of good presupposing the awareness of reality. The first thing that is demanded of an active man is that he should be knowing, as St. Thomas says (*Quaest. disp. de virtutibus card. 17*). Whoever does not know the true condition of real things cannot do good; for good is that which complies with reality. Naturally, here "knowledge" does not mean knowledge in the sense of the exact notions of modern science. What it does mean is real contact with objective reality. This contact, for instance, may be reached by a mode of revelation superior to the "scientific" mode. To prudence belongs also the quality of docility, which means an attentive submission to the genuine knowledge of a superior mind. In prudence the unbiased perception of reality is decisive for our actions. So the prudent person, on the one hand, looks at the objective reality of things, and on the other hand, concerns himself with the willing and doing. But it is the reality at which he looks in the first place. And then, in virtue of the knowledge of reality he decides what is to be done and what not, and how it should be done and how not. So, really, all virtue depends upon prudence. And somehow all sin contradicts prudence, *omne peccatum opponitur prudentiae* (*Summa Theologica,* II, II, 119, 37). Our habit of language, which is also our habit of thinking, has rather considerably deviated from this statement. According to our usage, prudence seems to be an evasion rather than a presupposition of good. It is hard for us to believe that it should always and necessarily be prudent to be just and true. And prudence and bravery above all seem to be most incompatible: to be brave is mostly imprudent.

But we have to remember that the true sense of this connection is as follows: acting justly, bravely, all acting well, is not just and brave and good unless corresponding to the truth of real things; it is the virtue of prudence in which this truth of real things becomes effective, fertile, and decisive. This doctrine of the priority of prudence has an immense "practical" importance. It includes, for instance, the educational principle that education and self-education aiming at moral development must be rooted in the virtue of prudence, that is to say, the ability to see objectively the realities surrounding our acts, and to make them decide our course of action. Furthermore, the classical doctrine of the virtue of prudence offers the only chance to overcome radically the phenomenon of "moralism." The substance of moralism, which most people regard as a thing peculiarly Christian, is that it severs what we are from what we ought to do, that it proclaims a duty without perceiving and without showing that duty is rooted in what we are. On the contrary, the nucleus as well as the proper concern of the doctrine of prudence is as follows: to prove as necessary the coherence of what we ought to do with what we are; in the act of prudence what we ought to do is decided by what we are. Moralism says: good is what should be, because it should be. The doctrine of prudence says: good is what agrees with reality; it should be because it corresponds with reality. (It is perhaps important to perceive here the distinctly inner connection of "Christian" moralism with modern voluntarism.) And a third "practical" and "actual" point must be intimated. The fundamental attitude of justness (in the sense of agreement with reality), of objectivity, as expressed in the classical doctrine of prudence, was summarized in the Middle Ages in the following sentence, a sentence both grand and simple: Wise is man if all things taste to him as they really are. Now it is an important experience of modern psychology or, more exactly, of modern psychotherapy that a man to whom things do *not* taste as they are, who instead tastes in all things nothing but himself because he looks only at himself—that this man has lost not only the real capacity for justice (and for all moral virtue) but also his psychical sanity. Thus a whole group of psychical

24

diseases is substantially due to such egotistic lack of objectivity. Such experience sanctions and illumines the ethical realism of the doctrine of the priority of prudence. Prudence is one of the spiritual regions where the mysterious connection between sanity and sanctity, between illness and sin becomes visible. A psychological theory which does not wilfully overlook them is likely to see very deep connections here. The ethical doctrine of prudence should be able to illumine in an amazing way the central notion of self-deception (which is nothing but a lack of objectivity in perceiving reality, and which is rooted in the will).

III

Prudence and justice are more closely connected than appears at first sight. Justice, we have said, is the ability to live truly "with others." Now it is easy to see that this ability to live in community (which nearly signifies the ability to live at all) depends upon the objective perception and acknowledgment of reality. This means that this ability depends upon prudence. Only an objective man is just; and injustice and the lack of objectivity mean, even in the very usage of language, almost the same thing.

It is prudence in which the real capacity for being good is rooted; only the prudent man has, in presupposition, the capacity for being good. This is why prudence ranks so high. But the rank of justice is based on the fact that justice is the highest and truest mode of this goodness itself. Such a statement must be emphasized since "Christian" middle-class people have for some generations proclaimed altogether different things as the primary and true criterion of a good man, specifically, "morality" so-called. A good man is primarily just. Man as a member of the community has the task of realizing justice. One can almost say that it is not so much the individual who represents justice (although, naturally, and strictly speaking the person alone can be "virtuous"), but We, the social entity, the people; which means that justice is the perfection of the We.

Now, the structure of each commonwealth is based on three fundamental relations; and if these three relations are right we can say that justice rules in it. First, there are the mutual relations of the members; the justness of these relations corresponds to the exchange of justice (*justitia commutativa*). Second, there are the relations of the whole to the members; the justness of these relations corresponds to distributive justice (*justitia distributiva*). Third, there are the relations of the individual members to the whole We; the justness of these relations corresponds to "legal" justice (*justitia legalis*). These things may sound very natural, as if they were a matter of course. But they are not a matter of course. The social doctrine of individualism, for example, sees only one of these three relations, namely, the mutual relations of the individual members. Individualism does not acknowledge the true independence of the social whole, and, therefore, it knows of no actual connection of the individuals to the whole, nor of the whole to the individuals. And accordingly the *justitia commutativa* is the unique form of justice which individualism knows of, if it is consistent. On the other hand, anti-individualism has created a "universalistic" social doctrine which frankly denies any existence of relations among individuals as individuals, and which, in consequence, declares the *justitia commutativa* to be an "individualistic misconception." The reality of the "totalitarian state" shows that such an "academic theory" is not inclined to remain on the level of mere "theory"; its coercive power hardly admits "private" relations among individuals who merely come together as functionaries to serve the ends of the state.

St. Thomas Aquinas also says that the whole moral life of man is closely bound to the *bonum commune;* the *justitia legalis,* therefore, really has a very particular rank and place. But we must not overlook the ambiguity of this statement of St. Thomas. One of its senses is this: there is a true obligation of the individual with respect to the common weal, and this obligation comprises the whole man. The other sense is this: all individual virtue has an importance for the common weal. This means that the common weal needs the virtue of all individuals, that it cannot be realized unless the individual members of the community are good, not only just, but good, virtuous in the most individual and secret and, so to speak, "private" way.

IV

Another error about justice (at bottom quite liberalist but not at all limited to the era of liberalism) declares: it is possible to be just without having to be brave. This is not so much an error about the nature of justice as an error about the real structure of "this" world, in which justice is to be realized. For "this" world is constructed in such a manner that justice, and good generally, could not be successful of its own accord without the fighting man, ready to die for it. Evil is mighty in "this" world: this fact becomes manifest in the necessity for fortitude which means readiness to endure injuries for the sake of the realization of good. So, St. Augustine says, fortitude itself is an irrefutable witness of the existence of evil in the world. Now it is a bad and false answer to the liberalist error to believe that it is possible to be brave without being just. Fortitude as a virtue is present only where justice is intended. Who is not just cannot be brave in the strict sense. Thomas Aquinas says: "The praise of fortitude depends upon justice" (*Summa Theologica,* II, II, 123, 12). This means: simultaneously I may praise anyone for his fortitude only if I can praise him for his justice. True fortitude, therefore, is essentially connected with the will to justice.

It is no less important to perceive that the idea of fortitude is not identical with the idea of an aggressive fearlessness at all costs. There even is a sort of fearlessness which is opposed to the virtue of fortitude. Here we must consider the place occupied by fear in the structure of human existence. The common and mitigating foreground-talk of everyday life is based on the denial of the existence of anything terrible. The terrible is pushed back into the realm of mere appearances. This mitigation, effective (or not effective) at all times, today finds a remarkable counterpart in the fact that in the philosophical, psychological, and poetical literature of our time no conception plays such a large part as the conception of fear. Another counterpart of that everyday attempt at making human existence harmless and "fearless" is a new stoicism which has found an imposing human representation and a fascinating formulation in literature. This new stoicism is "proclaimed" above all by a group of men who consider the events of the last wars as a destruction which includes the promise and the threat of new, still greater, and apocalyptic catastrophes. And the thesis is: life is always terrible, but there is nothing so terrible that a strong man could not endure it with greatness. But if you read the books, for example, of Ernst Juenger, who is one of the most remarkable heads of this new "Stoa," you have to agree that nearly all dreams of these "adventurous hearts" are dreams of anxiety.

To this question the ultimate and most profound Christian answer is: the notion of the fear of the Lord. But this conception runs the risk of being depleted, deprived of its reality, and concealed by the Christian common-consciousness. The fear of the Lord is not the same as "respect" for the absolute God, but real fear in the strict sense of the word. The common signification of fear, anxiety, fright, horror and terror is that they are all different answers to the different manners of the diminution of being, the ultimate one of which is annihilation. It is not at all the way of Christian theology to deny the existence of the fearsome in human life; furthermore, the Christian doctrine of life does not say that man should not or must not fear the fearsome. But the Christian asks for the *ordo timoris;* he asks for what is really and ultimately fearsome; and he is afraid of fearing perhaps that which is not at all really and definitely fearsome, and afraid of considering perhaps as harmless that which is definitely fearsome. That which is properly fearsome comes to this: the possibility of man's voluntarily separating himself from his ultimate origin of being. This is the ultimate peril of his existence. And it is man's fear of this possible separation from the Ultimate Origin of being, to which the fear of the Lord is the adequate answer. This fear which accompanies all human life, even that of the saint, as a real possibility, is a fear that cannot be overcome by any manner of "heroism." On the contrary, this fear is the presupposition of all genuine heroism. The fear of the Lord as a fear is to be endured and suffered right up to the definite security of the Eternal Life. When fortitude saves us from loving our life in such manner that we lose it—then this implies that the fear of the Lord, as a fear of losing Eternal Life, is the basis of all Christian fortitude. It should be considered, however, that the fear of the Lord is the negative counterpart of the hopeful love of God. St. Augustine says: all fear is the feeling of love.

The fear of the Lord is the "fulfillment" of the natural anxiety of man with respect to the diminution of being and of annihilation. All moral goodness is likewise a sort of extension of natural inclinations. And man fears the *nihil* by nature. And as the natural desire for life in community is accomplished in the virtue of justice, and as the natural desire for self-dependence is perfected in the virtue of magnanimity, and as the natural impulse for enjoyment is perfected in the virtue of temperance—so the natural anxiety of annihilation becomes also destructive, unless perfected in the fear of the Lord. The fact that the fear of the Lord in its proper form as *"timor filialis"* is a gift of the Holy Ghost and not, as for example, with the cardinal virtues, the natural fulfillment of a natural human faculty—this fact implies that only realized supernatural perfection is able to free man from the tyranny of unsatisfied anxiety. As it is, the destructive effect of this unsatisfied anxiety and its tyranny are proved not only in ethical spheres but also in the sphere of the natural psychical life—as psychiatry may confirm. Here is once more a point clearly revealing the coherence of sanity and sanctity. The distinctness, however, is limited to the fact of this coherence: in what precise manner sanity and sanctity and above all guilt and illness are interwoven and on which terms this connection becomes effective—a statement about this is hardly possible. In any case the "sanity" of justice, of magnanimity, of temperance, of fear of the Lord, and of all virtue consists in their conforming to the objective reality, both natural and supernatural. Compliance with reality is the principle of both sanity and goodness.

V

Earlier we noted that the natural desire for enjoyment can become destructive. This fact is concealed by the liberalist thesis: man is good. Enlightened liberalism, by virtue of its most fundamental presuppositions could not acknowledge the possible existence in man of a revolt of inferior spiritual forces against the government of mind; it denies that man has lost the spontaneous inner order of his nature through original sin. And so, judged from this aspect, the virtue of temperance necessarily passes for something nonsensical and objectless. For the virtue of temperance presupposes that the above-mentioned destructive revolt of the senses against the mind is possible and is perceived as possible. This depletion of the virtue of temperance by enlightened liberalism the common doctrine of many Christians (I will not say the doctrine of the Church, nor even theology) has countered by an over-accentuation of this very virtue. So for the Christian common consciousness the virtue of temperance, in its typical forms of chastity and abstinence, has become the conspicuous and all-dominating trait of the Christian idea of man. Now this answer of Christianity has, nevertheless, remained a child of its adversary, that is, of liberalism. This dependence upon the liberalistic-individualistic adversary becomes manifest in so far as the virtue of temperance is the most "private" among the four cardinal virtues; temperance refers to the individual as an individual. So the most "private" virtue passes for the most Christian virtue. In classical theology, however, this "private" character of temperance was the very reason for declaring this virtue to be the last instead of the first of the four cardinal virtues.

The overvaluation of temperance has had very considerable effects and extensions. The fact, for example, that in our everyday usage of language the words "sensuality," "passion," "desire," "inclination" have received a very negative meaning although they are ethically neutral conceptions, is partly due to this overvaluation of temperance. But if by the word "sensuality" is exclusively meant sensuality as revolting against the spirit, and by "passion" exclusively bad passion, and by "desire" exclusively mutinous desire—then, of course, there are no names left for the non-mutinous sensuality, which St. Thomas says, belongs to virtue. And this defect of the usage of language strongly inclines toward a dangerous confusion of notions, even of life itself. On the other hand, this defect of the usuage of language has arisen from a confusion of notions and of life.

Perhaps it may be good to cite here an example from the *Summa Theologica* which shows what the "Universal Doctor" thinks of this matter. It is an example, not a principle, but an example which illustrates a principle. In the *Summa Theologica* (*Summa Theologica,* I II, 22–48) there is a chapter about the *passiones animae,* the passions of the soul. The expression involves all motions of the sensuous faculty, such as love, hate, desire, delight, sadness, fear, and anger. One of the approximately twenty-five questions of this chapter deals with the "remedies against grief and sadness" (*Summa Theologica* I, II, 38). In five special articles St. Thomas enumerates five such remedies. Before mentioning them we should like to pose the question: What information could be given today by the moral common consciousness of Christianity concerning the "remedies against the sadness of soul?"

Everyone may answer the question himself. The first general remedy mentioned by St. Thomas is: any sort of delight, for sadness is like a weariness of the soul, but delight is like a rest. The second remedy: tears! The third remedy: the compassion of friends. The fourth: the contemplation of truth (which is more able to alleviate grief the more a man loves wisdom). As to the fifth remedy mentioned by St. Thomas, we should bear in mind that we have a textbook of theology before us, and certainly not an ordinary one. The fifth remedy against sadness of soul is: sleeping and bathing, for a sleep and a bath cause a feeling of well-being in the body which reacts upon the soul. Naturally, St. Thomas is well acquainted with the possibilities and necessities of a supernatural overcoming of human sorrow; he is even of the opinion that there are forms and degrees of human sorrow which can only be overcome by supernatural energies. But St. Thomas, on the other hand, does not think of putting aside natural possibilities—for example, sleeping and bathing. And he does not at all feel embarrassed to speak about them in the midst of a theological discourse.

VI

All four of the cardinal virtues—prudence, justice, fortitude, temperance—are principally connected with the natural sphere of human reality. But as Christian virtues they grow out of the fertile ground of faith, hope, and charity. Faith, hope, and charity are the answer to the reality of the Triune God, which is supernaturally revealed to the Christian by the revelation of Jesus Christ. And the three theological virtues are not only the answer to that reality, but they are at the same time the faculty and the source of this answer; they are not the answer itself but they are, so to speak, also the mouth which alone is able to give this answer. All three theological virtues are closely connected one with another; "they are," as St. Thomas says in his tract about hope, "flowing back into themselves in a holy ring; who by hope has been led to charity has also a more perfect hope, just as his faith is stronger than before" (*Quaest. disp. de spe, 3 ad 1*).

As the cardinal virtues are rooted in the theological virtues the supernatural ethos of the Christian differs from the natural ethos of the gentleman, that is, the naturally noble man. This origin itself, the manner and means of the coherence of natural and supernatural virtue, is expressed in the well-known sentence that grace does not destroy nature but presupposes and perfects it. This sentence seems to be very clear and really is so. But its clarity cannot affect the impossibility of making a mystery comprehensible by a simple statement. And there is nothing more mysterious than the manner in which God acts in man, and man in God.

Nevertheless, the difference between a Christian and a gentleman becomes clearly manifest and in many ways. The Christian can, for example, appear to act contrary to natural prudence because in his acting he must conform to realities which only faith perceives. Incidentally, about this supernatural prudence St. Thomas has written a sentence which, I think, is particularly important for the Christian of today. "Obviously," St. Thomas says, "the natural virtue of prudence presupposes quite a degree of acquired knowledge." Now, when the theological virtues augment in a supernatural manner the cardinal virtues, what about prudence? Does grace replace the natural knowledge of natural things? Does faith supersede the objective estimate of the concrete situation or the concrete deed, or does it replace it? In this case, how can grace and faith be useful to the "plain man," who does not possess this knowledge which is sometimes rather difficult? To these questions St. Thomas gives, I think a quite grand, and also most consoling, answer: "The men who require the advice and counsel of others can, providing they are in a state of grace, advise themselves in so far as they ask for the advice of other people and they (this is most important) are able to distinguish a good counsel from a bad one" (*Summa Theologica,* II, II, 47, 3). If they are in the state of *grace!* It goes without saying why this answer is consoling in the present situation of the plain Christian.

The difference between a Christian and a gentleman is especially evident in the gap dividing Christian fortitude from the natural bravery of the gentleman. This point really closes the consideration of the Christian idea of man. The difference between a Christian fortitude and a merely natural fortitude lies eventually in the theological virtue of hope. All hope says: it will turn out well, it will end well. Supernatural hope says: for the man who stays in the reality of grace it will turn out well in a manner which infinitely exceeds all expectation; for this man it will end with nothing less than Eternal Life.

Now it may come to pass that in an era of temptation to despair, all imminent and secular prospects for a "happy end" become gloomy. So it can come to pass that there is nothing left to the natural man limited to nature than the desperate fortitude of an "heroic end." And particularly the true gentleman will consider this way as the only possibility; for he of all persons will be able to renounce the "way out of happiness" (as Ernst Juenger says). In short, sometimes it may happen that supernatural hope remains the unique possibility of hope at all. This is not to be understood in any sense of "eudaemonism," it is not a question of anxiety about a last possibility of subjective happiness. The Biblical sentence "Although he would kill me, I would not tremble, but would plead my ways in his sight" (*Job,* 13, 15.) is far from a "eudaemonic" anxiety about happiness. No, the Christian hope is first and above all the existential adjustment of man to fulfillment, to the ultimate realization, to the fullness of being (to which, of course, the fullness of happiness or rather of beatitude corresponds). If then all natural hopes sometimes become senseless, it means that supernatural hope for man remains truly the unique possibility of adjusting his being. The desperate fortitude of the "heroic end" is at bottom "nihilistic," since it believes that it can suffer the unknown. Christian fortitude, however, is fed by hope for the abundant reality of Life, for the Eternal Life, for a new heaven and for a new earth.

THE PHILOSOPHICAL

BACKGROUND OF

CHRISTIAN DEMOCRACY

Luigi Sturzo

[1947]

CHRISTIAN DEMOCRACY AND THE CHURCH

IT IS common to confuse Christian democracy with the social movement of Catholics on behalf of the working classes, according to the papal teachings, among which the most noted are taken from the encyclicals *Rerum Novarum* of Leo XIII and *Quadragesimo Anno* of Pius XI. (I do not cite the *Graves de Communi* of Leo XIII because it is superseded by the *Quadragesimo* from the point of view of social questions). In fact, Christian democracy, having assumed a political character, with the formation of Christian Democratic or Popular Parties (and the adhesion given by the old Catholic parties which were orientating themselves toward democracy, adopting broad social programs), has passed the stage of simple activity on behalf of the working classes and placed itself on the political plane with its own program and action. This program and action are quite distinct from those of other Catholic nuclei, for the most part conservative, interested—either as a party or party pivots, or as participants in other parties, or merely as eminent and independent personalities—in the public life of their particular countries, concerning themselves in a special way with the religious interests endangered by the liberal and socialist parties of anti-clerical flavor.

To arrive at the technical plane of Christian democracy, it is necessary also to distinguish it from the Catholic Church as a teaching hierarchy and as the mass of faithful. The Christian democrats have been and are, in their largest majority, faithful Catholics devoted to the Church and attentive to the observance of Christian precepts; they have had the help of bishops and of popes, according to time and place; they have also been held in suspicion, criticized, eliminated from positions of responsibility in the Church or in Catholic Action, always according to time and place. (Whether through their own fault or the fault of others makes no difference). It is enough to cite the French Abbé Naudet who was prohibited from writing or speaking in any way; his obedience was total for the twenty years before he died. It is enough to mention Marc Sangnier of Paris, who endured the condemnation of his association "Le Sillon" (soon changed into an organization dependent upon bishops), to which is due the flowering of Christian democratic youth in France from 1900 on. In the same way, reviewing history, we find likewise the condemnation of the *Avenir* of Lammenais and Montalembert in 1832, the exile from Rome of Father Giachino Ventura (then General of the Theatines) in 1849; also, in Italy, the condemnation of Don Murri (who left the Church, but was reconciled in 1943); in Argentina, the old bitter struggle against Monsignor Michele de Andrea (Bishop *in partibus*).

All this is cited, not to justify those who come under the provisions of Church discipline, or to cast any shadow on the hierarchy of the Church, but to show how the Christian democrats shaped their experience and created a basic theory which, although always in the framework of Catholic thought, was actuated in a proper form.

Indeed, without the basis of Christianity a true form of Christian democracy could not develop, particularly because modern democracy is the fruit of Christian civilization and has little in common with the pre-Christian classic-Mediterranean forms of democracy. In the second place, because it gave prevailing value to morality in public life, it was natural, indeed, that Christian democracy should found itself on the Judaeo-Christian tradition of thought which is the historic and ideological basis of modern civilization.

The problem which confronted Catholics in the nineteenth century and which still confronts them even in our own century and after the tragic experience of two world wars, is precisely that of morality in public life. The problem presents itself to us, from period to period, as unsolved in its practical applications, and even in the theorems which influence resolutions, notwithstanding the fact that, ascending to general principles, it finds perfect coincidence with the teachings of Christianity. The reason for the disparity between the general principles of public morality and their practical applications, is derived above all from the complexity of political questions, and from the conflicts of the rights and duties of the individuals and social nuclei among themselves and in their concurrent relationship with the various communities to which, of necessity or freely, they belong. From this springs the difference not only in accentuation on one or an-

34

other social problem, but also the difference in theorization, to the point of finding bearable today that which tomorrow will be esteemed unbearable, and of regarding as not repugnant to nature (for instance, slavery) that which tomorrow will be judged against the rights of the human personality, as that which is most elevated in nature itself.

This is due not only to the usual difficulty of overcoming social prejudices based on established facts and the effects of traditions themselves, but also to the somewhat slow and insecure process by which the human understanding makes practical truths its own and brings them into complete correspondence with theoretical principles. What we have here is *video meliora proboque, deteriora sequor* (I see the better and I try it, but I follow the worse) which torments us even in the quest for truth; it is also that dark zone which separates the two extremes of intellectualism and pragmatism, and which often makes incomprehensible the connection between "theoretical reason" and "practical reason."

It is not to be wondered at if, even today, there are those who do not take account of the ethical value of democracy, ideally conceived, because they do not see the possibility of the practical realization of true democracy. They are bound down under the weight of rationalism or intellectualism or even scholasticism. As yet there has to be dispelled the influence of those who stand against political or social democracy, who have upheld and defended the authoritarianisms of absolute monarchies, the monopoly of historical aristocratic governments, who have chained the destinies of the people to the patrimonial rights of dynasties, and who have condemned the representative forms of government actuated by the bourgeoisie of the last century and have feared the advent of another estate (the working classes) either because they considered it a social extremism or because they judged it inactualizable, and hence anarchistic.

MODERN DEMOCRACY AND ETHICAL PRINCIPLES

Historical events were stronger than theories; the American and French Revolutions marked a new phase in the history of humanity.

Unfortunately, before a permanent political separation between Church and state was brought about, there was ripening a profound separation between public morality and Christian thought. The modern democracies were born under the stars of humanitarianism, naturalism, and positivism. American democracy itself (which was not, in fact, conceived as true democracy until later), although it maintained a Deistic inspiration in the Declaration of Independence and a widespread religious tradition among the people (a thing which, aside from anti-clericalism, a reaction connected with historic facts, was not lacking in France), suffered the effects of rationalist and even positivist political philosophies.

In the practical field there was on one side the separation of the state from the Church (a step which was historically implicit in the denunciation of the regime of the absolute monarchies bound to the established churches), which had, as its result the development of religious agnosticism in the ruling classes and in the schools, the abandonment of the conception of a natural ethics and religious morality, and a veering in the direction of the theories of historical, relative, fluctuating morality, independent of religion in general and of positive religion in particular.

The process was neither rapid nor constant, nor, in various zones, perceptible. But permeating the intellectual or professional milieu in the teaching of sociology and of political sciences and in the prevailing social conceptions, it invaded the realm of legislations, took the place of Christian traditions and created its own public and private morality which was defined as the "way of life" of each people or nation.

Nevertheless, the patrimony of Christian morality was not completely lost; it still lived as a natural morality in the premises of the codes and laws of each state, connected with those of the ten commandments concerned with commutative justice, with certain aspects of family life, and certain spheres of social life. From the Christian spirit (consciously or not) were being imbibed not a few of the modern social institutions dealing with the relationships between capital and labor, and with public institutions of assistance and social welfare.

But three modern heresies combined to make public morality more and more precarious and unstable: that of the independence of man from God either in the name of Hegelian idealism, or under the spreading influence of Comtean positivism; that of the historical materialism of a Marxist character; and finally that of agnostic pragmatism and historical relativism, which strip human acts of all ethical value.

Consequently, there was the search for a political *absolute* as an anchor to the wavering bark of society. First in the order of time, the state: the absolute state as an expression of the collective will: inspiration for this was found in Rousseau. Placing the state outside all ethical limits, it was then made a font of ethicality; either the ethical state or the Hegelians, of which (under Fascism) the philosopher Giovanni Gentile was high-priest—or the national state preached by Charles Maurras in France. The second *absolute* was the proletarian class, as the unifier of all political interests, re-expressed in economic terms: Lenin was its prophet. But with this the Russian communist experiment ended; Stalin's continuation of it is already on the nationalist-imperialist plane. The third *absolute* was the race, deified in the German conception: Fichte was its prophet and Hitler its demon. Public morality, in the three cases, identifies itself respectively with the divinity of the state or nation, of the class, of the race, subjugating the individual to the totalitarian and uncontrollable will of the dictator.

As nature has its forces which work together against all illnesses (except the last and the mortal one), so also in totalitarian experiments the interior forces of opposition and of revolution are influential (here more, there less) in diminishing the ethical and political effects, and in creating healthy reactions, as soon as the play of opposing forces produces the margins of evasion or resistance. It is because of the strength of such natural forces of resistance that even totalitarianisms cannot create true, stable, and profound pantheistic convictions of the state, nation, race, or class. Human reason seeks by instinct those ethical laws which are based on the rights of human personality, and goes even more deeply to the roots, asking for that principle which is the animator of true personality.

DIFFERENCES BETWEEN CHRISTIAN DEMOCRACY AND MODERN DEMOCRACY

Some believe that the search for a "Prime Ethics" in political relationships would be a return to an obsolete metaphysics, to mediaeval scholasticism, to rationalism, and to the 'natural law' of the seventeenth and eighteenth centuries; a looking backward and not a going ahead. They do not perceive that involutions of thought serve for further developments, in which the past is reflected, under other aspects, in the present, and prepares the future. The search for a "prime ethics" was once regarded either as pure philosophic speculation, or as a spiritual necessity of the individual, and in this second case it was confused with the religious needs of each of us. Today the "prime ethics" is looked at from the sociological viewpoint: if an absolute basis is lacking to ethics, society is without moral orientation; and if the ethics is a pure product of society in the concrete (granted that there does not exist an ideal society outside of our *a posteriori* abstraction, from fact to idea), the ethics will be variable according to the variety of social nuclei and their development.

Thus we are obliged to review the entire theory of society and to discover that fundamentally society is only the simultaneous and progressive projection of the activity of man's personality concretized in the multiplicity of individuals who, either necessarily or voluntarily, cooperate among themselves. From such a revision emerges, as a social factor and an ethical constant, the human personality; whence the fundamental problem is, how society can be reduced to human personality, and how personality can be the power animating society. These processes, in their reciprocal influences, acquire balance on cultural, political, and economic planes, when rationality prevails over pseudo-rationality (which plays its social role posing as rationality); and when, in the practical field, the equation between rational law and its ethical application is discovered.

Thus is achieved that transcendence—necessary in the human process of rationality—and that ethicality, which transports the various activities of life in society to their meaning and their permanent and interior value.

The special characteristic of Christian democracy differentiating it from every other political conception of modern times lies, above all, in its particular idea of democracy (some have called it "moralistic" making an unfounded criticism of it), which, theoretically and practically, has a different basis from that of modern democracy, notwithstanding certain historical and technical coincidences.

Let us pursue this special characteristic along certain lines:

1) That modern democracy and Christian democracy coincide in stressing that true democracy is government of the people, by the people, and for the people.

2) That democracy of any kind would not be real without the political freedoms of speech, of press, of assembly, and of the vote, admitting, however, that such liberties must be actuated with proper regulations so as not to become through abuse dangerous to society itself.

3) That modern democracy cannot exist and function without parliaments, and must guard and preserve as distinct the state powers: the legislative, the executive, and the judicial.

4) That real democracy cannot be conceived except as based on social justice, so as to avoid the economic exploitation of certain classes or social groups, and to give to all the opportunity for their well-being and betterment.

This scheme, which all modern democrats hold in common, if analyzed closely, is either formalistic or intentional, to the point of being able to include all forms of democracy, which from the end of the eighteenth century on have been established in all parts of the world; or, on the contrary, (as is done by certain purist democrats, in the manner of Rousseau) it excluded the historical experiments of democracy, thereby denying that true democracy ever existed under the sun.

Some Catholic thinkers, in the face of the prevailing naturalistic theorization of modern society, have been inclined to condemn those tendencies which are called liberal and democratic, often confusing the philosophical theories with political institutions. From this it has followed that the representative and democratic regimes have been realized outside the influence of the Church, making their own experiments, through a series of crises, now in conjunction with and now in opposition to certain Catholic-political wings. The usual Catholic criticism (transferred from the field of principles to the polemic field of daily politics) has been credited, in many instances, with being a denial of political liberties themselves and of democratic forms of government.

This unfavorable position of Catholics was influenced by the fact that their greatest writers have been men of the Church, who because of their mental training are more given to logic than others (and are sometimes even in some degree *Consequentiarii*, as scholars call them, being accustomed to evaluate facts from the pure viewpoint of principles). Thus, given that Rousseau was the father of democracy, there are those who have prejudged French democracy from 1789 on, as an application of a mathematical theorem (outside the realm of historical events), in the light of the words and ideas of the *Social Contract*.

In America, the idea prevails, in Church circles, that the democracy of the United States is not derived in any way from Rousseau but from the Christian spirit of the Founding Fathers, who were most felicitous in including theistic phrases in the Declaration of Independence. Thus American democracy, which has not many fundamental differences from European democracy (government of the people, freedom of speech, press, and assembly, and the vote) and which differs from it only in mechanism, has had the open support (although expressed with theoretical qualifications) of Catholic thinkers. I say "expressed with theoretical qualifications" because, given the attitude of the Papacy during the European and American revolutions, and the religious struggles which followed in Catholic countries, it was natural that many should have the attitude of looking more upon the past which they wished to preserve than upon the future to be won.

On the other hand, those Catholics who participated in the public life of free countries, whether in representative or governmental posts or as exponents of parties, realized the importance of the new popular institutions and the advantages which religion might derive from them, if the Church or the local clergy would abandon negative criticism and the conservative concept of a past which could not return. These were called, in the last century, "liberal Catholics" from the political viewpoint, and "Christian Socialists" from the social viewpoint. Only after the publication of the encyclicals of Leo XIII (especially *Libertas, Humanum Genus* and *Rerum Novarum*), did there spring forth the courageous movement of Christian democracy which inherited the spirit of the *liberal* (in the sense of popular government) and *social* (in the sense of economic reform) currents of the progressive Catholic wing. *Personalism, Pluralism, Institutionalism,* mark this beginning of the revision of political thinking.

For this very reason, we have had, and have, even today, a cultural and practical separation of the Catholics on political questions, with some crises, and at the same time with intense revision of the philosophical positions of Catholic thought. Such thinkers as Maritain and Blondel, who have not directly participated in political movements and in Catholic social activity—have largely contributed (each from his own viewpoint) to the philosophical re-examination of traditional theories.

One of the points granted today in Catholic thought is that of the right of the human person, which has caused the coining in France of the word "personalism" and also has given rise to a "personalist" group as well as a somewhat personal group. In the main, it has served to clarify some aspects of the ethical problem of society. In face of the state-worshiping tendencies of the nineteenth century and the totalitarianism of our own times, this revaluation of the person, not only in the purely naturalistic sense, but also in the historic-Christian sense (which has synthesized the natural with the supernatural), has been a step forward in human accomplishment and a positive affirmation against monistic theories of the Spirit, in the manner of Hegel, or of Humanity, in the manner of Comte, or of historical materialism, in the manner of Marx.

The fundamental revaluation of personality is indeed due to the great Christian tradition; but politically this value was obscured by the absolutism of the monarchs of the *"ancien régime,"* by the political conception of the state-religion, by the economic exploitation of the working classes, by the theory of a democracy in the manner of Rousseau, based on the tyranny of the supposed collective will.

Liberalism meant the liberation from such a past, but it tended to disorganize society, resolving it in the individual; so that afterwards to reorganize that society it had recourse theoretically to the system of an omnipotent state, and practically accentuated the defense of the bourgoisie as the ruling class, identifying the economic interests of such a class with those of the nation as a whole, whence the strong and decisive socialistic reaction. The personalist theory utilizes, out of liberal and socialistic experiences, those which are sound, and synthesizes their contrast in the prevailing value of human personality, seeking to actualize them with essential reform of the social organisms and to make them interdependent and effective.

Another step was taken in order to affirm the principle of liberty without falling into theoretical agnosticism and into practical individualism; this occurred in France after the first World War when the theory of *pluralism* was accepted by Catholics as a characteristic of modern society. It is not opportune here to analyze the juridical or legislative basis of this theory, or to discuss it from a sociological viewpoint. The point, above all, to be disputed is the affirmation that only modern society can be called pluralistic; all complex forms of society are in a certain sense pluralistic. It is also to be disputed that society can function without the process of dualization of social forces and without the tendency towards unification. *Pluralism* is an analytical formula (happy enough) of the nuclear state of society and of the need of individual initiative to form always a new series of nuclei, in agreement or in opposition. This is a centrifugal dynamism truly necessary to counterbalance centripetal dynamism. That which *liberalism* interpreted as a purely individual right (which, if it were really *pure* as certain liberal thinkers conceive it, could be a pure anarchy), *pluralism* analyzes more realistically and justifies more rationally. Catholics, on their part, (after a century of incomprehension of the true historico-sociological essence of liberalism, and after so many direct conflicts especially with naturalistic premises and with the agnostic consequences of liberalism) prefer to speak of *pluralism,* which contains a principle of social organicity, and which can have as presuppositions both theories, the naturalistic of the liberals as well as the ethico-sociological of Christian tradition.

Another theory, also of French origin, which has played a part in the revision of modern thought is that of *institutionalism:* that is, of the organic value of the social institution (juridico-political), which transcends individuals and continues, in time and space with its own character and vitality, as an extra-personal reality. This theory must also be revised to be in full agreement with that of personalism and that of pluralism. The writer has presented his criticism of the extra-personal character given to the institution and has specified the importance of personal and voluntary activity in the creation of social organs. The question warrants a much deeper study, as a real contribution to the revision of modern sociology and also of the traditional positions of Christian philosophy.

It is an urgent necessity to dispel the misunderstanding between Christianity and modern society and to arrive at a just and sound evaluation of present social and political institutions and of their ethical quality. But no theoretical revision whatsoever has any real importance in life if it remains in the purely speculative field and lacks the proof of its concretization in the practical field.

Insofar as the political, economic, and social currents prevailing in modern life are imbued with materialism or are inspired by a relativistic and basically hedonistic moralism, the corresponding actualizations, notwithstanding the high-sounding names of liberalism, democracy, radicalism, or socialism, will remain within the circle of naturalism and can pass into the sphere of permanent human values only through extrapolation, or through the traditional habits of thought and life.

From the other side, Christian theories will bear no weight, even as theories (apart from school exercises) if there are no politico-social currents which give them actualization and experimentation. The action of Christian democracy has contributed, in the present field, towards carrying the masses of Catholic people into political life, without diffidence or *"arrière pensée"* or recriminations for the past; it has enabled them to face with courage, strength, and personal sacrifices modern leftist or rightist totalitarianisms, even when the opinion expressed by the Catholic press was (either with few reservations or many eulogies) on the side of the dictators; and to accept the way of liberty and modern political institutions as a common basis for reform according to Christian ethics.

If there is still among the progressive groups of Catholics on one side a certain poverty of thought and on the other uncertainty of movement, this is due in part to the fact that the most noted writers have looked on Christian democracy with contempt, preferring polemics against the enemies of the Church to the slow and practical construction of a modern and democratic society. Catholic education has not contributed to the best preparation for political life because of the very fact that, to the principles of individual morality and traditional principles of society, it has not added the intellectual and practical formation suited to the needs of a new democratic society.

In view of the destructive effects of the Second World War, a larger and more generous contribution must be drawn from the studies of ethics and the philosophy of society, which inform the ideals of Christian democracy and which serve for a Christian reorientation of modern society, without laments for the past and without antihistorical wishes for a return to the Middle Ages.

MAN AND HISTORY

ASPECTS OF MEDIAEVAL

THOUGHT ON

CHURCH AND STATE

Gerhart B. Ladner

[1947]

"Two loves," St. Augustine says in *De Civitate Dei,* "have made two cities, love of self unto contempt of God the Earthly City, love of God unto contempt of self the Heavenly City," the City of God. These "cities"—*civitates*—are, of course, not states, but societies; St. Augustine himself tells us that the term *civitas* is an equivalent of the term society. They are societies, however, of a special kind. The *Civitas Dei* is a "mystical" society of all the elect, past, present, and future. The *Civitas Terrena,* the Earthly City, is identical neither with the earthly state nor with any particular earthly state such as the Roman Empire, nor with any merely human society, it too is a "mystical" society, that of the impious, the damned.

St. Augustine's concept of the City of God is a specifically Christian ideal of community life. Its true nature appears very clearly if it is confronted with Aristotle's famous definition of the state at the beginning of the first book of *Politics:* "The state or political community which is the highest of all and which embraces all the rest, aims at good in a greater degree than any other, and at the highest good." For Aristotle, then, the state is the form of community life which aims at the highest good. For Augustine the community which pursues the highest good, that is God, is not a state, but a supra-natural society, mixed on this earth, it is true, with the earthly or worldly society, but, nevertheless, extending beyond, to embrace its members in heaven.

It is only natural that notions of such perfection as that of the City of God or of the Church itself, which in one of its aspects is "the only human society engaged in building the City of God," tended to depreciate the state as conceived of by pre-Christian antiquity. St.

Augustine is indifferent towards the state as community and territory. He is not interested in the Roman Empire as a state thus defined—even the christianized Roman Empire is to him only of very relative value; he denies to any community except the City or Society of God the character of a commonweal in the strict and true sense: Cicero's *res publica,* lacking true justice towards God and men, was not a *res publica* in the highest sense for St. Augustine, and similarly, Aristotle's *polis* would in St. Augustine's eyes not have been the community aiming at the highest good.

And yet, St. Augustine does accept certain elements of the ancient notion of the state, namely the ideas of law and justice, order and peace which the Roman Republic and the Roman Empire had tried to make a reality within their limited conception of the true aims of mankind. He admits the nobility of these concepts of metaphysical origin even in their application to political life by the Romans, emphasizing how much more Christians, who have the full truth, ought to follow them than the pagan Romans. Thus, terrestrial *imperium* and terrestrial *regnum,* in so far as they are evaluated in a positive sense by St. Augustine, are for him not states as communities or territories, but forms and functions of just government in the mixed condition in which the City of God finds itself on this earth.

This last-mentioned Augustinian view was rather generally held in the patristic period and was an important factor in the development of early mediaeval political theory. While there were, of course, boundaries within which princes, kings, or the Emperor could command, and people over whom they could claim to rule, these principalities, kingdoms and, especially, the mediaeval Empire were conceived of not primarily as territories or political communities, but rather as governments, that is to say as functions fulfilled by persons. At least from the fifth to the late eleventh century this concept of the state, which for convenience's sake we might call the *functional* concept, prevailed.

Two generations after St. Augustine, at the end of the fifth century, Pope Gelasius I made his famous statement about the two forces that rule the world, the priestly authority and the kingly power. From that time onward for several centuries, *regnum* and *imperium* in political theory continued to be kingship and emperorship rather than kingdom and empire. It is significant that the mediaeval literary genus that accommodates political theory consists not of works on the state such as Plato's *Republic* or Aristotle's *Politics,* but of works on government: that is true especially for the long series of "Mirrors of Princes" or ruler's manuals of the earlier Middle Ages; but the tradition persists even when the functional concept of the state is being gradually eclipsed from the twelfth century onward: the form of the great political treatises from the twelfth to the sixteenth century, from John of Salisbury's *Policraticus* to St. Thomas Aquinas' *De Regimine Principum* and even to Dante's *Monarchia*, to Machiavelli's *Prince*, and to Erasmus' *Education of a Christian Prince* shows clearly their lineage from the old Mirrors of Princes.

It must not be forgotten, of course, that this functional notion of the state is due only in part to the specifically Christian component of mediaeval political theory and in part to general and practical political developments. These developments tended to substitute personal loyalties of various types—the best known is the feudal relationship of vassal to lord—for impersonal and objective relations between citizens and state. Instead of being the embodiment of a commonwealth, the early mediaeval ruler received different types of allegiance from different social groups. The material basis which enabled him to function as guardian of right and law, order and peace, was mainly his power over his own vassals and his position as one of the greatest, if not the greatest, of the landowners.

In the political theory and the actual political life of the earlier Middle Ages the Holy Roman Empire represents a special, but particularly important and paradigmatic case. The Holy Roman Empire was emphatically not a territorial state. When on Christmas day 800 the King of the Franks, Charlemagne, was crowned as Emperor by the Pope and when later in 962 the imperial dignity in the west was renewed a second time by Otto the Great, neither of them acquired additional territory or additional subjects with their imperial crowns. What they did receive, were additional rights and duties, functions of government. It was these rights and duties, not the territories or populations, which gave the mediaeval Empire its universal character, as can be seen, for instance, from the fact that the Holy Roman Empire of Otto the Great and his successors was considered a continuation of the Carolingian Empire, even though it did not include the western part of the latter, namely France, but only Germany, Italy, and later the Kingdom of Burgundy. The most important of the universal imperial functions was the protection of the Universal Church, and especially of the Roman Church, that is to say, of the Papacy, a task which was fraught with all the latent possibilities of conflict surrounding the ever problematic relationship which we today call the relationship between Church and state.

To put the relation in such terms, however, would not have made sense to men who lived in the ninth and tenth century; it was definitely a relationship between the Emperor and the Pope, not between Church and state. The age between Charlemagne and St. Gregory VII merely continued the terminology and ideology of Gelasius I, but only in this respect. If we compare relevant texts of the ninth century with the corresponding ones of the Augustinian-Gelasian age, we observe a very essential change. The intoductory words from Bishop Jonas of Orléans' *De Institutione Regia,* "On the Institution of Kingship," written around 830 for one of Louis the Pious' sons may serve as an example: "All the faithful must know that the Universal Church is the Body of Christ, that the same Christ is its head and that there are in it mainly two exalted persons, the priestly and the kingly."

While for Pope Gelasius I priestly authority and kingly power had been two forces or principles by which the world is ruled, in the Carolingian age this neutral concept of the world is firmly and clearly replaced by that of the Church which, as the Body of Christ, is the only possible all-embracing community and milieu in which government temporal, that is political, as well as spiritual can function.

This then was the great political idea of Christian unity in the Carolingian age, and on the whole, in the succeeding centuries down to the era of St. Gregory VII. Empire as the apex of kingship coordinated with the Papacy as the apex of priesthood, but—and this is most important for the history of political theory and reality—empires and kingdoms were *in* the Church, not *beside* the Church, as in St. Augustine and Gelasius, and not *above* the Church, as in the caesaropapism of the Byzantine Empire.

In comparing the idea of the Holy Roman Empire with Byzantine caesaro-papism it may be granted that in the west too the Emperors felt they were half-spiritual rulers—the terms "King and Priest," "Vicar of God," "Vicar of Christ" were not infrequently used as imperial attributes and titles. Yet even when the Papacy was most powerless, its mere existence prevented outright caesaro-papism in the west. It might even be argued that the Western Empire as the highest function of the lay order in the Church was the providential tool that saved the Papacy in the truly dark tenth and early eleventh centuries from losing its universal character through identification with the interests of the terribly corrupt Roman aristocracy. Looking at early mediaeval Europe in general, it would be wrong to underestimate the "functional" phase of political development when the ruler's chief concern was not national or territorial unity and centralization, but justice in an ordered world.

Yet there came the moment when this system no longer worked. The man who realized this most clearly and acted accordingly was the great archdeacon of the Roman Church, Hildebrand—Pope Gregory VII. It is the main object of the remainder of this study to show how the return in the latter part of the Middle Ages of the notion of the state as a self-sufficient community was prepared by certain transformations that took place in the Hildebrandian or Gregorian era.

The reason why the pre-Gregorian conception of double leadership within the Church, of priest and king, Pope and Emperor, and with it the notion of the state as a function of the Church, could not last, was that the demarcation-line between the two supreme powers and authorities was in practice very difficult to define. Even though the superiority of the spiritual over the temporal was undisputed on principle, the right order between the two was not easy to maintain in the contingencies of history. This difficulty caused the eleventh and twelfth century struggles between the Papacy and the leading European states, the most formidable of which was the Investiture Contest with the Holy Roman Empire, which concerned the question of who should invest or endue bishops and abbots with their spiritual offices and appertaining possessions. As a result of these struggles, great changes occurred in the relationship between Church and state; and now we are actually more justified in using this modern term for the relationship.

From St. Gregory VII to Innocent III more than a hundred years later, the Popes came to consider kings and emperors less and less as functionaries of the Church; instead of encouraging rulers of the priest-kingly type they themselves would at least from Innocent III onward claim the title Vicar of Christ. They made it increasingly clear that for them rulers were simply the leaders of peoples and holders of territories. These the Popes tried to tie to themselves in addition to the membership of all Christians in the universal Church by connecting them with the Roman Church through a special bond which might assume various forms, but most effectively the feudal relation of vassal to lord. In the case of the Holy Roman Empire, too, they tried to make the Emperor's protection of the Roman Church exclusively a matter of duty gradually eliminating all imperial claims of control over the Papacy. Between Gregory VII and Innocent III a vast system of states subject to the Roman Church was built up. To this system belonged at one time or another almost every kingdom of Europe and also some of the city communes which began to develop political forms of their own at that time. It is outside the scope of this essay to describe the actual development from the twelfth century onward of territorial and national kingdoms and of the Italian city states or of their relationship with the Papacy. The reasons for this development were manifold. The Papacy almost immediately recognized its importance. From the Hildebrandian era onward papal letters to rulers and bishops are—to an extent unheard of before— concerned with *lands* and *peoples* and thus give expression to a change in the notion of the state, now conceived of as an entity distinct from, but still subject to the Church, still within the Church, but in a new sense.

Among the many transformations in political theory and ecclesiological doctrine that occurred between the late eleventh and the early thirteenth century, three are of particular importance.

The first has already been touched upon. It is the unprecedented emphasis placed upon the *Roman Church,* the Pope's Church, as the Head and Mother of all churches and of all Christians. The doctrine of papal primacy, of course, goes back to the beginnings of Church history, but from the era of Gregory VII onward the Universal Church is much more clearly than before identified with the Roman Church in the wider meaning of this term—with the Church subject to the Pope. The relationship between the terms *Ecclesia* and *Ecclesia Romana* during the Middle Ages has not yet been fully studied. It seems that the term *Ecclesia,* mere and simple, was increasingly often used in the sense of Roman Church—for instance in *terrae Ecclesiae,* lands of the (Roman) Church—and in the sense of clergy, that is to say for that part of the Church which is most closely connected with the supreme teaching and governing authority of the Universal Church, with the Bishop of the Roman Church. The terms *Ecclesia* and *Ecclesia Romana* thus appear to coalesce into one concept comprising the Church both as an institution, that is, as an essentially clerical "corporation," and as the community of all the faithful, the Body of Christ. It was, perhaps, the formation of a "corporational"—institutional aspect of the concept of the Church which gave increasing importance to the concept of a Christian "temporal" society (*Christianitas, populus Christianus, politia* or *respublica Christiana*), not simply identical with the Church. The history of the expression *Christianitas* for "Christendom" is particularly significant. It seems to occur in this sense first in papal letters of the ninth century (of Nicholas I and John VIII), that is to say in a period which in many respects anticipates developments of the Gregorian era. In the letters of Gregory VII the term appears very often and from then on remains in use. It signifies the Christian people and peoples as distinct from the Church as the supranatural Body of Christ and from the Church as the "corporation" of the clergy. "Christendom then is the entirety of all Christians . . . who in temporal life cooperate with the religious ends of the Church." Thus the idea of *Christianitas,* understood in the sense of "Christendom" or Christian temporal society, and, at a later date, other similar concepts, became important contributions to mediaeval social thought.

Returning now to the new relationship between Church and state, discussed above, it is necessary further to emphasize the role of the institutional or "corporational" aspect of the Church—connected especially with the Roman Church. It was not easy to lower the status of the rulers as half-clerical functionaries in the Church; it would, for instance, have been impossible to eliminate their influence upon the churches in their Kingdoms. There was only one Church which could attempt to effect this great change, that was the Church of the Pope, the Roman Church, which being at the same time universal and territorial (anchored in the Papal States), at the same time the Body of Christ and the "corporation" of the clergy, could more easily meet the nascent political bodies, that is to say, the rising territorial and national states, on their own ground. Thus the Roman and Universal Church began to enter into a new type of relation with the states as political bodies.

And this leads to the second of the three great transformations alluded to above: the evolution of the organological or corporational or body politic theory of the state which marks the transition from the functional notion of the state to that of the state as self-sufficient community. The first mediaeval example, known to me, in which a state—in this case the Holy Roman Empire—is compared with the body, dates precisely from the Gregorian era. It is to be found in the *Liber de Unitate Ecclesiae,* the author of which asserts that the Emperor Henry IV strove to unify the ecclesiological body, *corpus ecclesiae,* so that the *corpus rei publicae,* too, might be made one. Half a century later, in John of Salisbury's *Policraticus* the conception of the state as political body composed of members with specific functions is well established: the state, comparable to the human organism, is made up of various functional members. But this body politic as a whole is considered to be more than a mere function of rulership, it is a sociological entity, a community of people consisting of rulers and ruled. The use of the body metaphor was part of ancient political theory. It can hardly be an accident that in Christian times before the Gregorian era it was as a rule not applied to the state but to the Church. The Church was the Body of Christ beside which or in which the "states" functioned as governments rather than as autonomous bodies. It is only from the era of Gregory VII that the states were seen as bodies politic, while at the same time the Roman Catholic Church developed its institutional-corporational side as one aspect of its being the Body of Christ.

The third point, which must be discussed at least briefly in an appreciation of the transformations that took place in the political thought of the Gregorian and post-Gregorian era, is an important parallel change in ecclesiology where the terms and concepts *Corpus Christi* and *Corpus Mysticum* almost reversed their meanings in a most significant manner. This development can now be easily followed, thanks to the illuminating study of the history of the term *Corpus Mysticum* by Father de Lubac, S.J. He has shown that before about 1150 the expression *Corpus Mysticum* and similar terms were generally used to designate the greatest "mystery" of the liturgy, the Holy

Eucharist, whereas the Church was called *Corpus Christi* in accordance with the terminology of St. Paul. After 1150 the sacramental *Corpus* came to be called *Corpus Christi Verum,* while the term *Corpus Mysticum* was gradually transferred to the Church. The explanation of this change is to be sought on the one hand in the necessity of stressing the real presence of Our Lord in the Sacrament of the Altar, which had been threatened by the heresy of Berengar of Tours, and on the other hand in the desire to connect the Church as closely as possible with the eucharistic life in the liturgy for which, as just stated, the term "mystical" had been customary. Thus the term *Corpus Mysticum* of liturgical origin, superseded by the term *Corpus Verum* in liturgical language, became the instrument of a more liturgical conception of the Church as the Body of Christ, as the effect, so to speak, of Christ's Sacramental Body in the communion and community of the Christians.

If I venture to continue de Lubac's line of thought by applying the results of this investigation to the history of the relationship between Church and state after the eleventh century, I am aware of the somewhat tentative character of my interpretation. Consciously or unconsciously, it would seem, twelfth century theologians felt the necessity of enriching St. Paul's formula *Corpus Christi quod est Ecclesia* by joining it more closely to the Eucharistic Mystery. They adopted the formula *Corpus Christi Mysticum* at a critical moment in Church history, when there was some danger of too much stress being laid on the institutional, corporational side of the Church. At the moment, in other words, when, with the eclipse of the functional concept of the state and with the re-emergence of the state as body politic and, a little later, as self-sufficient community, the Papacy, too, in a world of nascent sovereign powers had to emphasize the role of the Roman Church as a "corporation," supreme among all the bodies politic because of its spiritual foundation and divine institution, but not less concrete than they on the political and sociological level. All the more important was the attempt to deepen the concept of the Church also in the opposite direction through connecting it more closely with the Eucharistic Sacrament, as evidenced by the adoption of the originally liturgical term *Corpus Christi Mysticum* for the Ecclesiological Body. The mystical Body of Christ thus was firmly linked to His Eucharistic Body—both exalted as never before in the Dogma of Transubstantiation (1215) and the Institution of the Feast of Corpus Christi (1264): this was the way in which the Church transcended the new world of self-sufficient communities, of bodies politic, and also transcended her own political role in it.

The deepest justification for the Gregorian and post-Gregorian consolidation of the Church as the clergy within the whole Church, as the Mystical (Liturgical) Body of Christ, is to be found no doubt in the fundamentally sacerdotal and hierarchical character of the Church: "For in fact everything in the Church is founded on sacrifice. And first of all, Her hierarchic constitution. . . . All Her other functions are only a prolongation of Her Priesthood. . . ."

It is in the light of such thoughts that St. Gregory VII himself should, perhaps, be understood. The "secret" of this greatest among all mediaeval Popes still remains to be fully elucidated. His exaltation of the Roman Church was hardly meant as a "maximum program" of world-conversion, but rather as a guarantee of the preservation of the Church's sacerdotal and hierarchical essence in doctrine and Liturgy, the "minimum" and, truly, the "saving grace" to be defended in a wicked world which had rashly tried to identify itself with the Church.

However this may be, a large share in the elaboration of a new concept of the state in the twelfth and thirteenth centuries must be attributed to the development of the relation between Church and state since Gregory VII.

It remains true, nevertheless, that the terminology in which the state is defined as a community, self-sufficient and perfect in itself with regard to population and territory, did not re-emerge before the redis-covery of Aristotle's political thought in the thirteenth century. Also, the functional notion of the state was much too deeply rooted to be very quickly superseded. In fact, new variants of the Gelasian-Caro-lingian two-power-doctrine developed in the twelfth and early thir-teenth century, especially the doctrine of the two swords, the spiritual and the temporal, a doctrine which reflects the conflicting claims of royalists and imperialists on the one and papalists or curialists on the other side, by assigning either one or both swords to the Pope. While twelfth and thirteenth century political theory remained in many re-spects transitional, the beginnings of that notion of the state which was to be rationalized through the reception of the Aristotelian con-cept of the self-sufficient perfect community may, as we have seen, be traced to the events of the Gregorian era and to the discrediting of the functional idea of the state which started them.

The revival of the study of Roman Law in the twelfth century, to which is sometimes attributed the largest role in the early stages of the process here described, rather complicated the development. For the *Corpus Iuris Civilis* was dominated by the idea of the Empire to such a degree that lawyers of kings and jurists of cities from the twelfth to the fourteenth century had some difficulty in applying Roman Law principles to the non-imperial political bodies, to the self-sufficient national states and city states. Here again the Church showed the way. In the struggles with the Holy Roman Empire and the resulting disparagement of the latter's ideological foundation canonists and popes found the formulae which made it possible to reconcile Roman law with the new notion of the state and which culminate in the famous postulates of the thirteenth and fourteenth centuries: *Rex superiorem non recognoscens est imperator in regno suo,* "A king who does not recognize a superior is emperor in his kingdom," and *Civitas sibi princeps,* "The city state is its own ruler."

Some popes and canonists of the twelfth and thirteenth centuries attempted to define the new position of the papacy in front of the autonomous states by assigning to the Roman Church itself the role and office of the Roman Empire, declaring the Pope to be the true Emperor. But this idea had on the whole been given up by the time Boniface VIII pronounced his doctrine on papal supremacy over all states and, in fact, all human beings—there was no real need to make the Pope Emperor, he stood equally high over the Empire and the other forms of political life.

It is very interesting and significant that St. Thomas Aquinas in his discussions of the relation between Church and State ignored the Holy Roman Empire, except, perhaps, in the *Exposition of the Second Letter to the Thessalonians* which seems to have been written down by Reginald of Piperno after notes taken in the Saint's lectures on the Epistles of St. Paul. The passage in question comments on *II Thessal.* II 1–8, which in the earlier Middle Ages had been by some interpreted as denoting the duration to the end of the world of the Roman Empire or rather of its continuation, the Holy Roman Empire, while others had rather referred it to the eternity of the Church.

Putting his seal, as it were, on the end of the Hohenstaufen Empire in 1250, on the entire new situation, in fact, as it had developed since the Investiture Contest with regard to the relation between the Church and the states, St. Thomas, or one of his pupils, clearly states that the Roman Empire had been transposed from the temporal to the spiritual order (*commutatum de temporali in spirituale*) and infers that the prophecies concerning its eternity now apply to the Catholic Faith of the Roman Church.

In concluding it might be well to emphasize that the mediaeval notion of the state as self-sufficient community, expressed in Aristotelian terms, remained a Christian idea as long as it was limited to the natural and inferior to the supernatural order, as long as the self-sufficient community was embedded in the superabundant communion of the Church. St. Thomas, in this respect as in many others, combines the thought of St. Augustine and that of Aristotle when, in his *Commentary to Psalm 45,* he defines the Church both as the fully and truly self-sufficient community and as the City of God.

The real break in the mediaeval notion of the state or, better, the transition to one of the several modern sets of political ideas came, perhaps, with Dante who posited a realm of secular civilization (*humana civilitas*) not subordinate to, but—as far as terrestrial life is concerned—coordinate with the Church. It came in any case with Marsilius of Padua who created a mockery of the Church as the Body of Christ by making the laymen more important in it than the clerics, in other words by using the identity of the faithful and the citizen in a Christian society as a pretext for reserving all exercise of government in spiritual as well as in temporal matters to the political community, to the state. In doing so, Marsilius did not fail to play off a distorted concept of the Church as Mystical Body against that of the Church as a clerical, that is to say, essentially sacerdotal institution. His Paulinian definition of the Church as *Corpus Christi* in the twenty-second chapter of *Dictio II* of the *Defensor Pacis* must be read in conjunction with chapter two of the same *Dictio* where he gives important definitions of the meanings of the term *Ecclesia:* as clerical corporation or institution, further as the Roman Church or Roman-Catholic clergy, directed by the Pope, and lastly as "all the faithful (*universitas fidelium*) who believe in Christ and invoke His name." The first two definitions mentioned reflect two true aspects of the Church as it had developed since the days of Gregory VII; the third and, according to Marsilius, truest definition uses the expression *universitas fidelium* where one would expect *Corpus Christi Mysticum,* and thus represents a characteristic attenuation of the doctrine of the Church as the Body of Christ. Marsilius, in spite of his numerous references to St. Paul, could no longer conceive of the Church as a true supranatural society, but only as a corporation, if not of the clergy only, then of all believing individuals, a corporation in any case existing on the same sociological level as the state.

THE PHOTIAN SCHISM

IN WESTERN AND

EASTERN TRADITION

F. Dvornik

[1948]

THE problem of the Patriarch Photius involved one of the most tangled and bitter differences that hamper friendly relations between Eastern and Western Christianity. Since the Renaissance, Photius, a Greek scholar of the ninth century, has been venerated by philosophers and philologists alike as the genius who among others was instrumental in transmitting to later generations classical Greek and Hellenic culture. On the other hand, Photius' name has been associated with the rise of the first schism in the ninth century when, under Pope Nicholas I, Photius played a prominent part in the first clash between the papacy and the East. The result is that the same man who is venerated as a saint by the Eastern Church, and as one of the last living witnesses of the tradition of the early Christian Fathers, has been for centuries regarded by the Christian West as the father of the great schism, as a prevaricator who falsified papal letters and conciliar Acts, and as a symbol of pride and lust for ecclesiastical domination. It is evident that both views cannot be right. Hence, the history of the Patriarch still stands as the greatest stumbling block barring the way to a better understanding between eastern and western Christendom. The apparent impossibility of reconciling such contradictory estimates has left historians with the feeling that history in this case finds itself in a cul-de-sac.

Yet, the problems connected with Photius are in no way insoluble. I am confident that in a not too distant future historians and churchmen will be amazed that such a simple case should have been so hopelessly misunderstood. Their main mistake has been to approach the study of Photius solely from the religious and ecclesiastical angle: he is supposed to have occupied the See of Constantinople illegally, after conspiring with the government to expel the rightful occupant, Saint Ignatius, and to have defied papal protests against this violation of canon law by falsifying the Pope's letter, bribing his legates and inducing an eastern council to depose the Pope.

In spite of appearances, the origin of the conflict was not religious, and it is misleading to give it a solely religious meaning. The mistake can only be excused on the ground of ignorance of the political evolution of Byzantium. But in recent years, Byzantine studies, so long neglected, have made remarkable progress. One of the principal discoveries made in Byzantine political evolution is the role which political parties played in Byzantium. Ever since the transfer of Imperial Rome to the banks of the Bosphorus, there had existed in Byzantium a deep-seated incompatibility and open rivalry between the two main groups, the one moderate or liberal, the other conservative and reactionary, respectively called the Greens and the Blues. They were originally two semi-sporting factions of the Hippodrome, the successor in Byzantium of the Roman circus. The Blues included the bourgeois elements, usually conservative in Church and state matters; the Greens were more radical, eager to support new doctrines and new pretenders. They found their main backing among the popular elements.

The first centuries of Byzantine history were constantly troubled by incessant struggles between these two groups, and what is more, these political factions took a hand and had their say in all the theological conflicts that came their way. This spirit of partisanship never left the Byzantine stage. Even after the Blues and the Greens had lost their political influence, probably in the seventh century as part of the administrative reforms introduced by the Emperor, Heraclius, the two tendencies continued to exist and to fight for the upper hand in state and Church affairs. They came into the picture again during the image or icon conflicts, and later in a different form after the victory of orthodoxy over the iconoclasts.

Finally, about the middle of the ninth century, we find two powerful parties in Byzantium fighting for the control of Church and state: the intransigents and the moderates. The former were the devout zealots who, elated by their victory over the enemies of image worship, rejected every compromise in the treatment of the heretics. The moderates, who shared the same orthodox belief, preached moderation in the treatment of heretics, or to use the technical term current in Byzantium, they stood for *oikonomia*.

After the victory over iconoclasm, the two factions were again at each other's throats. The moderates first got the upper hand and the monk Methodius, orthodox but a partisan of *oikonomia*, was elected patriarch. But the intransigents did not consider themselves beaten, and they criticized Methodius' religious policy with such violence that the patriarch felt obliged to anathematize the refractory monks of the monastery of Stoudios, the leaders of the zealots. After the death of Methodius, things got decidedly worse, and the Empress Theodora did not consider it safe to summon the usual synod for the election of a successor. She appointed one herself, and chose the monk, Ignatius, son of the Emperor Michael II, whose memory was cherished by the intransigents. It was a concession to the extremists, but Ignatius, although by temperament a zealot, appears not to have been implicated in the intransigents' intrigues against Methodius.

To spare the feelings of the extremists, Ignatius thought it best to exclude from the ceremony of his enthronement the man who had probably been mainly responsible for the condemnation of the Studites, Gregory Asbestas, Bishop of Syracuse and champion of Methodius. As there had been no synod to elect the patriarch and to settle the schism created by the excommunication of the Studites, their case had to come before the court of the patriarch. In his anxiety to be impartial, he ordered Asbestas out of the meeting place, for the excommunicated party held him responsible for their condemnation.

But it was a tactical error. The moderates, who had accepted Ignatius' nomination in spite of his uncanonical promotion, felt aggrieved out of respect for the deceased patriarch who had canonically condemned the Studites. They accused the new patriarch of favoring a policy which his predecessor had condemned. Therefore in their eyes Ignatius could do nothing right.

Political complications embittered the incident. The Empress Theodora, who was regent during her son Michael's minority, appointed the eunuch Theoctistos, an able man, as prime minister; but her brother Bardas, no less able, resented this transfer of power to a stranger whose interest it was to keep young Michael and his uncle at a distance. At the beginning of Theodora's reign, Theoctistos had seen the necessity of practicing a moderate policy, as evidenced by Methodius' appointment to the patriarchal throne, but he also saw how popular Theodora was among the intransigents, who venerated her as a second Irene, the restorer of image worship. With their assistance, he hoped to keep her and himself in power. The choice of Ignatius was the result of this change of front.

Bardas had some reason to fear a repetition of the tragedy that had befallen Constantine V, who had been dethroned and blinded by order of his own mother, Irene, who wanted to govern alone. He looked among the moderates for supporters of Michael, in whose name he expected to reign. They were only too glad to oblige him, seeing the way the new patriarch was leaning on the extremists. Irritated by the criticisms of Asbestas and other leaders of the moderates, Ignatius felt driven to suspend and excommunicate them. But the condemned prelates appealed to Rome, as the Council of Sardica gave them the right to do. In Rome it was felt that the condemnation of these men was not canonically correct and confirmation of the sentence without a preliminary examination was refused. The moderates made the most of this opinion against the intransigents.

Further complications arose in the political field. It soon became evident that either Theoctistos or Bardas had somehow to be eliminated. Theoctistos fell, Michael III was proclaimed emperor, and Bardas succeeded his rival. But the intransigents refused to take this quietly. As long as Theodora remained in the palace, there was hope of seeing her again on the throne and the Empress lent herself to the plan. At the same time, the extremists tried to discredit Bardas in public opinion by inventing and spreading the absurd story of his incest with his daughter-in-law. Ignatius believed the calumny and insulted the regime by publicly refusing Bardas holy communion.

The extremists' success was short-lived. Their plot against Bardas and Michael was detected and Theodora was ordered out of the palace into a convent. In order to test Ignatius' loyalty, he was asked to bless the imperial novice's veil, and being loyal to his benefactress, he refused. To make matters worse, he took up the defense of a monk and an imposter who pretended to be Theodora's son in order to cause a riot. That was enough: Ignatius, without ceasing to be the patriarch, was interned on the island of Terebinth. His position became intolerable, and he was urged by the government and the episcopate to submit his resignation. A careful examination of contemporary accounts affords ample evidence, whatever has been said to the contrary, of the undeniable fact that he yielded to the request to save his church from worse difficulties. He even urged his supporters to elect a successor.

But his resignation brought no peace. Intransigents and moderates had each their candidates and one checkmated the other. It appears that thereupon the government proposed to follow Theodora's example by appointing Photius as its own candidate. But the intransigents protested and a synod was summoned which began by settling the cases of Asbestas and his friends. Our sources confirm the fact that after giving a certain satisfaction, probably by apologizing to Ignatius, they were restored to favor. After lengthy discussions, it was decided to discard the two party candidates and to accept the candidate proposed by the government. Photius was then canonically elected, before Christmas, 858.

This was a compromise, accepted by all the bishops, including the most refractory, who, however, put down the condition that the elected patriarch should sign an understanding to the effect that he would respect Ignatius' ecclesiastical dignity and defend him against calumnies. Photius was moreover asked to be consecrated by Asbestas and by an Ignatian, the names of this consecrator and of a third having remained unknown. The Acts of the council of 869–870 make it clear that Asbestas was not the only consecrator, although later the extremists tried to prove the invalidity of Photius' ordination on the ground that he had been ordained by an excommunicated bishop.

The Byzantine clergy agreed to the compromise. No one protested against the fact that Photius, like his patriarchal uncle Tarasius, was a layman and had received all the degrees of the priesthood within the space of one week. Everything looked promising and the new Patriarch enjoyed universal recognition for about two months.

The trouble started again in February, 859, when the intransigents found fault with the Patriarch's policy. It appears that Photius tried to prevent certain members of the clergy from agitating against the new political regime, and judging from a decision taken by the "first-second" council of 859, 861, he tried to check abuses that had in the past been partly responsible for the iconoclastic reaction and had crept both into the monastic and devout world at the time of Ignatius. On the pretext that Photius failed to observe the conditions of the compromise, some members of the higher and the lower clergy met in the church of St. Irene to declare that Photius had forfeited his right to the patriarchal throne and that Ignatius was restored to his rightful place.

The text of the sources that record the incident shows that Photius first tried canonical proceedings against the malcontents by summoning the clergy of the city to the church of the Holy Apostles; but before the synod had time to take a decision, riots broke out necessitating government intervention. The disturbance was quelled rather severely and Photius protested and threatened Bardas with his resignation.

Ignatius seems to have had nothing to do with the incidents, but police precautions were taken to prevent his communicating with the fomenters whom he had refused to condemn. When after an inquiry ordered by Bardas, Ignatius' innocence was proven, the old Patriarch was allowed to return to his monastery and a synod declared his second "promotion" to be null and void.

Not until then could the Patriarch send to the Pope and the other patriarchs the synodical letter announcing his nomination. As the recent trouble was nothing but an aftermath of the iconoclastic conflict, the Emperor conceived the thought of summoning a synod to condemn once more the iconoclastic errors and to check certain abuses of the monastic world. Michael III then invited the Pope and the other patriarchs to send their delegates to Constantinople and to lend their authority to the synod's decisions.

Nicholas I, who had done so much to raise the prestige of the See of Rome, saw in this move an opportunity to reassert his authority in the East. He gave his consent to the despatch of legates, but refused to acknowledge Photius as the legitimate patriarch before his delegates should have examined on the spot the circumstances of Ignatius' dismissal and reserved the final decision to himself. He hoped at the same time to recover his jurisdiction over the ancient Roman province of Illyricum which Leo III, the iconoclastic Emperor, had placed under the jurisdiction of Constantinople.

The Pope's decision was not welcomed in Constantinople where it was felt that instead of settling anything, it only gave the intransigents a pretext for further intrigues. The delegates, the Bishops Rodoald and Zachary, soon perceived that Byzantine apprehensions were not ill-founded. Their examination of Photius' appointment showed that the canonical rules concerning the election of bishops had been observed. It appears that the Emperor and Bardas gave them the choice between judging Ignatius in Constantinople in the Pope's name, to the obvious benefit of the Holy See, or cancelling the synod altogether. The legates appreciated the concession, since the Byzantines considered Ignatius' case as settled locally, and they consented to take their own counsel and to judge his case on the spot.

The synod was held. The Acts have survived only in an extract copied in Deusdedit's collection of Canon Law (eleventh century) and have so far not been studied by historians in due earnest. The extract of the Synodical Acts are undoubtedly authentic, and the Acts are of supreme importance in the history of Ignatius and Photius. Ignatius protested against the procedure and emphatically stated that he had never appealed to Rome. Thereupon the intransigents found another chance to fish in troubled waters. To forestall their attempts to recall Ignatius to the throne, the moderates fell back on the argument of the irregular method of his appointment without the procedure of a synod, while Photius had been elected canonically. The legates had also the satisfaction of settling Asbestas' appeal and of concluding a case that had already been settled independently of the See of Rome.

Ignatius apparently submitted to the verdict and—contrary to what is generally believed—no contemporary record confirms the generally accepted opinion that he appealed to the Pope. The latter had his misgivings about the happenings in Constantinople, but he did not blame his legates. This proves that he did not object on principle to their having taken matters into their own hands. Worthy of note also were the declarations of reverence for Rome by the Byzantine prelates and their readiness to recognize the right of appeal to Rome, a readiness which the Pope, in reading the Acts, must have noted with great satisfaction.

One card was left to Nicholas, the right he had reserved to himself to confirm the verdict of his legates, and this he was determined to play for the recovery of the jurisdiction over Illyricum which he took so much to heart. The subject had not been mentioned in his letters to the Emperor; but he had good hopes in the arrival in Rome of refugees from Constantinople, some pious monks headed by Theognostos, one of the intransigent leaders who complained that they had been persecuted by the Emperor. Their version did not quite tally with what the Acts and the official letters had to say about the whole affair; but they found it all too easy to exaggerate the opposition to Photius in Constantinople, the more so as they displayed such zeal for, and such subservience to the Holy See.

In Constantinople, a policy of silence was deemed to be the best, and not till 865 did the Emperor send a letter to the Pope to put before him the Emperor's own point of view. Fearing for his recent gains in Constantinople, the Pope took alarm. However, Bulgaria's withdrawal from the patriarchal jurisdiction (866) heartened him again, and as his letter to the Emperor had remained unanswered, he chose to credit the accusations of Theognostos and to dismiss Photius. The numerous letters he wrote to Constantinople and to the oriental patriarchs to inform them of his decision make it evident that the Romans completely sided with the extremists. The result was that the two legates were condemned. Zachary gave way, but Rodoald stuck to his opinion: to the end of his life, he maintained that his policy had been the only possible one, that the Pope should not have listened to a handful of obstreperous monks.

It was felt in Constantinople that the intransigents had scored a victory in Rome, and Photius under these circumstances should have held his tongue and said nothing. But the defection of Bulgaria had dealt a blow at the prestige of Byzantium and the empire. It seems that in order the better to sever Bulgaria from Byzantium, the Roman missionaries had indulged in some exaggerations and painted some innocent Byzantine customs as a danger to the faith. The Byzantine missionaries retorted by applying the same method to some Roman customs. For the purpose of impressing Boris, the Bulgarian Khagan, and to silence the Franks, the Emperor decided to summon a synod of all the patriarchs of the east and Photius announced the purpose of the synod in a synodical letter. The synod, held in 867, condemned the Frankish usages, and what was worse, Pope Nicholas' manner of acting.

He was accused of disregarding the customs of the Church of Constantinople, of abusing his rights and of listening to the calumnious gossip of the Emperor's and the Patriarch's enemies. Nicholas was deposed and Louis II was appointed to carry out the sentence.

This cavalier treatment did Photius no good. With fate seemingly working in his favor, he should have kept his peace. Nicholas I died the same year, and as some documents show, Rome was on the eve of a change of oriental policy, away from that of Nicholas. Hadrian II, the new pope, seriously considered the adoption of a more benevolent attitude to Photius to the disgust of the monk Theognostos, who feared the collapse of his schemes.

But before steps could be taken, a messenger arrived in Rome from Constantinople with the news that Michael III had been punished for his misdeeds by Basil I, and that the new Emperor had replaced Ignatius on the patriarchal throne following the instructions of Nicholas I. This bombshell fully justified in the eyes of the Romans the oriental policy of Nicholas I, since the Byzantines themselves had adopted it. Nothing was known in Rome of the rivalry between Basil and Bardas and no one knew that by assassinating Michael, Basil had to rely on the assistance of the intransigents. He had therefore to accept their conditions and replace Ignatius on the throne. He, of course, needed Rome's approval to stabilize his usurpation.

Impressed by these events, Hadrian stiffened his attitude toward Photius, who was duly condemned by a Roman synod. The sentence was to be made public before a synod in Constantinople and the pontifical legates had strict orders to see to its execution. It was at this juncture that Basil's interests clashed with the Pope's orders. Having no desire to exasperate the party of the moderates, the Emperor wished the synod to pass a second judgment on Photius in order to rally the whole clergy to the cause of Ignatius. But the legates persistently maintained that the case had been judged in Rome, and that the absence of Photius' representatives was immaterial. Sentence had been passed and the bishops had only to submit. Such obstinacy exasperated both the Emperor and Ignatius. What also aggravated them was that the legates asked every member of the synod to sign a document that proclaimed the Roman primacy too bluntly to suit Byzantine tastes. The synod (869–870)—called the Eighth Oecumenical Council—left Basil sadly disappointed. Most of the bishops remained loyal to Photius and Ignatius found himself unable to provide for the needs of his flock. The Byzantine Church was more divided than ever.

Disgusted with the stiff attitude of the Pope and the intransigents, Basil turned to the moderates, recalled Photius from his exile, entrusted him with the education of his children and, so it seems, appointed him Rector of the University. Reconciliation between Photius and Ignatius followed soon after. Of this we have incontestable evidence. Peace was to be sealed by a new council and an embassy left for Rome for the purpose.

The Photian legend would never have been born, if that council had been able to meet in Ignatius' lifetime. But when the Pope's legates arrived in Constantinople, Ignatius was dead and according to the terms of the arrangement between the Emperor and the late Patriarch, Photius was again at the patriarcheion. Seeing that the position was so different from what they had imagined in Rome, the legates wondered what they should do, and the Emperor had to send a second embassy to Rome. The new pope, John VIII, seized the occasion to settle the quarrel and turn it to his own advantage.

In his instructions to his legates and in his letters to Photius, Basil and the Council, he stated he was ready to acknowledge Photius as the legitimate incumbent, on condition that he should apologize to the Council for his past conduct and renounce the jurisdiction of Bulgaria.

The legates examined the position and saw the hopelessness of the first condition, laid down in complete ignorance of the situation in Byzantium for which Theognostos was responsible. Photius could not possibly comply with the Pope's wish without *ipso facto* approving the attitude of the extremists toward him. The mission was therefore doomed to failure if they should insist on an apology.

This being so, the pontifical letters that were to be read before the council had to be modified accordingly. They were actually expurgated, all reference to the apology being suppressed. The gap was filled with a few compliments to Photius. The historians who analyzed the two versions overlooked the fact that Photius left untouched most of what the Pope had written about the Roman primacy, which proves that the alterations were not made in a spirit hostile to Rome, and that Photius was not opposed in principle to the idea itself.

It has looked suspicious to many that the last two sessions of the council of 879–880 should have followed a different procedure from the other sessions, and that the Emperor only presided at the last but one. The inference was made that Photius tampered with the minutes of the session on the ground that the symbol of faith was read out without the *Filioque*. But the anomaly is easily explained. The Emperor Basil had lost his favorite son, Alexander, in the autumn of 879, and as all preparations had been made the council could not be put off. The court being in mourning, Photius was commissioned by Basil to take his place as chairman of the debates. But as the Emperor had to be present at one session at least, the delegates met at the imperial palace for the recital of the Symbol. This session was held towards the end of the period of official mourning.

The council solemnly confirmed the rehabilitation of Photius and his clergy and declared the council of 869–870—the Eighth Oecumenical—to be null and void. In fact, its Acts vanished from the archives of the Greek Church. The ultra-intransigents who refused to acknowledge Photius were excommunicated.

Until 1933 the conviction prevailed that John VIII never approved the Acts of the council of 879–880 which rehabilitated Photius. It was alleged that he protested against the alteration of his letters by Photius, that he disowned his legates, as Nicholas I had done, and sent the Deacon Marinus, the future pope, to make an inquiry on the spot. Marinus, so it was alleged, was imprisoned by the Emperor; and the Pope, on learning what had happened and on being told that the majority of the clergy had refused to acknowledge Photius, excommunicated him again. Hence the second schism, more serious than the first, which was to last till the second downfall of the Patriarch. All the successors of John VIII, so we were told, Hadrian III, Marinus, Stephen V, and Formosus, renewed the excommunication of Photius.

These allegations, which have been credited for centuries, must be flatly denied. Historians were really misled by some passages in anti-Photianist writings. What is true is that Pope John VIII found it strange that the conditions he had laid down were disregarded and that his letters had been altered. But as can be proved from his letter to Photius, though it has been misread, he eventually accepted Photius' explanation and those of his legates and ratified the Acts of the council, including the canon which annulled the so-called eighth oecumenical synod of 869–870. Photius was never re-excommunicated either by John VIII or by any of his successors. There was no other embassy sent from Rome to Constantinople and Marinus' imprisonment happened at the time of the Eighth Oecumenical Council of 870, when Marinus displayed too much zeal for the pope in Byzantium. Therefore, the two Churches were at peace.

It was notable also that Basil sent John VIII a strong military contingent to help him against the Arabs and that the two Churches made important concessions to each other in the south of Italy which then belonged to the Byzantine empire. Also, that the Byzantines surrendered Bulgaria to Rome, presumably on condition that the Greek clergy who had been working there should be allowed to stay. Not Photius, therefore, but Boris, was responsible for Rome's final failure in that country.

When Photius was forced in 886 to relinquish his see, it was Pope Stephen V who defended him and the Emperor Leo VI was asked to send a signed copy of Photius' abdication. Not till then did the Pope acknowledge the Emperor's brother as the patriarch.

There was indeed a schism in Byzantium, but it was internal. A small minority of the clergy set up a "Small Church," which remained obdurate even after Photius' fall and refused to hold communion with his successor, the Emperor's brother, because he had been ordained deacon by Photius. This "Small Church" vainly attempted to draw Rome to its side, but Rome continued to acknowledge Photius and his successors. This local schism collapsed at the end of the ninth century, towards 898, under the patriarch Cauleas, not as the result of a synod, as it has been alleged, but as the result of a correspondence between its leader, Stylian of Neocesarea and Pope John IX. The last downfall of Photius was due to Leo's change of policy. He turned to the intransigents at the beginning of his reign, till exasperated by the radicalism of their extremists, he followed his father's example and turned to the liberals.

This account, as measured by the complexities of the subject, is too short, yet makes it clear, I hope, that our notions on the schism of Photius need revising. If these findings are based on facts, then we must be ready for the complete rehabilitation of a man whose character has been blackened for centuries. By the same token, a formidable obstacle to a better understanding between the Western and Eastern Churches will be removed.

But some questions remain to be answered before the case can be closed. How are we to explain the origin and growth of the Photian Legend which, in East and West, so distorted the facts we have restated? If it is true that John VIII rehabilitated Photius and ratified the abrogation of the council that condemned him, how is it that this synod continued to be listed among the oecumenical councils and to be acknowledged as such by the Western Church?

The first factor to contribute to the birth of the Photian Legend was the unfriendly attitude adopted towards the Greek Patriarch by Pope Nicholas I. In his time and after him, nothing was known in Rome of the rivalry between the politico-religious factions in Byzantium, and it was generally assumed that Nicholas' handling of the Photian incident had been fair and was justified by the Byzantines themselves. Even John VIII, after rehabilitating Photius, seemed unable to get rid of misgivings. The Byzantines were satisfied with the reconciliation and content to drop the matter, but John's successors, who apparently accepted his decision, remained convinced that the first condemnation by Nicholas had been to a large extent well founded.

In this lay a serious threat against the truth of Photius' history; all the more so, as Nicholas expounded his ideas on the Roman See in the letters that dealt with the Photian incident and which for that reason obtained wide acceptance throughout the Middle Ages and down to our days.

I have looked for a solution of these problems in all the historical accounts bearing on Photius and on the conciliar question that were published in the West during the Middle Ages, with the following results. In the matter of councils, most of the chroniclers follow the ancient tradition of the Church as inspired by the synodical letter of

St. Gregory the Great and the Ecclesiastical History of Bede by count-
ing only four councils, six at most. The Frankish Church in particular
seems to have inherited Charlemagne's distrust of the Seventh Council
which restored image worship and as late as the tenth century the
Frankish bishops enumerated only six oecumenical councils in their
professions of faith. Even in the thirteenth century, a Frank, discussing with the Greeks of Constantinople, exclaimed: "No, the Seventh
Council is not acknowledged by our Church." Hence, few are the
chroniclers, most of Lombard or Roman origin, who mention seven
councils, and none mentions eight.

The indication is important, though not absolute evidence, for
what we must find is the tradition of the pontifical chancellery in this
particular matter. Now, we possess official documents issued from that
quarter proving that until at least the twelfth century the same chancellery respected the decision of John VIII and numbered no more
than seven councils. In the tenth century, Pope Marinus II threatened
the bishops of Capua with excommunication in virtue of the powers
conferred on the See of Rome by God, St. Peter and St. Paul, and the
authority of the seven oecumenical councils, a threat that would have
carried more weight with the addition of an eighth council.

A second document dates from 1055—the famous letter of Leo IX
to Peter, Patriarch of Antioch, defining the faith of the Church of
Rome. Therein the Pope enumerated all the councils his Church accepts as oecumenical and the last is the seventh. It has been objected
that the Pope only wished to spare the Greeks' feelings, as they did not
acknowledge the Eighth Council—not a very complimentary statement to make about the supreme head of the Church. A strange pope
indeed, who would drop an oecumenical council even to please the
Greeks.

Another document of the same period is the excommunication
launched again Michael Cerularius in Constantinople by Cardinal
Humbert: the redoubtable cardinal excommunicated the patriarch and
all his partisans in the name of the seven councils! Humbert was a
good canonist and no plea of tender feelings can hold in his case, since
he was in the very act of excommunicating the Greeks. We know him
too well to admit that he might have forgotten an oecumenical council,
whose authority would have given additional punch to his passionate
anathema.

Again, another testimony dates from the period of Nicholas II,
successor of Leo IX. In 1059, Nicholas sent St. Peter Damian, venerated today as a Doctor of the Church, to Milan as a legate on a mission
to reform a concubinary and simoniacal clergy. Among the documents
appended to the interesting report Damian wrote of his mission, we
find the copy of an oath which he imposed on all suspect ecclesiastics

who desired to do penance: they had to profess the faith defined by the seven councils. And, surely, Peter had no more reason to spare the priests in Milan than Humbert had to spare the feelings of the Greeks in Constantinople. Moreover, the formula served on them had certainly been drawn up by the pontifical chancellery. Would the experts responsible for it have forgotten the exact number of councils officially acknowledged by the papacy? There being no need to belittle the Roman theologians of that time, it is safe to admit that Peter Damian and his companion, Anselm of Lucca, the future Pope Alexander II, simply translated the Roman belief in seven oecumenical councils and no more.

This is by no means the last of our documents. Here is another also dating from the eleventh century and preserved in the famous *Liber Diurnus,* a formulary that served the Pontifical Chancellery as a handbook. We possess three manuscripts of this document, representing slightly different traditions and marking developments realized by the end of the eighth century and the beginning of the ninth. Among the formulae contained in the work there is a profession of faith which popes had to copy out on their election and sign with their own hand, the copy to be placed on the tomb of St. Peter and finally filed in the Pontifical Archives. The three manuscripts under consideration only enumerate six councils, which is strictly correct, as the seventh council was officially included in the list of the oecumenical councils only towards the end of the ninth century, after 880, the date of Photius' reconciliation with John VIII.

I have also found a new edition of the same profession of faith dating from the eleventh century and preserved in the famous canonical collection of Cardinal Deusdedit. It contains some clauses that may have been added only in the eleventh century and which we also came across in other formularies copies from the *Liber Diurnus* by Deusdedit, evidence that this work was considerably altered in the eleventh century. The popes' profession lists seven oecumenical councils, the same number being found at another place in the formula in connection with the profession of faith imposed on each bishop before his consecration. It all goes to show that the Roman Church upheld the decision of John VIII and that till the end of the eleventh century, she was at one with the Greek Church in this matter.

How then explain the different practice that prevails today? The responsibility for this lies with a curious error committed by the canonists of the end of the eleventh century and the beginning of the twelfth, the period called Gregorian.

Gregory VII, in looking for corroboration to vindicate his notions, so resolutely contested by the imperial jurists, threw open the Pontifical Archives and invited the canonists to search it for new documents, with the result that the Acts of the Councils dealing with the Ignatian and Photian incidents were then discovered and for the first time utilized for purposes of canonical documentation. Deusdedit thus happened to rescue an extract from the synod of 861, mentioned above, and of the Photian synod of 879–880. But to their great joy, the canonists also discovered in the Acts of the Council of 869, which called itself oecumenical, a certain canon XXII which forbade laymen to meddle with episcopal elections—exactly what they were looking for—that is, a decisive argument to corner the imperialists, who obstinately defended lay investiture. In their excitement, the canonists increased the number of Fathers present at the Council by a hundred—133, to be exact—to enhance its importance, and clearly forgot that this assembly, which did call itself oecumenical, had been annulled ten years after it was held.

It is true that the first school of canonists did make some reservations. Deusdedit, for instance, dared not go so far as to call the council oecumenical, but very properly designated it as "the council calling itself oecumenical," or "called oecumenical by some." He also copied out without any alterations the popes' profession of faith which only recorded seven oecumenical councils. But the copyists, not being gifted with the same critical sense and the same learning, did not adopt his discretion. In this respect, a Latin manuscript in the British Museum, is very suggestive. The copyist who worked on this collection included also some extracts from the cardinal's work, and among them the profession of faith which Deusdedit had taken from the *Liber Diurnus* in the Roman Chancellery. The copyist, who could not consult the original personally, noticed that the cardinal, in reporting the sayings of the Fathers of the Council of 869, called this council oecumenical. He thought the figure seven in the profession of faith must have been a mistake and coolly rectified it by adding to the seven oecumenical councils the council John VIII had officially cut out of the list.

Not all misgiving were thereby removed. The great Frank canonist, Ivo of Chartres, did consult the extracts from the Acts of the Photian Council which must have been in circulation in different versions and actually quoted in his work the canon by which the so-called Eighth Council was suppressed, and he quoted it for the purpose of establishing that popes had the power to annul even universal synods: but this did not prevent him (after he had consulted an extract from Cardinal Deusdedit's work, perhaps the one preserved in the manuscript of the British Museum) from copying from it the passage of the popes' profession as amended by the copyist, that is, with the addition of the Eighth Oecumenical Council. It is a strange paradox, showing the embarrassment of a canonist as eminent as the bishop of Chartres when he has to choose between two contradictory statements.

Another canonist, the author of the collection known as *Caesaraugustana* of Saragossa, which dates from the same period, and has so far remained unpublished (I consulted it in two manuscripts at the National Library of Paris), copied the canon quoted by Ivo which annuls the Eighth Council; yet being one of the few who may have consulted not only the work of Ivo of Chartres, but also the original collection of Deusdedit instead of a mere extract from the cardinal's work, he may have thought that the cardinal was in possession of a more accurate version of the profession of faith in question and omitted the document concerning the number of councils quoted by Ivo from his collection.

I have also looked over all the important canonical collections of the period, nearly all unpublished, to find out their mutual affiliation, and I have been able to establish that no other factor has entered that tradition, that all those collections cease to quote the original pontifical archives and depend solely on the great canonists of the Gregorian period, Anselm of Lucca and Ivo of Chartres.

An important stage in the growth of the Photian Legend is reached by the *Decretum* of the best known canonist in the Middle Ages, Gratian. In the twelfth century, he was nothing more imposing than a compiler, who did not consult the original documents and used the works of Ivo of Chartres as his favorite source. He copied out in his *Decretum* the popes' profession of faith as Ivo had it, with its eight councils; only, faithful to his principle and practice of reconciling the canons among themselves, he eliminated the canon of the Photian Council which annulled the Eighth Council, since it contradicted the popes' profession of faith.

Gratian's *Decretum* remained the standard work on the subject and it was from him that the Middle Ages took their canonical, patristic, and even their scriptural arguments. To none at the time did it ever occur that not eight, but seven councils only were oecumenical; the number was officially ratified by the Council of Constance at the beginning of the fifteenth century and to the first eight councils were then added those of the Lateran, Lyons, and Vienna.

But since Gratian included in his collection a canon of the Photian Council, it is evident that the memory of this synod was not completely obliterated in the Western Church, and it is still possible to find some historians and chroniclers—for instance, the Czech Martinus Opaviensis and the Doge of Venice, Dandolo—who admitted its validity together with Photius' rehabilitation by John VIII.

Not until the fifteenth century, that is in the course of the conciliar controversy, did theologians rediscover the Acts of the Eighth Council, and it is revealing to see how both sides made capital of the find for their respective claims. This again made the Eighth Council extremely popular, for directly its oecumenicity was admitted, all its decisions were assumed to be irrevocable and the very existence of the Photian Council which had abrogated the Acts of the eighth synod passed into oblivion. There is at best some hesitation on the part of Schedelus, Flavius, Flaccius and the authors of the Magdeburg *Centuries* and a few canonists like Agustin Antonio, but that is all; so that, when Cardinal Baronius, in looking about for answers to the Centuriators, began searching the Vatican Library, and there came upon the documents, so far unknown, bearing on the Photian case, he could not help accepting them in perfectly good faith. Whatever Nicholas, Photius' bitterest enemy, had said and whatever in other documents issued from the same milieu, was taken for granted, since it agreed with the decisions of the Eighth Council, so famous throughout the Middle Ages. It was then that Baronius' fluent pen gave the Photian Legend its definite shape, drew a portrait of Photius as striking as it was unfair, invented, and proved the existence of the second schism of Photius and made of the poor patriarch one of the greatest antagonists of the papacy and of the Western Church.

No one at the time could have withstood the avalanche of arguments that poured out from the cardinal. He had discovered so many new documents that it seemed impossible to question his inferences. But Photius' posthumous career did not end there. Protestant writers, who generally accepted Baronius' deductions, considered it, nevertheless, their duty to defend the Patriarch, since on Baronius' own showing, Photius had been the first to show up the popes' pretensions so gallantly. That, of course, was sufficient commendation to the Protestant writers. Thus the unfortunate Patriarch's name became the shibboleth that labelled the difference between Catholics and Protestants in the seventeenth and eighteenth centuries, the Gallican theologians keeping midway between the two extremes. One scholar only, M. Hanke, one of the first Byzantinists, came near to historical truth.

The discoveries of Cardinal Hergenröther did not substantially alter the portrait of Photius as drawn by his predecessor Baronius, and learned scholar that he was, he failed to shake himself free from the prejudices that had been nurtured throughout the Middle Ages until the final codification by Baronius in his *Ecclesiastical Annals*. Even he looked upon Photius as the first and foremost champion against the papacy.

If then we turn to the East, we find that even in Byzantium the historical truth of Photius' case was soon blurred by prejudice, and those first responsible for this were the writers belonging to the circle of Constantine Porphyrogenetos, the imperial writer of the tenth century. Constantine was interested in praising the achievements of his ancestor Basil, the founder of the Macedonian dynasty, the same who had murdered his friend and benefactor Michael III in order to seize the throne. His victim had therefore as a matter of political consistency to be painted as an immoral drunkard, whose reign spelled ruin to the empire, and a monster whose suppression could safely be credited to Basil, portrayed by inference as the saintly tool of Providence. Photius, who had been made patriarch under Michael and was deposed by Basil, was presented in a bad light.

Other writers, however, show that the memory of this great Patriarch remained very much alive in Byzantium. Past troubles were all the sooner forgotten, when Photius had made his peace with Ignatius before his rival's death, thus clearing the way for his disciples and admirers to venerate him as a saint. Evidence of this cult is found as early as the ninth century. Nicetas, the so-called biographer of Ignatius, confessed that the purpose of his biography, which after all was little better than a political manifesto, was to unmask Photius' deceit and prove that he did not deserve the title of saint.

Today, it is admitted that the Byzantine Church officially approved the cult of St. Photius, not in the fourteenth century, as was often alleged, but in the tenth century at the latest. It should be remembered that at the time the canonization took place, the Byzantine Church was on the best of terms with the Roman Church, for whatever has been said to this day about a schism between the two Churches from the end of the ninth century till the eleventh is pure fabrication. Nor should we forget that in those days canonization, even in the Western Church, was the responsibility of the bishops, for the popes did not reserve that power to themselves till after the eleventh century.

It has been generally assumed that Photius was always looked upon by the Orientals as the author of the doctrine that makes the Holy Ghost proceed from the Father only, not from the Son, and that all the Greeks' criticisms against the Latins in the Middle Ages were made, so to speak, in the name of Photius as the chief anti-Roman protagonist. I have gone through the whole of the Greek polemical literature and found that the polemicists of the eleventh and twelfth centuries were far from looking on Photius in that light. Granted that they often find inspiration in his writings; but they seldom quote his name and they are not at all sure that Photius was responsible for the differences in question. They merely assume that the doctrine on the Procession of the Holy Ghost is the true and genuine Greek doctrine. As to the relations between Photius and Rome, they are aware that he was reconciled with the Pope, the opinion to the contrary and to Photius' discredit not having developed till the thirteenth and fourteenth centuries, when the Greek Uniates were mainly responsible for its spread. Down to the sixteenth century Greek writers know nothing of a second Photian schism; and all the Greek polemicists, both Uniates and schismatics, are firmly convinced that Photius was not again excommunicated by Rome after his reconciliation with John VIII.

Regarding the Acts of the Photian Council which annulled the Eighth Oecumenical Council, the tradition of the Greek Church has been clear and consistent down to the modern period and all, even the Uniates, have considered them to be perfectly authentic. We know that efforts were made to create an impression that at least the Acts of the last two sessions of this Council were tampered with by the Greeks in the fourteenth century, but such an opinion is groundless. I had the good fortune at the London British Museum to come upon a long unpublished Greek treatise on the Councils attributed to Patriarch Euthymius, a manuscript dating from the fifteenth century whose authorship seems to me beyond dispute, and this Patriarch, forty years after the Council, quotes the two last sessions. I may add that I have found other quotations of a similar kind dating from the twelfth and thirteenth centuries, which should settle the question once and for all. It should also be noted that Greek writers never mention the Eighth Council, its fate in their opinion having been definitely decided by the Photian Council.

Even the Greek Uniates, for all their unfriendliness to the memory of Photius, refuse to acknowledge the Eighth Council, being at variance in this with the Roman Catholics. For instance, I found at the National Library of Paris a Greek manuscript of the fifteenth century belonging to this class: it gives the list of the oecumenical councils and to the first seven of them adds the Council of Lyons as the eighth, the Council of Constantinople which ratified the Council of Florence as the ninth, and the Council of Florence as the tenth.

But in spite of the veneration the Greeks always had for the Photian Council, the Byzantine Church never officially numbered it among the oecumenical councils. On this point, I consulted at least fifty Greek manuscripts in Paris, London, Brussels, Vienna, and Rome and all I can say is that not until the fourteenth century did some polemicists attribute oecumenicity to the Council of Photius. And this was not out of any partisan spirit against the Catholics who listed as oecumenical the Council that indicted Photius. We also know that the two traditions collided at the Council of Florence. There is evidence that the Greek writers had kept the original tradition about Photius in accordance with historical truth. But even the Orientals eventually fell under Baronius' spell and from the seventeenth century onward accepted his legend about the second Photian Schism.

Many more details could be added to make the argument more convincing, but I trust that this short account of the Photian Legend and of the tradition of the number of the first oecumenical councils will justify the results of an impartial study. Hence, for the two Churches which for centuries have pulled their different ways, there is but one thing to do, and that is to return to the historical truth about the great Patriarch and to the old tradition which they both upheld from the ninth to the twelfth century. These findings may lead to practical consequences of some importance. We are called upon to defend Western civilization and to bring about a lasting peace. But the worst danger that threatens the very foundations of Christianity lies in the division of the Churches. The survival of Christian civilization is then irrevocably bound up with the problem of reunion. If that is the case, history should show us the way to the goal: we must retrace our steps and go back to the time when the two Churches were one and could stand together in the defense of their ideals.

THE SIGNIFICANCE

OF MEDIAEVAL

INTELLECTUAL CULTURE

Alois Dempf

[1947]

MORE than twenty years ago Nicholas Berdyaev, the noted religious philosopher and sociologist, wrote *The New Middle Ages*. In this work he naturally did not imply that history is repeating itself. Nor did he imply that, by reason of a cyclical recurrence of identical periods in history, following our age of enlightenment, there would dawn a new age of predominantly religious authority concurrently with which state authority would almost disappear—a new age wherein philosophy and science would exercise a far greater general influence upon life than they do today. History, indeed, does not repeat itself. If it did, its story would be a poor *carmen universitatis*, a poor drama of world progress, unworthy of the Lord of history and of human freedom.

But we can and must learn from history. There is no necessity for repeating the same mistakes in political and cultural planning which were made in the incompetent attempts of the totalitarian state to regulate the whole of life. The totalitarian state was certainly a repetition of the absolutism of earlier history, but it was a repetition which had at its disposal many more efficient instruments. Totalitarianism used religion for its purposes—as absolutism had its *"cujus religio ejus regio"*; it manipulated public opinion by means of a monopoly of propaganda—an invention of Campanella and Richelieu; and it pursued its economic policy by establishing a gigantic mercantilistic machinery which put into its hands the exclusive rule of all production and consumption.

It is extremely difficult for us to understand the spirit which existed before the advent of absolutism. Indeed, it was absolutism, as

Max Weber has shown, which, by means of a strong national administration and judiciary, created the most significant premise for that unique phenomenon in the history of mankind—the modern industrial system. And this development certainly was heightened by the new advances in the natural sciences and in technology. It was by means of its intelligence department and the increased possibility of communication that the centralized state was able to intensify its influence upon all the circumstances of life. This fact all too frequently has led us to believe, erroneously, that through state action and state planning everything is possible. A decentralized cultural life, in which, according to the great Platonic theory of justice, everybody minds his own business, has become almost inconceivable to us. And yet, the normal situation in a society of free men is one in which it is the right of the competent, freely creative forces to conduct their own business within their own spheres. If we really want to draw any lesson on this matter from the history of ideas, we should realize that it is this freedom which has been the optimum of cultural history since Plato. In the Middle Ages, that cultural optimum actually was realized in a far-reaching manner. This is not to say that Plato's *Republic* was known or heeded, nor that the progress of cultural life was known to depend essentially upon the free choice of a profession and the subdivision of its work. The beautiful survivals of art which we have not equalled, in spite of our progress, prove that the cultural optimum must have been developed spontaneously by means different from cultural planning.

Now it is very easy to discover the secret of this so-called automatic self-regulation of the cultural community. It consists simply in the fact that those existing forces which tried to exercise the sole responsibility for the formation of all of the culture failed to do so, one after another. First, the Emperor and the Pope struggled for supremacy and both failed: the Emperor in the Interregnum and the Papacy in the Babylonian Captivity of Avignon. During the struggle, however, there grew up a third main party: the bourgeoisie of the city-states, which eventually brought about the glorious flowering of city-culture in the Renaissance, until in its turn it, too, was defeated by the religious battles of the Reformation and its outgrowth, absolutism. Only after the failure of absolutism did bourgeois culture recover, in the eighteenth and nineteenth centuries.

Besides these chief forces in the mediaeval community there is yet another, a fourth power, far too little noticed—the free intellectual culture of the Middle Ages and the powerful development of occidental learning in the free European universities. The blossoming of the universities can only be understood sociologically as caused by the weakness of the mediaeval states which had not yet taken the educational system completely in hand, and by the possibility of free corporations developing without any state law governing associations. The universities at that time were indeed without church or state support; they were simply communities of teachers—"university" originally meant "community." The teachers lived by their audiences and therefore only successful teachers flourished. That was the self-regulation of the life of learning toward the cultural optimum, at least within the field of intellectual culture.

It is very interesting and important for us to see how that condition was reflected in the formation of political and cultural ideas. Such a relationship has so far gone without full recognition because the free equilibrium of the community life of that time has not been noticed, owing to the misconception of the predominantly religious cultural unity of the Middle Ages. At the most the struggles of the Emperor and of the Pope have been investigated, because these struggles had great influence in political history, and because the political and not the cultural aspect was predominant in the writing of history.

As a result the enlightenment of the Middle Ages and the growth of bourgeois and scientific culture have not been sufficiently realized. Above all, the significance of the free university in the heightened consciousness of the educated class has been overlooked. Thus, it was thought impossible that Abelard (1080–1142) had already presented, in the twelfth century, the deism of the eighteenth century in all its principal features. The explanation for this opinion may be that after Abelard had been twice condemned, in 1121 and 1142, by the Provincial Councils for the all-too-free exposition of his ideas, he was obliged to conceal them completely. Whereas, or perhaps just because of this, Gregory VII, in the previous generation, had claimed for the spiritual authority the right of being solely answerable for the entire culture, while Gerhart of York (1108) had claimed this right for the temporal power, for his king, as *summus episcopus*.

The ideology of the supremacy of the state was represented at that time just as it was presented later under Henry VIII and James I, and it was doubtless this situation that caused Abelard to reserve this right of being answerable for the entire culture to the philosophers. His thought was anti-clerical and anti-political because his free and extraordinarily successful teaching had created within him the passionate consciousness of an autonomous intellectual aristocracy. He regarded himself, to use his own words, as the *summus philosophus*. Like Toland in the eighteenth century, he was convinced that the natural law was the highest principle of freely formed associations and of corporate law, and that it was much higher than the positive law of the state and of the Church. Indeed, Abelard already used the same garbled formula that Toland did for the presentation of his enlightened ethics, namely, that Christendom was only a reformation of the original natural law based upon and following the positive divine law of the Old Testament. This can be read in his dialogue between a heathen, a Jew, and a Christian, in which apparently Christ has the last word only because the dialogue was intentionally left incomplete. Thus Abelard's concept is precisely the historical concept of the age of enlightenment: following upon antiquity and the dark Middle Ages, a new era appeared. Only then is the true meaning of natural law, which in the original teaching was hidden in parables, recognized with spiritual understanding.

> *Advenit veritas, umbra praeteriit,*
> *Post noctem claritas diei subiit*
> *Ad ortum rutilant superni luminis,*
> *Legis mysteria plena caliginis.*

Such exaggerated optimism concerning the progress of culture through freedom of knowledge and research, and through the leadership of mankind by an intellectual aristocracy necessarily leads to deism. It becomes a belief in the benevolent architect of the universe who has ordered everything for the service of mankind—*fit ergo mundus optimus ac perfectus in omnibus*—just as the pessimism which does not accept the independence of the masses and their capacity to achieve a sensible social order, leads to a totalitarian state and atheism. Abelard denies the Trinity. In it he seemingly sees the three Divine Persons as modes of operations of the one, as the masks and faces of divine power, wisdom, and goodness.

This radical intellectual and aristocratic cultural ideology was very quickly dissipated, as were the other exclusivist claims to determine the cultural order. It was forthwith transformed into pure politics by one of Abelard's pupils, Arnold of Brescia. In 1147, Arnold raised up a rebellion of the Roman people against the Pope, the lord of the city, in order to reestablish the old Roman republic. He, too, failed and in 1155 he was hanged and burned, and his ashes were scattered to the winds. But his ideals of the republican autonomy of the Italian city in opposition to the lords of the city, at that time usually bishops, continued as a strong influence on the rapidly developing new city-states.

Abelard's ideas of independent learning and of a free management of teaching, independent of Church and state, were to find an entirely different fate. His method of free scientific research in philosophy through the harmonizing of opposing propositions was transferred to theology, canon law, Roman law, and the medical tradition. It was the scholastic method which already in the early thirteenth century had become the foundation of the four faculties and of the free European universities such as Paris, Bologna, Oxford, and Montpelier. Scholasticism took education, which had been formerly imposed upon the various classes of society in an authoritarian manner, and handed it over to autonomous corporations of teaching and learning. Thereby arose that intellectual aristocracy which, it is true, for the time being remained connected with the theological, legal, and medical professions until the invention of printing made possible the rise of a group of independent writers and intellectuals. But the universities of the Middle Ages were ultimately the principal sources of that technical, scientific, economic, and political development of the West whose rise Max Weber put about 300 years later.

Yet a scientific academic education for all the main classes had intellectual effects of even greater consequences: for the first time in the history of mankind there emerged the idea of unified cultural planning, not planned by one class alone. This idea was not dominated by class prejudice, that one social force alone could assume complete responsibility for culture. That fact was almost as epoch-making as the discovery of the ingenuous mythical symbols of history which stand at the beginning of all periods in the history of philosophy, and which inaugurate the transition from cultural bloom to cultural maturity. Thus, the constitution of an all-embracing culture became the most important problem at this stage of intellectual history.

In order to be able to see this it was necessary to acquire a scientific and sociological understanding of the classical philosophy of Catholicism, of Thomism. This primarily required an interpretation of the greatest of all political ideas, the idea of *lex aeterna*. It is not yet entirely clear what that idea meant to Cicero and to St. Augustine. But its decisive position in the gigantic construction of the Thomist doctrine has become evident to us. The Thomist idea of *lex aeterna* was defined through the personalist turn which Aquinas gave to the traditional conception. He first understood the whole cultural life with the help of personality types, especially of the political man. This man was responsible for the community, for he had the *cura communitatis,* just as the infallible Pope who had the supernatural illumination of the Holy Spirit was responsible for the conservation of pure Christian doctrine. Aquinas expected the cooperation of the scientifically-educated representatives of the classes because he independently adopted as the most significant heritage of ancient politics and ethics the concept of social man active in politics. That was the true beginning of the autonomous political renaissance in the West. There is no doubt that this beginning was due to the new self-consciousness of the teachers as opposed to the mere practitioners from the classes in authority. In intellectual matters that was the first fruit of the university, then scarcely a century old.

This development explains the ingenious turn of the *lex aeterna* idea into the realm of practice. There it became creative as a fundamental primary institution of the entire world order. For previously the norms of interchangeable custom and the order of living had to be considered static. Only by combining an understanding of the natural norms—ultimately founded upon the absolute spirituality and rationality of the Divine Being—with the activity of practical realization was the spiritually active personality completed. Thus the *lex aeterna* became the *forma institutionis mundi,* the basic plan of the arrangement of the world, of the whole community of the universe, and the *ratio gubernationis mundi,* the rational basis of world government as the *regula regulantis,* the establishment of the norm of the norm-giver.

Politically viewed, this idea went far beyond natural law. Natural law indeed only projected, within the given order of the positive right of the ruling classes, a change of order in the sense of the higher rationality of social life corresponding to the right norms of collective life. It was the idea of the *lex aeterna* which showed that Aquinas' work, *De regimine principum*—addressed to the princelings of Cyprus—was the first humanistic utopia. Of course, we must be familiar with many such fabled states, from the *Utopia* of Thomas More to the *City of the Sun* of Campanella, if we are to rediscover the old Platonic *Politeia,* the first utopia, as Aquinas' inspiration in his sober, completely reasonable system for a perfect state.

In Aquinas, even the idea of natural law received for the first time an entirely new and much higher meaning of still unexhausted range. It was the personal, active *regula in regulato.* The norm was discovered in that which has received from eternal wisdom its rational and social nature along with its ontological powers and standards of moral and spiritual development. Intellectual, creative men whose natural and supernatural fulfillment was in the supreme joy of the vision of God, became now full members of the *tota communitas universi;* but they had at the same time various capacities as businessman, physician, scholar, jurist, theologian, so that in the diverse realization of their gifts the free cooperative interplay might produce the cultural optimum. Again, there is no doubt that the faculties of the free European universities must have existed before this ingenious formulation of natural law could have been produced. The natural law was comprehended as being rooted in the nature of man, who mirrors the Creator. This likewise provided the foundation for the rule of the hierarchy of values. It was also understood as a basis for the natural differentiation of character which was so important for the fulfillment of cultural harmony. It has been recognized that Aquinas explained the natural law as a just and righteous law, a measure of the inner worth and obligatory character of the positive law. But it has been little noticed that he also understood it as a *vis directiva,* as a formative power of the person which has only to take into consideration the particular, special, and historic circumstances, but which is inferior to the fundamental and responsible arrangement of the mature culture. Ought the philosopher to stand above the king and the spiritual culture above the political? So Aquinas held, as well as Campanella after and Plato before him. Here the historical sequence of the great conception became evident, the still dominant significance of the ancient inspiration of Aristotelian politics which did not enable this conception to achieve a clear exposition and transfiguration of the mediaeval actuality. Thus the constitutional elective monarch, the *persona publica,* retained the responsibility for the *civitas perfecta,* the whole bourgeoisie, the whole life of the earthly community.

But the new intellectual environment partially asserted itself. It was revealed in the conception of the *lex divina,* the divine revelation and institution of religion (*lex* in the sense of a total order of culture as understood by the Jews and Moslems), as only an emergency intervention of God to help man after his original fall. God's help was necessary to assist human frailty to see more clearly, amidst the tangle of particulars in human development, all that involved responsibility and guilt.

The longest articles of the *Summa Theologica,* the powerful treatise on the *Old Testament*—100 articles out of the 900 of general ethics (I.II.98–105)—are undoubtedly the most gifted sociological performance of Aquinas. Such a comprehensive attempt to view the whole of Jewish culture as a fully rational form of divinely ordained stage between the natural law and the final perfect law of Christ had not been conceived either before or after Aquinas. It is a well-directed and normative exposition of the concrete and possible cultural optimum, in its liturgical, ethical, and politico-social order, which is inserted in a definite part of the divine world plan for total historical development. The law of the *New Testament* can only improve men further through the freedom of God's children in a law which they understand and through God's merciful help of the redeemed.

It is clear that Aquinas was hierarchical in a comprehensive sense. He believed in a spiritual leadership of mankind through the infallible Pope. This leadership is based on natural law and is supported by the social appreciation of the best cultural planning that is concretely possible and that is best adapted to human nature. This emphasis came first. Only thereafter did Aquinas stress the political responsibility of the constitutionally elective monarch for the perfect state, a political responsibility based on positive law.

But no less than Rousseau did Aquinas raise the question: Who in a particular case should interpret the *volonté de tous,* since in political life only the will of the community (*volonté générale*) counts? But how is it possible to discover this will of the community amidst the conflicting claims of individuals (*volonté de tous*)? Perhaps that is today the decisive question of mankind's political life. In the time of Aquinas there did not exist that free intellectual aristocracy of which Abelard had dreamed, which he too rashly saw in the community of his pupils, and all too one-sidedly assigned to the supreme philosophers alone. The primacy of philosophy would be just as wrong as the absolute power of the Pope in temporal matters and as the absolutist pretensions of totalitarian states to the formation of the whole culture. As Aquinas saw with superb clarity, only the divine abundance of intellectual gifts, freely operating within their own strictly observed sphere with each platonically able to do and doing its part, can lead to the cultural optimum.

Institutionally the independence of the intellectual aristocracy somehow must be anchored between church and state. All periods of philosophy begin with the emergence of an independent teaching profession which must take its place beside the church and the state because an evaluation of the world's course also involves the assumption of an aggregate responsibility for the cultural optimum. The struggles which developed from this situation alone can explain the beginning of all philosophical periods and even their further progress in cosmology and anthropology. Only thus can the historical foundations of major cultures be understood, as this writer has shown in his *Self-criticism of Philosophy*. In this way, too, the intellectual development of mankind can be critically analyzed in quite another manner than by evolutionist constructions.

The most noble philosophers fell for these ideas, beginning with Justin the Martyr, if indeed we should not first list Socrates and Seneca, up to Boethius, Thomas More, and Campanella. But the fate of Abelard, Arnold, and Rienzi is a warning. A rational philosophy of history which does not take into consideration the interplay of the forces of life in their proper sequence brings forth only utopias and intellectuals who dabble in politics, and does not produce that community of serious and spiritual men capable of caring for the multiplicity of conscious and responsible cultural planning. Dante, insofar as we can laboriously understand his secret language of Joachistic and Templar Wisdom of an intellectual conception of the Church (an intellectual leadership of mankind through a poet-philosopher as prophet and through political, elective monarchs chosen by God) had historically and philosophically ushered in the Renaissance by fulfilling the testament of Aquinas. He first recognized at the beginning of the bourgeois epoch the community of gnostic friends of science as the most weighty assurance against the excursions of church and state into fields outside of their competence, and thereby he already anticipated the further development of humanism.

Unfortunately, the tragedy of the master-pupil relationship, as with Abelard and Arnold, repeated itself, in that Rienzi again sought to renew the great ideas of Dante in the Roman republic. Indeed, we must conceive the relationship of Erasmus and More in the same fashion. Erasmus, with considered humor in his *Praise of Folly,* had wished to educate the supra-partisan community of the truly educated into a free intellectual literary class which had been made possible by the development of printing. To that end, More projected a political organization, even though it was well veiled in his *Utopia,* and this certainly contributed to his downfall. In this way, every subsequent utopianist has wished to place all classes of spiritual leaders within an overall political organization. But the chief lesson that can be drawn equally from the mediaeval and the humanist development of ideas, and especially from the recognition of the laws of the free development of philosophy and science as a free and invisible spiritual kingdom, is that intellectual men should constitute an independent community, such as arose of itself in mediaeval society. That is now possible in the form of independent universities and research foundations which already exercise an extensive influence in the United States, and are a pressing need in Europe. The synthesis embracing all the sciences which in the past produced pseudo-philosophic and pseudo-methodological monisms and some very disastrous *Weltanschauungen,* will in any case make necessary a new type of university. A critical synthesis of the leading sciences is already coming into being, a theoretical physics, biology, and anthropology, a critical synthesis which is in the course of producing a natural philosophic picture of the world of entrancing magnitude: the corresponding intellectual-philosophical synthesis will not be long in coming. That, however, implies a union of faith and knowledge whose character cannot be foreseen.

Now philosophical studies must no longer be confined to the beginning of specialized education, but must also come at its close to crown it, after its completion, with full maturity, and to contribute to the acceptance of a picture of the world and of mankind. It would also lay the foundation for a metaphysically secure ethics and sociology.

When the Prince de Broglie received the Nobel prize for atomic research, he expressed the belief that this vital power should not be handed over to irresponsible politicians. It was certainly to be expected that the scholars would not be able to preserve this *arcanum imperii in naturam*—in Francis Bacon's phrase—against the demands of military technology for the most effective weapons of destruction. But research always goes on its logical way, and in a few years the peaceful exploitation of atomic energy, with boundless consequences for economics and for the social strata, will so increase the reverence for science that the scientists will be put into golden cages. And only then will they learn to organize themselves independently.

RICHELIEU

AND RUBENS

Reflections on the Art of Politics

Otto Georg von Simson

[1944]

A DISCUSSION of the "art of politics" requires no justification at a time when the potentials of publicity and propaganda have made it abundantly clear that successful government is not identical with application of the results of a Gallup poll. It is for this very reason that we have also become distrustful of the *ars politica* which has been more and more identified with the modern arts of persuasion. Although the engineers of political publicity assure us that with the right technique the ruler can get anything "across," we turn rather to those who assert that good government is not an art but an active prudence, directed by such steady instruments of control as popular representation. However, even the most perfect technology of government is not a substitute for the art of governing. Guizot, no friend of absolutism, has pointed out one of the most astonishing manifestations of this "art": the ability of the *ancien régime* to maintain between people and ruler an intimate understanding without parliaments in the modern sense.

The "art" behind this success certainly deserves an analysis—if only to set it off from the clumsy tricks of modern propaganda. We turn to Richelieu as the founder and most powerful exponent of the ancient monarchy—only to discover that the secret of his statesmanship lies far less in that ability to persuade which every modern executive wields, than in what one may almost call his sensibility to experience. While directing the people according to his will, he remained uncommonly sensitive to their aspirations (like the artist to the touch of his medium), so that his State appeared as the fulfillment of the nation's will. One thinks of Condivi's remark on Michelangelo: in watching him at work the onlooker felt that his chisel did no more than free the design waiting in obscurity for its liberation. With this analogy we do not mean to attempt a moral revaluation of Richelieu's work. The art of politics, like the other arts, is by its nature amoral. The unremitting autonomy of statecraft, however, can be brought into strong relief by pointing to its artistic aspect. The following pages, devoted to an important, though neglected, side of Richelieu's personality, will also throw some light upon the nature of politics.

I

Even the casual student of Richelieu will be surprised to find in him an artistic disposition quite unsuspected in this master of political realism. One is at first inclined to consider the Cardinal's quite unusual taste, his continued and by no means purely receptive interest in the fine arts (his interest in the drama has been unduly stressed at the expense of other interests, as my paper will show) as hobbies, diversions of a mind otherwise occupied with entirely different subjects. This impression has caused historians to treat Richelieu's literary and artistic inclinations as biographical *marginalia,* significant only as collateral evidence of his political career. Even Sainte-Beuve, sensing the extent to which the artistic element colored the Cardinal's political vision, offered no explanation other than the literary and rhetorical training the young ecclesiastic had received. Yet, the further one penetrates into Richelieu's mind, the more inextricably we find his political realism and his artistic vision interwoven. One is finally compelled to ask, if we have not here two aspects of his statesmanship, if the blending of those two faculties does not constitute the essence of political genius.

A remark by Richelieu himself seems to attest the correctness of this interpretation. "I admit," he wrote justifying the time and effort he had spent on his never completed history of Louis XIII, "that it gives greater satisfaction to provide the matter of history instead of merely giving the latter its form; nevertheless, it has given me no little enjoyment to re-create here that which only with difficulty has become political reality." One is at first struck by this almost Goethean pleasure in "recreating" reality through the power of the word. The work of the statesman, however, is unthinkable without the desire and power to transform reality according to the clear pattern of vision, an impulse perhaps never entirely satisfied within the "matter" of history. It is no coincidence that most great statesmen, whether Caesar, or Gregory VII, or Bismarck, were great writers. Political genius seems to require such "formal" expression.

I I

The foregoing remark of Richelieu, of great importance, we believe, for his biography, has prompted the following investigation into his share in Rubens' greatest work, the Medici Gallery. We know something about the Cardinal's firm—though consistently secret—direction of some notable literary enterprises of his time. We also know, from references in the correspondence of Richelieu and Rubens, that the former directed the execution of the Medici Gallery. Yet in doing so, he took great care—even more than usual—to remain "back stage," so that we know almost nothing regarding the extent of his "collaboration." Yet the answer to this problem promises to be all the more interesting since the Medici Gallery occupies a special position in the history of art. It is the greatest work of art created in Richelieu's lifetime. It is the greatest and most astonishing example of painting in the service of politics. And in its subject matter it is intimately connected with Richelieu's career.

For our purpose it will suffice briefly to recall the facts. In 1621 Rubens received a commission to paint a number of large canvases for the new palace (the later Luxembourg) of Marie de Medici, widow of Henry IV and mother of Louis XIII of France. The paintings were to commemorate the life and political activities of the Queen in a blending of allegory and portraiture, eloquently expressive of the political philosophy of the *baroque*. By sheer dimensions alone—the pictures are over eleven feet high, the three largest more than 21 feet wide—art was here placed in the service of hero worship on a scale the Renaissance had never dreamed of. Patronage of this kind may seem understandable, in a scion of the Medici though nothing in the Queen's political career can justify its scope. What renders the commission entirely fantastic, however, is its political background.[1]

The regency of the widowed Queen, during the infancy of her son, had been a complete failure. She had ignominiously tried to buy internal peace from the great nobles of her realm. In foreign affairs, following not political considerations but personal sentiments, she had sought to draw France into the orbit of the Habsburg power surrounding her frontiers. A helpless victim of her courtiers, she had finally been surprised by an open revolt led by her son, had seen her favorites executed or exiled (Richelieu among the latter); banished

[1] Today the paintings are in the Louvre. Good reproductions may be found in the separate edition of the *Editions Tel* (Paris, 1935), and in R. Oldenbourg, *Rubens* (Stuttgart, 1921), pp. 243 ff. The reproductions in the Rubens book of the Phaidon Press are, unfortunately, not up to standard. The program was devised by a group of men, among them, besides Rubens, Peiresc, one of the great antiquarians of his age. On Richelieu's close supervision see Ruelens-Rooses, *Codex Diplomaticus Rubenianus* (Anvers, 1887), III, 37 ff. and *passim*. To save space we quote the subjects of the paintings here; the reader of the following pages may refer to this note. 1. *Marie's Birth;* 2. *Marie's Education;* 3. *Henry IV receives Marie's portrait;* 4. *The Wedding by Procuration;* 5. *Marie enters Marseilles;* 6. *The Marriage;* 7. *Birth of the Dauphin;* 8. *Marie appointed Regent;* 9. *Marie's Coronation;* 10. *Henry IV's Death and Marie's Regency;* 11. *The Council of the Gods;* 12. *Marie's Triumph;* 13. *The Spanish Marriages;* 14. *The Government handed to Louis XIII;* 15. *Happiness of the Regency* (substituted for *Flight from Paris*); 16. *Flight from Blois;* 17. *Treaty of Angoulême;* 18. *Hostilities Resumed;* 19. *Reconciliation.* Besides these pictures the Gallery included portraits of Marie de Medici's parents, an allegorical portrait of the Queen as Bellona, and two allegorical panels as prologue and epilogue of the cycle though not part of the actual series. The writer has discussed the Medici Gallery at length in his *Zur Genealogie der weltlichen Apotheose im Barock* (Strassburg, 1936).

to Blois, she had escaped, not like a queen but like a rebel, in order to embark on a career of veiled and eventually open hostilities on the side of the selfish enemies of a king who was her own son. Only a year before the Medici Gallery was begun, and not until her own forces had been decisively defeated in open battle, was the final reconciliation of mother and son effected.

Despite all this, Rubens' commission now provided for far more than a conventional glorification of the wife of Henry IV. According to the program given to Rubens in 1622, the master was to dwell precisely on those events which, one should think, the Queen must have been anxious to erase from memory: five out of nineteen pictures were to be devoted to Marie's estrangement from, and final reconciliation with her son.

Neither the plan for the Gallery nor the selection of these topics can be entirely explained by the Queen's very human and very feminine desire "to win the argument," to defend her policies *post festum*. The Queen Mother was no private individual. A monumental series of political paintings in her official residence was a political gesture. It was a political gesture at a decisive moment of French, and, indeed, of European history, and as such not to be misunderstood. During the seven years of her regency, the eleven of her political life, Marie de Medici, a granddaughter of the Emperor Ferdinand, had become identified with a definite political pattern: with the idea of peace and collaboration among the Catholic powers which, under Habsburg leadership, was to have revived the unity of the Middle Ages. However feebly and irrationally conceived by the Queen, here definitely was one alternative of French politics. But another was about to emerge, already envisaged by Henry IV though cut short by his premature death: that of consolidating French national power for an ultimate showdown with the Habsburgs in Germany and Flanders and Spain. History has identified Richelieu with this concept as it has Marie de Medici with the other. The Cardinal's ascendancy in French politics began at the very time Rubens received his commission. It seems certain that Richelieu had already set himself the twofold goal of consolidating the monarchy and of humbling Spain. From 1621 to 1624 it was his persistent criticism of the pro-Spanish policies of the existing cabinet which battered down the barriers that kept him from power. Yet at this critical time he allowed Marie de Medici, whose mind he controlled completely, to propound her political ideals in the Medici Gallery. The program we mentioned provided that four canvases were to be devoted to what the Queen considered her greatest achievement in the field of foreign politics, the "Spanish Marriages," of the Dauphin to Donna Anna and of his sister to the future Philip IV of Spain. If we add these topics to the five mentioned above it appears that more than half of the Medici Gallery was to be devoted to the opposition to royal authority and to the propagation of friendship with Spain—a travesty of the principles of Richelieu's *Testament Politique!*

But, if it seems paradoxical that the Cardinal permitted such a work of art to herald his advent to supreme power, the selection of the artist appears even more incomprehensible. Rubens was not only a Spanish subject, but the greatest representative of "Christian universalism" in the generation before Leibniz. In his art this ideal has found its last monumental expression. But he did not serve it with his art alone. A trusted servant and friend of the Infanta Isabella Clara Eugenia, regent of the Netherlands, he placed his remarkable diplomatic skill at the disposal of a political design diametrically opposed to that of Richelieu. In 1623, while working on the pictures for the Queen of France, Rubens negotiated for a prolongation of the truce between the Spanish Netherlands and the United Provinces of Holland. In view of the pivotal position of the Netherlands in European politics it is no exaggeration to say that Rubens, had he succeeded, might have averted the general conflagration which changed a religious struggle within the German Empire into the Thirty Years' War. In that event the great painter would have thwarted Richelieu's foreign policy on one of its decisive issues—and perhaps forever. But the Cardinal was fully awake to the danger. He had hardly seized the supreme power (April 29, 1624) when he opened negotiations with the United Provinces. Three months later he signed with that power a military alliance against Spain.

Thus, Richelieu's first diplomatic victory meant the defeat of the man with whom he was just then corresponding about the apotheosis of the Queen of France. The Cardinal knew, moreover, that both the Infanta and her minister in Paris had had a hand in securing for Rubens the commission to paint the Medici Gallery, and that the painter's visits to the French capital did not serve artistic purposes only. During the four years the painter was at work we have ample evidence of Richelieu's vigilance and distrust. Why then did he allow this man, whom in modern language he would have called a Fifth Columnist, to plead the case of Spain emphatically and spendidly within the heart of France?

III

The following attempt to answer this question would be mere conjecture without the existence of Richelieu's *Mémoires.* To modern scholarship we owe a conclusive evaluation of this puzzling work, as regards both its authenticity and its literary character. The *Mémoires* are not, as Sainte-Beuve thought, a literary *oeuvre* of the Cardinal, but rather a collection of material for the monumental *History* he planned to write as an apology and an apotheosis of his career. The documents were assembled by the Cardinal and partly revised by himself; but comparatively few pages have that lucidity, tenseness, and precision of style which mark them as his own. Apart from its literary merits, however, the work is invaluable as Richelieu's own interpretation of contemporary history.

The student of the Medici Gallery will be tempted to compare it with the narrative of the *Mémoires,* parts of which cover the same events. The result is quite unexpected: both works, in emphasis, in selection, one may even say, in style, show a very close similarity. In fact, so convincing is this similarity between Richelieu's apotheosis of himself and that of his opponent, the Queen, by Rubens, that we are led to assume that the Cardinal's "share" in the Medici Gallery is far greater and far more decisive than was believed, and that we suddenly understand why he permitted and furthered the work at this particular moment.

Richelieu's *Mémoires* of the years 1615–1625 reveal three basic facts: his keen realization of the weaknesses and potentialities of France's external and internal position; the difficulties and perils which threatened his own career as a result of the part he had played in the years covered by Rubens' narrative (1615–1620); the amazing skill with which he used these same disadvantages to pave his way to power during the following period (1621–1625) in which the Medici Gallery was completed.

Throughout the 1620's the French situation remained precarious from the viewpoint of Richelieu's designs. The "prelude" to the Thirty Years' War had ended in a complete victory for the Emperor. The battle of the White Hill forced the dissolution of the Protestant Union (May 14, 1621) while in the following year the storming of Heidelberg, "citadel of German Calvinism," terminated the Palatinate phase of the struggle. To the Cardinal's unflinching eye it must have been clear that no German coalition was strong enough to defeat the Habsburgs. At the same time he was compelled to realize that France was as yet far too weak to throw in her lot with the anti-imperial forces. The expedition into the Valtelline (1624), a first probing of Spanish military preparedness, had to be broken off hurriedly when the Huguenots rose again in France. Worst of all, Richelieu could hardly consider himself the right man to attempt the internal consolidation of France. The part he had played as the Queen's adviser during the civil war was too fresh in everyone's memory. His appearance on the political scene in the early 1620's would have looked almost like an encouragement to dissension. The King himself pointed at his mother's protégé, saying: "There is a man who would like to join my Cabinet; but I cannot persuade myself to take him in after all he has done against me."

Thus, for Richelieu, the time for action had not yet come. In evaluating the Medici Gallery one should bear in mind that during the years 1621 to 1625 the Cardinal was pleading his case. And from this viewpoint the glorification of the Queen Mother served a three-fold purpose. Inside France it was what we would call good publicity for her and her cause. To have her thus extolled as the Mother of France, and in the emphatic vision of Rubens which often blended the features of the Queen with those of the Blessed Virgin, served well the man who had risen in her shadow. The belief in Marie de Medici's moral and popular prestige had been voiced by no one more strongly than by Richelieu—so long as this belief could be useful to him.

It was certainly useful at this moment. We must recall that the reconciliation between Marie and Louis XIII had been achieved only in 1620. All credit for this accomplishment had gone to Richelieu; indeed it gained him the cardinalate. With his own career depending upon this family truce, it was extremely expedient, for the time being, to impress the still suspicious King with the political importance of his mother, with the implication that any less conciliatory attitude towards her and her party might involve serious risks for the monarchy. This argument one should bear in mind in studying the Medici Gallery, notably the *Reconciliation* picture: a heroic meeting of mother and son in heaven, deliberately borrowing from the traditional iconography of the assumption and coronation of the Virgin.

The Medici cycle was equally good publicity abroad. The two virtues Richelieu considered more essential in diplomacy than any others were secrecy and patience. Thus, as long as France was too weak to attack Spain it was necessary to mark time and to convince her of the peaceful designs of French politics. A curious dialogue *La France Mourante,* written around 1622 and unquestionably inspired by the Cardinal, reflects his view that the consolidation of France temporarily required peace with Spain. When entering the King's cabinet in 1624 he consequently advocated—and carried out—a policy of dissimulation with such success that at the time there were many Spaniards who believed in the friendly and peaceful intentions of the French Government and of Richelieu. The fact that the Spanish Ambassador in Paris was apparently among those deceived is incomprehensible unless we evoke the diplomatic atmosphere of the French capital during those years. And the Medici Gallery was a part of this atmosphere. One can hardly think of a more impressive (and less costly) way of convincing foreign observers that the pro-Spanish faction at Court was by no means dead than this glorification of Marie de Medici's reign by an artist known to be in the service of Spain. Spain, so often a victim of illusion, was rudely awakened only when the Cardinal, deciding that the time for

91

comedy was over and that for action was at hand, threw off his mask. It is significant that the Medici Gallery was completed on the eve of the emergence of France as a world power.

Dissimulation alone, however, is a two-edged weapon, especially if entrusted to a genius as independent as Rubens. And it is as paralyzing for the artist as it is for the statesman. The Cardinal's ability to conceal his intentions reveals of course as little of his *ars politica* as of his more subtle mastery of the fine arts. The stuff he is made of appears in the way he employs and inspires the great painter, his political enemy, blending the painter's vision with his own, in a masterful, ambiguous, and eloquent interpretation of politics—the only one that fitted him at this time. Richelieu's sensibility to the possibilities of propaganda through art would make him merely a modern man. His share in the work of Rubens reveals his ability to transform reality into fiction, an ability proper only to the artist and the statesman.

IV

This side of Richelieu's genius as well as the third and paramount purpose of the Medici Gallery from the Cardinal's viewpoint becomes apparent if we study the paintings more closely. Rubens' paintings were to dwell on three periods of Marie de Medici's life: her youth and early life as Henry IV's Queen; the regency; the struggle and final reconciliation with her son. The first had ended abruptly with the assassination of the King, the second with that of the Queen's favorite, the Marshal of Ancre, the third with the death of her enemy, the Duc de Luynes. The success of any "apology" for the Queen depended on her advocate's ability to prove that she had consistently pursued the traditional policies of France, that in all upheavals this policy had neither required nor undergone any modifications, and that Marie's estrangement from her son was nothing but the work of contemptible intriguers. This was Rubens' task in the Medici Gallery, but in reading Richelieu's *Mémoires* we realize that in a vital sense it was also the Cardinal's task.

The revolt of 1617 had surprised Richelieu in the wrong camp. He had found himself on the side of the Queen, whose character and political illusions he despised, who was soon to be his mortal enemy, and of whose exile and lonely death he was one day to be the cause. But from 1617 to 1624 their destinies were linked together, her cause was his. It is characteristic of Richelieu that he very coolly accepted his predicament. Identified with the rebellion, hated by the all powerful Luynes, and mistrusted by the King, he saw his ambitions barred by obstacles that would have proved insurmountable to any lesser man. Richelieu's *ars politica* not only overcame them, but turned them to his advantage. The Medici Gallery is an essential part of his strategy.

On first looking at these paintings one asks oneself: what made the King consent to this majestic exposition of political views that were neither his nor his father's, to the glorification of this Queen he had had to vanquish in battle before he could rule himself, to this transformation of revolt into innocent martyrdom? The answer is: Richelieu. His *Mémoires* show that during those years of pleading—we would say, campaigning—he built up the fiction—extraordinary in its mixture of oratory and realism—that France's well-being depended upon the close understanding between mother and son, that this understanding had been marred by a traitor, Luynes, but happily restored by himself, Richelieu; that, furthermore, it was essential to follow a political course represented by neither of the two opposite factions at Court but rather by a compromise, a golden mean. This course alone could claim the sanction of *Henri le Grand,* it alone would guarantee greatness and stability for France—it also happened to be the course he, Richelieu, had been pursuing all along. This is the argument the Cardinal presented to the King during their decisive interview in Compiègne, March, 1624. Let us compare with it the argument of the Medici Gallery.

Rubens received his commission for the Medici Gallery only one week after the Connétable's (Luynes) death. Beyond doubt we must see an immediate connection between these events. The grandiose project to glorify the Queen Mother marked her triumphant re-entry into her former dignity and into her son's favor. Contemporaries could not help seeing in Luynes' death, so closely followed as it was by the reunion of mother and son, the cause of the reconciliation as they saw in the Connétable's life the cause of the estrangement between mother and son. This argument, so contrary to the truth, but advantageous to the Cardinal, King, and Queen alike, is used with supreme skill in Richelieu's *Mémoires.* But the Medici Gallery was an even more effective way of presenting it. Marie de Medici's return to power was here officially confirmed, her political ideals were allowed magnificent expression in the creations of Rubens.

This interpretation of the purpose of the Medici Gallery is not at all disproved by the fact that the first program, handed Rubens in February, 1622, does not yet mention the topics related to the estrangement. Out of the nineteen pictures commissioned, the subjects of only fifteen were fixed, the remaining to be decided on later. Richelieu preferred, so soon after Luynes' death, to await the final repercussions of this unexpected event. It seemed more prudent to wait and see exactly how far he could go in denouncing his master's deceased favorite. But six months later, with Richelieu's ascendancy secure, Rubens received his final instructions. The remaining five pictures—one, significantly, has been gained by reducing the Spanish subjects from four to three—are all to be devoted to the struggle between mother and son. These are the titles: *Marie's Departure from Paris; The Flight from Blois; The Treaty of Angoulême; The Hostilities Renewed; The Reconciliation after the Connétable's Death.* This last title, with its distortion of historical truth, is perhaps the most revealing. True, the instructions stipulated that these events were to be treated in "mystical figures and with all respect for the son (Louis XIII)." But the topics are selected with such boldness that we may assume that even the King had by now accepted the "scapegoat" theory. In 1625, when visiting the completed Gallery, he expressed to Rubens his lively satisfaction over this work—neither the first nor the last monarch to sacrifice one he had once loved to his own prestige.

The subject matter alone, however, cannot give an adequate idea of the kind of argument, a terrible indictment of his dead foe, which Richelieu propounds in the last five pictures of the Medici Gallery. Let us also examine his style. The first of those paintings, *The Flight from Paris,* recalled the period when Marie's blind and complacent favoritism had brought France to the brink of ruin. The Queen had surrendered her powers only after the Marshal of Ancre, the most powerful of her Italian favorites, had been murdered; faced with the fury of the populace she had deemed it advisable to retire to Blois. Richelieu's *Mémoires,* however, give a very different interpretation of this event. In this passage, painstakingly revised by the Cardinal as well as by his "editor," Harlay de Sancy, and in its dramatic oratory one of the most impressive of the whole work, he depicts the Queen as a truly heroic figure. She was driven to flight, he says, by what some thought to be Fear at the sight of her friend's assassination; others, Astuteness, and still others, spiritual Strength. Richelieu does not write these "affects" with capital letters, but they assume an almost mythological reality in his recital, so remarkably similar to Rubens' rendering of this event. Only Rubens' sketch for this picture has been preserved, however. Unquestionably at the command of the King, the actual painting was eliminated at the last moment—Rubens replaced it, in a few days, by *The Happiness of the Regency,* one of the finest pictures in the Gallery. But he was not to blame for the political *faux pas.* He has shown himself a master of diplomacy in the dextrous handling of the four remaining topics, all potentially as dangerous as *The Flight from Paris: The Flight from Blois* (recalling a foolish and disloyal undertaking which Richelieu, however, justifies by the alleged sinister designs of Luynes); *The Treaty of Angoulême,* and *The Hostilities Resumed* are so clever in their use of allegorical ambiguities that they could be all things to all men. The final picture, *The Reconciliation,* we have already mentioned. The transfigured images of mother and son, an infernal monster, unmistakably the Connétable of Richelieu's

Mémoires, hurled forever into the abyss—one cannot dispute the eloquence of this vision. Rubens could report a complete success after the Gallery had finally been opened. He was probably right in adding that whatever murmur and sensation the pictures had caused (to the irritation of Richelieu) might easily have been avoided, had the entire program been left to his discretion. The diplomatic dexterity with which the master handled the Medici cycle—in the opinion of his contemporaries one of the great merits of this work—has rendered it a puzzle of the first order for modern scholarship.

V

Our discussion of the subject matter and the style of the Medici Gallery does not suffice to determine Richelieu's share in, and the political character of, this work. These become fully apparent only if we look at it through the eyes of those who viewed it for the first time and recall the occasion of this *vernissage.* This occasion, deliberately chosen by the Cardinal, was a momentous one: the magnificent feast —alleged to have cost him 40,000 livres—he gave in celebration of the marriage of Marie de Medici's daughter, Henrietta of France, to Charles I of England, May 27, 1625. Richelieu says that he wanted to show his satisfaction over this alliance which had required "so much pain and prudence" to conclude successfully. It is significant that he chose for this celebration the Palais du Luxembourg, official residence of the Queen Mother. And equally significant—though the haughty Cardinal fails even to mention Rubens' name—that the great hall in this palace was adorned by the *Histoire de la Mère et du Fils,* a picture of such a France as Richelieu wanted the world to see on this occasion which he himself has called the turning point of European history. He explains in his *Mémoires* (and it is noteworthy that he lets Marie de Medici deliver this argument) that with this marriage the danger of an Anglo-Spanish alliance with its vast repercussions had been definitely averted. We may add that the marriage also guaranteed the continuation of the Thirty Years' War. According to Richelieu, Charles's originally planned marriage to a Spanish Infanta would have implied the restitution of the Palatinate to his brother-in-law, with England suspending her subsidies to Holland in turn. Thus the two "powder kegs" of Europe, so essential for continuation of the war against the Empire, would have been neutralized. Charles was furthermore important to France as brother-in-law to Christian IV of Denmark. Richelieu puts great emphasis upon the latter's influence with Holland as well as with the Hanseatic cities of Germany. Had Charles I moved into the Spanish camp, he might conceivably have influenced those powers in favor of the Empire. Instead, the marriage with France, though barren of lasting results, was the event which then tipped the scales. Backed by France, English emissaries enlisted King Christian of Denmark against the Empire. Less than two months after the ceremonies in Paris, the "Danish" phase of the Thirty Years' War had begun.

The pivotal position which France, only yesterday weak and neglected, had suddenly assumed in Europe, was very adroitly demonstrated by the glorification of the Queen Mother. Already mother-in-law of the King of Spain and the Duke of Savoy and now in the same relation to the English sovereign, she had become the mother of Europe. One cannot think of a more impressive and at the same time more reassuring way of convincing Europe of the new power of France than the image of this princess who had always been a champion of peace. Richelieu was even now loath to joining openly the war against the Empire, a step "which would have thrown the German Catholics into the arms of Spain." It seems that he still hoped for an opportunity in which France might assume the leadership of Europe by arbitrating between both parties—a strange analogy to his own role between mother and son. If the Cardinal entertained such hopes, Marie de Medici's prestige was extremely useful. And in any event the Medici Gallery gave impressive evidence of the internal consolidation of France. While proclaiming the Queen Mother legitimate heir to Henry IV, it belittled the recent revolt as the work of one who could no longer do any harm. With the reconciliation of mother and son all opposition appeared quelled, and the unity of France more assured than ever before. Lastly, the "mythology" of this mother presented perhaps an even more ingratiating argument in favor of absolutism than the usual one of "paternalism."

Few of those, however, who first viewed the Medici Gallery could have failed to notice the role in which the Queen was celebrated here and on this occasion. In a strange world of allegory and fable, she appeared by no means as the *spiritus rector* of recent French history, but at best as its personification—allegory among allegories—and at worst as its marionette. Whether or not the Cardinal wanted her to appear in this role, the Medici Gallery thus sheds a singularly truthful light upon his relation to the Queen: the all powerful and merciless "back stage" director of the proud and helpless actress. He, for whose inexorable calculation all human and personal aspects of life fell into the political pattern he was carving, has used Marie de Medici with her passions, virtues, and faults, the indignities she had suffered as well as the dignity to which he had helped restore her, to achieve his own purposes. Now in this work of art, whose design and execution he had directed, her history appeared finally as his creation, not merely as a plea on his behalf, but as a drama of which he was the maker. Was the language of the Medici Gallery perhaps eventually more powerful

96

and truthful than he himself had intended? The work does much to explain the genius of the man who, though neither desiring nor requiring artistic fame, knew the pleasure of moulding the "form" as well as providing the "matter" of history. There is no better evidence of Richelieu's mastery over actors as well as interpreters, than the fact that he has so far never received any credit for his part in the Medici Gallery and that in a work which shows history as his work, he has remained invisible.

VI

Has the Cardinal really remained invisible in the Medici Gallery, as he seems to have wanted posterity to believe? One scene at least seems to require his physical presence, not only for the sake of historical truth, but in Richelieu's own interest. We refer to *The Treaty of Angoulême,* an illustration of the protracted negotiations preceding the reconciliation between Marie and Louis XIII. One wonders at first why this subject was selected at all. The negotiations had no lasting result, and peace was established only after the renewed hostilities to which the following picture alludes. It was neither in the King's nor the Queen's interest to stress the difficulties that had to be overcome before their final reconciliation. But Richelieu had so stressed them. We have seen the importance he attributed to his own role at that time. Referring to it in his *Mémoires,* he for once speaks out frankly for himself instead of putting his thoughts into the mouths of others and disclaiming his responsibility as he does so often. And, indeed, the negotiations mark the turning point of Richelieu's career. At no time has his mastery over men and events appeared more complete.

What exactly was his role at this time? The Cardinal's own *Mémoires* provide a far less complete answer to this question than the painting of Rubens. The master represents the negotiations by showing the Queen seated and accompanied by Prudence, while Mercury, messenger of peace, tenders her an olive branch. A Cardinal, identified by all writers as La Rochefoucauld, the King's ambassador at Angoulême, seems to plead emphatically that the Queen accept the offer. Does she accept? The answer to this question Rubens has put up to the second Cardinal at Marie's right. He puts his hand on her right arm in a gesture which is such a masterpiece of ambiguity and dissimulation that it remains altogether uncertain whether he intends to restrain her or to urge acceptance. Who is this Cardinal? The two early eighteenth century descriptions of the Gallery call him Guise and La Valette, respectively. Of these attributions the first can be discarded right away. The second is based on more weighty evidence, that is, the only contemporary description of Rubens' work, Morisot's *Porticus Medicaea,* published in Paris (1626). Now the introduction of La Valette, son of the rebel Epernon, into this picture would be meaningless as well as tactless. No one has ever held him responsible for the Queen's obstinacy on that occasion. Fortunately for us, however, Morisot issued a second edition of his rare work in 1628, this time revised by Rubens himself and thus unquestionably authentic. And here the Cardinal is called Richaeleus! The earlier insertion of a different name is not even surprising in view of the ambiguity to which, as we have seen, Rubens often had to resort in the Medici Gallery. His later "revelation," made at a time when his relations with Richelieu had already become strained, cannot but have irritated the latter. Even his usual secrecy apart, the Cardinal, as we shall find presently, had good reason to consider his "incognito" in this picture preferable.

However that may be, it is certain that Rubens has introduced Richelieu's portrait into *The Treaty of Angoulême*. As such it is not only the greatest portrait of the Cardinal—one has to compare this younger, vicious, and noble profile with the one by Champaigne to realize differences and resemblances; it is also the greatest political picture we know, the truth about Richelieu's role at this historical moment.

This role was as ambiguous and as sinister as the picture shows. His very career depended upon the reconciliation between King and Queen—provided he was the mediator and provided he was in this capacity able to "straddle" both parties. There was only one way this could be achieved: he must give the Queen the means to wage war, yet compel her to make peace. The King, on the other hand, must be persuaded that the Queen's forces menaced the existence of his State, and nevertheless be persuaded to forgive her. In other words, Richelieu had to create not merely the bogey, but the physical prerequisites of civil war, he had to make certain that the decision went to the right side at the right moment, and all the while he had to keep King and Queen, as well as the ever-suspicious Luynes convinced that he was working for nothing else but peace. Had this seemingly impossible scheme failed the schemer would have lost his head. But Richelieu succeeded well. The reconciliation earned him the purple in token of Marie de Medici's gratitude and eventually opened for him the door to the King's cabinet. Neither of them knew how completely he had deceived them.

The negotiations of Angoulême terminated Richelieu's exile. In his *Mémoires* he credits Father Joseph, the famous Grey Eminence, with the opinion that the King could have done no better than to send him to the rebellious Queen "pour adoucir son esprit." But as a messenger of peace he acted strangely indeed. In her first conciliatory letter to the King, written after Richelieu's arrival, Marie declares that before thinking of herself she wishes him to provide for those who have assisted her. In other words, she requests certain guarantees for her party which includes Richelieu. In quoting the letter, the latter does not tell us that he himself has dictated it, nor that at the same time he has managed to slip into the opposite camp! With the knowledge of Luynes he wrote the letter with which Father Arnoux, the King's confessor, replied in his master's name. Louis XIII remained convinced that the Connétable had hated Richelieu to his very end, as we, too, would believe in reading the latter's *Mémoires*. The truth is that Richelieu edited Luynes' letters to the Queen at this time, lavishing, as has well been said, his services upon both parties.

But he did not yet want reconciliation. That this is the meaning of his gesture in Rubens' picture, one learns from an *exposé* of the military and political situation which he delivered at this time before the Queen. Here he impressed the bewildered woman alternately with the dangers of war and the necessity of backing a good cause by force; with her moral right to defend herself in battle; and with the precariousness of her military situation, owing to the untrustworthiness of her allies: "thus, in defending herself against the tyrant [Luynes, not the King], she might become enslaved by her own supporters." This last argument is important. The Cardinal has tried to defend himself against the charge that he himself had incited the Queen to war, with the assertion that he had acted under compulsion and had merely given way to the storm "imitating the prudent pilot"—though one does not see who could or should have compelled him to do anything against his will. But he has never attempted to refute the more terrible charge levelled against him by the great Rohan, that he manoeuvred his mistress into a position where she was forced to give battle and was at the same time certain to lose. This charge it seems impossible to deny. Siri himself, as an admirer of Richelieu's "realism" certainly a reliable source, asserts that the Cardinal dissuaded the Queen from moving to a more secure and strategically far more advantageous position, and further, that he prevailed upon her to dismiss as unreliable Epernon, one of the best generals of his time! Siri's words are worth quoting: "Richelieu," he says, "was the real cause of the destruction of this powerful party, as well as of the ruin of the Queen, his mistress. For he kept her in Angers, cut off from the major forces of the insurgents, in order to manoeuvre her into a position where she would have to sue for the peace he so ardently desired as the means to his future greatness." In the ensuing battle Marie's forces were completely routed—and now the situation was ripe for Richelieu's plans. When peace negotiations were renewed he played the part he had so long desired and so carefully prepared. While everyone put the blame for the defeat on Marillac—a fact the Cardinal mentions with cool pity—the Queen considered Richelieu her savior. The King, on the other hand, had, perhaps, even more reason to show him gratitude than he knew. By dissuading Marie de Medici from accepting the peace offered her at Angoulême, Richelieu had induced her to assemble the forces of malcontents he now made surrender to the King as the prize for his own aggrandizement. No accomplishment is perhaps more characteristic of Richelieu than the way he gained the purple, no moment of his life shows him more possessed of Machiavelli's *virtù*. It is the moment Rubens selected to immortalize his enemy.

We have discussed *The Treaty of Angoulême* at some length because this picture provides the first major contribution to clarifying the nature of collaboration between Richelieu and Rubens. It would be altogether wrong to assume that the painter merely executed a program handed to him by the Cardinal—the very nature of art precludes such neat distinction between "content" and "form." The Flemish master was as keenly aware of the political import of his work as was the French statesman. And he had not come to Paris to be the tool of the man he knew to be the inexorable enemy of Spain. But not in every part of the Gallery can we distinguish Rubens' "voice" from that of Richelieu. Of the three sections of the Medici cycle mentioned above, the first, dealing with Marie's youth and married life, was handled in the thoroughly conventional fashion of the *baroque*, which for that time must have had the same psychological significance as the "human interest" element in modern political reporting. The seven subjects of this part presented no opportunity for either propaganda or disagreement. They are the only ones completed without change in the original program. The last part of the Medici Gallery, on the other hand, that referring to the civil war, presented a version of those events which, in absolving the Queen from all guilt and hailing her as the good genius of France, was as acceptable to Richelieu as to the "Spanish" viewpoint. Only in the *Angoulême* picture did Rubens find it necessary to introduce an interpretation differing subtly though unmistakably from the Cardinal's.

The middle section of the Medici Gallery devoted to the Queen's regency, gave room, however, for dissension. This part has undergone radical changes, not without Rubens scoring some significant victories for his political views.

Two different problems presented themselves in this part: the arrangement and distribution of its seven pictures, and the treatment of the relations with Spain. Both were essentially political and warrant a brief discussion. First it may be recalled that at the extreme end of the Gallery three wall compartments, each three times as large as those available for the other paintings, provided an aesthetic focus much like the high altar in a baroque church. The Queen, without vision in artistic and political matters, had selected as the subject for the central place, an event that was at best meaningless from the viewpoint of her own apotheosis. It was mostly due to Rubens' objections that this plan was dropped and the artist was advised that *The Capture of Jülich* was to be placed in the center. The campaign referred to had been undertaken by Henry IV as a kind of dress-rehearsal for his anti-Habsburg designs. A general war may have been prevented only by the King's sudden death and his wife's anxiety to terminate the hostilities with the Empire as soon as possible. But the anti-Spanish faction at court never tired of pointing to that event in justifying its own designs and in proving the illegitimacy of Marie's peace policies. In the center of the Medici Gallery *The Capture of Jülich* would have introduced a strangely ominous, or at least ambiguous, note into the whole cycle —perhaps not entirely against the Cardinal's will. Rubens' counter-proposal was simple, brilliant, and acceptable even from the Cardinal's viewpoint. He merely suggested that *The Capture of Jülich* be "shifted." Thus he obtained a threefold result.

In the first place, the picture which now occupied the center was *The Death of Henry and Marie's Regency*. To unite these two subjects had already been a happy thought. Now in the focus of the Gallery they emphasized the continuity of French policy where *The Capture of Jülich* would have suggested complete disagreement between both monarchs. Secondly, the shift brought *The Coronation of Marie* to one of the large wall spaces, increasing its importance three times, and perhaps more if we take a comprehensive view of the Gallery. Rubens had always wanted to do this but had to overcome the resistance of Richelieu, already determined to desert the Queen and, anyway, not interested in a triumph in which he had taken no part. The coronation of the Queen had been ordered by Henry IV, many said in a strange premonition, and had taken place the day before his assassination. Marie's supporters saw in the King's gesture supreme evidence of his confidence in his wife's political abilities. Rubens' painting of the solemn ceremony in St. Denis faithfully records what was still contemporary history and at the same time brings to mind those ancient coronation pictures by which the early Christian kings affirmed the divine origin of their authority. It is significant that Rubens' work is the last monumental representation of this kind (Napoleon's court painter could depict no more than the mockery of an emperor crowning himself and his empress), and equally significant that it was painted in the interest of peace.

Rubens, however, won his greatest success in disposing of *The Capture of Jülich*. His own proposal merely shifted this picture but still left it as the last of the three large paintings. This anti-Spanish demonstration was all the more disagreeable to the painter as he had been gradually compelled to reduce the "Spanish Marriages" to a single picture. Though this change indicates the political drift under Richelieu, the Cardinal's love of dissimulation gave Rubens his chance. He was not only allowed to shift the *Jülich* picture once more, this time to a far more modest place, but to treat it in such a way that the original meaning has become unrecognizable. The painting shows Marie as Bellona on a white charger, magnificently attired and accompanied by Fortitude, Fame, and Victory. Far in the background an unidentifiable siege is taking place, while in the air an eagle chasing smaller birds of prey introduces an allegory Richelieu himself has occasionally used to denote the victory of royal authority over rebellion. No existing description of this picture, least of all Morisot's, makes the slightest allusion to the capture of Jülich. The writer is inclined to see in this *trionfo* above all an allusion to certain successes over the dissatisfied nobility won by Marie early in her regency. No doubt, many interpretations could be given to the picture, a fact which reflects Richelieu's policy at the time as well as Rubens' political ideals.

VII

However, even during their collaboration a hostile tension existed between Richelieu and Rubens of which their polite correspondence gives hardly an inkling. Only a few weeks after the commission had been granted, the Cardinal had to deny the charge that he was intriguing to have another artist appointed in Rubens' stead. We have good reason to believe that this rumor was not entirely unfounded. Rubens' original contract provided that he was to paint a second Gallery, devoted to the life of Henry IV. It is certain that Richelieu busied himself from the beginning with preventing the master from completing this work, and that he was finally successful. He had taken no part in the achievements of Henry IV and was too "parsimonious" to permit a glorification that would merely have belittled his own position as he wanted it to appear in politics as well as in the Medici Gallery. Here again, Richelieu's sensibility to the psychological function of art was extraordinary.

Rubens, on the other hand, had never harbored any illusions as to the Cardinal's attitude towards him and his views. He had not forgotten the negotiations of 1623. In 1625, soon after his arrival in Paris, he informed the regent of Flanders that in his opinion there could be no hope of an understanding between France and Spain "because it has become a French maxim of State to keep the war in Flanders forever alive." "One must never forget," Rubens adds, "how completely the government is in the hands of the Queen Mother and of Richelieu." His appraisal of the relative strength of these partners was also shrewd. While working on the Henry Gallery he was constantly on his guard and even expected the sudden cancellation of his commission. Late in 1625 he asked a French friend to find out if he had fallen into disgrace at the French court, adding that he would not mind after the trouble he had had with the first Gallery. The next year the master was astonished at Richelieu's request to send him two pictures by his hand, as the Ambassador of Flanders had just informed him of the Cardinal's intrigue against the Henry Gallery. This work proceeded, however, but more and more haltingly, as Marie de Medici's prestige declined. The seventeenth century was too polite and too subtle to resort to an open breach of contract. The painter only met more criticism, more delays, more changes of mind. Then finally, in October, 1630, the Court interfered so rudely with the work already completed, that the master, in an outburst of rage, threw down his tools. Less than a month later, *Le Journée des Dupes* cost Marie not only her Palace, but her son's affection, her dignity, and her country as well. Richelieu had played his hand. Rubens' distemper, rare with him indeed, need not surprise us. He knew the French court well and realized that he was about to lose far more than his commission.

In these months, significantly enough, he hardly painted at all. He had again descended into the political arena, aware, as was his enemy, that the time for "fiction" had passed.

In 1629 the European situation resembled that of 1623. The peace of Lübeck ended the second phase of the Thirty Years' War, with the Emperor again victorious and the Protestants defeated. As in 1623, the hub of European politics was Flanders, and England was once more the power to which those who wanted to continue the war as well as those who wanted to terminate it, looked for help. The ensuing diplomatic duel which took place in London brought Rubens once more face to face with his great foe. This time, however, he appeared not merely as personal emissary of his regent, but as plenipotentiary of the King of Spain. He knew English diplomacy well. In 1626 he had negotiated with this power for a truce in Flanders, and even the year before, while in Paris with his "present" for the marriage of Henrietta and Charles I, he had attempted to enter into negotiations with the Duke of Buckingham—evidence of the diplomatic twilight in which the Franco-English alliance was concluded. Rubens had been unsuccessful on that occasion, but his chances had since improved proportionately to the deteriorations of the relations between France and England. In 1629 it looked as if he was to triumph over Richelieu. All efforts of the latter's ambassador Châteauneuf met with failure until he was recalled by his irate master. Rubens, on the other hand, was showered with tokens of Charles I's personal esteem and with assurances of the King's friendly intentions towards Spain. For a moment there seemed to materialize the vision of a European peace guaranteed by English neutrality. In a letter which with all its emotional eloquence strangely resembles Richelieu's cool exposition on the occasion of the English marriage, Rubens described the Anglo-Spanish alliance as the "nucleus" of a European federation, of which the mere possibility is already producing the greatest repercussions. "I admit," he continues, "that for the King (of Spain) the peace with Holland may appear more necessary, but I doubt if this will ever be achieved without intervention of the King of England. Peace between England and Spain, on the other hand, is a concrete possibility and would give the Dutch so much to think about that they may even make peace."

The letter concludes with a warning as to the grave consequences should the negotiations fail. Rubens was only too right in this regard, but it may be doubted if even the most generous concessions on the part of Spain would have achieved more. The great painter overestimated the internal strength of the Stuart regime—he similarly overestimated Marie de Medici's prestige in France once she had turned against Richelieu and had been defeated.

As the fugitive Queen crossed the French border into Flanders, Rubens' share in her struggle with the Cardinal became fully apparent. The artist was dispatched by the Infanta to open negotiations with the royal exile, and now he set out to achieve by force what all diplomacy had failed to accomplish. Soon there appeared upon the European horizon the shadow (it was no more than that) of a great Catholic League, composed of the Habsburgs, the Catholic princes of Germany and Italy as well as of Marie de Medici, Louis XIII's brother, Gaston of Orléans, and members of the great nobility of France. The league had one purpose: to drive Richelieu from power. The first and most passionate plea on behalf of a "war of intervention" came from Rubens. August 1, 1631, he wrote from Mons, where the Queen resided, to the Spanish Premier Olivarez. Rubens' arguments are noteworthy. He puts great emphasis on the Queen's prestige in France—much as Richelieu had on a different occasion—adding an evidently inspired list of great names in and outside France on whose support the Queen could count. Even Wallenstein is among them. Rubens urges speedy action, lest the whole Orléans party dissolve in smoke (one is strangely reminded of Richelieu's famous remark on the instability of the French character); he warns anxiously that delay will give the Cardinal time to resort to his usual "trickeries" and that the whole plan can succeed only in that utmost secrecy which is the soul of diplomacy—the very words Richelieu has used and which have so often been quoted to characterize the great statesman.

There follows, significantly, the assurance that intervention will by no means amount to an attack upon the legitimate authority of France. Orléans does not have to fight for a crown of which, after his brother's death, he is certain anyway, and both he and the Queen have promised to seek no help from the Huguenots. Their campaign has but one aim: to destroy the Cardinal "who with all his skill and strength is pursuing but one aim: to undermine, offend, and humiliate Spain, as the most terrible enemy of this power." Here Rubens is carried away completely by emotion. He declares non-intervention will be interpreted merely as cowardice in view of France's insolent and continuous support of the United Provinces—his words reveal that in all the years Rubens has not forgotten the defeat he and his cause had suffered in the negotiations of 1623. The fears, the hostility, and the forebodings of a lifetime explode in this letter, as if Rubens had realized that here was Europe's last chance to defeat his great enemy.

The margin of the letter bears Olivarez's contemptuous remark "useless to take this letter seriously, men like Rubens are blind in political matters." But we may question the sincerity of this remark. The Marquis d'Aytona, Spanish Ambassador in Brussels has seconded Rubens' request as "the greatest opportunity to act against France that had ever offered itself to Spain." It was not that the plan was bad, but that Spain was too weak to move—Olivarez himself admitted this before the Royal council, and Philip IV expressed a similar view in a letter to the Infanta. Richelieu was too great a statesman not to foresee and to neutralize any such danger to his regime. Again he had defeated Rubens, and this time decisively. A few months later the master notifies a friend that he has withdrawn from politics. "I have never less regretted a decision." With his defeat a European vision vanishes.

VIII

The purpose of this study was not to invite comparison between Richelieu and Rubens, for that could not do full justice to either of them. Yet it is their collaboration in the Medici Gallery which brings into relief the essence of what we have called *ars politica,* those elements it shares with the fine arts as well as those entirely its own. This is what renders the comparing and contrasting of the respective share of statesman and artist in the Medici Gallery instructive. As for Richelieu's share in this work, it is the authentic interpretation of history by its own maker and as such comparable to the *Testament Politique.*

The Medici Gallery covers Richelieu's struggle for power, the *Testament* surveys the second part of his career from 1624 to its end. Both should therefore be studied as component parts of one work, though they contrast significantly in form and style. The *Testament Politique* is the work of an aging man who looks back upon the past from the vantage point of success and supreme power. He sees his aims accomplished, his enemies destroyed, his fame secure. The Medici Gallery, on the other hand, depicts history in the making. It is the vision of a young man, thirsting for power, but still entangled in hostilities and intrigues, still struggling to persuade and to prevail. In the power of their oratory both works are clearly Richelieu's. One may well compare the emotional appeal of the Medici Gallery with the form of direct address to the King which the Cardinal chose for the narrative of the *Testament Politique:* he never allows his audience to waver in its approval of what he has done. The *Testament,* however, is addressed to the King of France, the Medici Gallery to the French nation as well as to Europe. The first work is a lucid demonstration of principles after the action is over, the second a warm, emotional, and almost popular appeal to the nation for support and appreciation of what Richelieu is about to undertake. These paintings may seem encumbered by the quaint erudition of the age as well as by the need for dissimulation, ambiguity, compromise. Nevertheless, the cycle is a great patriotic saga. Never again was the Cardinal so anxious to show that he spoke the language of France, that his designs were a continuation and a fulfillment of the past, that his vision of glory was also that of his compatriots. And never did he speak elsewhere with such warmth as here through the art of a stranger. In the *Testament Politique* he merely wrote history; in the Medici Gallery he made politics.

The political actuality of the cycle is somewhat difficult for us to realize today. But for the *grand personage* of the seventeenth century this world of fiction and erudition was no mere disguise. Among allegories and with the features of an antique deity, he saw himself in a kind of political heaven, with his immortality in history assured. The Musée des Arts Décoratifs preserves an old painting showing the performance of the *Ballet de la Prospérité des Armes de France,* presented by Richelieu in the theater of his palace to the King and Queen on the occasion of the marriage of his niece to the Duc d'Enghien. In this *ballet* the Duke himself appeared in the role of Jupiter, and to the courtiers in the galleries the solitary figures of the Cardinal and the Royal family alone occupying the *parterre* must have seemed not as part of their world but of the heroic fiction of the pantomime.

This is the light in which we must see the Medici Gallery. The commission for this work, even the selection of the artist and the first visitors, were all together part of Richelieu's *ars politica.* Yet, it is not by accident that the Cardinal's share in the Medici Gallery is forgotten. As *ars politica* the work died with the political moment for which it had been created. What has survived is Rubens' art. And thus it seems as if the artist did win the last round against the statesman. As a diplomatist Rubens, so blinded by his ideals, must compare poorly with Richelieu. But the latter's "art," while perfect in itself appears vitiated by contact with reality and its moral order, whereas the catholic universalism of Rubens' vision has remained alive in his art. Perhaps not only alive but more permanently active. One recalls a passage from Paul Claudel's *Le Soulier de Satin:* Rubens, and not the Duke of Alva, has saved Flanders "for Christendom against heresy."

THE HISTORIC

ORIGINS

OF LIBERALISM

Christopher Dawson

[1954]

THE history of the secularization of modern culture has yet to be written, and the reasons for this are easy enough to understand. For, on the one hand, the mind of the secularized majority has been so deeply affected by the process of secularization that it cannot view that process in an objective historical manner, while, on the other, the religious minority has been forced into an attitude of negative opposition which is no less unfavorable to dispassionate study. Nevertheless, it is emphatically a problem which requires an historical approach. The process of secularization was a historical movement no less than the Reformation, a minority movement which was gradually transmitted to wider circles until it eventually won the key positions of social and intellectual influence through which it dominated European society. This movement, which was already known as the Enlightenment in the eighteenth century, and the accompanying ideology, which later acquired the name of Liberalism, have long been studied by historians chiefly in Germany and France, though in a somewhat piecemeal fashion; but their work has not hitherto been fully assimilated by educated opinion in England and America. Here the tendency has been to concentrate attention on political and economic change, and, above all, on the American and French revolutions. But we have not paid enough attention to the intellectual revolution that had already taken place before there was any question of a political one. Yet it is this intellectual revolution that is responsible for the secularization of Western culture. This intellectual movement, like most of the movements that have changed the world, was religious in origin, although it was antireligious in its results. It owed its dynamism to the resistance of a religious minority and its diffusion to the ill-judged and unjust, though sincere, action of religious orthodoxy. It is indeed, the supreme example in history of the way in which religious persecution and repression defeats its own object and serves the cause it is attempting to destroy.

During the ten years of European peace which extended from 1678 to 1688 the power and prestige of the French monarchy reached its climax and the Catholic cause was everywhere in the ascendant. French Protestantism seemed to have received its death blow from the Revocation of the Edict of Nantes. The Protestant powers of Germany and Scandinavia were the allies and pensioners of Louis XIV. The Empire had recovered from the exhaustion of the Thirty Years War and had begun the reconquest of southeastern Europe from the Turks and the repression of Protestantism in Hungary, which Leopold I had vowed to make "The Kingdom of Mary." Even the Netherlands, the great stronghold of bourgeois civilization and Calvinism, had come out of the war with France weakened, disunited, and impoverished.

Nevertheless, the powers of authority and tradition were far weaker than they seemed and the moment of their apparent triumph really marked the turn of the tide and the rallying of the forces of opposition. The attempt of Louis XIV to exterminate French Protestantism by the Revocation of the Edict of Nantes, and that of James II to secure toleration for Catholicism in England, rekindled the flames of religious warfare and aroused a passionate spirit of resistance to the supremacy of Louis XIV. The Huguenot exiles who largely consisted of the ablest and most enterprising elements of the French bourgeoisie were the intellectual leaders of this movement. Wherever they settled in Holland and England and North Germany, they formed centres of militant anti-Catholic opinion and carried on an organized campaign of public propaganda and secret agitation against the government of Louis XIV and the Catholic Church.

In this way the Huguenot diaspora acted as an intellectual ferment in Western Europe and instilled a common purpose into the scattered forces of Protestantism. Nowhere was their action stronger than in the Netherlands, which were at once the centre of the new bourgeois economy and culture and of the old Calvinist spirit of opposition to Rome and the Counter Reformation monarchy. Here too they entered into relations with the exiled leaders of the English opposition who had taken refuge in Holland from the victory of the monarchical reaction in England. Here Jurieu and Claude, Bayle and Le Clerc and Basnage met Shaftesbury and Burnet and Linborch, and it was in this international atmosphere that both the plans for the English revolution and the philosophy that was to justify it were formed.

The Revolution of 1688 was the greatest victory that Protestantism had won since the independence of the Netherlands themselves, for unlike the earlier Puritan revolution which had been directed against a Protestant King and his bishops, it united Puritans and Episcopalians in defence of their common Protestantism. It found a leader in the foremost representation of continental Protestantism, the descendant of William of Orange, and it inaugurated the long struggle against Louis XIV which broke the strength of the French Monarchy and inclined the balance of European power for the first time in favor of Protestantism.

But if the Revolution of 1688 was a victory for Protestanism, it was very different from the triumph of the Kingdom of the Saints of which Milton and the Puritan idealists had dreamed. The children of the saints had become company promoters and financiers, like Nicholas Barbon, the son of Praise God Barebones, and Sir Robert Clayton, the "extorting Ishban" of Dryden's lines. They were allied with aristocratic traitors and renegades like Sunderland and Romney, and Shrewsbury and Montagu. And behind the whole combination broods the sinister genius of Shaftesbury.

Never has the influence of class interests and selfish greed been more nakedly revealed in political action. It was the victory of oligarchy and privilege over monarchy and prerogative. For the new regime was essentially a class state in which the government was controlled by the great Whig families, while the local administration was in the hands of the squirearchy. Nevertheless the new order was by no means exclusively an agrarian one. As the Revolution owed its success to the alliance of Churchmen and Nonconformists, so the resultant social order owed its stability to the union of landlords and business men, a union which was reinforced by intermarriage and the purchase of estates by wealthy merchants and bankers. In this way the new regime acquired a distinctively bourgeois character which gradually transformed the traditional structure of English society. Under the old monarchy the government had striven to keep the several orders of the polity within their appointed limits, to maintain the corporative system in industry, to regulate wages and prices, and to protect the peasants from eviction and enclosures. Now the rights of property were absolute, wages and prices were left to find their own level, and the principle of *laissez-faire* took the place of the old ideals of state regulation and corporative organization. The eighteenth century was the golden age of the great landlords and the squires, and the man of property enjoyed a freedom and social prestige such as he had never known in the world before.

But it was an age of ruin and decay for the peasants and the yeomen and the free craftsmen: it was the age of the enclosures of the commons and the destruction of the guilds; it abandoned the traditional Christian attitude to the poor and substituted a harsher doctrine which regarded poverty as the result of sloth or improvidence and charity as a form of self-indulgence. It made self-interest a law of nature which was providentially designed to serve the good of the whole so that the love of money was transformed from the root of all evil to the mainspring of social life.

This new view of life was not, however, merely the ideological reflection of the material interest of the bourgeois class and its state. It had behind it both the moral force of Puritan individualism and the prestige of an imposing philosophical tradition. The spiritual foundations of liberalism had been laid long before the rise of the liberal state. For the germs of intellectual revolution contained in Renaissance thought were not destroyed by the temporary triumph of authority in Church and state. In fact it was in the Baroque period rather than in that of the Renaissance that the new science and the new philosophy which revolutionized men's ideas of the universe and of human nature itself were born. And it is an important factor in the unity of European culture that at the moment when the religious unity of Christendom was passing away, a new community of thought which transcended national and religious frontiers arose in its place. The new physical synthesis on which modern science is based was an international achievement to which an Italian and an Englishman, a Frenchman, a Dutchman, and a German—Galileo, Newton, Descartes, Huygens and Leibnitz—each contributed his share. This cosmopolitanism is less strongly marked in philosophy, where national characteristics show themselves in the contrast between the empiricism of the English philosophers from Bacon to Locke and the Cartesian rationalism of France. Nevertheless, both of these movements met and exchanged ideas in Holland, the great intellectual clearing house of seventeenth century Europe, where Descartes and Hobbes, Spinoza and Locke found a home or a temporary refuge and whence their ideas were disseminated by Huguenot publicists and cosmopolitan adventurers like Bayle and Le Clerc, Coste and Desmaiseaux, Toland and Mandeville. Thus there grew up by the end of the seventeenth century a common tradition of liberal thought to which the partisans of a new social order could appeal in their struggle with authority.

This scientific and secular current of late Renaissance thought met with the Puritan movement for political rights and religious freedom to produce the new English culture of the period of the Revolution. It is true that the Revolution was an apparent defeat for the principle of toleration, since the King (whose attitude inspired by Penn in this matter was perfectly sincere, in spite of the Whig historians) stood for toleration, while the Whigs fought for the Test Act and the penal laws. But the Whig leaders did not as a rule share the religious prejudices which they used as their instruments. They were in full sympathy with the new secular culture, and they aimed at a state which should represent, not the domination of a particular religion, but the real social and economic forces of the nation. The philosopher of the Revolution, John Locke, was himself a believer in toleration and in a purely rational religion, and his theory of the state and of the origin of political authority in a social contract for the common good is purely secular in character. His whole philosophy, with its common sense rationalizing spirit, its rejection of all abstract ideas and its derivation of all knowledge solely from sensible experience, was one of the great formative influences in eighteenth century thought, and its influence extended far beyond the limits of English culture.

Even more important, however, was the work of Newton, to whom was due the final achievement of the work of Galileo and the completion of the new physical synthesis. His triumphant application of the law of gravitation to the movement of heavenly bodies justified Galileo's belief in the power of mathematics to solve the riddles of the material universe, and proved that the same physical laws held good in every part of the universe. In place of the Aristotelian doctrine that the heavens were moved by conscious spiritual substances, which derived their eternal motion from God, the unmoved mover, there was now substituted a conception of the world as a vast machine, consisting of material bodies situated in absolute space, and moved by mechanical physical laws. The ultimate realities were no longer spiritual substances and qualities, but space, matter, and time.

Thus at the same time that spiritual forces were being excluded from society and from human experience by the new philosophy of Hobbes and Locke, their control of the world of nature was also being denied by the new science. God was no longer seen as the heavenly King and Father who ruled His world by the unceasing interposition of His all-seeing Providence, nor even as the Renaissance philosopher saw Him, as the immanent spiritual principle of nature. He was the Architect of the Universe, a sublime mechanic who had constructed the cosmic machine and left it to follow its own laws.

Hence the new science was as hostile to supernaturalism and to the miraculous element in Christianity as was the new philosophy, and proved one of the chief factors in the secularization of European thought. It is true that the leaders of the movement were by no means hostile to religion. Newton and Locke were good Protestants, and even the "atheist" Spinoza was a profoundly religious man. But the religion of the philosophers was very different from that of Christian orthodoxy. It was inspired by a spirit of rationalism and naturalism which was equally hostile to the Augustinian pessimism of Calvin and to the mystical ecstasies of Baroque Catholicism. It was the product of the new lay culture that had been developing since the Renaissance and it inherited the Humanist distrust of clerical obscurantism and its resentment of the claim of the clergy to control education and thought. How widespread this anticlerical tendency was in the seventeenth century is shown not only by the ferocious anticlericalism of Hobbes and Bayle, but by the attitude of the defenders of orthodoxy themselves: for instance, Boileau's satire on the obscurantism of the Sorbonne, and Dryden's contemptuous dismissal of the ages of faith as

> Times o'ergrown with rust and ignorance . . .
> When want of learning kept the layman low,
> And none but priests were authoriz'd to know;
> When what small knowledge was, in them did dwell,
> And he a god who could but read or spell:—

The orthodoxy of the classical tradition was, in fact, only maintained by a severe moral discipline, and a strong sense of authority in the state was accompanied by a revolt against the principle of authority in religion and an assertion of the supremacy of reason and the freedom of thought. It was but a step from the "Reasonable Christianity" of Locke (1695) to the "Christianity not Mysterious" of Toland (1696) or from the negative scepticism of Boyle to the open incredulity of Collins and Mandeville. Already in the Augustan age religion in England was exposed to a campaign of anticlerical and anti-Christian propaganda which was satirized in Swift's brilliant "Argument against Abolishing Christianity."

Nevertheless the immediate dangers of this movement were less serious than they appeared to contemporary believers of the type of Charles Leslie and William Law. The excesses of Deism and infidelity alarmed the man of solid Protestant bourgeois opinion which was the real force behind the English Revolution, and produced the religious reaction which characterized the middle decades of the eighteenth century. The new society found its intellectual leaders not in cosmopolitan freethinkers of the type of Toland and Bolingbroke, but in men of moderate views like Steele and Addison, and Pope, who adapted the ideals of humanist thought to the needs of the English middle classes and thus gave the Protestant bourgeois culture a classical form which was completely lacking in the undiluted Puritan tradition, as we see it in New England at this period.

In eighteenth century England humanism came to terms with Puritan ethics, and rationalism with Protestant theology, as represented by Samuel Clarke, and Hoadly and Warburton. For the chief threat to the established order came from the Right rather than the Left, and the fear of a Jacobite counter revolution caused the supporters of the principles of the Revolution to adopt a conservative attitude in defence of the *status quo*.

Hence it was in France rather than in England that the revolutionary consequences of the new ideas were most fully realized, and the attack on the traditional Christian order was pressed farthest, though the French Enlightenment owed much of its success to the achievements of the English revolution and to the influence of English ideas. But in France there was no room for a Whig compromise. The majestic unity of French absolutism and Catholicism stood like a fortress which must be destroyed before the city could be taken by the forces of liberalism and revolution. The enforcement of religious unity after the Revocation of the Edict of Nantes left no room for freedom of opinion, and the energies which found an outlet in England in the communal life of the nonconformist sects and their theological controversies were in France driven below the surface and could only express themselves in negative criticism or in utopian idealism. Thus it is no accident that the age which saw the end of French Protestantism was followed by the age of the philosophic enlightenment; indeed the latter may be regarded as a second Reformation that carried the revolt against authority and tradition from the sphere of theology to that of secular culture. The Catholic Church still bore the brunt of the attack; indeed the new reformers repeated with monotonous insistence the abuse of priestcraft and superstition, of monkery and asceticism, of papal tyranny and scholastic obscurantism which had been the current coin of Protestant controversy for two centuries. But the state and the social order were now no longer immune. Every institution and every accepted belief were submitted to the test of criticism and were summarily dismissed if deemed unreasonable or devoid of social utility. In the eyes of the new philosophers the traditional social and religious order of Western Christendom was an antiquated Gothic structure which was no longer habitable. The time had come to demolish it and to construct on the *tabula rasa* of human nature a new edifice based on simple rational principles which would be suited to the needs of an enlightened society.

But the revolutionary implications of this reformation of society were only gradually realized. The earlier leaders of the Enlightenment like Voltaire and Montesquieu had no intention of promoting a social revolution. If they hated mediaevalism and clericalism, they had a profound admiration for the age of Louis XIV, and their ideal was that of a secularized and humanized classicism. When the Huguenot La Beaunell attacked the regime of Louis XIV as an intolerant and oppressive despotism, Voltaire himself arose in defence of the King and the achievements of his reign, which he declared to be the greatest age that France or any other European nation had known. Although the French Enlightenment was closely related to the rise of the bourgeoisie and the development of a new bourgeois mentality, the French bourgeoisie was a very different class from that which created the new capitalist society in Holland and England and America. In France the state had kept a tight hand on trade and industry, and the policy of Louis XIV and Colbert left no room for the development of an independent financial power like that of the financiers who ruled the Dutch and English East Indian Companies and the Bank of Amsterdam and the Bank of England. The typical French financier was a servant of the Government, a treasurer or tax farmer; and even the bankers, like Samuel Bernard, the great Huguenot capitalist under Louis XIV, were more concerned with the negotiation of public loans than with ordinary commercial or industrial credit.

Consequently the French bourgeoisie looked to the state rather than to private enterprise for employment and social advancement. It was the ambition of the rich merchant or lawyer to purchase some office which would open a career for his son in the public service. To a greater extent than any other European country France was a state of lawyers and officials. The French bureaucracy, "the order of officers" as it was called, formed a kind of bourgeois aristocracy distinct in character and origin from the feudal nobility, and even the great ministers of Louis XIV, such as Colbert, were often men of humble origin. It is true that in the eighteenth century the path of advancement grew more difficult and the *noblesse de robe* became more and more a closed caste. Nevertheless, wide as was the gulf between great magistrates like Montesquieu and Henault and lawyers like Mathieu Marais or the father of Voltaire, they possessed a unity of traditions, interests, and ideas similar to that which unites the commissioned and noncommissioned officers in an army, or the prelates and the clergy in the church.

The predominance of this legal and official class is reflected in the development of French society and culture during the seventeenth and eighteenth centuries. It showed itself in the sense of logic and order, the insistence on abstract principles and rights and the jealousy of clerical domination which inspired educated lay opinion. It was this class which created the classical culture and the absolutist state of the *Grand Siècle* by the administrative genius of the archbureaucrat Colbert and the intellectual leadership of men like Racine and Boileau, Pascal and Descartes, Bossuet and Malebranche, all members of the *noblesse de robe,* the bourgeois official class. In the eighteenth century this class remained as important as ever, but it was no longer controlled by the firm hand of a great king like Louis XIV, whose strict religious principles and intense devotion to duty made him the embodiment of the bureaucratic ideal of monarchy. The court of the Regent, on the other hand, outraged all the traditions of the bourgeoisie by its immorality and luxury, while the abortive attempt of the new government to restore the political role of the nobility antagonized the Parlement of Paris and the bureaucracy. The official class became animated by a spirit of opposition and disaffection which was a constant source of embarrassment to the French government throughout the eighteenth century. It was not atheists or demagogues who undermined the stately order of the *Grand Siècle*. Long before the Revolution the authority of the crown was challenged by the official representatives of legality, and the orthodoxy of the Church was discredited by the partisans of theological traditionalism. The two movements of political and religious opposition were closely related, and nowhere are the characteristics of the official parliamentary caste more clearly defined than in the leaders of the Jansenist movement like the great Arnauld and Nicole and M. de Sacy. But it was not until the eighteenth century that Jansenism became almost identified with the parliamentary opposition and degenerated into a narrow and bitter sect which did more to discredit the cause of religion than all the attacks of the philosophers. It was Jansenism which first created the bourgeois anticlericalism that appears so clearly in the journals of men like Mathieu Marais. And it was this spirit of Jansenist anticlericalism which prepared the way for the downfall of the Jesuits and thus shook the very foundations of the Baroque culture.

But though the Jansenist opposition divided and weakened the forces of tradition, it was powerless to create a new order. It was itself a lost cause—a kind of religious Jacobitism—which was condemned to struggle in vain against the rising tide of enlightenment. It was not in the dusty atmosphere of the Sorbonne and the Parlements that the spirit of the new age found expression, but in the great world of the court and the salons where the cult of pleasure and the pursuit of social success were too seductive for men to trouble themselves with the austere demands of Jansenist morality. As we have seen, the tradition of free thinking and loose living was already well established in French aristocratic society during the seventeenth century. But it was in the eighteenth century during the reign of Louis XV that it passed from the nobles to the bourgeois and developed into the great movement of ideas which secularized French culture. Voltaire, the foremost representative of this movement, was himself a member of the lawyer class who preferred the career of letters to the career for which his official father had destined him and who by sheer literary talent attained a position of greater wealth and social importance than any commoner in Europe had hitherto achieved. In this he served the interests of his class no less than his own, for he did more than anyone else to raise the profession of letters from the proletarian squalor of Grub

Street and its servile dependence on noble patrons to an independent power in European society—a fourth estate which could meet princes and ministers on an equal footing and influence the fortunes of nations. Voltaire graduated in the liberation society of the Regency—at the Temple and the salons of the Duchess of Maine—and his mind never lost the imprint of the Regency tradition. But his bourgeois spirit revolted against the arbitrary pride and inequality of aristocratic society and it was in the England of the Whig Revolution rather than in the France of the Regency that he found his philosophic vocation.

Here, it is true, he was following in the footsteps of many another French exile, like the Huguenots Leclerc, Coste and Desmaiseaux, but he was by far the greatest of the apostles of English ideas, and his visit to England in 1726, which was followed by Montesquieu's in the next year, marks an epoch in the history of French thought.

Voltaire and Montesquieu found in England a society that was the direct antithesis of all that they had known in France—one in which the crown had no control over the legislature or the administration of justice, and in which the greatest freedom of thought and expression prevailed, alike in political and religious matters. They were impressed by the vigorous individualism of English life and by the economic and social prosperity by which it was accompanied, but most of all by its frankly secular and anticlerical spirit. For they had discovered England in the age of the Deists and the Freethinkers before the great Wesleyan religious revival, the imminence of which they could hardly suspect. "Point de religion en Angleterre," says Montesquieu—and this was the feature of English life which most appealed to the mind of Voltaire. He ascribed it to the victory of the new philosophy of Newton and Locke, and accordingly he made this the basis of his own philosophic propaganda in France. His first influential work, "The Philosophic or English Letters," which begins with a discussion of the English sects and the praise of English toleration, finds its centre in an exposition of the ideas of Newton and Locke, whom he hails as the greatest minds of the human race. "From Plato to Locke, there is nothing," he says; and later D'Alembert summed up the judgment of his age when he declared Locke to be the creator of metaphysics as Newton had been the creator of physics.

This philosophic propaganda achieved an extraordinary success in France. The new ideas were taken up by the fashionable world, and were debated in the salons of great ladies and fashionable financiers. With the publication of the great *Encyclopaedia,* from 1751 onwards, they received as it were an official statement, and became the creed of an organized party, which gained adherents wherever the influence of French culture was dominant from Berlin to Naples.

But the movement had undergone a profound change in passing

from England to the Continent. As we have seen, the Whig Revolution was based on the sturdy individualism of Protestant bourgeois society, and the new English culture represented a compromise between the Puritan and the humanist tradition. In France, on the other hand, the new ideas were introduced into a society which had been drilled into uniformity by the combined influences of the Counter-Reformation Church and the Baroque monarchy, and which possessed a complete unity of culture and religion. The philosophers found themselves opposed, not to a fluctuating mass of warring sects, but to a single Church which claimed absolute authority over thought and morals. Hence the openly anti-Christian character of the philosophic movement, of which the watchword was Voltaire's "Ecrasez l'infame," and which ultimately led to the celebration of the Feast of Reason in the Cathedral of Notre Dame. Though they might invoke the principle of toleration, as practiced in England, their real aim was to replace one unity by another, to substitute the universal reign of science and reason for that of religion and authority. This absolutism of thought, so utterly unlike the cautious realism of the English thinkers, was due not only to the violence of the intellectual struggle, but to the whole tendency of the French mind. The men of the age had an unlimited belief in the powers of human reason and in the possibility of an immediate social transformation if only the legislature would be won over to the cause of reason and progress. But they had no desire for political or social revolution and little sympathy with democratic ideas. Almost to a man the philosophers, like their predecessors the English Whigs, were on the side of property and order. Their ideal was an authoritarian liberalism based on the union of the government and the intelligentsia, and they were never so happy as when they were acting as the confidential advisers of kings and ministers, as Voltaire did with Frederick II, and Choiseul and Diderot with Catherine the Great.

In spite of the vein of Utopian socialism which comes to the surface in writers like Morelly, author of the *Code de la nature,* and the Abbé Mably, the philosophers would have been horrified at the idea of transferring power from rulers like Frederick the Great and Catherine of Russia, or from ministers like Choiseul and Turgot to the common people. Voltaire in particular had an unbounded contempt for the populace, the "canaille that is not worthy of enlightenment and which deserves its yoke." He was himself a capitalist who had accumulated an enormous fortune by loans and speculation and careful investment and no one could have had a stronger sense of property or a greater desire to make the most of the social position he had achieved. He was a true liberal, but his liberalism had in it nothing visionary or utopian. In fact, as M. Lanson remarks, the Voltairean ideal found its realization in the bourgeois France of Louis Philippe.

Even in intellectual matters the philosophers were by no means in favor of universal enlightenment. Voltaire wrote

I doubt if the populace has either the time or the capacity for education. They would die of hunger before they became philosophers. It seems to be essential that there should be ignorant beggars. If you had to improve a property or if you had ploughs, you would agree with me. It is not the worker we must instruct, it is the bon bourgeois and the townsman.

In the same vein: "We have never pretended to enlighten shoemakers and servant girls, that is the portion of the apostles."

In fact, as David Mornet points out, it was the Church that worked almost alone, but not unsuccessfully, for the cause of popular education while the philosophers were content to devote their energies to the enlightenment of the "little flock" of rich, well born, well educated people who make public opinion. Here their propaganda proved extraordinarily successful. With the fall of the Jesuits the Church lost its influence over the mind of the ruling classes and the philosophers took the place of the confessor as the spiritual guide of kings and ministers. The movement reached its height during the generation before the French Revolution, the age of Joseph II in Austria and his brother Leopold in Tuscany, Catherine II in Russia, Gustav III in Sweden, Struensee in Denmark, Florida Blanca in Spain and Turgot and Malesherbes in France. Even before this time the new ideas were at work in France under Choiseul and Mme. Pompadour, in Prussia under Frederick the Great, in Austria under Kaunitz, in Naples under Tanucci, and in Portugal under Pombal. Throughout Europe statesmen were engaged in sweeping away the debris of the Middle Ages and carrying out administrative, social, and economic reforms according to the principles of the new philosophy.

But though the success of this movement was rapid and widespread, it was also limited and superficial. Underneath the surface of rational enlightenment the life of the peasants and the craftsmen followed the old ways of social and religious traditions. While the courtiers of Catherine II or Joseph II read the latest books from Paris and adopted the fashionable rationalism of cosmopolitan society, their peasant serfs still lived in the world of Baroque Catholicism or Byzantine Orthodoxy. And hence there developed a spiritual cleavage in society which contained the seeds of class conflict and social revolution. In the old Christian order nobles and peasants had shared a common faith and a common service. But now that Christianity was regarded as only good for the lower classes, as Voltaire so often asserts, the spiritual foundation of social unity was destroyed. In spite of all that the enlightened despots and their ministers did for the cause of civilization and progress they had lost the sacred character of the old Christian kingship which invested even the unimpressive exterior of the later Habsburgs with the aura of divinity. And with the loss of this tradition the heart went out of the *ancien régime* and left it a hollow shell.

It is true that in certain respects European culture has never reached a higher level than it did in France during the Age of the Enlightenment. Never has the art of living been more cultivated, never has society been more open to ideas and more ready to appreciate and reward intellectual talent, but all the graces of life—the famous *douceur de vivre* of which Talleyrand speaks—were often a brilliant facade which had nothing but a spiritual void behind it. The men who were loyal to the old tradition, like Dr. Johnson, had their hearts in the right place, however narrow and bigoted they were in their views. But there is a repellent heartlessness about the leaders of the Enlightenment, like Frederick the Great and Voltaire and Chesterfield and Horace Walpole and Talleyrand, which is the peculiar weakness of a purely rational culture. Hence there arose a reaction against the Enlightenment, which asserted the rights of the heart against the dictatorship of reason and created a new religion of feeling which did more than all the reasonings of the philosophers to create a new social order. The answer to Voltaire came neither from the Sorbonne nor the Jansenists, but from Rousseau.

THE YEAR 1848 IN GERMAN

HISTORY: REFLECTIONS

ON A CENTENARY

Friedrich Meinecke

[1948]

THE popular uprising of the March Days of 1848 in Berlin, superficially viewed, remained an episode, and the men who were fighting for progress along various lines failed, and were bound to fail, in their aims. The German revolution, said Friedrich Engels in his instructive articles of 1851–52 (which he published in America above the signature of Karl Marx), was a necessity, but its temporary suppression was similarly unavoidable. We shall still have to substantiate this, but must turn our gaze first upon the Berlin revolution, and upon the positive comment which it may offer for our contemporary historical situation. Yet for this too it is necessary to search somewhat deeper.

We must set before ourselves today more sharply than before, the problem of critical alternatives in the history of Germany, in order to gain a deeper insight into the infinitely complex web of her dark destiny. The natural task of Germany in the nineteenth century was not only to achieve unification, but also to transmute the existing authoritarian state (*Obrigkeitsstaat*) into a commonwealth *(Gemeinschaftsstaat)*. To that end, the monarchial-authoritarian structure had to be made elastic—if possible, through peaceful reform—so that the result would be an active and effective participation of all strata of society in the life of the state. This was imperatively demanded by the new configuration which was in process within the German society, and which was undermining the former aristocratic foundations of the authoritarian monarchy. An upper middle class arose, the lower middle class increased in large strides, and the beginnings of the industrial proletariat in the middle of the century gave notice of its mighty growth to come. Now, the task of reorganizing and harmonizing within a new commonwealth a people in social transition, bursting with vitality, remained largely unfulfilled, although many liberal and democratic concessions were granted by the old authorities. Which then were the decisive points in this development? When were possibilities first seen, attempts made or frustrated, which could have brought Germany forward upon the path to the commonwealth?

I see, above all, three such moments. The first occurs toward the end of the Prussian era of reform, in the year 1819—the year of the Carlsbad Decrees—when with the dismissal of Wilhelm von Humboldt and Boyen, their most fruitful constitutional projects were also buried, and the authoritarian and militaristic principle triumphed in Prussia. The second crisis, when this principle once more won out in the end, was the year 1848. And the third point of decision was the Prussian era of conflict and the year 1866, which, while seeing some progress made toward satisfying the desire for national unity and strength, allowed the liberal and democratic ideas only a partial or apparent success. For it separated the way of the upsurging popular movements from the authoritarian-militaristic citadel of the entire national life.

Of these three fundamental decisions of the nineteenth century, the first was fought out in the more restricted circle of the ruling class itself, between high-minded and farsighted statesmen on the one hand and a monarch of limited understanding on the other. The third crisis developed as a duel between the liberal upper middle class and Bismarck, in which that tremendously skilful campaigner understood how to win over at last a large part of the opposition. At no time in the years before 1866, was the weapon of a revolution seriously considered by Bismarck's progressive antagonists; they were fearful of it, in accordance with the instincts of an upper bourgeoisie. The second crisis—that of 1848—offers therefore a unique, and for us today, a moving spectacle: here the whole people, not Prussians alone, but Germans of every class, stepped into the arena, and an actual revolution came about.

Revolutions, fearful as the invasion of irrational forces may be, or turn out to be, have in certain cases their deep historical justification. Such was the case in Germany, and especially in Prussia, in the year 1848. Admittedly the old order, now attacked by the revolution, was not in all aspects characterized by decay or ossification. The *Biedermeierzeit* with its lovely spiritual flowering had gone before. The Zollverein, since 1833 a work of the Prussian bureaucracy, had made secure the indispensable preconditions for the rise of modern economic forces, and thereby also for the social transformation from which the revolution itself had sprung. The psychopathic romanticist who now sat on the throne of the Hohenzollerns was himself inspired with a deep love for German civilization (*Deutschtum*), and was at some pains to bring about a German unity in its own way. But this way contradicted most sharply the urgent needs of the time. It was upon illusions that he based his attempts to reform the wretched organization of the German Bund and to fulfill the promise of a constitution (made in 1815) by the assembling of the united provincial diets in 1847. For the strongly aristocratic composition of these provincial estates, and the narrow powers which were all that the king would concede to them, were completely inadequate to satisfy the claims of popular representation which grew out of the process of social change. And in everyday life one felt everywhere the old absolutist-militarist police state, unbroken in spite of the isolated concessions to liberalism which the king, giving with one hand and rescinding with the other, might make. But behind the reaction against his personal and self-contradictory rule, and behind all individual grievances, there stood as the deepest source of discontent the feeling that the Prussian military and Junker state must be reorganized from the ground up—that the old authoritarian state must give way to a new commonwealth.

In fact this emotion, spurring on toward revolution, was not actually evoked but only powerfully stimulated, by the February revolution in France and the scattered revolts that were flaring up throughout Germany and even in Metternich's own Vienna. The remarkable circumstance that they succeeded everywhere at once, without encountering resistance, would demonstrate that the moral position of the rulers themselves was already noticeably shaken, that they no longer possessed an unquestioning and naive faith in the viability of the old order. Such a faith was necessary, if the governments were to use against the revolution the physical instrumentalities of power, still amply available to them. When later they realized that these resources were still at their disposal, the authorities did not hesitate to act accordingly, and to suppress the revolution with reaction. But as things were in March, 1848, they all, as Frederick William IV later expressed it, "lay flat on their bellies."

He, the king himself, most of all. And this in spite of the fact that he had actually launched, on the 18th of March, the physical auxiliaries of his power—his faithful army—successfully against the people's barricades in Berlin. Yet on the very next day, he permitted, through his own order, these troops—though undefeated—to abandon the inner city which they had conquered, and thereby exposed the person of the king to the severest of humiliations at the hands of the rebels. Let us leave aside entirely the tangled complexity of these events, which have been investigated time and again, and emphasize only this. So feeble and contradictory a policy could not have been conducted by any prince, who, with a pure and undiminished faith in his old world, was simply defending it against a new. This new world had already to some degree insinuated itself, secretly and unsuspected, into his own thinking, distracting and weakening his power for effective action. Sooner or later the new was bound to win out, in spite of many setbacks to come, and to replace the authoritarian state by some form of democracy.

Such an interpretation may be justified, as we look back over the whole century that separates us from the year 1848, and as we think of the task now before us—the task of casting aside all relics of the authoritarian state (of which the Third Reich was, in fact, but a malignant outgrowth), and building up a sound and vigorous democracy. The easy victory—to be sure, not a military but a political and psychological victory—by which the street-fighting in Berlin prevailed over the old military monarchy, suggested symbolically that the latter's downfall was written in the stars; that one day the sovereignty of the people would become a reality. But, at the same time, it was no more than a symbol. For the new world was as yet quite untested and immature, and the old world still possessed many unexploited resources —even the chance of remaining victorious for some time to come. Bismarck and his work, after all, had sprung from it, at once magnificent and ephemeral. But let us now mark clearly the indications of that immaturity in which the new world of democracy then continued to find itself.

First, a glance at Berlin. The men on the barricades of the 18th of March certainly fought bravely and fiercely, more fiercely than the Parisians before them had fought on the 24th of February. Such was the opinion of the Frenchman Circourt, who had come to Berlin as the representative of the new republican government, and had witnessed both engagements. But was it really the whole of the Berlin populace that stood behind the fighting or accompanied it with good wishes? Pastor Bodelschwingh, son of the minister whose task it was to pass on the royal command for retreat on the 19th of March, wrote in 1902: "We youngsters were running about on the streets that Sunday morning (March 19). With the uprising repelled, there reigned a joyful mood among the greater part of our population; everywhere from the houses the troops were plied with food." Of course, most of the individual bits of evidence which we possess concerning the 18th and 19th of March, are colored to some extent by the sympathies of the witness, and so this testimony of Bodelschwingh should not be taken too literally either. But even less does it deserve to be entirely discarded. And a glance at the general attitude of the German upper middle class in the years 1848–49 reveals all the more clearly that large sections of this class were still greatly desirous of tranquillity, and continued to be loyal to the old authorities.

It is necessary to go more deeply into these questions, in order to explain the paradoxical fact that the German revolution of 1848 could everywhere succeed so easily at first, and then in the sequence of events be overthrown with comparatively little effort. To understand this, the character, attitudes, and moral habits of the German people as it was at that time, and those of the various social strata within it, must be taken into consideration. And our contemporary need to attain to an inner relationship with this first attempt at German democracy gives this problem all the more importance.

The German people had only just emerged from the years of thinking, writing, and striving. But the thinking and dreaming continued likewise within the framework of new achievements and new desires. This ideological groundswell is common to all parties and classes within the German people, from Frederick William IV and his devout Christian-German friends—the extremists of reaction—all the way to the extremists of revolution: the men whose forceful minds conceived the Communist Manifesto of 1848, Karl Marx and Engels. For did not Hegel live on with them—a Hegel in reverse and yet preserved (*aufgehoben*)? Was it not true of both these thinkers, who claimed to regard all ideologies as merely secondary efforts of fundamental economic forces, that in them there came to life something distinctly ideological—an unqualified belief in the determining power of the laws of development—set up at a time when they themselves found only a tiny handful of followers? In any case, we ought no more gainsay the strong impulse of idealism which worked in these men, than that operating in Dahlmann and Gagern—the champions of the liberal nation-state—or in the brothers Gerlach, defenders of a divinely ordained corporative state. The German revolution of 1848, admittedly, shows not only an all-pervading spirit of idealism, which often outstripped reality and became ideological. It also brought to bear what in actual effect was more powerful—the reality itself, the massive and elemental interests of individuals and social groups. And, because it *was* a revolution, it likewise saw the release of base passions, and outrages of all kinds, perpetrated by the Right as well as by the Left. But if 1848 is compared with other revolutions—and particularly with the most ignominious of all revolutions, that of 1933—it can be stated that the factor of human depravity played a comparatively insignificant role. This must not be obscured by the fact that the extremist parties took pleasure in accusing one another of disgraceful conduct. Theirs were for the most part "atrocity stories." Neither was there anything which could be termed a "brutalized soldiery," nor were the barricades and the free corps of Hecker and Struve manned by a mere "mob." The German people, considered as a whole, kept in those days to a comparatively high moral level.

It must be admitted that their level of life no longer possessed the spiritual grandeur of the age of Goethe. This decline was unavoidable in any case, since the urgent task of establishing a new political and social way of life compressed men into mass or group patterns, and made it more difficult for the individual to gather within himself the creative force from which proceeds all great culture. But what mattered now was, whether this people would prove to possess the maturity, the strength, the insight, and steadfastness, that its new task demanded. Certainly, as we have noted, it was written in the stars that one day the new world would triumph over the old, popular sovereignty over the authoritarian state. But could the victory be achieved at this juncture? The fact that the revolution failed does not necessarily prove that the people were not ready; this may have been due to the coincidence of accidental factors. How bitter were the complaints, in the very midst of events, that just such a personality as Frederick William IV should have been for the revolution its "man of destiny"—a man who had actually, out of weakness, bowed before it at the outset, but who had then stubbornly resisted it; and by his refusal of the imperial office on April 3, 1849, had allowed the nation's call for the creation of the liberal nation-state to die away. Certainly another man in his place could have attempted another and possibly more propitious solution of the German problem. Then, however, the success of the attempt would once more have depended, in the last analysis, upon the world situation. This aspect of the problem we shall take up later. Suffice it now to ask again: was the German people really prepared for the task ahead?

Basic attributes and historical experiences, working together, had made the German people parochial, not only outwardly but inwardly as well, to a degree hardly equalled in any other nation of Europe. The princely territorial state, multiplied a hundredfold to the point where it exhibited absurd extremes of dwarfishness, depended everywhere upon a landed gentry which served the state and, in return, held sway over those beneath them. All this had mingled with the German bloodstream and had rendered the German people obedient and lacking in political self-reliance. In this very multiplication of authority, we see the chief means by which the mentality of the authoritarian state penetrated so deeply into the pores of German life.

One need only compare this with the development of England and France, where the royal absolutism—in England short-lived anyhow—had indeed helped to create a unified nation, but had never been able to instil so lasting and thoroughgoing a habit of obedience, as had the multiplicity of small German principalities. How far an original or native trait had helped to bring this about, can only be conjectured. Was it perhaps the spirit of fealty described by Tacitus? But the example of the Germans in Switzerland and their historical development since the Middle Ages indicates that there were other potentialities of a political nature inherent in the German character. Free of princely and therefore of rigid rule, subject only to patrician and—by the same token—more pliable authority, Switzerland was enabled to develop the native democratic tenet of her original cantons into the governing principle of her commonwealth, and thus to build upon historical foundations a modern democracy. No, the German need not submit to any fatalistic dread that because he is a German, he may for ever and ever be condemned to the habits of servility implanted by the authoritarian state. But it takes time, much time, again to tear free of it. Then too, this state has borne the German people, along with evil fruits, many and varied benefits, and thus fashioned much of ethical value that might well be carried over into the new world of the democratic commonwealth.

Good and evil alike, then, grew out of this disposition toward obedience, whose origin may well be placed primarily in the political fragmentation referred to above. Even where a larger political entity was growing up, as in Prussia, the extreme insistence upon this subservient attitude brought out in a manner especially striking the contrast between its good and evil effects. Prussia was, indeed, a state with two souls: the one austere and narrow, withdrawing into itself; the other culturally alive, striving, in Boyen's phrase, toward a threefold alliance of *"Recht, Licht und Schwert."* This Prussia, at once forbidding and attractive, now exerted her influence upon the rest of Germany. But how much was this influence again bound to confuse and distract all the aims of revolutionary Germany! The singleness of revolutionary purpose which would have been necessary for a victory over the old order, was thus rendered at the outset far more difficult to achieve. Now the German people, breaking loose from its previous subservience, did indeed reach out tumultuously for unity, power, and freedom—only to find itself divided anew when it sought to determine the methods by which these were to be accomplished. How deep was the disintegrating and paralyzing effect of the Austro-German (*grossdeutsche*) problem, which implied what to some seemed an avoidable, to others an inevitable sacrifice of a portion of their fellow-countrymen (*Brudersstamm*), and the break-up of a German national community; how strongly has this problem contributed to the negative result of the revolution! It is hardly necessary, in addition, to recall the particularism of the intermediate German states. In fact, it was not merely the egotistic instincts of the princes, of their court councillors and court provisioners, but particularistic tendencies as well, conscious or unconscious, in the people themselves, which came into conflict with the new yearning for unity.

These were the factors of secular growth, going back as far as the Middle Ages, which weakened and divided in advance any unified revolutionary purpose in the German people. To these, however, were now added problems of the most modern type, arising out of the new configuration of society. It is true that the one part of the people which now broke away from the old attitudes of obedience, and rose up against the authoritarian state and against the splintering apart of the nation, was agreed upon the demand for greater unity, power, and freedom; but it fell out once again over the emphasis and interpretation to be placed upon one or another of these three words. For behind the national revolution there was unfolding a social revolution, a class struggle between the old, the newer, and the newest social strata. This fact was recognized most clearly at the time by Marx and Engels, the champions of the newest class—the industrial proletariat—which had only just arisen and was still by no means very numerous. Between this youngest and (as Marx and Engels dogmatically proclaimed) potentially most important class, and that which had ruled so far—the nobility and the higher bureaucracy—there lay the two clearly distinct divisions of the bourgeoisie: the upper and lower middle class. The first was of more recent origin; the other dated far back, though it was not nearly as old as the peasantry—who, together with agricultural laborers, still made up by far the preponderant majority of the people as a whole. (The committee on economic affairs of the Frankfurt Parliament estimated that they constituted virtually four-fifths of the total population at that time.) The share of the rural population in the revolution was certainly not unimportant, but created no particularly complicated issue for the fate of the revolution as a whole. Since a general land reform through the dismemberment of the large estates was not yet seriously envisioned, the agrarian problem of 1848 entailed only the casting-off of all remaining feudal encumbrances upon the peasant class and the peasant holdings. That was a comparatively simple task. Even conservative statesmen realized the necessity of solving this question at once, and when the peasants saw that steps in this direction were being taken or being planned, they calmed down again. They still shared sufficiently in the old habits of subservience, in any case. The young Bismarck could well consider using them as tools in the counter-revolution.

Side by side with the working class, the lower middle class provided most of the revolutionary energy. Craftsmen and workers formed the bulk of the fighters on the barricades. Had they not risen up, the revolution could not have achieved dynamic force at all, and all the idealists and theorists of the general movement (reaching into the upper middle class) would have remained officers without an army. There would have been no parliament in the Paulskirche, no draft for a German constitution with an hereditary Prussian emperor at its head. The craftsmen in Germany at that time were badly off. It was related in the Paulskirche that there was one small town with seventy tailors, of whom only seven were able to find employment. Some hardship was caused by guild restrictions which continued here and there. But a genuine guild spirit revived again, as is evidenced in the desperate struggle waged against the new machine by workers who were losing their livelihood, in the excesses committed by the waggoners against the railroads and by the boatsmen against the Rhine river steamers. These were all, in fact, merely symptoms of the basic feature of an age in which the machine, and the modern technology, had revolutionized the entire life of the Western peoples, by creating new human masses and new, unsuspected, and distressing situations among these masses.

In such a crisis, the old authoritarian state proved unable for a long time to provide effective aid. Its officialdom was vacillating between benevolence and a narrow, pedantic attitude; its police a nuisance; its army—though possessed in the militia (*Landwehr*) of a more popular aspect—aroused bitter opposition by the arrogance and drill-ground manner of the regulars and their officers. Democracy as a cure for all these sufferings was the magic word that echoed through the ranks of the lower bourgeoisie—a class so quietist by nature and so restless now. The working classes took up the same slogan, and added to it their own socialistic demands. The younger generation within the upper middle class in many places espoused the democratic cause with enthusiasm, and imbued it with the impulse of idealism. It was, to be sure, an exceedingly immature and primitive democracy of which these Germans dreamed, more a rejection of the old authoritarian state than a positive affirmation of the people's state resting upon a fully developed common spirit among all classes. The distrust and arrogance with which the various classes regarded one another, once more divided the very groups which had just made common cause against the old authorities. Let us illustrate this and other facts aforementioned, with certain experiences which the young Rudolf Virchow had in the March Days of Berlin.

Eight days before the 18th of March, he had returned from Upper Silesia, where he had been sent as a doctor to study the "hunger-typhus." He was indignant at the inability of the magistrates to take effective measures, and had long been convinced that the absolutist system of government was untenable. He assisted in the building of barricades on the 18th of March, and, armed with a pistol, placed himself at the one which blocked the Friedrichstrasse from the Tauben-strasse. Only six days later, he had to admit in a letter to his father: "Already there begins a reaction among the citizenry (Bourgeoisie) against the workers (the people). Already they are speaking of a rabble, already plans are being made for withholding equal distribution of political rights among the various groups in the nation." But, he added, the popular party would be alert and powerful, and would see to it "that no bourgeoisie should enjoy the fruits of a battle it had not waged."

One realizes here the closeness of the relationship between events in Berlin and the revolutions of 1830 and 1848 in France. But the problems of the German revolution were nevertheless much more complicated than those of the French uprisings. For the social revolution in Germany and its underlying class struggle were intertwined with the national revolution in a way which finally led to the failure of both. France no longer had need of a national revolution. She had long since achieved her unity, and her centralized power apparatus remained through one regime after another. In Germany both social equality and national consolidation were still to be achieved, with endless pains. And the need of the nation for unity and power was just as elemental and as deeply rooted in history as was the cry for domestic freedom and equality arising from those classes which the authoritarian state had so far kept down. Dahlmann in Frankfurt even voiced the opinion that within the German desire for both power and freedom, the stronger impulse was now directed toward power, which had thus far been denied. The criminal excesses reached in our day by the need for power in Germany should by no means mislead us into condemning the elemental national craving of the men of '48. For theirs was a genuine hunger for something indispensable. Even Goethe had once acknowledged this fact, after the battle of Leipzig. "Art and science," he said to Luden, "are universal, and in view of these the bonds of nationality disappear. But the consolation they afford is but hollow comfort, and cannot replace the proud conscious-ness of belonging to a great, strong, feared, and respected nation." Basically all the cravings of the year 1848 were permeated by kindred feelings and experiences. There was a general desire to leave behind the constricting and now intolerable bonds of the past, as one leaves behind a dark and airless dungeon. Just as the little man felt himself generally neglected and mistreated by the authoritarian state, so did the more cultivated German, who saw himself as a member of a great national community, and yet hemmed in by the irritating boundaries and the often ridiculous parochialism of thirty-eight greater or smaller authoritarian states. And equally neglected and thrust aside did he feel himself and his whole people to be within the entire body of European states.

All three of these desires [the liberal, the national, the European] were now, it was fondly hoped, to find their fulfilment through the Frankfurt National Assembly which, elected by universal and equal suffrage, convened on the 18th of May. Let us consider its social composition; it was noticeably different from what one might have expected as the result of the democratic suffrage imported from France. It contained no workers, only one genuine peasant, few members of the lower middle class, but many lawyers and judges—and, as is well known, many professors; nor were representatives of business and industry lacking. This indicates the still remaining respect of the lower for the upper strata of society, especially for the academically educated and in general for what is termed the upper bourgeoisie. But the same masses who now cast their votes for these people, were simultaneously in a state of unruly and turbulent commotion, which must necessarily have boded evil for the upper middle class interests and ideals. One had to rely on such an energetic thrust from below, in order to succeed at all to Frankfurt and the Paulskirche. But now it was a question, indeed, whether one could continue to employ these energies as indispensable weapons against the rulers, and yet keep them within limits, so as to guard against anarchy and the overturn of the social order.

In the last analysis, it was the danger of communism which appeared to threaten the whole bourgeoisie—not only the upper but the lower middle class as well. How real even the latter felt this threat to be, is exemplified by the bloody clash between the civil guard and the workers in Berlin on October 16, 1848. Communistic slogans and demands rang out from the enraged masses. A clearly conceived program, such as that of Marx and Engels, was in truth limited at first to the narrowest circles. But in a broader perspective, it appears that the very existence of a communist movement was perhaps decisive, or at least instrumental, in determining the course of events in 1848— and, in the first instance, the attitude and policy of the Paulskirche. For it was in view of this communist threat that the middle class and its representation in the majority parties of the Paulskirche again and again were forced over toward the Right, toward some kind of compromise with the old authorities and their military resources. The same threat was instrumental in preventing the maintenance of a unified revolutionary purpose within the whole people, to which perhaps the government might at last have been forced to submit. We use the little word "perhaps," because historical questions of this sort cannot be treated like a mere problem in mathematics; because in every case where we have to consider the historical possibility of another kind of development than that which actually took place, an unknown "X" disturbs the calculation.

In any event, the parties of the majority—right and left center—which desired to establish a liberal, constitutional nation-state with an hereditary Prussian emperor as its head, found themselves in an extremely contradictory and precarious position. They needed the resources of a revolution just as much as those of a counter-revolution. But their position did not enable them to make full and unqualified use of either, without endangering the very basis of their undertaking. In their effort, however, to pursue a middle course and to bring both revolutionary and counter-revolutionary resources simultaneously or alternately into play, they incurred the danger, in turn, of becoming powerless themselves, and of seeing their cause wrecked against the forces of the stronger contender of the two—the counter-revolution. This, viewed as a whole, was to be their fate. Let us briefly point out here only the critical stages.

From France the signal had been given in February for the revolution; from France again the signal was given for the counter-revolution in June. In a terrible, three-day street battle, Cavaignac smashed the Paris workers. To be sure, the German middle class heaved a sigh of relief; but for them the ebbing of the revolutionary wave which now followed in Germany as well, was gain and loss alike—while for the reactionary forces of the authoritarian state, this turn constituted a clear gain. With the decline of communist fortunes, those of national liberalism sank as well.

This same dynamic course of events then unfolded during September. When the Prussian government concluded with Denmark the truce of Malmö, which seriously threatened the German claim to Schleswig, the aroused majority in the Paulskirche at first rejected it outright; but shortly thereafter, in view of the impracticable consequences of a refusal, the assembly, once more grown meek, ratified the agreement. And when an uprising from the Left now led to street fighting in Frankfurt itself and endangered the assembly, it was forced to turn for help to Prussian and Austrian troops (from the federal fortress at Mainz), in order to prevent a general landslide to the Left. Once more the fortunes of the authoritarian state rose, once more those of national liberalism sank. And they dropped still lower when the governments of Austria and Prussia, in October and November respectively, put down with their own military forces the rebellious democracy in Vienna and Berlin.

Under such circumstances was born the constitutional project of the Frankfurt National Assembly, culminating in the choice of the King of Prussia as hereditary emperor on March 28, 1849. Doubtless it was a proud achievement of the noblest aspiration toward national unity and freedom. But it lacked the basis of power which would have been necessary to put it through against the particularistic and reactionary forces of the authoritarian state. It was defeated at once when Frederick William IV, on April 3, 1849, refused to accept the new crown offered to him—a crown which in his view could appear only as a product of the revolution, a Danaean gift. And when the genuine revolution now reared its head again, and the disappointment which broad masses of the people experienced over the failure of Frankfurt exploded in the May uprisings in Pfalz and Baden, the equally disillusioned middle class—in order not to be engulfed altogether by revolution and the social upheaval that might follow—was forced once more, as in September, 1848, to lean on the authoritarian state. It had now exhausted its own role as an independent power factor, and had to be satisfied with the scant dole of liberal and national concessions which the insight of those who ruled Prussia might still be willing to grant. The May uprisings, on the other hand, were easily put down by Prussian troops. The fighters of the revolution, be they idealists of the urban educated class, little people of the lower bourgeoisie, or workers, proved completely inadequate to wage a military campaign against the disciplined and dependable fighting force of the authoritarian state.

Upon these rocks was wrecked the German revolution. Only a unified revolutionary purpose, reconciling workers with bourgeoisie and upper with lower middle class, might have been able (as we have noted) to force another result and so to weaken the army's tradition of loyalty as to overthrow the old authorities. But the social transformation of the people, which brought on disruption within the entire middle class, had in fact made impossible from the first the growth of such a spirit of revolutionary unity. Without this social transformation, however—without a rising upper middle class, a lower middle class threatened with disintegration, and an aspiring working class—the revolution itself would have been impossible. Thus strangely and tragically intertwined were the inner necessity of this revolution and its inevitable failure.

We have deliberately emphasized the question whether the year 1848 could have brought a commonwealth to the German people. For it is this very question which above all burns in our hearts in the dark situation of today. Only as a genuine and healthy commonwealth could Germany win in Europe and in the world a position strong enough to be maintained through all the crises of Europe. The Bismarckian Reich, magnificent as was its undertaking to combine the vital elements, old and new, within state and society, was yet unable to achieve that intense common spirit which is indispensable as an essential bond within the whole, and as the basis of any vigorous democracy.

There has been much talk since Ranke of a primacy of foreign policy, which is supposed to exercise a formative and dominating influence upon domestic affairs. I believe that this doctrine, while containing an indisputable kernel of truth, today requires revision and certain qualifications. The motives as well as the effects of foreign policy—and particularly whether its success is to be lasting or only temporary—depend to a considerable extent upon the inner coherence and sturdiness of the individual state; upon the type and degree of a common spirit which animates it. The Bismarckian Reich, it is true, was built up under a primary impulse of foreign policy—that is, out of the necessity to erect a strong and independent power in the center of Europe. In addition, it certainly lacked no appreciation of the fact that this power must also possess inner coherence, and rest on a sense of national community. But the synthesis which Bismarck attempted to forge between authoritarian state and commonwealth failed the test in the years of decision, when the world wars came. Too much of the authoritarian state remained in Bismarck's work.

But in what way, we must now inquire, is the year 1848 related to the primacy of foreign policy and to the world of European power politics in general? We have already seen that among the aims of the year 1848, there was also present the hope of raising Germany to the status of a great power. And this need was felt not only in the ranks of the middle class—of the party of liberal reform, the advocates of an hereditary imperial crown. More or less consciously, it inflamed also the will of many of those who wished to make of Germany "the republic one and indivisible." The Left too had its power politics—still a totally irresponsible variety—but one already spurred on in no small measure by desires and aspirations, though they were of course, assumed to advance democracy. Hence war was appraised as an instrument for winning a lasting peace among the democratically united peoples of Europe. This idea of forming an aggressive front is to be encountered often enough—for example, in the proposal of an alliance with democratic France against autocratic Russia. And was it not the Left itself in the Paulskirche—in the September crisis after the truce of Malmö—which demanded the continuation of a national war against Denmark, a war threatening to widen into a European war? It was the opinion of Karl Marx that a world war must assist his cause. Thus democrats were willing enough in such cases—though at first with merely verbal audacity—to take up the sword, the assumption being that in the future it should not be carried by the "brutalized soldiery" of an authoritarian state, but by a people's army. We realize now that an intensification, a victory of the domestic revolution in Germany, could have led—and perhaps necessarily—into the storm center of a great European war. A realization, once more, that is deep with tragedy.

This danger of a European war, in fact, was like a lowering black storm-cloud overshadowing the whole of the revolution of 1848, and even subsequent events. All the problems of this year which were specifically national, were inflammatory in the highest degree. To gain Schleswig, a war had to be started as early as April, 1848; but it stirred immediate opposition in Russia, England, and Sweden, which eventually did bar the way to this prize. The Polish-German problem of Posen led, even in its first stage, to bloody fighting within the province itself; but it could as easily have eventuated in a Russian intervention. The great Austro-German question, the exclusion of Austria from the federative state envisioned in the Paulskirche, was most clearly burdened with the heavy mortgage of an imminent war against Russia and Austria. And France? There from the outset a common conviction prevailed that a united and powerful Germany could not be tolerated. French "security," they felt, would be endangered by such a development. Thus a new struggle over the Rhine frontier was threatening. In the French mind, offensive and defensive motives were in this case —as, perhaps, ever since then!—inextricably intertwined. But were they not also similarly present in many ways in the German mind? There was no lack here either of expansionist fantasies, though at first they were confined to individual imaginations.

Thus did the German revolution of 1848, and especially the work of the Paulskirche—the imperial constitution of 1849—contain certain warlike possibilities, which through the succeeding century became realities, and finally ended in the collapse of Germany. At that time they remained mere possibilities, because the German revolution (with the exception of the Danish war) spent itself internally; because internally it could still be held in check through the exercise of the resources of authoritarian power. But by this means were restrained not only the war-breeding impulses toward unity and power, but also the urge to freedom of the German people; the insistence upon becoming a popular, national commonwealth. Once more an interrelationship altogether tragic—one whose significance seizes us especially today.

The fact must however be acknowledged that a large part of this fatal interaction lay in the existence of the Prussian military and authoritarian power. Only Prussia—as the party of the hereditary imperial crown at Frankfurt perceived—was able and destined to fulfill the hopes of the whole nation for unity and power; but at the cost of the nation's hope for freedom, if Prussia remained what she was. She was indeed a state with two souls; yet the Junker-militarist principle inherited from Frederick William I and Frederick the Great was stronger in her than the principle of the Prussian reform era, which had pointed toward the commonwealth. If Prussia should remain what she was, even within a Germany united under her leadership, then it was to be feared that the Junker-militarist principle would permeate the whole, in one way or another. Instead of Prussia merging into Germany, Germany would merge with Prussia—if not formally, at least in essence. This danger the sponsors of the hereditary imperial crown at Frankfurt clearly recognized—as I had occasion to point out more specifically forty years ago—and therefore they demanded that Prussia sacrifice her political unity and allow herself to be divided into provinces directly under the Empire. But this the strong and proud spirit of the Prussians rejected categorically, and thus the partisans of the hereditary imperial crown—as they cast their votes for Frederick William IV—had to comfort themselves with the uncertain hope that the force of events would some day take effect and integrate Prussia within Germany.

The force of events decided otherwise. The militaristic principle continued to dominate almost the whole of a century, until it overreached itself in hybrid form; and Prussia was not dissolved from within, but destroyed from without. The tormenting problem today is this: will *Finis Borussiae* also mean *Finis Germaniae?* To desire once more to become a great power in the traditional sense, would be to begin all over again the tragedy of the century gone by. This time let us learn at last from history! In order to avoid new catastrophes —not only for Germany, but for Europe, yes, even for the whole world—new forms of international solidarity must be discovered. And they are in fact already being sought today, with the purpose of safeguarding the morally justified and externally valid need of a nation for strength. Goethe's phrase (from which we quoted) has indeed expressed this demand: to exist as a nation, fully respected by other nations, to whom a like respect is due. The contribution which Germans themselves have to make to the accomplishment of this infinitely difficult task, is at the same time the permanent legacy of the revolution of 1848. The weaknesses resulting from time and destiny, from which this revolution suffered and through which it failed, we have brought honestly into the open. May we succeed, as men who have been tempered by misfortune, in reaching the goal of that pure and noble yearning: national unification within a democratic commonwealth.

MARXIST HISTORY

AND SACRED HISTORY

Jean Danielou, S.J.

[1951]

For Marxism * history is the process by which man transforms himself by transforming the economic conditions of his existence through work. The expression of this process on the social level is the class struggle through which the rising class, corresponding to the economic infrastructure of the future, tends to substitute itself for the exploiting class which is the expression of the outworn infrastructure. To exist is to engage in this conflict and thus participate in the movement of history. Now very often Christians, in order to oppose Marxism, remain on the Marxist plane. They are satisfied to set up one social doctrine against the order. We propose to show in this article that while it is true that there is a Christian social doctrine, and one superior to that of Marxism, the true superiority of Christianity does not lie in this. Its superiority consists, on the contrary, in the fact that it has not only a social doctrine but very different dimensions as well and is thereby capable of giving an integral interpretation of human existence while Marxism only touches on the surface.

We can show this by taking certain vantage points which will permit us to see, paradoxical though this may at first appear, that it is precisely in the most supernatural and the most essential realities, those most peculiar to Christianity, such as the sacraments, that we shall find the profoundest answer to the problems of the present world. All these realities will no longer then appear as *obiter dicta* in our lives, but, on the contrary, as at the very heart of life. They will no longer seem to be a sort of routine exercised so as to be in the good graces of God, but a real total commitment.

It is characteristic of the mentality of men today to conceive the world they live in as one history. We find it everywhere. This is be-

---

* This article was originally published in *Dieu Vivant*, No. 13, under the title, "Histoire marxiste et histoire sacramentaire." The English translation is by James A. Corbett, Professor of History in the University of Notre Dame.

cause humanity, with the increasingly great extension of its knowledge, is more aware of its growth and advancement. Science has also shown us that before our history there was a whole human prehistory. Thinking which does not consider this unfolding in time, this new dimension hardly suspected by the ancients, is ineffective. First developed in the philosophy of Hegel, this idea has assumed more and more importance in our world of today, and especially in Marxism.

But the expression given to this awareness by Marxism appears to be very narrow. The essential idea of Marxism is that the reality of history is dialectics by which man creates himself, that is, builds up humanity little by little through the transformation of the material conditions of his existence. Consequently, the most effective men and the true heroes of the modern world will be scientists and workers; poets, artists, philosophers, and saints are of secondary importance. Thus, for Marx two categories of men are absolutely essential; the scientist who invents and the worker who produces the conditions which ought to improve the life of man. This philosophy is obviously a dynamic one for those two classes of men because it makes them the essential agents of history. The stages in the history of humanity are the great ages of stone, of iron, of steam, of electricity, of radio, and of atomic energy. This is the only important reality. All the rest is superstructure. The levers which guide human progress are techniques, the only way to develop humanity is to develop technique.

What gives force to this position is that it is not only a matter of making man aware of things, but of helping him to commit himself by showing him the reason and value of this commitment. It is not simply a vulgar materialism, but a humanism, a conception of man. As such Marxism is the absolute contradiction of Christianity: man is the supreme value of man; he is his own creator. To recognize God is degrading and vilifying; to reject him is the essential condition of a realistic humanism.

Henceforth we cannot confront Marxism with a more or less pale Christian humanism. If Christian thought sometimes seems weak alongside Marxism, it is because Christianity does not rely enough on its essential principle, on the fact that it is a religion of God, a divine conception of history. For the Christian it is not only a human society which is built up in history but a divine destiny of man. We shall only overcome Marxism when we realize that it is Christianity which makes history real. Christianity is also fundamentally one history and not a conception of an ideal world more or less outside of human realities, and sort of added to them. As an interpretation of total history, Christianity gives history its definitive meaning.

The history of the world, in the Christian sense of the word, is essentially Sacred history, the history of the great works of God in time in which, with the irresistible power of His creative spirit, He builds the true humanity, the eternal City. Hence, if we wish to find the Christian meaning of history, we must know how to go beyond apparent and external history in order to penetrate to the real one which is built in the depths of man. Only the Holy Spirit can give us an understanding of this. We find the essentials of it in Scripture, an account of the great works of God and a description for us of the ways of God and of the manner in which He does things. It is, therefore, in the measure in which we live by Scripture as the true reality that we shall discover and understand the universe according to God.

Scripture begins with an historical affirmation of the creation then shows us the continual action of God through events: He chose Abraham as head of His people and made an alliance with him to lead his people in His ways. And here we come to an important idea: this Sacred history which God makes is opposed to that which man wishes to make (the one that Marx discovered). From the beginning there are two histories. There is the one men wish to make because of pride, the flesh, imperialism, and domination; it is the bloody history of wars, persecutions, and captivities. For many men this is the only history. But beside this human history there is the history which God makes. Through it God builds His kingdom and leads men according to His ways. The Old Testament gives a typical example of these two tendencies in the conflict between the prophets and the powerful who always persecute them. The prophets have the Christian sense of history and, through the spirit which enlightens them, they act as though introduced by God to the veritable meaning of the destiny of humanity.

In the middle of history, the Son of God Himself, by His Incarnation, came on earth to assume humanity, to unite Himself to it, to purify it with His blood and to lead it forever into the kingdom of the Father after having liberated it from death and sin. What man seeks is precisely a liberation; he wants to shake off the captivity which weighs heavily upon him. This captivity, however, is not economic but spiritual. Original sin is not capitalism, the essential evil for Marxism. Even a humanity freed of all social miseries would still remain in an integral misery: that of sin. When Marx said that once man was freed from his economic bondage he would be happy, Marx was wrong for there remains spiritual misery. Thus, in Soviet Russia, people may be liberated on the economic level, but they exist—and strikingly so—in a profound spiritual despair.

The Marxist effort is, therefore, superficial and does not descend into the veritable depths of human misery. Of course, we should fight against social misery; but such misery is simply the repercussion of another much more profound and intimate one: sin, death, Satan.

The one who liberates from this real captivity is Jesus Christ and He alone. The meaning of history as the Marxists say—and we agree with them here—is to free man, but we say that only Jesus Christ and those who live in Him can do it. These are the missionaries and contemplatives, the real saviors of humanity. As long as we fail to realize that social reaction against Marxism is inadequate, as long as we do not enter into the reality of Christianity and act accordingly, we shall retain an inferiority complex. Although we have our duties on the social and economic plane, they are not all. There is something more important and deeper: the continuation of the work of Jesus Christ in the salvation of humanity.

To be sure, Marxism does not deny absolutely that Christianity is a great and beautiful thing, that it brought a veritable revelation into the world. But Marxism says that what Christianity accomplished in the past is over and done with. Now it is in a state of crisis and a new humanity is beginning. We are beyond Christianity on the road to a religion of the new times. The Christian of today answers this with a profession of faith: one does not surpass Jesus Christ for in Him the end of things is reached. He alone is the last, the eternal youth of the world. He is always the new beyond Whom there is absolutely nothing, in Whom the end of all things is attained. With Him the essential event of humanity has occurred; consequently we should not expect from *progress,* whatever it may be, anything which has the importance we possess in Jesus Christ. We have infinitely more in Him than any technique or any revolution can bring.

For the Marxist, history has not yet set its course: he looks toward the future. For the Christian, history is substantially fixed and the essential element is at the center, not at the end. There is thus no total risk. The acceptance of salvation given by Christ—which is not our work—is an aspect, in the eschatological order, of this recognition of our basic dependence, a dependence constituting the fundamental religious attitude. Does this mean that there is nothing more to be done? Yes, *if,* after the event of the Redemption, no fundamental task remained to be accomplished. But the Redemption is a reality of incomparable dynamism; for what is acquired by right for all humanity remains indeed to be transmitted to all men. There is the mystery of missions and the grandeur of the missionary ideal. Sacred history is the history of the present in which we live, of which we are the instruments as the prophets once were who worked to extend to all peoples what Jesus Christ brought to us.

In *Christ and Time* Cullman observes that in war there comes a day when the decisive battle is won, and afterwards the day of the triumphal march under the arch of triumph. Between these two events there is a certain lapse of time. The Resurrection is the Stalingrad of the Redemption, the day when the battle is won. But Christ wished to permit us to participate in the victory—and some battles remain to be fought. Total victory, however, does not depend on them; it has already been won. Christian hope is the certitude of this victory with the expectation of our coming into possession of peace. Present history is that of combats through which God deigns to associate us with His work until Christ has taken on His full stature in breadth and depth in all hearts. This is what fills present history, much more than the conflicts or the alliances between nations and classes. If we act often like worldly men and allow ourselves to be taken in by apparent history it is because we do not see things deeply enough.

The sacraments are the historical actions, corresponding to the particular characteristics of the time which extends from the Ascension to the Last Judgment, that is to say, of the time in which we live. What characterizes this time is the fact that it comes after the essential event of Sacred history by which the world has already reached its end and hence—as certain Protestants clearly saw—it can add nothing to time. Jesus Christ is not surpassed. On the other hand, the glory of Jesus Christ has not yet been visibly manifested. This time, therefore, is characterized, secondly, by this non-manifestation, by this "hidden" aspect. And finally time's proper content is the extension to all humanity of the reality acquired by Christ.

Now these are precisely the characteristics which the actions of sacramental structure present. On the one hand, they are never anything but "imitations," "representations" of the Death and Resurrection of Christ: "We who have all been baptized in Christ Jesus have been baptized in death." The sacraments are simply a reproduction of the sacerdotal action of Christ by which all things have attained their end. Still, the sacraments have a hidden aspect. Only the sign is apparent; its reality remains invisible. For indeed the reality of the Resurrection is not yet visibly manifest. This is admirably explained by St. Paul (Col. III, 1–4): "Risen, then, with Christ, you must lift your thoughts above, where Christ now sits at the right hand of God. You must be heavenly-minded, not earthly minded; you have undergone death, and your life is hidden away now with Christ in God. Christ is your life, and when He is made manifest, you too will be made manifest in glory with Him."

Thus, the sacraments constitute the events of a time which is the tension between the Resurrection and the Parousia. They are a "memorial" of the Resurrection and the permanent "prophecy" of its manifestation. The Eucharist, as a "document" of the "New Alliance," prevents us from forgetting the essential event by which this alliance was definitely concluded: the union in the person of Jesus of the divine and human nature and the introduction of human nature purified by the Blood of the Cross into the sphere of the Trinitary life. And the Eucharist, as an eschatological meal, is the prefiguration of the heavenly banquet, of the communication by Christ of the fulness of His goods to His own in the House of His Father. Thus during the delay of the Parousia, the Eucharist prevents humanity, in this foretaste of celestial food, from tiring of waiting and from returning to terrestrial food.

But I have not dwelt so far on the last characteristic of our time. Between the Ascension and the Parousia its special function is missionary activity, begun at Pentecost and continuing until the return of Christ, since, the Gospel tells us, the condition of this return is the evangelization of the whole universe. Now the sacraments are the essential instruments of this mission which is the reality of present history under the appearances of profane history. The mission of the Apostles is, properly speaking, to baptize: "Go, teach all nations, baptizing them in the name of the Father, and of the Son and of the Holy Spirit." Indeed it is Baptism which unites one to the messianic community, to the Church, and which makes those who have received it participants in messianic gifts. Confirmation, participation in the anointing of Christ by the Spirit at the beginning of His public life furnishes the Christian adult, according to Cyril of Jerusalem, in a stable way, with prophetic charism which makes of him, by preaching and by witnessing, an active agent of the mission. And the Eucharist is the sacrament of unity which gathers about the Christ of glory, present in the community, all nations in order to offer them through His hands to the Father.

It is these sacramental actions which are the great events of the present world—much greater than great works of thought or of science, much greater than great victories or revolutions, which fill the pages of apparent history, but do not penetrate to the depths of real history. These are grandeurs of the order of intelligence or of the order of bodies. But the sacraments are the grandeurs of the order of charity. "Jesus Christ," Pascal said, "did not make any great inventions but he was holy, holy to men and redoubtable to the devil." This is what we have not sufficiently realized. And this is why we allow ourselves to be so impressed by the grandeur of the flesh or of the intelligence while forgetting that we are the trustees of the designs of Trinitary charity. By the importance we give them we make idols of human glories, of science, of money, of history, of the state; whereas the first commandment is: "Thou shalt love the Lord Thy God with thy whole heart, and with thy whole soul, and with thy whole mind, and with thy whole strength."

Now the works of the power of God among us are the sacraments. We said above that there was a greater captivity than economic captivity and capitalistic enslavement, that the greater captivity was spiritual captivity, enslavement not to the powers of money, but to the Powers of Darkness. Now Baptism alone delivers us from this captivity. One alone indeed liberates us from spiritual captivity, Jesus Christ, Who by His death descended into the kingdom of death, into the profoundest abyss of misery, and Who, by His resurrection, crashed forever the doors of death and came out the Conqueror of Hell, opening up to all humanity the road of spiritual liberation. Baptism, St. Paul tells us, makes us die with Jesus Christ in order to arise with Him and ascend with Him to the right of the Father. Given in the first Christian century during the Paschal night, Baptism appears clearly here as the continuation of those great works of liberation accomplished by God in delivering His people from the yoke of Egypt in the course of the first Easter and in the deliverance of His Son from the yoke of Hell during the second Easter. And the third Easter is thus not a simple liturgical commemoration of the two others, but the effective continuation of the same reality.

The mystery of liberation, Baptism is also the mystery of "creation." It is, according to St. Paul, *palingenesis,* a second Genesis. At the beginning of the world, the Spirit of God, hovering like a dove over the primitive waters, raised up in them the biological life of the first creation. It is this same Spirit which, the Gospel tells us, covered Mary with His shadow, *obumbrabit tibi,* to raise up in her by His all powerful virtue and second creation, that of the universe of grace, of the world of divinized humanity of which Christ is the Orient, the eternally rising sun. Now Baptism is this recreation of each man. Plunged into the waters vivified by the energies of the Spirit, he comes out regenerated, reborn; recreated in Christ and, henceforth, belonging to the second creation. Marxism sees in man the demiurge of humanity which it creates perpetually by transforming through work his economic infrastructures. But it can no more liberate man from his more profound captivity than it can raise up a really new humanity, for Jesus Christ alone is the really New Man, the *homo novissimus.*

What is true of baptism is likewise true of all the sacraments and of the economy of all Christianity which is sacramental. I shall note only one other example: the Mass. This is essentially the presence, subsisting under the sacramental mode, of the sacerdotal action of Christ. Now this sacerdotal action of Christ by which He glorifies perfectly the Father is the end of history, the fulfillment of creation, the success of the divine plan. The purpose of creation is, indeed, the glory of God, that is, the recognition of His sovereign excellence by means of spiritual liberties. It is to recognize the sovereignty of God that the sacrifice of all nations and of all religions has been made down through the centuries. But these were only figures, for in reality, the men who offered them belonged to the city of sin which, according to St. Augustine, is "built on love of oneself to the contempt of God." The Passion of Christ, on the contrary, manifests "the love of God to the contempt of oneself." He showed that the will of the Father is so lovable that everything is worth sacrificing to it, "becoming obedient until death and until the death of the Cross." The Father is thereby glorified for ever. Now the Mass is that sacerdotal action of Christ made present by the sacrament so as to hold human liberty in the movement which bears it to the Father and so to extend the glory of God. Again and again we discern the characteristic feature of sacramental times: it is situated within the end already gained which is the glory of God. God is glorified in Christ and nothing, surely no vicissitude of history, can alter this glorification. But this end must extend to all men and through Christ "all glory" must ascend to the Father.

The Mass is, therefore, the presence already of the consummation of things. And he who unites himself to the sacerdotal action of Christ in the Mass fulfills the absolute action, that in which the totality of his being expresses itself and in which the reason of his existence is made clear. Thus the Mass is the end to which Baptism is ordered; it is not the beginning but the fulfillment of the mission. The ultimate aim of all this is to constitute the total community offering the unique Mass by which all spiritual liberties, having been turned toward God, would recognize His sovereign excellence and unite with the Trisagion. But this presence remains a presence veiled in the sacraments, *velatum*. This sacramental status is that of expectation. It corresponds to the delay of the Parousia. This delay causes anguish for some. Daniel Halévy recently said that it was a great difficulty for him: "Christ said he would return—and yet he has not returned. And so nations have tired of waiting and have turned to other guides." But Christ also said that before His return His gospel had to be preached to the ends of the earth. The delay of the Parousia is that which the evangelization of the whole world requires. That is why the patience asked of individuals and peoples who were the first baptized is essentially based on charity. They are waiting for everyone to be there before entering. The Mass is the form of fulfillment of the human vocation appropriate to the time of expectation which is, as Pascal tells us, the order of charity.

Marxist history, Sacramental history—we have contrasted them as representing two levels of reality and we have tried to show that Sacramental history alone embraces the totality of human existence and reaches the extremities of it. Does this mean that there is no communication between them? Is this movement of history, this dialectic of infrastructures and suprastructures which Marxism described for us, completely foreign to the movement of Sacred history? The Marxist interpretation certainly is foreign in so far as it pretends to be a total explanation. But it is not foreign in so far as the elements of reality it uses constitute a certain human datum. In other words, if we consider that the dialectic of economic history ought to bring a total response to the human problem, we say and hope to have shown that it is an illusion. There is no salvation outside of Christ and His sacramental work. Man is radically incapable of saving himself. No invention, no revolution can solve the essential drama of his destiny.

But if profane history does not itself save, it is part of what is destined to be saved. Christ did not come to substitute another humanity for the one He has created. He came to liberate this humanity from its spiritual servitude. Hence, vain as is the pretension of human history to achieve the salvation of man, absurd as it is to think that in participating in scientific research or political action we help the salvation of the world and are agents of it, it is, nevertheless, legitimate to think that we are cooperating to build what will be saved. It is quite clear that the man who will be transfigured in glory will be the one that we make here below. It is as true to say that we constitute what will be transfigured as it is false to think that we work for its transfiguration. What is true on the individual plane is also true on the total plane. Profane history, the history of civilization and culture, comes into the realm of Sacred history in so far as through Sacred history, profane history constitutes the humanity which the sacraments heal of spiritual miseries and bear into the kingdom of the Son.

Thus profane history is assumed into Sacred history and the Church in this sense participates in its assumption. But profane history always remains of secondary importance. This is what Mounier does not recognize when he seems to make the "sacralization" of the new figures of the world the constitutive element of the Church, and when he charges those who oppose the liturgical cosmos to the scientific cosmos with "confusing outmoded form of representation with the eternal essence of the religious act." No one is less attached than ourselves to outmoded structures. That is why we denounce the illusion which "sacralizes" unduly momentary and dead structures in order to see in them the very finality of the history of our time. This is also the point on which we disagree with Father Montuclard when he writes: "We realize that the progress of the Church cannot be in the hands of purely spiritual men." If we understand by the progress of the Church its adaptation to changes of social structures it is quite clear that this is not properly the work of saints. But this conception of the progress of the Church remains on the surface of history, in the very zone in which Marxism moves and where the transformation of the economic infrastructures constitutes a progress in which the Church merely becomes incarnate. But the real story of the Church is not to be found there. The real progress of the Church is in the liberation of captive souls by Baptism and in the extension of the glory of God by the Eucharist. The real protagonists of this history are the saints.

III

MAN'S PLIGHT

IN

MODERN CIVILIZATION

WORLD POLITICS IN THE

MID-TWENTIETH CENTURY

Hans J. Morgenthau

[1948]

FROM the end of the religious wars to the First World War, the modern state system was kept together by the intellectual and moral tradition of the Western world. That tradition imposed moral and legal limitations on the struggle for power on the international scene and provided in the balance of power an instrumentality which, in a certain measure, maintained order in the international community and secured the independence of its individual members. What is left of this heritage today? What kind of consensus unites the nations of the world in the period following the Second World War?

The answer can only be that the limitations upon the struggle for power on the international scene are weaker today than they have been at any time in the history of the modern state system. The one international society of the seventeenth and eighteenth centuries has been replaced by a number of national societies which provide for their members the highest principle of social integration. In consequence, the international morality which in past centuries kept the aspirations for power of the individual states within certain bounds has, except for certain fragmentary restraints, given way to the ethics of individual nations which not only does not recognize any moral obligation above and apart from them, but even claims universal recognition from all the world. World public opinion is but an ideological shadow without even that substance of common valuations and reactions in which in other times at least the international aristocracy shared. The main bulk of the rules of international law owes its existence to the sovereignty of the individual nations. Far from restraining the aspirations for power of individual nations, they see to it that the power position of individual nations is not adversely affected by whatever legal obligations they take upon themselves in their relations with other nations. What national morality is in the field of ethics, what national public opinion is in the domain of the mores, sovereignty is for international law, the manifestation of the nation as the recipient of the individual's ultimate earthly loyalties, as the mightiest social force, as the supreme authority giving and enforcing laws for the individual citizen.

I THE NEW MORAL FORCE OF NATIONALISTIC UNIVERSALISM

The supra-national forces which bind individuals together across national boundaries are infinitely weaker today than the forces which unite peoples within a particular national boundary and separate them from the rest of humanity. This weakening of the supra-national forces, which must be strong in order to impose effective restraints upon the international policies of nations, is but the negative by-product of the great positive force which shapes the political face of our age: nationalism. Nationalism, identified as it is with the international policies of individual nations, cannot restrain these policies; it is indeed in need of restraint. Not only has it fatally weakened, if not destroyed, the restraints which have come down to us from previous ages, it has also supplied the aspirations for power of individual nations with a good conscience and a pseudo-religious fervor and has thus instilled them with a thirst and strength for universal dominion of which the nationalism of the nineteenth century knew nothing.

The nationalism of the mid-twentieth century is essentially different from what traditionally goes by that name and what culminated in the national movements and the national state of the nineteenth century. The latter pursued the goal of freeing the nation from alien domination and of giving it a state of its own, and this goal was considered to be a rightful one not for one, but for all nations. The national aspirations were satisfied, once a nation had united its members in one state, and there was room for as many nationalisms as there were nations which wanted to establish or preserve a state of their own. The international conflicts in which the nationalism of the nineteenth century was involved were, therefore, essentially of two kinds: the conflicts between a nationality and an alien master, such as the ones between the Balkan nations and Turkey, the Slav nations of the Danube basin and the Austro-Hungarian monarchy, the Poles and Russia, and the conflicts between different nationalities over the delimitation of their respective spheres of dominion, such as the ones between the Germans, on the one hand, and the Poles and the French, on the other. What led to conflict was either differing interpretation of the national principle or else the refusal to accept it at all. It was hoped as late as three decades ago that, once the aspirations of all nations for national states within which to dwell were fulfilled, a society of satisfied nations would find in the legal and moral principles of national self-determination the means for its own preservation.

To give the same name of nationalism to what inspired the oppressed and competing nationalities of the nineteenth century and what drives the super-powers of the mid-twentieth century into deadly combat, is to obscure the fundamental change which separates our age from the preceding one. The nationalism of today, which is truly a nationalistic universalism, has only one thing in common with the nationalism of the nineteenth century, that is, the nation as the ultimate point of reference for political loyalties and actions. Here, however, the similarity ends. For the nationalism of the nineteenth century the nation is the ultimate goal of political action, the end-point of the political development beyond which there are other nationalisms with similar goals and similar justifications. For the nationalistic universalism of the mid-twentieth century the nation is but the starting-point of a universal mission whose ultimate goal reaches to the confines of the political world. While nationalism wants one nation in one state and nothing else, the nationalistic universalism of our age claims for one nation and one state the right to impose its own valuations and standards of action upon all the other nations. These rival claims to universal dominion on the part of different nations have dealt the final, fatal blow to that social system of international intercourse within which for almost three centuries nations were living together in constant rivalry, yet under the common roof of shared values and universal standards of action. The collapse of that roof has destroyed the common habitat of the nations of the world, and the most powerful of them assert the right to build it anew in their own image. Beneath the ruins of that roof lies buried the mechanism which kept the walls of that house of nations standing: the balance of power.

II THE NEW BALANCE OF POWER

With the destruction of that intellectual and moral consensus which for almost three centuries confined the struggle for power on the international scene within its framework, the balance of power has lost the vital energy which transformed it from a metaphor into a living principle of international politics. Concomitant with the destruction of that vital energy, the system of the balance of power has undergone three structural changes which considerably impair its operations.

1 THE INFLEXIBILITY OF THE NEW BALANCE OF POWER

The most obvious of these changes is to be found in the drastic numerical reduction of the players in the game. At the end of the

Thirty Years War, for instance, the German Empire was composed of 900 sovereign states which the Treaty of Westphalia in 1648 reduced to 355. The Napoleonic interventions, of which the most notable one is the dictated reforms of the Reichstag of Ratisbon of 1803, eliminated more than 200 of the sovereign German states, and when the Germanic Confederation was founded in 1815, only 36 sovereign states were left to join it. The unification of Italy in 1859 eliminated seven, the unification of Germany in 1871, 24 sovereign states. In 1815, at the end of the Napoleonic Wars, eight nations, that is, Austria, France, Great Britain, Portugal, Russia, Prussia, Spain, and Sweden, had the diplomatic rank of great powers. With Portugal, Spain, and Sweden receiving such consideration only out of traditional courtesy and soon losing that undeserved status altogether, the number of actually great powers was really reduced to five. In the sixties, Italy and the United States joined their rank, followed towards the end of the century by Japan. At the outbreak of the First World War, there were then again eight great powers, of which for the first time two were located totally outside Europe: Austria, France, Germany, Great Britain, Italy, Japan, Russia, and the United States. The end of the First World War found Austria definitely, Germany and Russia temporarily, removed from that list. Two decades later one could count seven great powers, Germany and the Soviet Union having again become first-rate powers and the others having retained their status. The end of the Second World War saw this number reduced to three, namely, Great Britain, the Soviet Union, and the United States, while China and France, in view of their past or their potentialities, are treated in negotiations and organizations as though they were great powers. In the aftermath of the Second World War British power has declined to such an extent as to be distinctly inferior to the power of the United States and of the Soviet Union, which are then the only two great powers left at present.

This reduction in the number of states which are able to play a major role in international politics has an important effect upon the operation of the balance of power. This effect gains added importance from the reduction in the absolute number of states through the consolidations of 1648 and 1803 and the national unifications of the nineteenth century, a reduction which was only temporarily offset in 1919 by the creation of new states in eastern and central Europe; for these states have in the meantime disappeared either as states, for example, the Baltic states, or, in any case, as independent factors on the international scene. This development has deprived the balance of power of much of its flexibility and uncertainty and, in consequence, of its restraining effect upon the nations actively engaged in the struggle for power on the international scene.

In former times the balance of power operated in the main by way of coalitions among a number of nations, the principal of which, while differing in power, were still of the same order of magnitude. In the eighteenth century, for instance, Austria, France, Great Britain, Prussia, Russia, and Sweden belonged in the same class, insofar as their relative power was concerned. Fluctuations in their power would affect their respective position in the hierarchy of power, but did not affect their position as great powers. Similarly, in the period from 1870 to 1914, the game of power politics was played by eight players of the first rank of which six, the European ones, were always playing. Under such circumstances no player could go very far in his aspirations for power without being sure of the support of at least one or the other of his co-players, and of that support nobody could generally be too sure. There was virtually no nation in the eighteenth and nineteenth centuries which was not compelled to retreat from an advanced position and retrace its steps because it did not receive the diplomatic or military support from other nations upon which it had counted. This was especially true of Russia in the nineteenth century. On the other hand, if Germany, in violation of the rule of the game, had not in 1914 given Austria a free hand in her dealings with Serbia, there is little doubt that Austria would not have dared to go as far as she did, and that the First World War might have been avoided.

The greater the number of active players, the greater is the number of possible combinations. Thus uncertainty increases as to the combinations which will actually oppose each other and as to the role which the individual players will actually perform in them. Both William II in 1914 and Hitler in 1939 refused to believe that Great Britain, and ultimately the United States, too, would join the rank of their enemies, and both discounted the effect of American intervention. It is obvious that these miscalculations as to who would fight against whom meant for Germany the difference between victory and defeat. Whenever coalitions of nations comparable in power confront each other, calculations of this kind will of necessity be close, since the defection of one prospective member or the addition of an unexpected one cannot fail to affect the balance of power considerably, if not decisively. Thus in the eighteenth century when princes used to change their alignments with the greatest of ease, such calculations were frequently almost indistinguishable from wild guesses. In consequence, the extreme flexibility of the balance of power resulting from the utter impermanence of alliances made it imperative for all players to be cautious in their moves on the chessboard of international politics and, since risks were hard to calculate, to take as few risks as possible. In the First World War it was still of very great importance, for the ultimate outcome of the conflict, whether Italy would remain neutral or enter the war on the side of the Allies. It was in recognition of that importance that both sides made great efforts, by competing in promises of territorial aggrandizement, to influence Italy's decision; the same situation then prevailed, to a lesser degree, even with respect to so relatively weak a power as Greece.

This aspect of the balance of power has undergone a radical transformation in recent years. In the Second World War the decision of countries, such as Italy, Spain, or Turkey, or even of France, to join or not to join one or the other side were mere episodes, welcomed or feared, to be sure, by the belligerents, but in no way even remotely capable of transforming victory into defeat, or vice versa. The disparity in the power of nations of the first rank, such as the United States, the Soviet Union, Great Britain, Japan, and Germany, on the one hand, and all the remaining nations, on the other, was then already so great that the defection of one, or the addition of another, ally could no longer overturn the balance of power and thus materially affect the ultimate outcome of the struggle. Under the influence of such changes in alignments one scale might rise somewhat and the other sink still more under a heavier weight, yet these changes could not reverse the relation of the scales which were determined by the preponderant weights of the first-rate powers. It was only the position of countries, such as the United States, the Soviet Union, and Great Britain on the one hand, Germany and Japan, on the other, that really mattered. This situation, first noticeable in the Second World War, is now accentuated in the polarity between the United States and the Soviet Union and has become a paramount feature of international politics. The power of the United States and of the Soviet Union in comparison with the power of their actual or prospective allies has become so overwhelming that they, through their own preponderant weight, determine the balance of power between them, which cannot be decisively affected by changes in the alignments of their allies, at least for the forseeable future.

As a result, the flexibility of the balance of power and, with it, its restraining influence upon the power aspirations of the main protagonists on the international scene have disappeared. Two great powers, each incomparably stronger than any other power or possible combination of other powers, oppose each other. Neither of them need fear anything unexpected from actual or prospective allies. The disparity of power between the former and the latter, as we have seen, is such that changes in the allegiance of one or the other of the minor powers by themselves can have no decisive influence upon the balance of power. As a further result of that disparity of power most, if not all, of the nations ranking below the two big ones have lost that freedom of movement which in former times enabled them to play an important and often decisive role in the balance of power. What was formerly true only of a relatively small number of nations, like certain Latin-American countries in their relations with the United States or Portugal in her relations to Great Britain, is true now of most, if not all, of them: they are in the orbit of one or the other of the two giants who can hold them there even against their will by making use of their own political, military, and economic preponderance.

This is the exact opposite of the era of ever-shifting alliances and new combinations demanding vigilance and caution. Of that era the eighteenth century is the classic example. Its characteristics prevailed in the nineteenth and the first three decades of the twentieth century, and even during the Second World War played an important role at least with regard to the anticipated actions of the major belligerents. Today neither the United States nor the Soviet Union needs to be wary lest the defection of one ally or the addition of another upset the balance of power. Neither is any longer constrained to accommodate its policies to the wishes of doubtful allies and exacting neutrals. No such fears and considerations need restrain ambitions and actions. Each is, in a unique way, master of its own policy and of its own fate. The line between the two camps is clearly drawn, and the weight of those few still straddling the fence is so small as to be virtually negligible or is, as in the case of India, a matter of future development rather than of the present. There are no longer neutrals which, as "honest brokers," can mitigate international conflicts and contribute to their peaceful settlement or else, by maneuvering between the two camps and threatening to join the one or the other as occasion might require, can erect effective barriers to limitless aspirations for power.

2 THE DISAPPEARANCE OF THE BALANCER

The second change in the structure of the balance of power, which we are witnessing today, is the inevitable result of the change just discussed, namely, the disappearance of the balancer, the "holder" of the balance. It was both her naval supremacy and her virtual immunity from foreign attack which for more than three centuries enabled Great Britain to perform this function for the balance of power. Today Great Britain is no longer capable of performing it; for, on the one hand, the United States has far surpassed her in naval strength and, on the other, the modern technology of war has deprived navies of the uncontested mastery of the seas, has put an end to the invulnerability of the British Isles, and has transformed from an advantage into a liability the concentration of a population and industries on a relatively small piece of territory in close proximity to a continent.

In the great contest between France and the Hapsburgs around which the modern state system revolved, at least till the "diplomatic revolution" of 1756 when France allied herself with the Hapsburgs against Prussia, Great Britain was able to play the controlling and restraining role of the balancer because she was strong enough in comparison with the two contenders and their allies to make likely the victory of the side which she joined. This was again true in the Napoleonic Wars and throughout the nineteenth and the beginning of the twentieth century. Today her friendship is no longer of decisive importance and, hence, her role as the "holder" of the balance has come to an end, leaving the modern state system without the benefits of restraint and pacification which she bestowed upon it in former times. While even as late as the Second World War the neutrality of Great Britain or her alignment with Germany and Japan instead of with the United Nations might easily have meant for the latter the difference between victory and defeat, it may well be that, in view of the probable trends in the technology of warfare and the distribution of power between the United States and the Soviet Union, the attitude of Great Britain in an armed conflict between these two powers would not decisively affect the ultimate outcome. In the metaphorical language of the balance of power one might say, rather crudely but not without truth, that, while in the Russian scale that is a weight of seventy, the weight of the American scale amounts to a hundred of which seventy is on account of the United States' own strength, ten on account of Great Britain, and the remainder on account of the other actual or prospective allies. Thus even if the British weight were removed from the American scale and placed in the Russian, the heavier weight would still be in the American scale.

It follows from what has been said that the decline of the relative power of Great Britain and her resultant inability to keep her key position in the balance of power is not an isolated occurrence solely attributable to Great Britain, but the consequence of a structural change which affects the functioning of the balance of power in all its manifestations. It is, therefore, impossible that the privileged and dominating place which Great Britain has held for so long could be inherited by another nation. It is not so much that the power of the traditional holder of the place has declined, incapacitating her for her traditional role, as that the place itself no longer exists. Alongside giants strong enough to determine with their own weight alone the position of the scales, there can be no chance for a third power to exert a decisive influence upon that determination. It is, therefore, futile at the present moment to hope for another nation or group of nations to take the place vacated by Great Britain. France has entertained such hopes for a time through the eloquent voice of General DeGaulle. In a number of speeches he has advocated that either France alone or a United Europe under French leadership should perform the pacifying and restraining task of the "holder" of the balance between the colossus of the east and the colossus of the west. He made this point with particular emphasis in his speech at Bar-le-Duc of July 28, 1946, which he started with a brilliant analysis of the transformation of the balance of power by saying:

> It is certain indeed that, with respect to what it was before this thirty-year war the face of the world has altered in every way. A third of a century ago we were living in a universe where six or eight great nations, apparently equal in strength, each by differing and subtle accords associating others with it, managed to establish a balance everywhere in which the less powerful found themselves relatively guaranteed and where international law was recognized, since a violator would have faced a coalition of moral or material interests, and where, in the last analysis, strategy conceived and prepared with a view to future conflicts involved only rapid and limited destruction.
>
> But a cyclone has passed. An inventory can be made. When we take into account the collapse of Germany and Japan and the weakening of Europe, Soviet Russia and the United States are now alone in holding the first rank. It seems as if the destiny of the world, which in modern times has in turn smiled on the Holy Roman Empire, Spain, France, Britain and the German Reich, conferring on each in turn a kind of pre-eminence, has now decided to divide its favor in two. From this decision arises a factor of division that has been substituted for the balance of yore.

After referring to the anxieties caused by the expansionist tendencies of the United States and the Soviet Union, DeGaulle raised the question of restoring a stable balance of power.

> Who then can re-establish the equilibrium, if not the old world, between the two new ones? Old Europe, which, during so many centuries was the guide of the universe, is in a position to constitute in the heart of a world that tends to divide itself into two, the necessary element of compensation and understanding.
>
> The nations of the ancient west have for their vital arteries the North Sea, the Mediterranean, the Rhine; they are geographically situated between the two new masses. Resolved to conserve an independence that would be gravely exposed in the event of a conflagration, they are physically and morally drawn together by the massive effort of the Russians as well as by the liberal advance of the Americans. Of global strength because of their own resources and those of the vast territories that are linked to them by destiny, spreading afar their influences and their activities, what will be their weight if they manage to combine their policies in spite of the difficulties among them from age to age!

But the weakness of France in comparison with the United States and the Soviet Union incapacitates her even more than Great Britain.

Above all, General DeGaulle's argument leaves out of account the decisive fact that Great Britain was capable of making her beneficial contributions to peace and stability only because she was geographically remote from the centers of friction and conflict, because she had no vital interests in the stakes of these conflicts as such, and because she had the opportunity of satisfying her aspirations for power in areas beyond the seas which generally were beyond the reach of the main contenders for power.

It was that threefold aloofness, together with her resources of power, which enabled Great Britain to play her role as "holder" of the balance. In none of these three respects is France or a United Europe aloof from the centers of conflict; they are, quite to the contrary, deeply implicated in them in all three respects. For they are at once the battlefield and the prize of victory in an armed conflict between the United States and the Soviet Union; they are permanently and vitally interested in the victory of one or the other side; and they are unable to seek satisfaction for their aspirations for power anywhere but on the European continent itself. It is for these reasons that neither France nor Europe as a whole could enjoy that freedom of maneuver which the "holder" of the balance must have in order to fulfill his function.

3 THE DISAPPEARANCE OF THE COLONIAL FRONTIER

The balance of power owed the moderating and restraining influence which it exerted in its classical period not only to the moral climate within which it operated and to its own mechanics, but also in good measure to the circumstance that the nations participating in it rarely needed to put all their national energies into the political and military struggles in which they were engaged with each other. Since the possession of territory was considered the symbol of substance of national power, nations in that period had an opportunity, much less risky, of gaining power through the acquisition of land than in trying to take it away from their powerful neighbors. The wide expanses of three continents offered that opportunity: Africa, the Americas, and the part of Asia bordering on the Eastern oceans.

Throughout the history of the balance of power Great Britain found in this opportunity the main source of her power and of her detachment from the issues which involved the other nations in continuous conflict. Spain dissipated her strength in exploiting that opportunity and thus removed herself from the struggle for power as a force to be reckoned with. What for Great Britain and Spain was a constant and major concern attracted the energies of the other nations to a lesser degree or only sporadically. The policies of France in the eighteenth century present instructive examples of the reciprocal effect of colonial expansion and imperialistic attacks upon the existing balance of power; the more intense the latter were, the less attention was paid to the former, and vice versa. The United States and Russia were for long stages of their history totally absorbed by the task of pushing their frontiers forward into the politically empty spaces of their continents and during those periods took no active part in the balance of power. The Austrian monarchy was in the main concerned, especially during the nineteenth century, with maintaining her control over the non-German nationalities of Central and Southeastern Europe which made up the bulk of her empire. Thus she was incapable of more than limited excursions into power politics. Furthermore, until deep into the eighteenth century, the threat of Turkish aggression limited her freedom of movement on the chessboard of international politics. Prussia, finally, as the late-comer to the circle of the great powers, had to be satisfied with defending and securing her position as a great power and was too weak internally and in too unfavorable a geographical position to think of a program of unlimited expansion. Even after Bismarck had made Prussian power predominant in Germany and German power predominant in Europe, his policy was aimed at preserving, not at expanding that power.

In the period between 1870 and 1914 the stability of the status quo in Europe is the direct result, on the one hand, of the risks implicit in even the smallest move at the frontiers of the great powers themselves and, on the other, of the opportunity of changing the status quo in outlying regions without incurring the danger of a general conflagration. Professor Toynbee observed:

> At the center [of the group of states forming the balance of power], every move that any one state makes with a view to its own aggrandizement is jealously watched and adroitly countered by all its neighbors, and the sovereignty over a few square feet of territory and a few hundred "souls" becomes a subject for the bitterest and stubbornest contention. . . . In the easy circumstances of the periphery, quite a mediocre political talent is often able to work wonders. . . . The domain of the United States can be expanded unobtrusively right across North America from Atlantic to Pacific, the domain of Russia right across Asia from Baltic to Pacific, in an age when the best statesmanship of France or Germany cannot avail to obtain unchallenged possession of an Alsace or a Posen.

With the unification of Germany in 1870 the consolidation of the great nation states was consummated. Territorial gains in Europe could henceforth be made only at the expense of the great powers or their allies. Thus it was not accidental that for more than four decades the great issues of world politics were connected with African names, such as Egypt, Tunis, Morocco, the Congo, South Africa, and with the decrepit Asiatic empires of China and Persia. Local wars arose from these issues, such as the Boer War in 1899 between Great Britain and the Boer Republics, the Russo-Japanese War of 1904, and the Russo-Turkish and Italo-Turkish Wars of 1877 and 1911–12 respectively. But in all these wars one of the great powers fought against what might be called a "peripheric" power, which was either the designated object of the former's expansion or, as in the exceptional case of Japan, an outside competitor. In no case, however, was it necessary for a great power to take up arms against another great power in order to expand into the politically empty spaces of Africa and Asia.

The policy of compensations could here operate with a maximum of success, for there was much political no-man's land from which one could compensate one's self and allow others to do the same. There was always a possibility of compromise, without compromising one's vital interests, of retreat while saving one's face, of side-stepping, and of postponement. The period from 1870 to 1914, then, was a period of diplomatic bargains and horse-trading for other people's lands, of postponed conflicts and side-stepped issues.

The most persistent and the most explosive of the great issues of that period (from which the conflagration of the First World War arose): how to distribute the inheritance of the European part of the Turkish Empire, also called the Eastern or the Balkan Question, is significant in this respect. Located at the periphery of the circle of the great powers, the issue was closer to it geographically and weighed more directly upon the distribution of political and military power within it than any other of the great issues of that epoch. Where as the Balkan Question was more likely than any other issue of that period to lead to open conflict among the great powers—especially since the vital interests of one of them, Austria, were directly affected by the national aspirations of Serbia—it is, however, doubtful whether this outcome was inevitable. One might even plausibly maintain that if the other great powers, especially Germany, had dealt with the Balkan Question in 1914, as they had done successfully at the Congress of Berlin in 1878, that is, in recognition of its peripheral character, the First World War might well have been avoided.

When Bismarck declared in 1876 that, as far as the interests of Germany were concerned, the Balkans were not worth "the good bones of one single Pomeranian musketeer," he affirmed emphatically the peripheral character of the Balkan Question in view of the political and military interests of Germany. When the German government in July, 1914, promised to support whatever steps Austria would take against Serbia, it did the exact opposite, and for no good reason. Germany identified herself with the Austrian interest in the prostration of Serbia as though it were her own, while Russia identified herself with

Serbia's defense of her independence. Thus a conflict at the periphery of the European state system transformed itself into one which threatened to affect the over-all distribution of power within that system.

Bargaining had become impossible if it was not to be the bargaining away of one's own vital interests. Concessions at somebody else's expense could no longer be made. Because of the identification of one's own interests with the interests of the smaller nations involved, concessions at the apparent expense of others would have meant concessions at one's own expense. The conflict could not be postponed because of the overriding fear of most of the great powers that postponement would strengthen the other side for an armed conflict considered to be inevitable. For once the issues had been brought from the periphery into the center of the circle of the great powers, there was no way of side-stepping them; there was, as it were, no empty space into which to step in order to evade the issue. Russia had to face the Austro-German determination to settle the Serbian problem on Austria's terms; in consequence, France had to face the invocation of the Franco-Russian Alliance by Russia, and Germany had to face the activation of that alliance and Great Britain, the threat to Belgium. There was no side-stepping these issues except at the price of yielding what each nation regarded as its vital interests.

What blundering diplomacy brought about in July, 1914 has today become the ineluctable result of structural changes in the balance of power. It was possible in the period preceding the First World War for the great powers to deflect their rivalries from their own mutual frontiers to the periphery and into politically empty spaces because virtually all the active participants in the balance of power were European nations and, furthermore, the main weights of the balance were located in Europe. To say that there were during that period a periphery and politically empty spaces is simply a negative way of saying that during that period the balance of power was quantitatively and qualitatively circumscribed by geographical limits. With the balance of power becoming world-wide and the main weights being placed in three different continents, the American and the Eurasian, the dichotomy between the circle of the great powers and its center, on the one hand, and its periphery and the empty spaces beyond, on the other, must of necessity disappear. The periphery of the balance of power now coincides with the confines of the earth. The formerly empty spaces lie east and west, north and south, on the poles and in the deserts, on land, on water, and in the air, athwart the routes over which the two super-powers must approach each other for friendly or hostile contacts. Thus into those spaces the two remaining great contenders on the international scene have poured their own power, political, military, and economic, transforming these spaces into the two great blocks which border on each other and opposite each other at the four corners of the earth.

4 THE POTENTIALITIES OF THE TWO-BLOCK SYSTEM

These two blocks face each other like two fighters in a short and narrow lane. They can advance and meet each other in what is likely to be combat, or they can retreat and allow the other side to advance into what is to them precious ground. Those manifold and variegated maneuvers through which the masters of the balance of power would try either to stave off armed conflicts altogether or at least to make them brief and decisive yet limited in scope, the alliances and counter-alliances, the shifting of alliances according to whence the greater threat or the better opportunity might come, the side-stepping and postponement of issues, the deflection of rivalries from the exposed front yard into the colonial back yard—these are things of the past. With them have gone into oblivion the peculiar finesse and subtlety of mind, the calculating and versatile intelligence and bold yet circumspect decisions which were required from the players in that game. With those modes of action and intellectual attitudes there has disappeared that self-regulating flexibility, that automatic tendency of disturbed power relations either to revert to their old, or to establish a new, equilibrium.

For the two giants which today determine the course of world affairs only one policy seems to be left, that is, to increase their own strength and that of their satellites. All the players that count have taken sides, and in the foreseeable future no switch from one side to the other is likely to take place. If it were to take place, it would not be likely to reverse the existing balance of power. Since the issues everywhere boil down to retreat from, or advance into, areas which both sides regard as of vital interest to themselves, positions must be held. So the give and take of compromise becomes a weakness which neither side can afford.

While formerly war was regarded, according to the classic definition of Clausewitz, as the continuation of diplomacy by other means, the art of diplomacy now transforms itself into a variety of the art of warfare. That is to say, we live in the period of "cold war" where the aims of warfare are being pursued, for the time being, with other than violent means. In such a situation the peculiar qualities of the diplomatic mind are useless, for they have nothing to operate with and are consequently superseded by the military type of thinking. The balance of power, once disturbed, can only be restored, if at all, by an increase in the weaker side's military strength. Yet since there are no important variables in the picture from the inherent strength of the two giants themselves, either side must fear that the temporarily stronger contestant will use its superiority to eliminate the threat from the other side either by shattering military and economic pressure or by a war of annihilation.

Thus, as we approach the mid-twentieth century, the international situation is reduced to the primitive spectacle of two giants eyeing each other with watchful suspicion. They bend every effort to increase their military potential to the utmost, since this is all they can count upon. Each prepares to strike the first decisive blow, for if one does not strike it the other side might. Thus contain or be contained, conquer or be conquered, destroy or be destroyed, become the watchwords of the new diplomacy.

This political state of the world does not of necessity result from the mechanics of the new balance of power. The changed structure of the balance of power has made the hostile opposition of two gigantic power blocks possible, but it has not made it inevitable. On the contrary, the new balance of power is a mechanism which contains in itself the potentialities for unheard-of good as well as for unprecedented evil. Which of these potentialities will be realized depends not upon the mechanics of the balance of power, but upon moral and material forces which use that mechanism for the realization of their ends.

5 THE INFLUENCE OF TOTAL WAR

The French philosopher Fénelon, in his advice to the grandson of Louis XIV, gives an account of the different types of the balance of power and, while trying to assess their respective advantages and weaknesses, bestows the highest praise upon the opposition between two equally strong states as the perfect type of the balance of power.

The fourth system is that of a power which is about equal with another and which holds the latter in equilibrium for the sake of the public security. To be in such a situation and to have no ambition which would make you desirous to give it up, this is indeed the wisest and happiest situation for a state. You are the common arbiter; all your neighbors are your friends, and those that are not, make themselves by that very fact suspicious to all the others. You do nothing that does not appear to have been done for your neighbors as well as for your people. You get stronger every day; and if you succeed, as it is almost inevitable in the long run by virtue of wise policies, to have more inner strength and more alliances than the power jealous of you, you ought to adhere more and more to that wise moderation which has limited you to maintaining the equilibrium and the common security. One ought always to remember the evils with which the state has to pay within and without for its great conquests, the fact that these conquests bear no fruit, the risk which one runs in undertaking them, and, finally how vain, how useless, how short-lived great empires are and what ravage they cause in falling.

Yet since one cannot hope that a power which is superior to all others will not before long abuse that superiority, a wise and just prince should never wish to leave to his successors, who by all appearances are less moderate than he, the continuous and violent temptation of too pronounced a superiority. For the very good of his successors and his people, he should confine himself to a kind of equality.

In other words, the distribution of power which Fénelon envisages resembles distinctly the distribution of power which exists, as we approach the mid-twentieth century, between the United States and the Soviet Union, that is to say, a potential equilibrium with the preponderance at present on the side of the United States. The beneficial results which the French philosopher contemplated have, however, failed to attend this potential equilibrium between the United States and the Soviet Union and do not seem to be likely to materialize in the foreseeable future. The reason is to be sought in the character of modern war which, under the impact of nationalistic universalism and modern technology, has become total. It is here that we find the fifth and last of the fundamental changes which distinguish the world politics of the mid-twentieth century from the international politics of previous ages.

War in our time has become total in four different respects: with respect to the fraction of the population completely identified in its emotions and convictions with the wars of its nation, the fraction of the population participating in war, the fraction of the population affected by war, and the objectives pursued by war. When Fénelon wrote, at the beginning of the eighteenth century, war was limited in all these respects, and had been so since the beginning of the modern state system.

It is the revolution in the productive processes of the modern age that has made total war and world-wide dominion possible. Before its advent war was bound to be limited in its technological aspects; for the productivity of a nation was not sufficient both to feed, clothe, and house its members and to keep large armies supplied with the implements of war for any length of time. More particularly, national economies operated on so narrow a margin above the mere subsistence level that it was impossible to increase the share of the armed forces in the national product to any appreciable extent without endangering the very existence of the nation. In the seventeenth and eighteenth centuries it was not at all unusual for a government to spend as much as, or more than, two-thirds of the national budget for military purposes, which a few times during that period consumed more than ninety per cent of the total outlay of the government; for military expenditures had of course precedence over all others and the national product was too small to be taxed extensively for other purposes. Thus it was not by accident that before the nineteenth century all attempts at universal military service failed; for in the interest of keeping national production going, the productive classes of the population had to be exempt from military service and only the scum which was unable to engage in productive enterprises and the nobility which was unwilling to engage in them could safely be conscripted.

The Industrial Revolution and, more particularly, the mechanization of agricultural and industrial processes in the twentieth century have had a triple effect upon the character of war and of international politics. They have increased the total productivity of the great industrial nations enormously. They have, furthermore, reduced drastically the relative share of human labor in the productive processes. They have, finally, together with the new techniques in medicine and hygiene, brought about an unprecedented increase in the population of all nations. Since the increase in productivity thus achieved exceeds by far the increased demands upon the national product caused by the higher standard of living and the greater number of consumers, that excess in productivity is now available for new purposes and can be guided into the channels of total war. The new energy created by the machine and much of the human energy which a century and a half ago was still absorbed in the business of keeping alive can now be employed for military purposes, either directly by way of military service or indirectly through industrial production.

Nor is that human energy now available for war of a muscular nature alone. The machine age has lightened immensely the intellectual and moral burden of keeping one's self and one's dependents fed, clothed, and protected from the elements and from disease, which still a century and a half ago absorbed most of the vital energies of most men. Moreover, it has provided most men with an amount of leisure which only few men have ever had before. Yet paradoxically enough, by doing so, it has freed tremendous intellectual and moral energies which have gone into the building of a better world, but which have also gone into the preparation and the waging of total war. This concatenation of human and material forces, freed and created by the age of the machine, has given war its total character.

It has also given total war that terrifying, world-embracing impetus which seems to be satisfied with nothing short of world dominion. With his intellectual and moral energies no longer primarily concerned about this life nor deflected toward concern with the life thereafter, modern man looks for conquests, conquests of nature and conquest of other men. The age of the machine, which has sprung from man's self-sufficient mind, has instilled in modern man the confidence that he can save himself by his own unaided efforts here and now. Thus the intellectual and moral lifeblood of modern man streams into the political religions which promise salvation through science, revolution, or the holy war of nationalism. The machine begets its own triumphs, each forward step calling forth two more on the road of technological progress. It also begets its own victories, military and political; for with the ability to conquer the world and keep it conquered, it creates the will to conquer it.

Yet it may also beget its own destruction. Total war waged by total populations for total stakes under the conditions of the contemporary balance of power may end in world dominion or in world destruction or in both. For either one of the two contenders for world dominion may conquer with relatively small losses to himself, or they may destroy each other, neither being able to conquer, or the least weakened may conquer, presiding over universal devastation. Such are the prospects which overshadow world politics as we approach the half-way mark of the twentieth century.

Thus we have gone full circle. We recognized the driving element of contemporary world politics in the new moral force of nationalistic universalism. We found a simplified balance of power, operating between two inflexible blocs, to be the harbinger of great good or great evil. We discovered the menace of evil in the potentialities of total war. Yet the element which makes total war possible, namely, the mechanization of modern life, makes possible also the moral force which, through the instrumentality of total war, aims at total dominion.[1]

[1] This paper, in a slightly altered version, forms part of a systematic treatise which, under the title *Politics among Nations. The Struggle for Power and Peace,* was published by Alfred A. Knopf.

THE TRAGIC ELEMENT

IN MODERN

INTERNATIONAL

CONFLICT

Herbert Butterfield

[1950]

IN THE nineteenth century, when many people were optimistic in their views of human nature, and confident that the course of progress was going to be continued into an indefinite future, there were one or two prophets who feared and foretold that the twentieth century would see great wars of peoples, popular military dictatorships, and the harnessing of the machines of industry to the science of warfare. It is interesting to note that, without knowing whether one country or another was going to emerge as the chief offender, and without basing his prediction upon any view that Germany was likely to present a special problem to the European continent, a writer could still feel assured, a generation beforehand, that this age of terrible warfare was coming. He could see, in other words, that, apart from the emergence of a special criminal, the developments in the situation itself were driving mankind into an era of conflict. In the midst of battle, while we are all of us in fighting mood, we see only the sins of the enemy and fail to reflect on those predicaments and dilemmas which so often develop and which underlie the great conflicts between masses of human beings. And though these conflicts could hardly have taken place if all men were perfect saints, we often forget that many of the inhuman struggles that have divided the human race would hardly have occurred if the situation had been one of completely righteous men confronted by undiluted and unmitigated crime. Given the ordinary amount of cupidity and wilfulness in human beings, unmanageable uations are likely to develop and some of them may almost be guaranteed to end in terrible conflict. While there is battle and hatred men have eyes for nothing save the fact that the enemy is the cause of all the troubles; but long, long afterwards, when all passion has been spent, the historian often sees that it was a conflict between one half-right that was perhaps too wilful, and another half-right that was perhaps too proud; and behind even this he discerns that it was a terrible predicament, which had the effect of putting men so at cross-purposes with one another. This predicament is the thing which it is the purpose of this paper to examine; and first of all I propose to try to show how the historian comes to discover its existence.

If we consider the history of the historical writing that has been issued, generation after generation, on a given body of events, we shall generally find that in the early stages of this process of reconstruction the narrative which is produced has a primitive and simple shape. As one generation of students succeeds another, however, each developing the historiography of this particular subject, the narrative passes through certain typical stages until it is brought to a high and subtle form of organization. It would be difficult to give names to these successive stages in the development of the historiography of a given theme, but there is an early period in the writing-up of a subject, particularly when the subject itself is one form or another of human conflict, which seems to me to belong to the class of literature sometimes described as "Heroic." It does not matter whether the topic which the historian is writing about is the victory of Christianity in the Roman Empire, or the struggles of the modern scientists in the seventeenth century, or the case of either the French or the Russian Revolutions. There is a recognizable phase in the historical reconstruction or the chronicle writing which has distinctive features and shows a certain characteristic form of organization; and on more than one occasion in my life I have found myself saying that this kind of historiography bears the marks of the Heroic age. It represents the early period when the victors write their own chronicles, gloat over the defeated, count their trophies, commemorate their achievements, and show how righteousness has triumphed. And it may be true that the narrative has a primitive sort of structure that we can recognize, but it is a structure that requires little thought on the part of the writers of the history; for it was ready-made for them all the time— it is nothing more than the sort of organization that a narrative acquires from the mere fact that the author is taking sides in the conflict. We who come long afterwards generally find that this kind of history has over-dramatized the struggle in its aspect as a battle of right versus wrong; and to us it seems that these writers refused to exercise imaginative sympathy over the defeated enemy, so that they lack the perspective which might have been achieved if they had allowed themselves to be driven to a deeper analysis of the whole affair. In England our own whig interpretation of history is only a development from the "Heroic" way of formulating the issues of human conflict—as though the parliamentarians of the seventeenth century were provoked to war by mere personal wickednesses and deliberate aggressions on the part of Charles I and his supporters.

Though I have no doubt that the progress of historiography to a higher level than this is really to be regarded as a collaborative achievement, I have always understood that the name of S. R. Gardiner is particularly associated with the developments which led to a drastic refocusing of these English constitutional conflicts of the seventeenth century. It seems to have been the case furthermore that with him as with other people the refocusing resulted from what in the last resort might be described as the method of taking compassion on the defeated. Gardiner's mode of procedure led him to be careful with the defeated party, and he tried by internal sympathetic infiltration really to find out what was in their minds. And this is a process to which there ought to be no limits, for historical imagination comes to its sublimest achievements when it can succeed in comprehending the people not like-minded with oneself. Once such a process is embarked upon, the truth soon emerges that it is an easy thing to produce a whig history of a constitutional conflict or alternatively a royalist version of the affair; but it is no easy matter to compromise the two in a single survey, since clearly they cannot be just joined or added to one another. In reality you find that at every inch in your attempt to collate the outlooks of the two belligerent parties you are driven to a higher altitude—you have to find a kind of historical truth that lies on a higher plane before you can make the evidence square with itself or secure a story that comprehends all the factors and embraces the purely partial visions of the two opposing sides. Then, after much labor, you may achieve something more like a stereoscopic vision of the whole drama. Similarly, if an English foreign secretary and an Austrian ambassador give curiously divergent reports of a conversation that they have had with each other, the historian would not be content merely to add the two reports together. Collating them inch by inch he would use one document to enable him to see new folds of implication in the other. So he would be carried to a higher version of the whole affair—one which embraces the contradictions in the original accounts and even enables us to understand how the discrepancies should have occurred. In the long run the historian will not limit himself to seeing things with the eyes of the royalist or with the eyes of the roundhead; but, taking a loftier perspective which puts him in a position to embrace both, he will reach new truths to which both sides were blind—truths which will even enable him to see how they came to differ so much from one another.

When the historiography of the English seventeenth-century constitutional struggles has developed through the work of Gardiner and his successors, and has been brought to a higher state of organization by virtue of processes somewhat on the pattern that I have described, what emerges is a new and drastically different formulation of the whole conflict. And this new way of presenting the entire issue has a peculiar characteristic which I wish to examine, because it shows us what the revised perspective really amounts to—it provides us with almost a definition of what is implied in the progress of historiography as it moves further away from the events that are being narrated, further away from the state of being contemporary history. The progress of historiography takes us away from that first simple picture of good men fighting bad; and not merely in the case of seventeenth-century England but in one field of history after another we find that it contributes a new and most uncomfortable revelation—it gradually disengages the structural features of a conflict which was inherent in the dialectic of events. It shows us situations hardening, events tying themselves into knots, human beings faced by terrible dilemmas, and one party and another being driven into a corner. In other words, as the historiography of a given episode develops and comes to be further removed from the passions of those who were active in the drama, it uncovers at the basis of the story a fundamental human predicament —one which we can see would have led to a serious conflict of wills even if all men had been fairly intelligent and reasonably well-intentioned. Perhaps it was this reformulation of the conflict which Lord Acton had in mind when he suggested that it needs the historian to come on the scene at a later time to say what it was that these poor seventeenth-century royalists and roundheads were really fighting about.

In the new organization of the narrative the personal goodness or badness of Charles I may still appear to be operative but it ceases to be the central issue, ceases to be the basis for the mounting of the whole story. We see the English monarchy coming into a serious predicament in this period in any case; and something of a parallel kind is seen to take place as we study the conflicts of the reign of George III. The central fact—the one that gives the new structure to the whole narrative—is a certain predicament, a certain situation that contains the elements of conflict irrespective of any special wickedness in any of the parties concerned; and the personal goodness or badness of Charles I or George III operates only, so to speak, on the margin of this, and becomes rather a fringing issue. So, while contemporary ways of formulating the human conflict have the structure of melodrama, the white hero fighting the black villain of the piece in a straight war of right versus wrong, historiography in the course of time leads us to transpose the lines of the picture and redraft the whole issue, especially as we come to comprehend more deeply the men who were not like-minded with ourselves. The higher historiography moves away from melodrama and brings out the tragic element in human conflict.

If all this is true, then we who are so deeply engaged in an age of conflict, are under an obligation not to be too blindly secure, too wilfully confident, in the contemporary ways of formulating that conflict; and it is incumbent upon us not quite to forget how future historiography may expose the limitations of our vision. If all this is true, then an issue is drawn between the view which the contemporary historian so often tends to possess and the view associated with a higher and riper stage of historiography—the view of what I hope I may be allowed to call "academic history." The issue is drawn because the two kinds of history differ in the actual structure of the narrative and formulation of the theme, unless the contemporary history has been written after great prayer and fasting, which seldom happens to be the case. If what I have said is true, then the examination of the actual structure of a piece of historical narrative can be at any rate one of the tests of the intellectual quality of the work and the genuineness of its historical perspective. Furthermore, if any people should desire to envisage the events of their own day with a certain historical-mindedness, then we have at least a clue to the kind of direction in which they should move in their attempt to achieve the object. For if we realize the way in which historical science develops in the course of time— if we know even only one of the laws which govern its development as it proceeds further away from the merely contemporary point of view—then we have at any rate a hint of the kind of thing which historical perspective requires of us; and we can be to that degree more hopeful in our attempt to hasten or anticipate the future verdict of historical science. Behind the great conflicts of mankind is a terrible human predicament which lies at the heart of the story; and sooner or later the historian will base the very structure of his narrative upon it. Contemporaries fail to see the predicament or refuse to recognize its genuineness, so that our knowledge of it comes from later analysis—it is only with the progress of historical science on a particular subject that men come really to recognize that there was a terrible knot almost beyond the ingenuity of man to untie. It represents therefore a contribution that historical science itself has added to our interpretation of life—one which leads us to place a different construction on the whole human drama, since it uncovers the tragic element in human conflict. In historical perspective we learn to be a little more sorry for both parties than they knew how to be for one another.

The international situation of the present day is so difficult, and we are so greatly in need of a deeper vision that we ought to be ready to clutch at anything which might have a chance of leading us to fresh thoughts or new truths. We might ask, therefore, whether in the modern world there is any hint of the kind of human predicament that we have been considering and whether the idea can be of any use to us when we are seeking light on our contemporary problem. For the purpose of illustrating an argument I should like to describe and examine an imaginary specimen case in diplomacy—one which will enable me to isolate and to put under the microscope that very factor in human conflict which so often emerges at a later time, when historians have long been reflecting on the issue, but which is so often concealed from contemporaries in the heat of action and in all the bustle of life. For the purpose of assuring that the issue shall confront us more vividly I should like to present this imaginary instance in the guise of something real, something which will come to us as an actual problem of the present day.

Let us suppose then, that the Western powers on the one hand and Russia on the other hand have just defeated Germany and have reduced that country to total surrender. And let it be granted that the Western powers, confronted by the Russian colossus, feel that they cannot afford to allow the defeated Germany to be drawn into the orbit of the communist system; while Russia, for her part, faced by what to her is the no less formidable West, is ridden by the mathematically equal and opposite fear that the balance will be turned against her for all the future if Germany is enlisted in the non-communist group. Here then is a case in which the objects of the two parties are mutually exclusive, since if the one side is satisfied the other feels the situation to be utterly desperate; and it is a case not difficult to imagine, since it might be argued (though we need not commit ourselves to the fact) that it has actually existed in our world since 1945. If we can take this situation for granted for the purpose of argument, and then persuade our minds to perform a piece of abstraction, we may arrive at a result upon which we can do some mathematics. What is required is that we should stretch our imagination to the point of envisaging this particular international predicament in a purer form than either it or anything else ever exists in history. Let us assume that the Soviet group of states on the one hand and the western group on the other are absolutely level in point of virtue and in the moral qualities of the statesmen who conduct their affairs. Further, we will postulate that the level shall be a reasonably high one, that the statesmen on both sides are not saints, of course, competing with one another only in self-renunciation—a situation which would defeat our mathematics—but are moderately virtuous men, as men go in politics, anxious that their countries shall come to no harm, and moved by national self-interest to a degree that we must regard as comparatively reasonable. We will postulate that they have just those faults which men can have who feel themselves to be righteous and well-disposed—both sides anxious to avoid a war, but each desperately unsure about the intentions of the other party; each beset by the devils of fear and suspicion, therefore; and each side locked in its own system of self-righteousness.

Allowing for all this—which means that the problem before us is presented in what I should call its optimum setting—then I should assert that here is a grand dialectical jam of a kind that exasperates men—a terrible deadlock that makes ordinary human beings even a little more wilful than they ordinarily are. Here is the absolute predicament and the irreducible dilemma—for I shall have something to say later to those who assert that it is no genuine predicament at all, and that every schoolboy knows the solution to the problem. Even granting throughout the whole of human nature no more than the ordinary amount of human wilfulness such as we ourselves may be said to possess, here are the ingredients for a grand catastrophe. The greatest war in history could be produced without the intervention of any great criminals who might be out to do deliberate harm in the world. It could be produced between two powers both of which were desperately anxious to avoid a conflict of any sort.

Though the example that I have given is a purely hypothetical one, as I have said—for in the complicated realm of history so clear a pattern will never be found in its absolute purity—still there is a sense in which it typifies an essential human predicament; it illustrates a certain recalcitrancy that may lie in events as such, an intractability that can exist in the human situation itself. Here, in other words, is the mathematical formula—or perhaps one of the formulas—for a state of things which produces what I should call the tragic element in human conflict. As regards the real world of international relations I should put forward the thesis (which, if it is true, would seem to me to be not an unimportant one), that this condition of absolute predicament or irreducible dilemma lies in the very geometry of human conflict. It is at the basis of the structure of any given episode in that conflict. It is at the basis of all the tensions of the present day, representing even now the residual problem that the world has not solved, the hard nut that we still have to crack. So far as the historian is concerned, here is the basic pattern for all narratives of human conflict, whatever other patterns may be superimposed upon it later. Indeed, as I have said, when the historical reconstruction of a given episode has been carried on for generation upon generation, this is the structure the story tends to acquire as it becomes revised and corrected and reshaped with the passage of time. This tragedy of the absolute human predicament enters into the very fabric of historical narrative in proportion as we move further away from being mere contemporary historians.

Turning again to the hypothetical case which we have been using as our pattern, we may note that not only could the greatest war in history be produced between two powers both of which were moderately virtuous and desperately anxious to prevent a conflict, but such a struggle, far from being a nice, quiet and reasonable affair, would be embittered by the heat of moral indignation on both sides, just because each was so conscious of its own rectitude, so enraged with the other for leaving it without any alternative to war. It is the peculiar characteristic of the situation I am describing—the situation of what I should call Hobbesian fear—that you yourself may vividly feel the terrible fear that you have of the other party, but you cannot enter into the other man's counter-fear, or even understand why he should be particularly nervous. For you know that you yourself mean him no harm, and that you want nothing from him save guarantees for your own safety; and it is never possible for you to realize or remember properly that since he cannot see the inside of your mind, he can never have the same assurance of your intentions that you have. As this operates on both sides the Chinese puzzle is complete in all its interlockings—and neither party sees the nature of the predicament he is in, for he only imagines that the other party is being hostile and unreasonable. It is even possible for each to feel that the other is wilfully withholding the guarantees that would have enabled him to have a sense of security. The resulting conflict is more likely to be hot with moral indignation—one self-righteousness encountering another—than it would have been if the contest had lain between two hard-headed eighteenth-century masters of *realpolitik*. In such circumstances the contemporary historians on each side will tend to follow suit, each locked in the combative views of his own nation, and shrieking morality of that particular kind which springs from self-righteousness. That is one of the reasons why contemporary history differs so greatly from what I have called academic history. In all that I am saying I am really asserting, moreover, that the self-righteous are not the true moralists either in history or in life. Those who are less self-righteous may face the world's problems more squarely, even when they are less clever, than other people.

Pandit Nehru, when he was speaking at Columbia University, made a somewhat moving criticism of both East and West, because in his view they were intent upon what he called a race in armaments. Some people even say that a race in armaments is a cause of war—

but nobody actually wills a "race"; and I personally would rather pity both sides than blame them, for I think that the race in armaments, and even the war that seems to result from it, are caused rather by that tragic human predicament, that situation of Hobbesian fear. All that we can say is that the predicament would not exist, of course, if all the world were like St. Francis of Assisi, and if human nature in general were not streaked with cupidities. The predicament, the race in armaments and the war itself are explained in the last resort, therefore, as the result of man's universal sin. Similarly, suppose two great groups of alliances have been at virtual deadlock for some years, so that even neutral states have begun to assert that war is inevitable—meaning that war is inevitable, human nature being what it is. Suppose you have such a situation, and then one party to the predicament becomes over-exasperated and makes too wilful a decision; suppose in particular that he does it because he thinks that somebody must take a strong line at last; and we will say that he even intends to bluff, but the bluff does not come off and so a great war is brought about. Then, though this man has done wrong I could not personally agree that he should be charged as the sole author of the war and loaded with all the misery of it as though he were the only villain in a melodrama. I could not agree that he should be regarded as guilty in just the way he would have been if he had fallen unprovoked on a flock of innocent lambs. Ultimately the true origin of the war lies in that predicament; and on this basis the melodrama re-shapes itself, assuming more of the character of tragedy —the kind of tragedy in which it is so to speak the situation that gives one a heartache, and sometimes, as in the case of *King Lear,* what seem to be little sins may have colossally disproportionate consequences.

The truth is that when faced by this human predicament—this final unsolved problem of human relations—the mind winces and turns to look elsewhere, and statesmen, for their case, pile all the blame on the handiest scapegoat. Men fix their attention upon what in reality are fringing issues, and they remove these from their proper place on the fringe to the center of the picture—you can evade all problems by saying that everything is due to the wickedness of King Charles I. The point can be illustrated best perhaps by the process of looking for a moment at its converse. Let us make it clear to ourselves: if in our present-day crises Stalin and his colleagues could be imagined to be as virtuous and well-intentioned as the statesmen of the Western world, still our predicament would exist, and there would be the same dilemma concerning the future of Germany— especially as we, because we look at him from the outside, could never be sure that Stalin's intentions were as good as ours. In any case we could never be sure that if we put our trust in him we should not really be placing weapons into the hands of some villain who might succeed to his power next year, supposing he passed off the stage. Of course, if we are in this same international predicament and the Russians happen to be thieves or adventurers or aggressors or drunkards or sexual perverts to boot, then that is an extra boon which Providence throws into the lap, so to speak of the Western powers—the kind of boon which, to judge from our assertions over a number of centuries, Providence has generally vouchsafed to the British in their wars. Even in such circumstances, however, we are evading an essential problem if we lose sight of the basic predicament—a predicament so exasperating sometimes that it can be responsible for making people more wicked and desperate than they otherwise would have been. It is like the case of the person who owed his neighbor £5 and refused to pay it on the ground that the neighbor was an immoral man and would make a bad use of the money. The moralizing might not be without its justice but in this case it would be introduced as a screen to cover a delinquency of one's own. Or it is like the case of those people who so often, as in 1792, would judge a revolution entirely by its atrocities—evading the structural problem and pouncing upon an incidental issue. I have no doubt it would be a boon to me, supposing I were challenged in debate on a point of history, if I could say: "Take no notice of this man; he has just come out of prison after serving sentence for forging a check." I should be picking up a fringing issue and turning it into the central issue; and in this way I might use the other person's immorality most unfairly for the purpose of evading a challenge that happened to be inconvenient to myself.

Not only may the problem of war present itself in the acutest possible form irrespective of any difference in morality between the contending parties, but the whole problem and the whole predicament that we are discussing exists absolutely irrespective of any differences in ideology. All the evidence that we have—and it seems to me that we have had very much in the last one hundred years for this particular case—shows that the basic problem would not be fundamentally altered, and would certainly not be avoided, supposing what we were confronted with at the moment were all the power of modern Russia in the hands of the Tsars, instead of the regime of the Soviet. The predicament would not be removed even if there were no communism in the world at all, or supposing that every state involved in the problem were a Christian state in the sense that so many countries were Christian throughout most of the centuries of modern times. Even supposing Russia were liberal and democratic—supposing the great powers on either side were so situated that their populations could put pressure on the government in the very matter of foreign policy—still the populations would be just as fearful or suspicious or exasperated or angry as the foreign offices themselves. Indeed it seems to be generally the case that they are more so, unless the knowledge of the predicament is withheld from them.

In so far as international conflicts are concerned, therefore, I am suggesting that after many of the more incidental features of the case have been peeled away, we shall find at the heart of everything a kernel of difficulty which is essentially a problem of diplomacy as such. In fact I personally think that in the international crises of our time, we are muddying the waters and darkening our own minds and playing the very game the Russians want us to play, when we mix our drinks and indulge in a so-called "ideological" foreign policy, forgetting that the fundamental problems exist, as I have said, independent of the differences in ideology. The truth is that we could very well say to the Russians: "We would not have allowed you to steal this particular march on us, or to encroach in this particular direction or to dominate defeated Germany even if you had been a Christian empire as in the time of the Tsars." And, given the distribution of power which existed in Europe in 1945, the old Tsardom would have dominated Poland, Czechoslovakia, Hungary and the Balkans, just as the Soviets do now, though it would have used something different from the Marxian ideology to facilitate the execution of its purpose. All this carries with it the further corollary that we ought to attach very great importance to a study which in England at least has gravely declined and is woefully out of fashion, namely, pure diplomatic history regarded as a technique in itself; for it was just the characteristic of this technical diplomatic history to lay bare the essential geometry of the problem and isolate for examination the fundamental predicament that required a solution. Indeed what I am doing in this paper is to elicit the moral implications of that whole system of thought which is invoked in diplomatic history— and I am asserting that the new diplomacy of our time, as well as its dependent forms of historiography, though they are more self-righteous than the old, are in reality less moral, at any rate in certain respects.

We have already noted, however, that in the complicated realm of historical events, no pattern ever appears in a pure and unadulterated form—and certainly, when a diplomatic issue is presented to us for resolution, we can never say that both sides are exactly balanced in point of morality, exactly equal in the virtues of their leading statesmen. The original issue may be aggravated and greatly intensified by the aggressiveness of a politician in one country or the barbarism of a regime in another country; and our fear of the expansion of Russia is considerably increased if Russia implies either a Tsarist despotism or the communist system. All the same, it is wrong to overlook that original diplomatic predicament which forms the kernel of the problem requiring to be solved; and it is a mistake to allow the incidental matters or the attendant circumstances to drive that essential issue out of our minds. I could express the point, for example —or I could illustrate its implications—by noting that we should not like to be conquered by Russia even if Russia were not a communist state. Alternatively I might say that supposing it could be made out that there were general reasons for conceding that Spain had a right to Gibraltar, it is not clear that the British would be justified in withholding that possession merely because they disliked the present regime in Spain and disapproved of General Franco. It was perhaps one of the virtues of the older type of diplomacy that in time of war it did not allow itself to be entirely obsessed by the question of the responsibility for the resort to violence—did not merely hark back continually to the actual occasion of the outbreak—but recognized that the war itself was partly tragedy, that is to say, partly due to a predicament. Attention was concentrated rather on the kind of world which would be produced once the victory had been achieved, and the aim was not so much to punish the culprits, but rather to make sure that there was a tolerable balance of forces at the finish. Even after the battle of Waterloo, the enemies of Napoleon did not allow themselves to be moved by the desire of giving due punishment to France, though that country had kept the world at war for over twenty years and had given itself over to Napoleon for a second time, after his return from Elba. France in 1815 lost practically none of the territory she had held before the outbreak of war, and in a remarkably short time she was readmitted to the comity of nations; and yet now we know that even the creators of the peace of 1815 made a mistake in fearing still that France would always be the aggressor; in consequence of which they insisted upon installing a strong Prussia in the Rhineland to defend Germany against France, and so helped the coming giant to be stronger than ever, because they had been too rigidly obsessed with the danger that had troubled them in the past. The essential thing is to guard against the kind of war which, if you win it absolutely, will produce another "predicament" worse than the one you started with.

We of the twentieth century have not been as wise as the men of over a hundred years ago. The great diplomatic issue that emerged— or rather re-emerged—in Europe in the early years of this present century concerned the question whether Russia on the one hand, should dominate those countries of central and eastern Europe which run from Poland, through Czechoslovakia and Hungary to what we now call Yugoslavia and the Balkans. This is how it came about that the occasion for the war of 1914 was an episode involving Bosnia and Serbia, while the occasion for the war of 1939 occurred in regions concerning which Lloyd George had long before expressed his apprehensions—namely in Czechoslovakia and in Poland. Those two wars were embarrassing in certain respects for Great Britain, for though we claimed that we were fighting for democracy we were allied in the former case with Tsarist Russia, where the Jews had been oppressed, and the Poles were held in subjection, and the Baltic nations were prevented from achieving state-hood; while in the case of the second World War we were the allies of the Soviet System. So far as I can interpret European history in general, the line of central European states which were in question—Poland, Czechoslovakia, Yugoslavia, etc.—can flourish beautifully when both Germany and Russia are reduced to impotence, as they were in the fifteenth century, and as they came to be again for a period after 1919. The same states may preserve their independence provided both Germany and Russia are strong, so that when the giant on the one side seeks to oppress them they can look for help to the giant on the other side. It is bound to be sad, however, for Poland, Czechoslovakia, etc., if only one of these giants is left standing and there is no other great power in the vicinity to challenge or check this monster. Indeed, we have seen how even in the last few years America, England and the nations of Western Europe have been unable to prevent this whole line of states from coming quite into the power of the Russian bear. Supposing wars to be necessary and unavoidable—as indeed they seem to be sometimes—it might still be a question whether we have conducted ours with a right mentality or with a proper grasp of the essential issues. In respect of the great diplomatic problem of the twentieth century, we may wonder sometimes whether Russia was so much more virtuous than Germany as to make it worth the lives of tens of millions of people in two wars to insure that she (as a communist system—or even as a tsarist empire) should gain such an unchallenged and exclusive hold over that line of central European states as Germany never had in all her history, and never could have had unless Russia had first been wiped out as a great state. For it is just that kind of question—the question of the redistribution of territorial power—which war decides. We cannot spread democracy by war, which barbarizes peoples and tends rather to make democracy more impracticable over a greater area of the European continent.

The supporters of the new diplomacy, which has emerged since the opening of the epoch of world-wars, like to tell us that the whole problem we have been discussing does not exist, because it ought not to exist. In any case, there is no Chinese puzzle at all, they say, for, whatever the issue might be, we could easily dispose of it by referring it to a conference or sending it to the United Nations. Against these specialists in wishful thinking it must be asserted that the kind of human predicament which we have been discussing is not merely so far without a solution, but the whole condition is a standing feature of mankind in world-history. If the whole of Russia and the entire body of its satellites were to buried under the deepest oceans from this very night, the predicament would still be with us tomorrow, though the terms of it would be transposed by a regrouping of the remaining powers. Supposing there were no Russian power in existence, supposing Germany herself were lying prostrate as a beaten and ineffective nation, and supposing the help of America were not essential to everybody concerned—all that fine show of unanimity between the countries of Western Europe, all that cooperation induced by the threat of an immediate danger, would break down into bitterness and anarchy. And if the issue which divides the world at a given moment were referred to a conference-table, then, though many good things might be achieved, we should not have eliminated the predicament which was most crucial—we should merely find it transplanted into the bosom of the conference itself. Even the organization of the United Nations has not proved essentially different in this respect from the case of the former League which had its headquarters in Geneva; and though the problem is transposed somewhat, so that different nations and different problems now produce the stumbling-block, the new international order has not in fact prevented powers from remaining armed as never before, and racing one another in the development of the atomic bomb.

It was once my feeling that if, in a European crisis, Great Britain pressed for the assembly of a conference, while Germany rejected that procedure, then Germany was clearly in the wrong and my own country was plainly on the side of the angels. Unfortunately it comes to be borne in upon one's mind as one studies these matters that conferences themselves are only too liable to be the arena for a kind of power-politics; and the greater states, in the very nature of things, hold a predominance in them which bears some proportion to their might. It even became evident to me that sometimes it was calculable in advance how the votes would be distributed if a conference met, since these would be affected by the alliances and affiliations of the various governments concerned, and might even be decided by sympathies in ideology. Supposing it became clear that if a conference were assembled the result was a foregone conclusion and Germany was so to speak outvoted in advance. I began to wonder whether in such a case she was necessarily more selfish than anybody else when she refused to put her head in the noose—I began to wonder also whether the virtues of Britain were quite so much to boast about when they coincided so nicely with her interests. This argument might be projected onto a wider canvas altogether; for without doubting the good intentions of the men who have ruled England in the last few decades, one must note that if a Machiavellian imperialist statesman had happened to be governing us with purely egotistical purposes in view, he would have found the conference method the best way of promoting our national interests, indeed the only way in view of the decline of actual British power and in view of the general distribution of forces in the world. In other words Great Britain in our time has been in a position which we must regard as fortunate in a certain respect, in that the policy which altruism would have dictated to her happened to be the same as the one which self-interest would demand —so that, though the conference method has been promoted so often by Englishmen who were only conscious of it as a noble aspiration, it has also been described as the only method of *Realpolitik* left to us. The conference method is more advantageous to us than any decision to measure forces with a rival, even if the voting should go against us on occasion in a matter of some moment to us.

But when I take this crucial case and imagine a real predicament —when I think of the kind of issue which decides whether a state or an empire goes up or down in the world—then I find myself in a position of some doubt even in regard to Great Britain. Supposing it to be the case that the loss of our overseas possessions would bring about a serious reduction in the standard of living of the British people, and supposing a motion were to be proposed that all forms of colony or of subjection or of dependency were to be abolished through the wide world—I, in a situation of this kind, should like to know what the attitude of the government of my country would be. In particular, I should like to know what its attitude would be to the idea of submitting such an issue to a conference or assembly in which the communists were known in advance to have the majority of votes. I should like to know what my country would do on the assumption that we still had enough power to make a valid and independent choice. Where the conflict is really a cut-throat one it seems to me that the conference method does not put an end to the predicament but merely changes the locality and the setting of it. The whole method is liable to break down if either the communists or the non-communists can be fairly sure in advance that on critical issues the other party is going to have the majority. And in any case I am not clear that anybody has ever devised a form of political machinery that could not somehow or other be manipulated by ill-intentioned people in the possession of power.

Like the Germans, we sometimes allow the academic and professorial mind to have too much sway among us; and with us this has helped to give currency to the heresy that everything can be settled if men will only sit together at a table—a view which may be justified on many occasions but which does not prove to be correct when the conflicting parties are in the extreme kind of predicament we have been discussing. Where the predicament really exists and the question is one of those which decide whether states are to go up or down in the world, those who do have the power will not allow themselves to be talked or voted out of their strategic positions, any more than empires will go under without putting up a fight, supposing a fight to be possible at all. Europeans have had hundreds of years in which to discuss theological problems, but mere discussion round a table has not brought them into agreement on the disputed points. This was the kind of issue upon which men can at worst agree to disagree, though I note that ecclesiastical systems were slow to come to this arrangement and they went on fighting one another, using weapons that kill, as long as it was feasible to fight at all. But if two different countries are claiming Gibraltar it is not so easy to settle the matter by saying that the parties can agree to disagree. The conference method does not get rid of the difficulty—it merely transplants the whole predicament into another place.

While we are at war, and the conflict is a matter of life or death for us, we may hardly have any part of our minds free for devoting to a general survey of the whole predicament in which the human race is standing. When the war is over, however, a time of healing ought to come, and it is our duty to carry all our problems to further analysis. Politicians, in the hurry of affairs, and in the stress of conflict, may hardly have an opportunity to cover the problem in an all-embracing survey, for we must regard them as generally acting under great pressures. We in universities, however—and especially those of us who study history—have a duty to think in longer terms and seize upon the problem precisely where the difficulties are most challenging. We ought to be straining our minds to think of new things and to enlarge the bounds of understanding; for though our enlarged understanding of the problem will not necessarily prevent war, it may remove some of the unwisdom which has made victory itself so much more disappointing in its results than it otherwise might have been.

SOME REFLECTIONS

ON COLONIALISM

Hans Kohn

[1956]

COLONIALISM AS A HISTORICAL
PHENOMENON

THE meaning and implications of the word colonialism and of the
closely connected terms of empire and imperialism have undergone a
profound transformation in the last decades. Until the end of the
nineteenth century the word empire or imperialism was generally
used in a laudatory and not a pejorative meaning. The Roman Empire had been the model for Western political thought for one thousand years. The Americans at the end of the eighteenth century
proudly and hopefully spoke of their empire. The French revolutionaries proclaimed the imperial expansion of their leadership. Modern Western civilization was regarded as superior to other more stag-
nant civilizations, and to bring higher civilization to less developed
countries was considered a praiseworthy enterprise, in spite of the
fact that like so many human efforts this too was inextricably mingled
with all kinds of corruption and greed. Empire and colonialism
always implied dominion and power; and power, whether exercised
by "native" or "alien" governments, has a potency for abuse as probably no other relationship has. Yet liberal alien governments—and
liberalism means primarily restraint upon, and limitations of, governmental authority—will be more easily controlled by public opinion
against abuse of power than illiberal "native" governments.

Colonies may be of two different kinds: those of settlement and
those of mere dependence. The former ones are more dangerous
for the natives. The outstanding example is the United States where
the settlement of the vast continent meant the practical extermination
of the natives. Where the natives were not exterminated by settlement of immigrants but only driven out or relegated to subordinate
positions, as in Aryan India, South Africa, Palestine, and partly in

French North Africa, tragic situations have been created, factually for the natives, morally for the immigrant settlers where they were inspired by liberal ideals. Such inspiration was lacking among Aryan Indians and South African Boers.

In a much more fortunate position are the colonies where no large-scale immigrant settlement was attempted. There the dependent status has worked on the whole to the advantage of the natives, who have found themselves, or will find themselves at some future time, in control of a vastly improved native land. Such was the case in British India and in Malaya, to quote only two instances.

In those areas, thanks to colonialism, for the first time, capable native cadres for the administration of the country and for all walks of civilized life have come into existence. Many of the new "nations" like India, Indonesia, and Nigeria owe their existence and potential cohesion as nations to the colonial regimes.

The more liberal a colonial regime was, the more bitter an anti-colonialism did it produce. Therefore, there is practically no anti-colonialism in the Portuguese colonies or in the Belgian Congo. Anti-colonialism, as far as it exceeds simple xenophobia and is inspired by higher ideas, has been the child of the colonial administration and of the ideas of liberty which it spread. The anti-colonial leaders were educated in the schools of the colonial powers. Thus, anti-colonial sentiments are not necessary signs of oppression.

In that connection it should be stated that 1776 was not a movement of oppressed natives, but of North American Britishers who enjoyed more liberties and rights than Britishers in Britain. The Anglo-Americans had come as conquerors and settlers; they revolted against their motherland in the struggle for the interpretation of common constitutional rights. This struggle cannot be compared, for example, to the movement for Algerian or Moroccan independence but rather to any possible attempt on the part of the French settlers there to establish their independence from the French motherland in order better to exploit Algeria or Morocco.

LAND EMPIRES AND MARITIME EMPIRES

American thinking about colonialism has been largely influenced by emotional misunderstandings. For obvious reasons the United States felt itself striving for complete political, economic, cultural, and ideological independence from Britain, disregarding the interdependence and affinity existing in all these respects between the two nations which have developed from the same historical roots; the striving for independence led to competition and to over-compensation of existing cultural and political inferiorities by a feeling of moral superiority.

In addition, there exists the wide-spread though unwarranted assumption, which had its origin in the fifteenth century age of discoveries, that empires are established by sea powers, whereas expansion into contiguous land masses does not produce empires or colonialism. The then agrarian empire of Rome looked with contempt upon Carthage's maritime empire. But Rome was an empire too. And the United States in its war against Mexico and in its many wars against the various Indian tribes and nations created an empire as truly as did the sea-faring island states of Britain and Japan. Yet the United States, not considering itself an imperial power—even after 1898 when it occupied Pacific and Caribbean territories and established distant naval bases—applied similar criteria of non-"imperialism" to the military conquests and ruthless expansive policies of Russia and China.

These land empires were never regarded in the same way as the sea empires.

This American attitude was easily shared by the colonial peoples under British, Dutch, or French rule in Asia. It coincided with the reality which confronted them. As a result, these people did not regard Russia, in spite of her immense land conquests in Asia, as an imperial power comparable to the sea empires. Russia seemed in a different category. This feeling was strengthened by the fact that Russia, through her history and her isolation from Europe until the eighteenth century, resembled in its attitude toward authority and government, in its agrarian backwardness, and in the lethargy of its church and its masses, much more the countries of Asia than the dynamic, individualistic, and progressive West.

Russia was the first great "backward" country to be subject to the process of Westernization with its creation of a Westernized intelligentsia, which accepted the Western ideas and tried to apply them in a milieu which was socially and ideologically completely unprepared for it. At the beginning of the twentieth century Russia, like the Asian countries, lived politically under an autocracy and economically through the first stages of an early and under-capitalized capitalism. Thus the Russian Revolution of 1905, against the expectations of Lenin, made no impression among the workers in the West, where the political and economic conditions were totally different from what they had been in 1840. On the other hand, the Russian Revolution of 1905 started a chain reaction of revolutions throughout Asia. Lenin took good note of it.

CAPITALISM AND COLONIALISM

The American view distinguishing between expansion across land masses and across separating waters was now strengthened among Asian intellectuals by the Leninist theory, that imperialism and colonialism were the product of late and over-capitalized capitalism, seeking new outlets. On the one hand, the colonial relationship was regarded as primarily "capitalistic exploitation"; on the other hand a non-capitalistic nation by definition could not be imperialistic or exploiting. Thus, the U.S.S.R., in spite of having subjected so many peoples in Europe and Asia to a process of Russification and absolute control from Moscow, and Communist China, in spite of not liberating Tibet or Sinkiang from its imperial control and trying to restore its control over Korea, Annam, Burma, etc., do not appear as imperialist countries to the Asian nations.

ANTI-COLONIALISM AND POWER STRUGGLE

The issue of anti-colonialism has been used for some time in the international power struggle, and not only by the U.S.S.R. Anti-imperialism and anti-colonialism are widespread among the independent nations of Latin America, which for a long time have seen in the United States the leading imperialist and colonial nations, American imperialism being chiefly though not exclusively "dollar imperialism." Argentina, an independent nation for over a century, very proud of its independence and hardly in danger of imperialist aggression, has used the issue of anti-colonialism as a weapon in her struggle against the United States for leadership at least in the southern and middle parts of the western hemisphere. The United States has used the issue of anti-colonialism in its rivalry with, or dislike of, Britain for very many decades. Now the Soviet Union is using the same issue in her rivalry with, and hatred of, the United States. But there is hardly anything fundamentally new in it except that the Western nations, especially Britain, have by now set many nations in Asia and Africa free, and that it is above all among these nations which are now independent that the issue of anti-colonialism is raised.

IS COLONIALISM A WESTERN "CRIME"?

It is a widespread propaganda slogan that imperialism introduced wars, poverty, racial and economic exploitation to Asia and Africa. That is not the case. Poverty has existed in Asia and Africa since time immemorial, as it existed in Europe until the rise of liberalism and capitalism. Poverty in Asia and Africa was for reasons of climate and temperament greater than in Europe. There has been unremitting warfare in Asia and Africa, as far as historical memory goes; one Asian nation or king enslaved other Asian peoples; African tribes enslaved and exterminated other African tribes. Imperialism is no Western invention. For many centuries Asian tribes and empires have endangered Europe. An accident saved Europe, but not Russia, from Mongol domination in the thirteenth century. As recently as 1683 the Turks were at the gates of Vienna, and Turks and Berbers enslaved Christian Europeans.

Western imperialism has had only a brief day in history. Its sun is now setting, and though this sun has been shining over many injustices and cruelties, in no way worse than the normal cruelties in Asia and Africa, it has brought lasting benefits to Asia and Africa, as the imperialism of Alexander the Great and of the Romans did for their empires, and has awakened and vitalized lethargic civilizations.

Now the tide of Western imperialism is definitely receding, due not so much to external pressure as to Western ideas themselves— but it has been on the whole a period of which the West and especially Britain has not to be ashamed. It would be wrong to apply twentieth century standards and principles of international law to preceding centuries. By doing that—and it should not be forgotten that these new twentieth century standards were developed by the Western world and only by the Western world—the West suffers from a bad conscience; the anti-Western propaganda is exploiting these guilt feelings. The extension of European control into American, Asian, and African lands came not as the result of any peculiar iniquity, but as the result of a sudden great disparity in cultural energy and economic productivity. Today, largely due to Western influence, this disparity is vanishing. A difficult readjustment is due—it will not be helped by any feeling of guilt or need for indemnity.

After 1918 Germany successfully exploited Western guilt feelings about Versailles; this false historical perspective, imposed upon a wrongly contrite West, was one of the main reasons why Hitler rose to power and why the Germans started to threaten the West in their second hegemonial war of the twentieth century. The communists similarly have exploited the West's guilt feelings about many things, not only about colonies, for the last thirty-five years.

COLONIALISM AND NATIONAL INDEPENDENCE

Reduced to its barest outline colonialism is foreign rule imposed upon a nation. Apart from the fact that no nations existed in most cases where colonialism was established, often with the connivance of the colonial peoples themselves, it must be emphasized that this phenomenon of "foreign" rule has nothing to do with *European* control of Asia. Within Europe there has been rule by one people over another, or rather by one government over several peoples, and this has been resented as strongly and often, using the very same words as the anti-colonialists in Asia do today, who have learned their slogans and their tactics from European nationalist movements. This has nothing to do with race or race superiority, one of the most bewildering myths of the present time. Closely related peoples opposed each other; Norwegians against Danes or Swedes, Croatians against Serbs, Slovaks against Czechs, Ukrainians against Russians, Catalans aginst Castilians, etc., and most bitterly resented what they regarded as political dominion, economic exploitation and relegation to a status of inferiority.

Nor will Asian aspirations for independence and conflicts resulting from it be solved by the dissolution of the existing Western empires and their replacement either by nation states or by Asian empires. The recent riots in Bombay in which the Indian police had to intervene in the very same way as under the British Raj and in which the number of victims was apparently greater than in any single riot or uprising against the British Raj since 1857, were caused by the fact that the Maharashtri population found itself or believed itself politically and economically exploited by, and subordinated to, the Gujerati population. It should not be forgotten that it was a Maharashtra who assassinated the Gujerati Gandhi.

The people of southern India, who speak Dravidian languages, of which Tamil is the most important, have formed the Dravida Kazhagam and the Dravida Munnetra Kazhagam (Dravidian Federation and Dravidian Progressive Federation) to prepare their separation from Aryan India. They feel themselves exploited and wish to establish Dravida Nadu (the Dravidian nation). "The social exploitation," one of their leaders writes, "we have endured for so many decades from Brahminism and the decay of our cultural literature due to this force is responsible for our attitude. Not only does Brahminism result in casteism; it has kept us for many a century on the lower rungs of the social ladder. That is why we say that the poisonous teeth of the Brahmin snake must be taken out."

These words only repeat what the Brahmins said—with less justification—against the British. The Indian government will probably suppress any attempt for independence on the part of some of the peoples of India with much greater ferocity than the British ever tried. Nor would it be fair to compare the position of the Negro in the United States to that of the outcasts in India. Though the position of the Negro is by far not yet what it should be, it is infinitely better than that of the Indian Untouchables. In the new Asian nations movements for independence continue: the territorial conflicts between India and Pakistan, between Pakistan and Afghanistan, the independence movements of the Karens in Burma and of the South Moluccans in Indonesia, the division between south and north in the Sudan and in Nigeria—these are some examples of continuing unrest after "imperialism" has gone. The Indian element in East Africa and the Chinese in Southeast Asia may create great hardship for the natives, once imperial protection is removed.

If the anti-colonial issue is brought up, the Western speakers should not put themselves on the defensive, but state the facts as they are. There have been Mongol, Chinese, Indian, Ottoman Empires with their subject peoples as there has been a British Empire. Which was "better" history will tell. Much is bad in many colonies, but much is bad in independent countries too. The British colony of Basutoland is much more progressive and salutary for the natives than the independent Union of South Africa which nevertheless claims Basutoland. British Hongkong is an oasis of order and liberty in the Far East, entirely due to British efforts and ideas. In the case of Cyprus the strategic interests of the Turks and their well-founded fears should be taken as much into consideration as French interests and fears in the Saar. There is no reason to assume that the New Guinean Papuans would fare better under the administration of Indonesian rulers, with whom they have no affinity in race, language, or religion, than under Dutch administration. All that does not mean that all colonial countries or all dependencies, whether in Europe or in other continents, should remain in this status. *Change and reforms are due everywhere.* Some colonial administrations like the French in North Africa and in Madagascar have been bad for the last decade, partly on account of over-centralization and of staffing even the lower echelons of the administration with Frenchmen. The question about the desirability of national independence, of the formation of new nation-states is in no way confined to Asia or Africa. It may well be asked whether the application of the principle of national independence—instead of transformation and reform of supranational empires and political entities—has helped the cause of liberty and peace in Europe. The most important maxim guiding our actions in all parts of the world should be the recognition that gradual reforms are necessary everywhere, that there is no panacea, and that each case must be judged on its own merits, according to its historical setting.

The people of the United States should not only renounce the use of the anti-colonial slogans, they should also give up the vain endeavor of competing in promises and panaceas with the Soviets. The Soviet short cuts for achieving economic well being and social happiness are naturally attractive, and they provide spiritual satisfaction to an intellectual elite which has abandoned its own traditional values and has turned against those of the West. But the Soviet heaven can come only *after* the total revolution which is not reversible. We cannot promise a Utopia like that either for ourselves or for others, and should in all decency stress the fact. Sound progress can come only slowly and by great efforts and self-control. In Asia the moral and social conditions do not exist to make the Asians in any foreseeable future as rich as we are. This fact may be deeply regrettable, but it cannot be attributed to our or to anybody's fault. Yet the only thing which would apparently satisfy the emotional dissatisfaction of some Asian intellectuals seems to be the lowering of American and British standards to theirs. That we cannot do. We are not free because we are rich; it has been our long and hard developing tradition of individual liberty and responsibility which has made it possible for us to become rich.

THE WEST AND NEUTRALISM

Besides Utopian promises the Soviet leaders since Stalin's death play upon the vanity of the non-committed people. Under Stalin, Tito was a Fascist traitor and Gandhi a lackey of British imperialism. Now all that has been changed. The change may be very agreeable to Nehru's and Tito's ears, but it would be a mistake if we tried to compete in that way. We do not wish to force people into the camp of modern Western civilization. We recognize the diversity of human conditions and civilizations and the right of this diversity. We have to be respectful of the civilizations and attitudes of others, but we have also to respect our own traditions and dignity.

Nehru is a neutralist and he has the right to be one. He believes that only in such a way can he build up the Indian leadership in the world to which he looks forward. In addition, Nehru who is *not* a communist, has always been, under the influence of the English Left (the *New Statesman,* Harold Laski, etc.), rather vaguely pro-Soviet and deeply distrustful of American capitalism. He has expressed these opinions clearly in his autobiography published in 1937. He feels that Indian moral superiority as against capitalistic depravity entitles India to world leadership. The second great neutralist leader, not only not a communist but not a socialist intellectual at all, Nasser in Egypt, regards himself as a successor of Mehemet Ali, another Egyptian soldier of fortune and energetic reformer, who wished to renew and regenerate the Arab and Islamic world through Egyptian leadership. The third neutralist leader, Tito, is a communist but one who does not wish to be ruled by Moscow any more than by Washington. Tito believes in Tito first. Again only as a neutralist can he gain, personally and for his country, an influence out of all proportion to his real strength. Americans are shocked at their neutralism. According to American folklore one has only to remove "foreign" rule for the "liberated" peoples to become "democrats" and above all friendly to the United States. The sooner we abandon that mistaken view, the better it will be for our relations with the non-committed areas of the world and for our understanding of the forces and drives behind anti-colonialism.

We should consider the non-committed areas without too much

excitement. We know that Nehru and Tito can afford to be neutralist only because there is a strong Western union under Anglo-American leadership forcing the communists to treat the neutralist nations and leaders with great circumspection. If the West should disintegrate or weaken, Yugoslavia might face the fate of Poland and India that of China. It is Western unity and strength which save the neutralists; it is not the friendliness of the neutralists which will save the West.

SECRET SOURCES OF THE

SUCCESS OF THE

RACIST IDEOLOGY*

Yves R. Simon

[1945]

To UNDERSTAND the extraordinary fortunes of racism, it is necessary first of all to see the paradox in the success of this ideology. Racism has been condemned over and over again by the Church; it has been refuted a thousand times—and without any great difficulty—for never has a theory with scientific pretensions produced such an accumulation of inconsistencies, of manifestly arbitrary affirmations, of fantastic generalizations and of grotesque constructions. In the course of the last few years racism has been guilty of colossal crimes, crimes that must fill with indignation every soul in which there exists the slightest sentiment of justice or of charity. We are today witnessing the defeat of those temporal powers in which it is incarnate. For all that, racism still flourishes, and nothing would be more unwarranted than to say that this plague is in decline.

The Nazis have built up a philosophy in which racism finds a normal place and plays a role of prime importance. This philosophy can be described as a vitalistic and intuitionistic materialism, animated by a great communal passion which plunges its roots into a soil of legends and myths and culminates in an exaltation of individual pride, immeasurably inflated by the exaltation of collective arrogance. Such a philosophy does not need proofs, and laughs at refutations. Pseudo-scientific absurdity erected into a science, gross immorality erected into a system of ethics, find their place in this eruption of unreason. Follies and crimes of every description will find their place in it when those

* This study is a translation by V. M. Hamm of the second chapter of a book entitled *Par delà l'expérience du désespoir* (Editions Parizeum, Montreal, 1945.)

follies and crimes have a chance, because of favorable circumstances, to add impulsive force and cohesion to that great drive in which men enjoy intoxication as a substitute for salvation.

But outside the system of life constructed by the Nazis, racist ideology presents itself as the lucubration of pretentious intellectuals, issuing from cracked heads amidst the fumes of laboratories and the dust of libraries—a thing awkward and artificial, opposed to common sense, and uncongenial to the most natural and common moral feelings. What, in effect, is the essential characteristic of racism? The racist profession of faith is complete the moment one admits that there exists, apart from individual and sociological causes of infamy, a mark of degradation which is properly biological, permanent, transmissible by physical generation, inherent in the chromosomes, independent of all good will and all good conduct, ineffaceable, fatal in the way death is fatal.

By a mark of degradation I mean every stain which renders a man, in the eyes of his fellows, subject to punishments, eventually to capital punishment. A man has a mark of degradation as an individual when he has committed a crime against society; he is branded with a mark of degradation on sociological grounds when he belongs to a society engaged in criminal action and when he himself participates in the criminal action carried out by the group of which he is a member. An individual German soldier and an individual Japanese soldier may be men of good faith; considered as individuals they may be entirely innocent. It is nevertheless legitimate and necessary to strike them down so long as they are belligerents, that is to say, active members of societies engaged in an unjust war. Once taken prisoner they cease to be belligerents, having been snatched from the injustice practiced by their countries and cleansed of the collective infamy which a moment before rendered them worthy of death. We do not demand even that they prove their individual innocence; we want them to be treated the way we want our comrades to be treated if they happen to be made prisoners of war.

This sociological mark of infamy and degradation has, in all times and in all parts of the world, been the occasion for innumerable abuses, for massacres of innocent persons in which ordinary men have shown themselves no less cruel than their ideological leaders. When the common man found justifiable the massacre of entire populations, including newborn infants, the false reason which his perverted conscience avowed was the idea that only death could prevent the members of the guilty society from persisting in those wicked actions to which that society appeared irremediably dedicated. The infamy adduced to justify the extermination of a people was not essentially distinct from the cause which justifies armed resistance to aggression. There was simply a criminal misunderstanding about the application of a general principle.

The idea of a mark of infamy attached to a biological strain, the idea that there exist within the human species certain cursed groups the members of which are culpable because of the blood which they have inherited from their fathers whatever their personal merits or religion or social status may be—this idea has no attraction for the common man: it has an attraction only for a certain school of biologists. Racism in itself has nothing to make it popular.

To account for its popularity many interested persons have not failed to point out the wide diffusion of materialism in contemporary societies. People who have lost the sense of the supernatural vocation of man and the sense of his spiritual dignity, come to accept and finally to find alluring a philosophy which treats man as one treats beasts; that is to say, in terms of biological properties. To throw the blame on materialism is to let one's self off cheaply when one does not profess a materialistic philosophy. But in the case with which we are concerned, this kind of exculpation is a flagrant hypocrisy which should deceive no one. Men who have nourished from the Renaissance to our own times prejudice against Negroes, who have excused, justified, and practiced the slave trade and slavery, were not all materialists; those who today excuse, justify, and practice the most iniquitous discrimination are not all materialists. They were not materialists who unleashed in France the anti-Semitic tempest of the Dreyfus case. In Germany, in France, and in many other countries, Nazi anti-Semitism found the ground prepared. But who would dare to say that the writers, the journalists, the politicians, who prepared the ground, were all, or even a majority of them, materialists?

It is true that the materialists, the naturalists, the vitalists of the Nazi type, are almost alone in making open profession of the racist philosophy. The other racists, especially if they claim to accept the teaching of the Church, reject this philosophy ostentatiously, and go ahead within the shelter of their denials. It is necessary to know what we are talking about when we speak of the success of racist ideology. The days of racism in uniform are numbered. Its defeat is mostly the business of the military operations which are being prosecuted on five fronts. Except in Germany, avowed racists have never been very numerous. But how can any one contest the enormity of the evil accomplished by discreet, moderate, and camouflaged racists, even by perhaps unconscious racists? In one sense they are responsible for the whole evil, for they are the ones who rendered possible the coming into power of the radical racists and the implementing of their principles. It will require more than military victory to finish off the moderate racists. They are everywhere busy among us, from one end of the world to the other, tenaciously working at their task, silent or loquacious according to circumstances, sometimes indiscernible, and sometimes ignorant of the true meaning of their activities. They represent the future of racism. It is they whom we must now strip of power to do harm.

It is necessary to repeat: racism cannot successfully make its biological arguments prevail except in the framework of a group already given over to a materialistic and vitalistic philosophy. It cannot extend its conquests beyond this limited circle except by appealing to motives completely strange to biology, to motives which have nothing specifically racial about them. But it will destroy itself if it admits that the efficacious motives of its influence are borrowed motives, that its popularity is a borrowed popularity. The right way of combatting it is to bring to light the motives which it studiously avoids declaring.

Let us consider in the first place motives of an economic character.

Commutative justice, or what comes to the same thing, equality in the exchange of goods and services, has this unpleasant feature that it makes life hard for everybody, with very few exceptions. It does not suppress inequality of conditions and fortunes, but it tends to confine it within such limits that a man would have to be lucky to escape the rigors of an industrious life and a frugal economy.

In a society where farmers, workers, and domestic servants are constrained to accept the wages and market prices which employers and consumers are willing to grant them, it is enough to have a little money, a small holding, some investments, to enable one to unload on others the most painful and menial tasks. Commodities are cheap, and daily consumption leaves to the small property-holder a margin of revenue sufficient to permit him to have his house kept and his kitchen cared for by hired servants, to get a locksmith to repair his locks and a gardener to look after his garden. So long as working men and women are content with wages that will barely enable them to eat poorly, dress poorly, and provide some slight protection against sickness and premature death, it is not necessary to be rich in order to have a pleasant life; it is enough to have a little property. In these circumstances the class that is freed from menial tasks will be relatively numerous. What would happen if farmers, servants, and workmen obtained wages that would enable them to lower the death-rate in their class to the level of the rate of mortality in the property-owning classes? There is no question here of providing luxuries, but simply of those advantages necessary to prevent children from dying and adults from dying prematurely. Just to prevent children from dying you need a prodigious amount of money. In the end you would get what you have in countries where wages are high: with the exception of rich families, everybody works—all women are housekeepers, all young mothers are nurse-maids, all the men are locksmiths, carpenters, gardeners, scullions, and laborers. It is not at all astonishing, then, that the propertied class and those who aspire to its status are desperately opposed to a process which means for such a large number of its members the end of an easy life.

Now, in order to assure cheap labor it is not enough that the privileged classes control money, administration, the police, education, and industry; it is also necessary that the public conscience, and above all the collective conscience of the privileged classes themselves, accommodate itself to a conception of society which considers extreme poverty on the part of the working classes a normal and even a good thing. The rich, the men of property, the petty bourgeois, are not as hard-hearted as they have been accused of being. In order to enjoy in peace the advantages of cheap labor they have need of an ideology which represents the working classes as men of a subordinate kind, whose sufferings, maladies, and premature death have only secondary importance. The experience of every society shows that such an ideology can very easily be constructed, maintained, hardened, and finally venerated, without any consideration of race entering into it. But wherever it has the slightest chance of appearing, the idea of racial inferiority will make incomparably easier and more effective the efforts of the public conscience to find obvious justification for the advantages of cheap labor.

In order to understand fully the point of insertion and the manner of operation of the feeling of racial inequality, it is fitting to consider the psychology of cheap labor in societies where the question of race does not arise. Western Europe, towards the end of the nineteenth century furnishes an ideal field of observation. The privileged classes then included not only, as in the Old Regime, a rich aristocracy and middle class; it also comprised (I am thinking, above all, of France) a large lower middle class. Wages were in general very low; agricultural products could be bought very cheaply. The diseases—and also the vices—incident to destitution, made enormous ravages among the working population. The privileged were aware of these things, and many of them felt sincere compassion.

Notwithstanding, the system still continues to function and will not be seriously impaired until the combined forces of labor organizations and political democracy improve the conditions of the worker. Then, and only then, will the collective conscience of the privileged classes be open to the idea of just wages and a just price. Until the day that this process of education by force is accomplished, the ideas of just wages and just price will be ineffective. Yet, these ideas will not be absent entirely. The good bourgeois mother who provides medicines for the sick children of her housekeeper can with difficulty avoid the thought at times that a wage which does not give sober and honest people the means necessary to rear their children is not a just wage. But the housekeeper, granted alms for her sick children and finally an extra allowance for funeral expenses, can hardly hope for a substantial increase of salary. For such an increase to be substantial it would be necessary in many cases that the wages be doubled or tripled, and that would mean, for the middle class family, the end of ease: no more oriental rugs, no more boxes at the theatre, no more private tutors, no more elaborate parties and receptions, and above all no more money to invest regularly. Either the employee will live in misery, or the employer will learn to know the meaning of a hard life. The second part of the alternative is evidently impossible; the first alternative must be in conformity with reason, nature, and justice.

We who have, without any merit on our part, shared in the recent progress of the social conscience, do not find the second alternative impossible. That a great number of people should know the meaning of a hard life so that a greater number of people may escape a miserable life, appears to us altogether natural, and we accept with good will our share of servile work. We wonder, indeed, how it has ever been possible for people who were otherwise just and charitable to enjoy in peace a system of cheap labor which assured them an easy life only by denying to working men the possibility of a normal life. So manifest and cruel a rupture of the balance of exchanges would have troubled consciences had it not been skillfully disguised. In order not to be exceedingly unhappy the conscience of the propertied classes had to fabricate a system of screens or blinds. This is the interesting point: what is the spiritual outlook, the judicious construction, the consistent fiction, that permits society to enjoy without remorse the advantages of a false balance of exchange?

Léon Bloy accused Paul Bourget of having written that the poor suffer less than the rich because they have less refined souls. He gave no reference. We have no time to run through the complete works of Paul Bourget in order to verify the exactitude of the citation, and we have little confidence in a reference from memory made by Léon Bloy. What is the difference? If the quotation is not exact, it ought to be. It sums up with remarkable precision a postulate which operates every time that a society of privileged persons sanctions the quest for cheap labor. According to this postulate, which is the more efficacious as it is the more confused, society naturally divides itself into two categories: there are the people who have refined souls, and the others who have not. If the values exchanged between the one and the other are unequal, this exchange, in spite of appearances, remains equitable, since the less refined, in receiving much less than he gives, receives all that he needs. Is not the exchange of glass trinkets for gold perfectly equitable if he who gives the gold desires nothing but trinkets? Similarly, to exchange the advantages of an easy life for the simple maintenance of a life of bare subsistence will seem to be an honest operation if we suppose that our customer is destined by nature to lead a miserable existence. That existence is good enough for him since nature has not assigned him a better. Is it not a fact that many people who are badly paid, badly fed, and badly clothed appear to be overflowing with gaiety and satisfied with their lot?

Such are the arguments which privileged people in all ages use to justify the employment of cheap labor. As long as the question of race does not raise itself, these arguments form an imperfect screen, and no matter how slightly the force of tradition may be relaxed, the truth has a chance of coming through. Everything becomes much easier and more certain when a difference of race, real or supposed, traces a line of obvious demarcation between the refined and the vulgar, the civilized and the barbarian. There is no doubt that the Prussian Junker feels much more at ease in his relations with the Polish peasant than in his relations with the Prussian peasant. Too often the white employer feels himself altogether at ease with the black workingman. To falsify the accounts with an easy conscience, we should imagine that our fellow does not belong to the human species, that between him and us there is no unity of nature and no common brotherhood. Even under its most discreet forms racism does us the inestimable service of bringing us near to this ideal. This ideal is completely attained and even surpassed by the radical forms of the racist philosophy: the screen has become altogether opaque when one admits, according to the celebrated formula of the Nazis, that there is less distance between men of an inferior race and animals than there is between men of a superior race and men of an inferior. If a Negro has the incontestable right to make use of a beast of burden, a white man has the even more incontestable right to make use of a Negro without furnishing him other compensation than the pittance necessary to retain his services. These shocking propositions derive logically from the principle admitted when one has granted that, independently of all consideration of race, one part of society has the absolute right of escaping from a hard life and that this right is valid even if it involves as an inevitable concomitant a reward for labor that is insufficient for the bare necessities of life.

The quest for cheap labor does not favor the racist ideology except in the propertied and controlling classes. But racism excels in exploiting another economic motive the attractions of which are particularly great because they exercise themselves on all classes and all social categories. To soften the rigors of competition by eliminating those competitors for whom we feel no sympathy and so to reserve the monopoly of the market to the group which we call "ours" by excluding those groups which we consider alien, provides a motive which has without doubt contributed more than any other to make racism popular in our age. Like the motive analyzed earlier, it does not involve any necessary connection with the idea of race; we see it at work in circumstances where the problem of race does not arise.

But the idea of a distinction of races considerably facilitates its functioning by providing an easy way of tracing a line of separation that will be clearly recognizable, between what is ours and what is alien. Lawyers short of cases, doctors short of patients, bankers embarrassed in their operations by the great number of banks, business men who would like to increase their volume of business, professors who covet positions for which there is a surplus of candidates, workers who are experiencing or are threatened with unemployment, civil servants anxious for advancement, politicians in quest of votes, would like it if there were less lawyers, less doctors, less bankers, and so on, on the market. It has long been noted as one of the sorrows of military life that the death of a comrade has the advantage that it creates a chance of advancement. Lawyers, bankers, professors, and the like—all these poor fellows exhausted by the competition which keeps them breathless and prevents them from enjoying life start to dream from time to time, especially in periods of economic depression, of selective epidemics or, what is more practical, of drastic purges which would cleanse the field by relieving them of their most annoying competitors. The important thing is to find a criterion on which one can agree for distinguishing the undesirable who are to be excluded, and the desirable who are to be protected, without submitting oneself to the menace of the operation proposed. A doctor cannot permit himself to declare, without more precision, that it is indispensable to refuse a certain number of doctors the right to exercise the medical profession: he must be able to designate, without any possible ambiguity, a group to which he does not himself belong.

The criterion varies with circumstances: sometimes it is nationality, sometimes it is religion, sometimes social origin, sometimes political affiliation, and sometimes race. Measures of exclusion sometimes take the form of an unofficial boycott, sometimes of a boycott officially organized by private groups, sometimes of legislative action; sometimes they go to the extreme of extermination. It would be superfluous to cite examples which are present memories.

The cleansing of a field or market by the elimination of undesirable races generally needs no further justification than an appeal to the egoism of the majority, or of a powerful minority, if the power is in the hands of a minority. Nevertheless, it is always preferable to fortify oneself with an argument which will move people of moral excellence to whom egoistic considerations might appear indecent. This argument is furnished by the fact that so-called racial groups often have a tendency to invade certain professions to the point of exercising a virtual monopoly, a fact that can easily be exaggerated. Thus, in all countries containing large Jewish populations, it is true that there is a strong proportion of Jews among lawyers, bankers, actors, shopkeepers, theatrical people, journalists, and professors of philosophy. Now, if the Jewish population does not constitute more than .7% of the total population, a majority or a strong minority of Jews in a profession is represented as an imbalance harmful to the general interest. Thus the cleansing of the market which is to the advantage of doctors without clients and lawyers without cases easily passes for a measure of public welfare. This begins by a *numerus clausus*. We know today how it ends.

If the principle of the closed number is to have the slightest appearance of justification, it is evidently necessary to suppose that the members of the "race" to which it is applied form a group which has internal unity and is at the same time separated from the rest of the community. If these two conditions are realized, the invasion of a profession by a "race" ends by placing in the hands of a group which is unintegrated or poorly integrated, a power which threatens to play the role of a force of disintegration. The whole argument rests on the notion that the members of the race in question are incapable of integration, or as one says ordinarily, of assimilation.

Let us accept the principle, in order to see what happens when we develop its consequences. If the *numerus clausus* is justified in the case of the Jews, by reason of their pretended unassimilability, logic and honesty demand that there be a *numerus clausus* for every group which persistently preserves its identity within a community and refuses to allow itself to be assimilated. Thereupon we see the *numerus clausus* multiplying. Even in nations whose unity is ancient and who present a degree of integration never surpassed, certain professions are invaded by definite groups conscious of their distinction. The mutual aid which is practiced within these groups is never without certain dangers, of which the most evident is the tendency to exclusiveness which inevitably accompanies it. Is it necessary to establish a *numerus clausus* for each of these groups? Now, in a country like France, it would be necessary to limit the number of Bretons in the navy, the number of Corsicans in the police force, the number of reactionary professors on law faculties, the number of sons of noble families in the colleges of the Jesuits, the number of doctors' sons in the medical profession, the number of country squires in the diplomatic service, and so on.

In societies of more recent foundation and till recently open to extensive immigration, like the United States, the principle of the closed number would find more obvious, more numerous, and more voluminous applications. One could no doubt apply the principle to Jews in the motion picture industry, in banking, and in small business. But logic would demand that, on the other hand, Germans be limited in breweries, Catholics in municipal administration, Poles in symphony orchestras, Irishmen in fire departments and police forces, and whites in well-paying jobs of all sorts. And what of the Church? Gallicans and other nationalists have long demanded a form of *numerus clausus* for Italians in the college of cardinals and in the succession to the Holy See. (If they dared, they would reproach Our Lord for not having limited the number of Jews in the Body of the Apostles.)

With the logical application of the principle of the closed number we should see a savage conflict shaping itself: a merciless war between hardened and irreconcilable groups, a maniacal discord which no community could withstand. But it has never been a question of applying this principle logically, honestly, and consistently. I believe, with Pascal, in the sincerity of witnesses who allow themselves to be martyred; I shall believe in the sincerity of the partisans of the *numerus clausus* when they demand that their principle be applied with a rigor fatal to their own interests. Until we see white workers demanding a limit on the number of white workers in well-paid positions, we shall refuse to believe that the advocates of the *numerus clausus* are really interested in the common good and in the harmonious distribution of the various parts of the community.

As we have already said, the desire to reduce competition has succeeded in making racism popular in certain proletarian groups; powerful labor organizations in South Africa, in Australia, in the United States, have practiced, in varying degrees, a policy of racial discrimination. It is necessary to insist on the extreme gravity of these facts, and on the particular importance of all action designed to protect the working classes against and to deliver them from the infection of racist ideas. We believe, indeed, that every social class, and more generally every section of society, has the historic mission of promoting a certain moral idea, a certain aspect of public morality. Thus the body of magistrates has the mission of maintaining and increasing the sentiment and the value of relations legally defined, and the respect for legal forms; professional soldiers have the mission of preserving and if need be, arousing the interest of the nation in national defense. If property-holders relaxed their energies in affirming the principle of property, by whom would this principle be maintained? If the ruling class lost its faith in the principle of authority, the sense of authority would soon be compromised in society as a whole. It demands, perhaps, a little more attention and historical knowledge to understand the great role which the working class plays in the preservation and promotion of the idea of equal justice for all. It is not by accident that the modern labor movement, even when it refrained from substituting the class struggle for the struggle of nations, has spontaneously organized itself on an international plan. The concerted action of men without property who are constantly menaced—should their solidarity be relaxed —by the imperialism of the better provided classes, the labor movement is the natural ally of all those whom the accident of social relations particularly exposes to the forces of exploitation. A union which refuses to accept Negro workers and demands measures of discrimination against them transforms itself into a society of exploitation and gives the lie to its very fundamental idea; most efficaciously it works for the coming of an era when the whites themselves will no longer have the right to organize and make the principle of equal justice for all work to their own advantage.

Today racism is everywhere at work. No part of our society escapes its ravages. The fight against racism is, therefore, among all groups and in all places an enterprise of extreme urgency. Yet there is an order in this urgency. Most pressing of all is the task of purifying of all racist influence those groups charged with the duty of teaching true ethics. Second place must be given to anti-racist action in the world of organized labor. If racism should establish itself on a large scale and as a permanent feature in the practice of unions, it would have an excellent opportunity of penetrating into the morals of society as a whole and of holding in check, for an indefinite period, the forces of justice and of charity.

The popularizers of Marxism have given currency to the idea that all social and international conflicts can be explained by the play of economic rivalries. This over-simplification of the problem has served only to produce deception and confusion. One would like to believe, for example, that circumstances permitting all workers to get remunerative employment would lead at once to a cessation of conflict between white and Negro labor. The experience of several industrial centers in the United States during the present war has demonstrated that a demand for great masses of labor at exceptionally high wages can very well coincide with an exasperation of the struggle between races. This does not prove that these conflicts have nothing to do with the facts of competition; it simply proves that the factor of economic competition is not the only one at issue, and that the circumstances which decrease the intensity of this factor, and of all other economic factors as well, can favor the play of certain uneconomic factors too.

A large demand for labor on the industrial market often provokes an influx of workers belonging to a race considered inferior. These workers risk the chance of being very unwelcome. Is there a fear that they are going to be definitely established and that they will some day offer strong competition? Possibly there is something to this, but much stronger than the fear of future difficulties is the irritation of the so-called superior race of being jostled by the inferior. We are here touching on a motive which cannot be reduced to economic grounds, even though it may often be associated with economics: the desire for aristocratic distinction.

Nothing is more universally human than the need to feel oneself a member of a community of distinguished people, of an elite. We want the distinction we seek to be easily recognizable, permanent, and transcending our own petty existence; we want it to be attributable to our fathers and transmissible to our children, participated in by our kinsmen and relations. There are many notes of aristocratic distinction: they are not all equally accessible. It is not possible for every one to bear a name rendered illustrious by glorious ancestors and to be received into the society of grand dukes and peers; to possess the money necessary to defray the expenses of conspicuous consumption which displays with brilliance the distance between those blessed by fortune and simple mortals; to excel in intellectual pursuits and take one's place in the pedantic circle of the age's luminaries; to participate in the functions of high society; to dress elegantly, eat, talk, and behave according to the best usage, to speak correctly a language, to have one's children educated in schools notorious for their snobbishness. There is, however, a mark of obvious, permanent, and transmissible aristocratic distinction which is open to all—I mean to all those who have taken the trouble to be born on the right side of the line of demarcation between the races. Not to be a Negro, not to be a Jew, these are aristocratic distinctions which one can possess without having noble ancestors, or fortune, or education, or power, or good manners. The only thing one has to do is to think about it. The superior race is an aristocracy like any other. Racism is the consciousness of this aristocracy.

Reared as I myself have been in a middle-class environment where aristocratic pretensions abounded, and where the feeling of class-differences was extremely marked—to tell the truth, it invaded the whole of life—I have often been struck by the analogies existing between race prejudice as it appears in the United States and the class prejudices of old Europe. The European traveller, especially if he is a Frenchman of liberal stripe, becomes indignant when he observes the segregation occasionally imposed on Negroes in America. In his virtuous indignation he forgets that many analogous measures are currently applied in Europe to the proletariat and the peasantry. In all railway stations of any importance in France there are two waiting rooms, one for travellers of the first and second classes, the other for travellers of the third class. Is the reason for this division that the former should have a degree of comfort proportionate to the price of their tickets?

The main reason is that they should be spared the company of the common people who travel third class. In order to avoid this company many of the lower middle class, in spite of their poverty, go to the expense of buying a second class ticket. This is very much like the separation of whites and Negroes in the railways and waiting rooms of the Southern States. In churches attended by whites, even in the Northern States, colored people would be looked at askance if they sat in the front seats. I think of my own native parish in France, and I imagine a working-class family installing itself in the transept at High Mass in the midst of the notables of the town: such a scandal would not occur twice, and I doubt seriously if it has ever occurred. In the Northern town where I live now the public schools are open to all children without distinction of color; this is not to everyone's taste. I know quite well some fathers who would look with horror on the possibility of their son sitting next to a little Negro boy in school. I have known these people for a long time; I knew them in France fifteen years ago, when the middle-class, conscious of its dignity, revolted against laws destined to facilitate the entry of children "of the people" in the *lycées*. In many cities of the United States the settlement of Negro families in a certain district causes the value of real estate to drop: this reminds me of the importance which the French bourgeoisie attached to living in a quarter that was "well inhabited," that is, inhabited by bourgeois families. Interracial marriage is the nightmare of white families. Now, in the upper middle-class in Europe a man who marries a workingman's daughter is very much looked down upon. In American society where, in spite of the sharpness of the conflicts of labor, the feeling of class differences is incomparably less widespread, less keen, and less pervasive than in the old societies of Europe, racial consciousness is often nothing but the substitute for a non-existent class consciousness.

Provided we are personally indifferent to the desire for aristocratic distinction, we shall be strongly tempted to attribute all the abuses to which this feeling gives rise to pride and stupidity. But this would argue a superficial and sterile psychology. Pride is everywhere present in man, yet in order to increase our chances of limiting its obnoxious results, it is very important to recognize the nature of the legitimate, or at least excusable, tendencies which it perverts by exploiting them. Perhaps we should say that the need of belonging to a distinguished group proceeds from the overpowering sense of our misery, and that the role of pride often consists in relieving us, by fraudulent means, of a burden of suffering which we would bear more willingly if we clearly knew what is involved. But these things take place in the propitious shadow of a conscience which has been obscured by anguish.

Nothing is more insupportable to man than loneliness, and of all forms of loneliness the most painful is that which we feel in the midst of our fellows. There is something enraging about the feeling of loneliness when one is living in the midst of men—especially if one has to endure the hardships of a complicated social life: innumerable laws, regulations, conventions, and usages, submission to bureaucratic formalities, the payment of taxes, and all sorts of sacrifices. To be an individual lost in a mass, in an organism so large that all its parts remain strange to us, to work with numerous people, for oneself and for them, to suffer with them and at their hands and never to have the joy of saying "we," that is an intolerable ordeal. It is generally admitted, with reason no doubt, that this ordeal is much more frequent and much more painful in contemporary societies than it was in the societies of the past which were less voluminous, less mobile, less centralized, less regimented, and more differentiated. To escape from loneliness we seek differentiation and distinction, and in this anxious search we take what we can find. The big thing is to be *somebody,* to belong to a group which does not comprise everybody—such a group would leave me lonely—which would gather round me people who are like me and unlike others, tracing around me a very distinct circle so restricted that I can see and touch its limits. This would allow me to feel that a society lives in me. It is necessary, moreover, that this salutary incorporation present guarantees of permanence, so as to prevent the threat of a fall back into loneliness. All will be for the best if my membership in a differentiated and distinguished group precedes my existence in that of my forefathers and survives it in that of my descendants. However little pride intervenes here, all the abuses of the aristocratic conscience inevitably follow. The myth-making faculty of the group brings to birth in the spirit of everyone arrogant images big with all the desires for exploitation which the human heart can conceive. Thus the distinguished group which saves me from loneliness becomes a chosen group, a race of masters to whom everything is permitted: titled nobility, nation, white race, Aryan race, Nordic race, or even, as in the days of the Russian Revolution, the proletarian class, bearer of the hopes of humanity, incarnation of the genius of history.

If it is true that the search for aristocratic distinction is related to the intolerable sufferings which man undergoes when he feels himself alone and deprived of community life in the midst of his fellows, it is logical to think that the greater the evil of solitude the more imperious, general, and ready to yield to vulgar satisfaction will the desire of aristocratic distinction show itself to be. Indeed, to find a source of comfort in the sentiment of belonging to a community of men whose only merit is that they are neither Negroes nor Jews, one must be singularly in need of community life. It is not by accident that racial passions have undergone an unprecedented development in the age of masses and of mass despair. A man must be without a home, without a village, without a province, without a church, without a country, without faith, and without hope; a man must feel in his heart a deathlike loneliness, in order to have the idea of seeking a refuge in the fictitious community of a sub-species of animals distinguished by highly doubtful biological properties. A man must have the soul of a poor fellow indeed, to feel proud of belonging to an aristocracy open to every scoundrel.

At this precise moment of our inquiry, contemporary racism with its unheard-of scope, its logic, its cynicism, its bestial cruelty, takes on the aspect of a convulsion brutally agitating a society that has been exhausted by a long process of atomization. To reverse the movement which has produced this disintegration so often observed in modern societies, to promote the institutions best fitted to multiply centers of community life—this would undoubtedly be a line of action capable of contributing to the decline of racism and also of protecting our societies against other products of mass despair.

When we consider racism as the consciousness of a cheap aristocracy we can easily understand how this ideology has had particular success in that fraction of modern society in which aristocratic pretensions are over-sensitive, that is to say, in the lower middle class. By the very fact that it finds itself in the immediate vicinity of the working class, the lower middle class experiences—more vividly than any other part of society—the need of affirming its distinction and superiority. The social structure has placed it along an uncertain and fluctuating frontier: to maintain this frontier is for it a vital necessity and at the same time a difficult task. Putting even the best face on it, its titles to distinction are not brilliant. It has no ancestry, or if it should have, the memory of it serves only to provoke resentment by producing a feeling of debasement; it has not much money, perhaps even less than its neighbors of the working class; it has only a minimum of culture and good manners, and the vanity which it feels in these things is open to ridicule; it makes great sacrifices to preserve the external signs of its dignity: lodgings relatively costly, domestics, neat clothes, and the like; the least additional title of distinction would be very welcome, especially if it were clearly defined and permanent.

The great economic changes of the last thirty years have made the situation of the lower middle class more precarious than ever and have intensified its insecurity. At the very moment when the spirit of conquest of the lower classes was affirming itself with growing audacity, important sections of the lower middle class lost their last economic means of distinction and slipped down into the proletariat without other hope than to provide an elite of the masses. Under these conditions the aristocratic sense of the lower middle class was admirably prepared for the seduction of racist propaganda. To these desperate people, who had the feeling of losing everything when they lost their frontier, racism meant that everything was not lost: another frontier, to which only mediocre importance had been attached hitherto, became all at once the great line of division, the only one which really mattered in the eyes of the new society. This was the frontier of races. Irritated at being elbowed by the working man, the lower middle class man, or the ex-lower middle class man, received in compensation the privilege of racial distinction, which did not cost him very much and which no one could take away from him. Passing by the yellow benches reserved for Jews in the public parks, the petty bourgeois blessed the destiny which had spared him the misfortune to be born of an impure race. While despair led more and more members of that impure race to suicide this class enjoyed the consciousness of its racial purity: henceforth it was race that condemned men to despair. The man who the year before had thought of taking poison, could again take heart.

It is necessary here to complete what we said at the beginning of this study about the paradoxical character of the success which racist ideology has had with ordinary people who are indifferent to the metaphysics of the biologists. As we said before, the idea of a mark of deterioration which is neither personal nor sociological, but biological, is strange to the ordinary man; nevertheless there exists a way of making him accept it in a confused fashion, and this way is precisely the exaltation of his aristocratic feeling. It has often been observed that the idea of heredity, before it was cultivated, with or without moderation, by scientists and philosophers, had constantly been cultivated without any moderation by aristocracies. This is easily understandable. Let us remark once more that aristocratic distinction seeks permanence and demands titles which transcend in every way the dimensions of individual existence. Any distinction which could not be transmitted from generation to generation would leave it unsatisfied.

Now there are two possible ways of conceiving the transmission of any excellence from generation to generation. It can be thought of as above all a matter of education, tradition, example, and imitation —a hypothesis that is not very reassuring. In order to maintain the excellence of the lineage it would be necessary to begin anew with each generation the laborious task of raising the young man above the common level; moreover, the result would remain doubtful, for it is not at all certain that my son would allow himself to be influenced by the good example and the virtuous instruction of his father. It is much more comforting to imagine that aristocratic distinction transmits itself through the blood, that a biological fatality forces it to perpetuate itself and assures its permanence in spite of the frequent failure of education. Here as elsewhere the tendency to materialism identifies itself with the tendency to follow the line of least resistance. Every aristocracy is tempted to construct a materialistic and racist conception of its destiny. In order not to succumb to such a temptation it would have to accept all the rigors of a heroic conception of human greatness; it would have to admit that there is no royal road out of the misery of our condition, that all excellence is transitory and cannot be perpetuated except by being perpetually reconquered. The materialistic imagination, in order to sustain what we find excellent in ourselves, invents principles of permanence, independent of what is not human in man, and thus arranges matters less expensively. To feel the seductions of the materialistic imagination it is not necessary to have been indoctrinated by philosophers; it is enough to be a man and to have common sense. For if it is true that common sense "in so far as it is natural, that is to say, in conformity with the essential inclinations of our intelligence, is naturally right, flexible, and intuitive," it is equally certain that common sense, in so far as it is "exposed to the ordinary dangers which threaten our intellect, has a certain natural propensity to stupidity, to materialism, to incomprehension of the spiritual." For the ordinary man to be interested in racism, it is enough to make a skillful appeal to the stupidity of common sense.

The proscription of the Jews changed profoundly when it ceased, rather recently, to be a religious matter, and became a racial issue. Nevertheless, in changing its principle, anti-Semitism has continued to benefit by many of the psychological dispositions which contributed to its force in the past. Among these dispositions a place apart belongs to the complex of beliefs and passions which compose *the psychology of accursed groups.* An accursed group may be a religious group, an ideological group, a racial group, a social group, or a national group. The following are, as far as we can make out, the essential properties of an accursed group: 1) there is involved a rather small and clearly defined minority; 2) rightly or wrongly, there is attributed to this minority an exceptional importance; there is ascribed to it the power of exercising a decisive influence on the destiny of the majority; 3) it is held for certain that this minority is perfectly unified, that all its actions are deliberate and concerted, that it acts like a single man. Much is made of the contrast apparently existing between its perfect unity and the lack of unity in the majority; 4) finally, the accursed group is enveloped in mystery. Its unity is assured by certain elusive persons who are generally anonymous. Because of this mystery, legends multiply about it and from time to time sensational revelations are made. An illustration at once typical and comic, of the psychology of accursed groups, is furnished by the adventure of Leo Taxil. Towards the end of the last century an individual answering to this pseudonym, notorious because of his anticlerical, pornographic and blasphemous publications

(*La Bible amusante, Les amours secrètes de Pie IX*, etc.) underwent at Paris a remarkable "conversion," and undertook, by means of a new series of publications, to open the eyes of Catholics to the activities of the Freemasons (*Les assassinats maçonniques, Les soeurs maçonnes*, etc.). He had enormous success. A priest has told me that he was called a "liberal" because he had refused to believe, on the word of Leo Taxil, that there was at Gibraltar a lodge where the devil appeared in person and played the piano with his tail. Then one fine day Leo Taxil gathered a large audience in order to reveal the best of his secrets: all his revelations were nothing but an imposture intended to demonstrate how far the stupidity of his readers could go. Note well that this happened in Paris, by general consent the most keen-witted city in the world.

The Christians of the first centuries formed an accursed group. In our day, the most famous accursed groups are the Jesuits, the Freemasons, and the Jews. One might also include the Trotskyites.

Whatever the truth of the accusations of which they are the object, an accursed group renders many services, and it is good, prudent, and comfortable, always to have one at hand.

The accursed group renders intelligible many events which, without its intervention, would confound the mind by the mystery of their contingency. We are here dealing with a particular case of the psychology of chance. Philosophers have often remarked that every chance event consists in the intersection of causal lines independent of one another. If it happens, for example, that a man discovers a treasure while he is digging a ditch, one says that this discovery is the result of chance, because there is no connection between the series of causes which led the unknown ancestor to conceal his treasure on this spot and the series of causes which led the digger to make a ditch in the same place. At the centre of the chance event there is an irreducible plurality; chance is unintelligible because unity alone is intelligible.

Now it is supremely unpleasant to remain without explanation in the face of a fact that imposes itself on our interest. That is why all human thought, philosophic, scientific, and vulgar, feels the constant temptation to deny the reality of chance by supposing the existence, beyond the manifest multiplicity of causes and effects, of principles of unity which render fortuitous coincidences intelligible. If a villager finds a treasure while digging a ditch, the entire village will be induced to believe that the villager was advised of the existence of the treasure and of its location. Philosophers who reject the notion of chance and appeal to "universal necessity," scientists who reject the same notion and affirm a "rigorous determinism," are yielding to the same tendency which makes the gossips of the village chatter. Similarly, it is the belief in a principle of unity and finality hidden under the appearances of chance which permits the liberal economist to think that the spontaneous play of economic atoms will infallibly produce the greatest good of the greatest number. And it is the same belief that renders the mind of the gambler impenetrable to the lessons of experience and of the calculus of probabilities: whatever you may tell him, he remains persuaded that he can draw profit from it. He believes in his run of luck. This gambler's "run" is an odd sort of demon, subject to fits of humor, but a good fellow, all things considered, who operates secretly in the series, apparently orderless, of lucky and unlucky plays, re-establishes order, and gives the lie to the calculus of probabilities in favor of his protégé.

Harnessed to the heavy task of making our way across the accidents of history, disconcerted at every instant by the incomprehensible rigors of fortune, what relief shall we not feel if we can imagine that all our misfortunes, or at least the principal ones, arise from a single intelligent cause which is faithful to its evil designs, a kind of inverted providence, a diabolic providence? This cause must be a relatively small minority: otherwise it could not accomplish this marvel of unity and purpose. Furthermore, it must work secretly: otherwise the majority would not permit it to perpetrate so much mischief. The high cost of living, crushing taxes, ruinous competition, difficulties of advancement, political crises, strikes, riots, wars: the simplest method of standing up against the mystery of all these accidents without losing one's reason is to recognize everywhere, without bothering too much about evidence, the hand of the Jesuits, the concerted action of the Jews, the sinister plans of the Trotskyites, and so on.

To satisfy the mind so simply and cheaply does not trouble those who cannot secure any greater satisfaction in these matters. Since the amelioration of our lot is the chief concern in this business, the notion of the accursed group promises dazzling possibilities. Thanks to this notion, we can hope in a confused way one day to free ourselves from the grim cares of a perpetual conflict against the many difficulties of life. Our difficulties are numerous only in appearance, since they all come from the same cause. There is no reason why they should be perpetual, since it is only necessary to destroy their unique cause in order to put an end to them. Thanks to the accursed group, the exalting vision of a Herculean achievement, or a Napoleonic battle replaces in our minds the unattractive image of an endless strife. All the heads of the Hydra will fall at one fell swoop; the entire coalition will be sent packing in one night and will never re-form again. Order will be established for ever and we shall, at last, be able to start enjoying life. The psychology of accursed groups thrives on utopian optimism.

Finally, the accursed group serves to confine within reasonable limits the horror of the human condition, and especially to keep that horror at a respectable distance from our own persons. We encounter here one of the deepest problems of the psychology of evil. Very few people dare to hold consistently an optimistic conception of the human will; there would be too much risk of passing for an imbecile if one showed oneself unaware of the immensity of evil and the scarcity of good in human nature. The most optimistic people, those temperamentally and systematically so, have the habit of directing attention to certain great agents of corruption, clearly defined, which they hold responsible for the discrepancy between that good humanity which their philosophy expects to find in reality and that bad humanity which the history of all ages reveals. Thus, according to the optimistic anarchist, the state and property are the true and only causes of dishonesty, murder, and evil passions in general; for the devotee of the philosophy of enlightenment, it is ignorance; for the romantic agrarian, it is city life, with its machinery and its newspapers. These folk pass their time discussing the evils of the machine, of obscurantism, of property, and of the state; thanks to this artifice they avoid passing for nit-wits, while at the same time they preserve for themselves the intimate joys of an optimistic conception of human destiny. In an age like ours, which has suffered so many disillusions, it is more necessary than ever to speak the language of pessimism; parties and schools—especially literary schools—outdo one another in pessimistic phraseology. The conservatives had to distinguish themselves in this competition, for it is generally admitted that progressive and revolutionary ideas are bound up with a naive belief in the imminent triumph of the forces which will make life happy and beautiful.

Nevertheless, in the midst of this debauch of pessimism, in the midst of all these black and gloomy pictures of human misfortune, every one is careful to preserve around himself a privileged circle in which the good is supposed greatly to outweigh the evil. Decent people, respectable and right-thinking people, people like you and me, who have never been accessory to the murder of a banker or played cards with a crook, cultivate with particular care this garden of illusions where they find a refuge against the excessive miseries of the human condition. To maintain their circle they are ready to deny many truths. This is no doubt the reason that people of means often become the best instruments of deception. They are not always as culpable as one may be tempted to think; their weakness and timidity are more to blame than actual perversity. Indeed, it takes great strength of mind and strong nerves to live without protective screens among men and amidst the infernal powers which lurk in our hearts. The respectable man is afraid he will be struck dead if crime and horror should dare show their faces within two feet of him, if he should ever see blood on hands he loves to clasp, to say nothing of his own hands. To suppress the distance between the fact of evil and our conscience would be to expose ourselves to a frightful crisis capable of making us fall into despair and losing our reason, if we are not possessed of a hope stronger than all the world.

It is therefore easy to understand why we neglect no precaution in order to preserve that circle of decent existence in which we want to pass our days. It is a complicated business, not to be managed in our time without great subtlety. In the days when an optimistic philosophy of human nature and of history prevailed in the public mind, in the good old days of enthusiastic rationalism, many people could, in considering their situation in space and time, feel themselves at a sufficient distance from those horrors which respectable people do not like to see too close at hand. Mass executions, refined torments, the proscription of the best citizens, general insecurity, highway robbers, poisoning and dagger blows, secret dungeons and feuds, enslavement, the deportation of peaceful populations, judgments without appeal and taxes without control, all these horrors seemed very remote to the bourgeoisie of the West in the nineteenth century. That class at that time vaguely referred such things to antiquity, also, and more insistently to the Middle Ages, to the Renaissance and the darkness of the Old Regime, to backward places whither civilization had not yet penetrated: Siberia, Turkey, China, Ethiopia, Equatorial Africa, or the Pacific Islands. When it thought of these things, its dominant feeling was one of happiness in belonging to a civilized society with a police force to protect property, a parliament to adjust taxes, and courts to make the rights of the miller of Sans Souci prevail against the might of the king of Prussia.

These good old days ended in the month of August, 1914. Then the Western world began to understand that the civilization of which it had been so proud formed a very precarious guarantee against that which is infernal in the heart of man. Those soldiers who burned towns, massacred populations, killed the wounded and prisoners, tortured the vanquished, were men like us; we had associated with them only lately when they wore civilian clothes much like our own, when they earned a livelihood for their families as we did for our own, were interested in Greek and Latin poetry, in music, and in the beauties of the earth. Thus we had been deceived; we had not known how to recognize the monster under its civilized form. All the Western world was seized with a paroxysm of insecurity. Then came the Russian revolution and the great convulsions of the post-war years, the years of economic depression, the years before this war! It became more and more imperative to retrace the frontiers of our circle of decent existence while taking into account factors alien to space and time. Horror swarmed in our very midst.

Who does not see that such circumstances create conditions exceptionally favorable to the psychology of accursed groups? Since space and time in the final analysis play no part here, it is necessary to drive back into groups clearly recognizable and not very numerous that terrifying evil whose proximity we dread and whose traces we secretly fear to discover in our own souls. We insist on this point: the groups in question must not be numerous; a handful of men would offer an ideal solution. If they were of large dimensions I should fear lest they contained individuals close to me and might finally engulf me too. (In the Germany of Hitler and the France of Pétain it takes a minimum of three Jewish grandparents to make one a Jew. If one or two had been sufficient there would be too many Jews among the Nazis, their partisans and imitators, and no one would any longer feel secure against the unforeseeable expansion of the accursed group.) In defining these groups one will make use of ideological, political, social, and racial criteria. When a man finds himself in a situation so distressing as that described above, he cannot afford to be too exacting; he takes what he can find.

Several months after the beginning of the Spanish War, a famous French historian gave a speech entitled "How crime becomes possible." The speaker suggested a parallel between the massacres of September 1792 and the great massacre of priests recently perpetrated in Spain. Both cases called for an explanation of how it could happen that people should suddenly pass from "extreme civilization" to barbarism. A handful of ringleaders gave the answer. In 1792 these were the members of intellectual societies, of the revolutionary clubs. In 1936 they were, according to secret but incontrovertible information, a corps of sixty Russian Jews dispatched by Moscow in order to organize the terror in Spain.

Thus respectable people preserved their peace of mind in default of any other peace: the bourgeois and artisans of 1793 and the Spaniards of 1936 only played the role of semi-conscious instruments of crime. They belonged principally to "extreme civilization," in spite of their occasional lapse into barbarism. *The crimes of the Spanish War were to be explained in terms of sixty Jews.*

In spite of everything that distinguishes it from the old anti-Semitism, antisemitic racism today also appeals to religious feelings, and so preserves a certain continuity with the old anti-Semitism. Let us repeat that racism lives only on borrowing. It takes its borrowed strength where it finds it, but also from the higher region of the moral sentiments and even from that sublime region in which time unites with eternity. The uncompromising purity of the Church in the face of outrages perpetrated by racism against Christian faith and morals, the great charity dispensed by the Church to the victims of racist persecution, are nowadays exploited by legions of hypocrites in order to conceal the responsibilities of the Christian world in regard to the infamies of racism. This is only a particularly odious case of a current practice. Every time that the bad Christian fears lest his own impurity be uncovered, he tries to save face by taking refuge in the purity of the Church. A simple verbal equivocation, and the thing is done. In using the word "Christian" we can indeed intend to describe an ideal type which is realized perfectly only in the saints; one can also describe any member at all of a group defined by a minimal participation in this ideal. If the word Christian is taken in the first sense, one is speaking the truth when he says that the Christian does not lie or steal or commit adultery, that he does disapprove of racism and that his charity is without limit. But if the word is taken in the second sense, if one understands by Christian every individual who has been validly baptized, or baptized in the Catholic Church, or every individual who, having been baptized and made profession of the Catholic faith, frequents his parish church and receives the sacraments, one lies when he says that a Christian does not lie or steal, or the like. The fallacy of identifying the ideal-typical sense of a word with the vaguest and widest sense of the same is extremely crude; but the very crudeness of a fallacy is sometimes a factor in its success.

Honest minds which will not let themselves be perverted by fallacies of this caliber, will not allow the inflexible doctrine and charity of the Church to be employed as instruments of camouflage to protect against deserved denunciation the most secret though not the least efficacious of the sources of the success of racist ideology.

Nobody can deny that Christian circles, orthodox as well as heterodox, have played a role of prime importance in the maintenance, the development, and the renewal at opportune moments of that moderate anti-Semitism which, after having directly committed many iniquities, has perpetrated the crime of rendering possible the triumph of radical anti-Semitism, from the laws of Nuremberg to the extermination camps. It is certainly not as Christians that Christians have participated in the success of doctrines so manifestly contrary to Christian faith and morals and so clearly condemned by the Church. Nevertheless it would require a most suspicious kind of naivete, to suppose that this scandalous participation is a matter of pure coincidence. It would be to ignore the fact that the religious sentiments, like all that is best in man, can undergo formidable perversions. Pharisaism and the aberrations of the mystical aspiration are the best known of these perversions. It is quite possible that a certain perversion of the religious sense has something to do with the success of anti-Semitic racism in Christian circles. The question urges itself all the more vigorously since Christian circles are not clean of all responsibility in the bad treatment of Negroes at various times, our own included, and in various parts of the world. Let us dare to say that contemporary experience in the matter of racial conflicts, whether involving Jews or Negroes, strongly suggests the presence of a perverted religious sentiment in the leaders of racist persecution.

Concerning the Jews, it is necessary here to consider the characteristics of the old anti-Semitism. In the Middle Ages the Church prescribed in regard to the Jews certain measures of discrimination and segregation which it would be equivocal and ridiculous to call anti-Semitic. There was no question of making a certain race or people suffer; it was simply a matter of protecting the Christian faith against dangers to which they were exposed by the proximity and proselytism of a religious group which had become infidel the day it refused to recognize the Messiah who had been announced by the prophets. Whoever left the infidel group and entered the Church through a sincere conversion, by the same token escaped from a discrimination which no longer had any sense, since it never had had any but a religious sense. Around these measures issuing from the love of the Church for souls, the malice of men, the covetousness of princes and peoples, the follies of popular credulity constructed a long history of crimes which properly constitutes mediaeval anti-Semitism and whence modern anti-Semitism nourishes itself with powerful memories.

From the day when Catholic unity was broken, from the day when all varieties of infidelity began to multiply in societies once unified by the Catholic doctrine, the problem of the defense of the faith against the errors of the Jews changed its character. In Germany or France of the nineteenth century, the Jewish professor (who, moreover, generally had renounced his religion) perhaps menaced the faith of his students, but no more and no less than the Aryan and atheistic professor, no more and no less than the Aryan and agnostic, rationalist, pantheist, materialist; perhaps less than the fallen-away Catholic in revolt against the Church and the doubtful Catholic whose errors gained him an audience of believers because they were covered by official submission to the Church. If one adds that modern Judaism, even when it preserves its religious fervor, has generally renounced all proselytism, it is clear that the defense of the true faith against the errors of the Jews has vanished in the more general and differently difficult task of defending the faith against a multitude of errors that have no elective affinities for any racial or ethnic group: against the error of the rationalists, Jew or Aryan; against the error of the positivists, Jew or Aryan; the atheists, Jew or Aryan; the racists, Aryan or

Jew (for it is not impossible that there are some Jews among these); against all the monsters of error which have devoured so many souls. Anti-Semitism no longer can, as it could in other times, construct itself around a program of the defense of the faith. To those who are interested in the life of truth in the souls of men, it is not highly important that an enemy of God had only one Aryan grandparent, or two or three or four; or that a fervent believer had three or four Jewish grandparents. If anti-Semitism is to continue to exploit the religious sentiments of Christians to its ends, it will henceforth be forced to address itself, at least mainly, to a perverted form of these sentiments.

We shall understand without difficulty what perversion is in question here if we at all know how to apply the data of the psychology of accursed groups. The hatred and persecution of the hated group have this comforting feature about them, that in driving evil back into the interior of a group to which we know or believe that we ourselves do not belong, we free ourselves from the embarrassment of the insupportable presence of evil in our neighborhood and in our own hearts. Now, among all the crimes committed since the beginning of the world, there is one which infinitely surpasses all the others in malice. We are using the adverb *infinitely* in the strictest sense, for the crime involved is the crucifixion of the Son of God. Of this crime we are all guilty. The Christian cannot forget this; he can only try to forget it. Insofar as we have not forgotten it, our greatest joys—and precisely our purest and most elevated joys—will be mingled with the profoundest sadness. At every instant of our lives we shall have present in our minds this thought: my sins have made Jesus die on the cross. Behold here an abyss of anguish from which it would be well to remove oneself. The thing is easy to do. It is sufficient to put one's hands on an accursed group which will discharge us of the greatest of crimes by assuming the entire responsibility for this crime. The hated group is found. Is it not the Jews who crucified Our Lord? But then we, who are not Jews, evidently have nothing to do with that affair. We had no part in that ugly business. Our sins have only a limited importance. We again become capable of joys free from every sadness. Let others hold vigil while Jesus is in agony, that is to say to the end of the world. Rather than live in anguish with Jesus, we have chosen a peace which is not His. A pogrom from time to time, and the illusion will be complete.

These are hard words. Each one of us, however, whatever may be his own unworthiness, has the right of pronouncing them, for in doing so he accuses himself. There is no Christian in the world, anti-Semite or not, who does not feel the constant temptation of breaking company with Christ in His agony. The assistance given by an accursed group simplifies matters, but if this assistance is wanting, we shall nonetheless find some means of forgetting our role as deicides unless we renew, at every moment of our lives, the choice of living in agony with Christ rather than enjoying a peace which is not the peace of Christ.

The reader has seen that in the course of our exposition of the psychology of *accursed groups* we have constantly taken the expression *accursed group* in an entirely human and psychological sense, not in the sense in which it is taken when one speaks of a "divine malediction" resting on a people. In the case of the Jews the psychology of accursed groups functions towards a people which is considered to be the object of a divine curse; but the same psychology functions likewise in regard to the Jesuits and the Trotskyites, against whom no one has ever invoked a text drawn from Holy Scripture.

The problem of divine maledictions, which belongs entirely to theology, is alien to the object of this study. But we cannot prescind from the manner in which racism in all its manifestations—popular, literary, and scientific—which laughs at theology, makes that idea serve its own ends, in the case of the Negro as well as in the case of the Jew. Father Albert Perbal points out that certain writers suspect that a curse rests on "the Mohammedans, the Hindus, and the Chinese" also. Thus the picture is complete: wherever the white Aryan turns in quest of cheap labor, of economic monopoly, of aristocratic distinction, and the like, his bad conscience salves itself with a justification drawn in appearance from the highest sources of justice:

"I get my sailing orders from the Lord," says Stephen Vincent Benét's slave-trader:

> He touched the Bible: "And it's down there, Mister,
> Down there in black and white—the sons of Ham—
> Bondservants—sweat of their brows." His voice trailed off
> Into texts. "I tell you, Mister," he said fiercely,
> "The pay's good pay, but it's the Lord's work too."

In any case, it remains to be demonstrated that the members of non-accursed races have the right to designate themselves the executors of the divine vengeance and to pursue its accomplishment under the most profitable conditions for themselves, while they violate the commandments which denounce theft and homicide without distinction of race. The least one can expect of exterminating angels is that they will put no money in their pockets. Now, they do not even take the trouble of concealing their designs, and there is no poetic hyperbole in the frankness of Stephen Vincent Benét's slave-trader. See for example what we read in an article by M. Hubert Beuve-Méry, the well-known Catholic political scientist, on the Slovakia of Monsignor Tiso, the ally and protege of the Nazis:

The Jews, very ill-treated in the effervescence of the outset, still remain under a threat. They are no longer stripped and robbed by the Hlinka guards, their synagogues are not burned as at Trnava; their shops are not sacked; but they cannot have many illusions. In order to put a stop to the depredations, the official organ of the party, the *Slovak*, published these lines which will today no longer surprise anyone: "Our program comprises a *radical* solution of the Jewish question, *in the spirit of Christianity*. A law will be voted to this effect by the Diet. But it would be useless to have the law integrate into the national patrimony such and such properties if these properties have already been burned or pillaged. Whoever breaks the show-cases or windows of Jews *destroys the property of Slovakia*" (11 December, 1938). A little later the same journal warned the favorers of the opposition: "We ought to proceed in a purely *Christian fashion. . . . The guards of the concentration camp will unify those whom we have not succeeded in unifying*" (February 7, 1939).

M. Hubert Beuve-Méry observes that Msgr. Tiso "represented at the head of the Slovak government a relatively honest and moderate element." Compared with the Nazis of Germany the Christian anti-Semites of Slovakia certainly look like moderate racists, even though they seek a "radical" solution, and their friends the world over will not be slow to make the most of the fact that there have never been, in Slovakia or other "Christian" countries, extermination centers provided with chambers of carbon monoxide gas for producing rapid death. What the *Slovak* wrote, any moderately anti-Semite journal sincerely desirous of making a "Christian" solution of the Jewish problem prevail would have written in similar circumstances and is ready to write as soon as circumstances are equally favorable. Driven by force of arms from positions where it could express itself in a radical form, racism is soon going into strategic retreat towards moderate positions, just as the Nazi chiefs will try to find refuge in moderately totalitarian countries. Tomorrow there will no longer be a racist citadel at Nuremberg or Berlin, but racism will continue to occupy innumerable semi-underground fortresses, better camouflaged than the forts of the Maginot Line, which will have to be taken by assault, one after the other, regardless of the cost.

Some readers will perhaps be tempted to think that this essay sins through over-simplification, and that in our radical anti-racism we fail to recognize all the problems that are aroused by the diversity of races. Let me state simply that I think myself aware of these problems, and that in order to render possible their exact statement and then their solution, the first thing to do is to annihilate the least vestige of the racist spirit. Who would deny, for example, that the effective access of American Negroes in the Southern States to the liberties guaranteed by the Fifteenth Amendment raises grave problems? Who would deny that the establishment of an equitable order in the relations between French citizens and native Mohammedans in Algeria presents extreme difficulties? These problems, however, will not receive the slightest beginnings of solution, these difficulties will not cease to be insurmountable, until the day that the representatives of the so-called superior race cease to see in the Negroes and the Arabs precious reservoirs of cheap labor and a contrast ready-made to enhance their aristocratic dignity.

Moreover, the men of our generation have good reasons for not attaching too much importance to the reproach, humiliating above all others, of over-simplification. We intellectuals have loved our subtlety, our nuances, our politeness, overmuch. At the time when the great catastrophes of the present were preparing and already beginning to unfold, we remained anxious not to be taken for people who think like brutes. Sometimes the adversary himself was forced to render homage to our sense of the delicacy and complexity of problems, to our conscientious way of weighing one thing against the other, to the serenity of our judgments, to our art of remaining friendly with everybody. Then came a day when circumstances permitted the good gentlemen with whom we had conversed so courteously to reveal their true character. Concentration camps filled up, innocent people died by thousands and millions, and among those most immediately responsible for the atrocious situation, traitors, executioners, influential accomplices, we recognized the persons whom our polite dialectic had merely grazed. A more vigorous dialectic, and one less concerned with good manners, would have beaten them down. The blood of innocents cried for vengeance against our timidity. To oppose to the power of crime triumphant nothing but muffled arms suitable only for academic controversies—that has been the disgrace of our youth. The war now drags us out of this shame.

Now, this international civil war will not be finished when the statesmen have signed treaties. The ideologies which are incarnate in the Nazi state and in those of its satellites will continue to work—more secretly perhaps, but we know that secrecy often favors the success of these ideologies. The cause of racism will not be definitely shaken until the day when our moderate, secret racists, will find, facing them, not smiling analysts and hair-splitting "logicians," but men with tightened fists, determined to commit themselves thoroughly, determined to run risks, determined to call people and things by their right names; men who refuse to enjoy a life from which justice is absent; men who have for their motto *justice or death*.

IDEOLOGY AND TERROR:

A NOVEL FORM

OF GOVERNMENT

Hannah Arendt

[1953]

I

THE following considerations have grown out of a study of the origins, the elements and the functioning of that novel form of government and domination which we have come to call totalitarian. Wherever it rose to power, it developed entirely new political institutions and destroyed all social, legal, and political traditions of the country. No matter what the specifically national tradition or the particular spiritual source of its ideology, totalitarian government always transformed classes into masses, supplanted the party system, not by one-party dictatorships, but by a mass movement, shifted the center of power from the army to the police, and established a foreign policy openly directed toward world domination. Present totalitarian governments have developed from one-party systems; whenever these became truly totalitarian, they started to operate according to a system of values so radically different from all others, that none of our traditional legal, moral, or common sense utilitarian categories could any longer help us to come to terms with, or judge, or predict its course of action.

If it is true that the elements of totalitarianism can be found by retracing the history and analyzing the political implications of what we usually call the crisis of our century, then the conclusion is unavoidable that this crisis is no mere threat from the outside, no mere result of some aggressive foreign policy of either Germany or Russia, and that it will no more disappear with the fall of Soviet Russia than it disappeared with the fall of Nazi Germany. It may even be that the true predicaments of our time will assume their authentic form—

though not necessarily the cruelest—only when totalitarianism has become a thing of the past.

It is in the line of such reflections to raise the question whether totalitarian government, born of this crisis and at the same time its clearest and only unequivocal symptom, is merely a make-shift arrangement, which borrows its methods of intimidation, its means of organization and its instruments of violence from the well-known political arsenal of tyranny, despotism, and dictatorships, and owes its existence only to the deplorable, but perhaps accidental failure of the traditional political forces—liberal or conservative, national or socialist, republican or monarchist, authoritarian or democratic. Or whether, on the contrary, there is such a thing as the *nature* of totalitarian government, whether it has its own essence and can be compared with and defined like other forms of government such as Western thought has known and recognized since the times of ancient philosophy.

Questions of this sort have been out of fashion for a long time and for reasons which may have more than a little to do with those modern developments which eventually brought about a crisis of Western politics no less than of Western political thought. More specifically, such questions have been thought superfluous, if not meaningless, ever since the social sciences established their rule over the whole field of politics and history. Interesting in this development, which easily can be traced back to Marx, was that sociology from its beginnings showed a marked tendency to explain political institutions and historical developments in terms of psychological types; all the well-known clichés of the lower middle classes, the bureaucracy, the intelligentsia have already that particular tinge of typification which shows itself openly in categories such as "the authoritarian personality." More recently, with the growing disappointment in the strictly Marxist explanation of history, psychology itself with its new Freudian concepts of super-ego, father-image, and oedipus complex, has invaded the social sciences and continues to provide them with their chief tools of "evaluation" to such an extent that it has become difficult to tell the two sciences from each other.

This new-fangled mixture of sociology and psychology is no accident. Both sciences have their origin in a liberalism that viewed politics (and more or less all human affairs) under the dual category of society and individual. Men became mere parts of a society that conditioned or determined the individuals, as the whole determines its parts. In this sense, sociology and psychology have always been two sides of the same medal, the one dealing with the functioning of the whole (society), the other with the functioning of the parts (individuals). The trouble came when psychology, notwithstanding its respect for society, discovered that even these individuals, whose whole interior life was supposed to be conditioned by, or to react against, social circumstances, possess a "soul." But we have souls only as long as we are more than mere members of society where this psychological side of our being has always created disturbances. Manners and conventions, all public morals and *mores* help us to control our souls so that we can function on a merely social level. Individual psychology, since it looked on man as though he were nothing but an individual part of society, has developed into a science which deals mostly with abnormal behavior patterns: all "psychological" attitudes become abnormal when they occur in society because they have been stripped of the privacy in which alone a man's soul can function "normally." Individual psychology became fashionable wherever customs and conventions, the whole texture of morality which is the lifeblood of society, lost their authority. The modern individual is the surviving member of a society which no longer exists; it is a part that lost its place in the whole. In this situation, the psychological sciences have become increasingly social-minded and direct their greatest efforts toward the re-adjustment of isolated individuals. The trouble is that society as a whole, that is, as something which is greater than the sum total of its parts, no longer exists. The best demonstration of this is that the social sciences can conceive of society now only in terms of individual behavior patterns, which they indiscriminately apply to collective bodies where such behavior never occurs.

The great merit of this confusion is that it somehow has awakened us to the fact that political bodies, to quote a long-forgotten remark of Plato, do not spring from oak and rock (Rep. viii, 544D). Yet, they do not spring from within our particular and individual selves either. The old Roman distinction between *res publica* and *res privata* is still valid. Political forms of organization concern matters which are of equal concern to each of us because they occur *between us*. Our question whether there is such a thing as the nature of totalitarian domination means actually whether the entirely new and unprecedented forms of totalitarian organization and course of action rest on one of the few basic experiences which men can make whenever they live together, and are concerned with public affairs. If there is a basic experience which finds its political expression in totalitarian domination, then, in view of the novelty of the totalitarian form of government, this must be an experience which, for whatever reason, has never before served as the foundation of a body politic and whose general mood—although it may be familiar in every other respect—never before has pervaded, and directed the handling of, public affairs.

If we consider this in terms of the history of ideas, it seems extremely unlikely. For the forms of government under which men live have been very few; they were discovered early, classified by the

Greeks and have proved extraordinarily long-lived. If we apply these findings, whose fundamental idea, despite many variations, did not change in the two and a half thousand years that separate Plato from Kant, we are tempted at once to interpret totalitarianism as some modern form of tyranny, that is a lawless government where power is wielded by one man. Arbitrary power, unrestricted by law, yielded in the interest of the ruler and hostile to the interests of the governed, on one hand, fear as the principle of action, namely fear of the people by the ruler and fear of the ruler by the people, on the other—these have been the hallmarks of tyranny throughout our tradition.

Instead of saying that totalitarian government is unprecedented, we could also say that it has exploded the very alternative on which all definitions of the essence of governments have been based in political philosophy, that is the alternative between lawful and lawless government, between arbitrary and legitimate power. That lawful government and legitimate power, on one side, lawlessness and arbitrary power on the other, belonged together and were inseparable has never been questioned. Yet, totalitarian rule confronts us with a totally different kind of government. It defies, it is true, all positive laws, even to the extreme of defying those which it has itself established (as in the case of the Soviet Constitution of 1936, to quote only the most outstanding example) or which it did not care to abolish (as in the case of the Weimar Constitution which the Nazi government never revoked). But it operates neither without guidance of law nor it is arbitrary, for it claims to obey strictly and unequivocally those laws of Nature or of History from which all positive laws always have been supposed to spring.

It is the monstrous, yet seemingly unanswerable claim of totalitarian rule that, far from being "lawless," it goes to the sources of authority from which positive laws received their ultimate legitimation, that far from being arbitrary it is more obedient to these suprahuman forces than any government ever was before, and that far from wielding its power in the interest of one man, it is quite prepared to sacrifice everybody's vital immediate interests to the execution of what it assumes to be the law of History or the law of Nature. Its defiance of positive laws claims to be a higher form of legitimacy which, since it is inspired by the sources themselves, can do away with petty legality. Totalitarian lawfulness pretends to have found a way to establish the rule of justice on earth—something which the legality of positive law admittedly could never attain. The discrepancy between legality and justice could never be bridged because the standards of right and wrong into which positive law translates its own source of authority—"natural law" governing the whole universe, or divine law revealed in human history or customs and traditions expressing the law common to the sentiments of all men—are necessarily general and must be valid for a countless and unpredictable number of cases, so that each concrete individual case with its unrepeatable set of circumstances somehow escapes it.

Totalitarian lawfulness, defying legality and pretending to establish the direct reign of justice on earth, executes the law of History or of Nature without translating it into standards of right and wrong for individual behavior. It applies the law directly to mankind without bothering with the behavior of men. The law of Nature or the law of History, if properly executed, is expected to produce mankind as its end product; and this expectation lies behind the claim to global rule of all totalitarian governments. Totalitarian policy claims to transform the human species into an active unfailing carrier of a law to which human beings otherwise would only passively and reluctantly be subjected. If it is true that the link between totalitarian countries and the civilized world was broken through the monstrous crimes of totalitarian regimes, it is also true that this criminality was not due to simple aggressiveness, ruthlessness, warfare, and treachery, but to a conscious break of that *consensus iuris* which, according to Cicero constitutes a "people," and which, as international law, in modern times has constituted the civilized world insofar as it remains the foundation-stone of international relations even under the conditions of war. Both moral judgment and legal punishment presuppose this basic consent; the criminal can be judged justly only because he takes part in the *consensus iuris,* and even the revealed law of God can function among men only when they listen and consent to it.

At this point the fundamental difference between the totalitarian and all other concepts of law comes to light. Totalitarian policy does not replace one set of laws with another, does not establish its own *consensus iuris,* does not create, by one revolution, a new form of legality. Its defiance of all, even its own positive laws implies that it believes it can do without any *consensus iuris* whatever, and still not resign itself to the tyrannical state of lawlessness, arbitrariness, and fear. It can do without the *consensus iuris* because it promises to release the fulfillment of law from all action and will of man; and it promises justice on earth because it claims to make mankind itself the embodiment of the law.

This identification of man and law, which seems to cancel the discrepancy between legality and justice that has plagued legal thought since ancient times, has nothing in common with the *lumen naturale* or the voice of conscience, by which Nature or Divinity as the sources of authority for the *ius naturale* or the historically revealed commands of God, are supposed to announce their authority in man himself. This never made man a walking embodiment of the law, but on the contrary remained distinct from him as the authority which demanded consent and obedience. Nature or Divinity as the source of authority for positive laws are thought of as permanent and eternal; positive laws were changing and changeable according to circumstances, but they possessed a relative permanence as compared with the much more rapidly changing actions of men; and they derived this permanence from the eternal presence of their source of authority. Positive laws, therefore, are primarily designed to function as stabilizing factors for the ever changing movements of men.

In the interpretation of totalitarianism, all laws have become *laws of movement*. When the Nazis talked about the law of Nature or when the Bolsheviks talk about the law of History, neither Nature nor History is any longer the stabilizing source of authority for the actions of mortal men; they are movements in themselves. Underlying the Nazis' belief in race laws as the expression of the law of Nature in man, is Darwin's idea of man as the product of a natural development which does not necessarily stop with the present species of human beings, just as under the Bolsheviks' belief in class-struggle as the expression of the law of History lies Marx's notion of society as the product of a gigantic historical movement which races according to its own law of motion to the end of historical times when it will abolish itself.

The difference between Marx's historical and Darwin's naturalistic approaches has frequently been pointed out, usually and rightly in favor of Marx. This has led us to forget the great and positive interest Marx took in Darwin's theories; Engels could not think of a greater compliment to Marx's scholarly achievements than to call him the "Darwin of history." If one considers, not the actual achievement but, the basic philosophies of both men, it turns out that ultimately the movement of History and the movement of Nature are one and the same. Darwin's introduction of the concept of development into nature, his insistence that, at least, in the field of biology, natural movement is not circular but unilinear, moving in an infinitely progressing direction, means in fact that nature is, as it were, being swept into history, that natural life is considered to be historical. The "natural" law of the survival of the fittest is just as much a historical law and could be used as such by racism as Marx's law of the survival of the most progressive class. Marx's class struggle, on the other hand, as the driving force of history is only the outward expression of the development of productive forces which in turn have their origin in the labor *force* of men. Labor, according to Marx, is not a historical but a natural-biological "force," namely man's "metabolism with nature" by which he conserves his individual life and reproduces the species. Engels saw the affinity between the basic convictions of the two men very clearly because he understood the decisive role which the concept of development played in both theories. The tremendous intellectual change which took place in the middle of the last century consisted in the refusal to view or accept anything "as it is" and in the consistent interpretation of everything as being only a stage of some further development. Whether the driving force of this development was called nature or history is relatively secondary.

In these theories, the term "law" itself changed its meaning: from expressing the framework of stability within which human actions and motions can take place, it became the expression of the motion itself.

II

By lawful government we understand a body politic in which positive laws are needed to translate and realize the immutable *ius naturale* or the eternal commandments of God into standards of right and wrong. Only in these standards, in the body of positive laws of each country, do the *ius naturale* or the Commandments of God achieve their political reality. In the body politic of totalitarian government, this place of positive laws is taken by total terror, which is designed to translate into reality the law of movement of History or Nature. Just as positive laws, though they define transgressions, are independent of them—the absence of crimes in any society does not render laws superfluous but, on the contrary, signifies their most perfect rule—so terror in totalitarian government has ceased to be a mere means for the suppression of opposition, though it is also used for such purposes. Terror becomes total when it becomes independent of all opposition; it rules supreme when nobody any longer stands in its way. If lawfulness is the essence of non-tyrannical government and lawlessness is the essence of tyranny, then terror is the essence of totalitarian domination.

Terror is the realization of the law of movement; its chief aim is to make it possible for the force of Nature or of History to race freely through mankind, unhindered by any spontaneous human action. As such, terror seeks to "stabilize" men in order to liberate the forces of Nature or History. It is this movement which singles out the foes of mankind against whom terror is let loose, and no free action of either opposition or sympathy can be permitted to interfere with the elimination of the "objective enemy" of History or Nature, of the class or the race. Guilt and innocence become senseless notions; "guilty" is he who stands in the way of the natural or historical process which has passed judgment over "inferior races," over individuals "unfit to live," over "dying classes and decadent peoples." Terror executes these judgments, and before its court, all concerned are subjectively innocent: the murdered because they did nothing against the system, and the murderers because they do not really murder but execute a death sentence pronounced by some higher tribunal. The rulers themselves do not claim to be just or wise, but only to execute historical or natural laws; they do not apply laws, but execute a movement in accordance with its inherent law. Terror is lawfulness, if law is the law of the movement of some suprahuman force, Nature or History.

Terror as the execution of a law of movement whose ultimate goal is not the welfare of men or the interest of one man but the fabrication of mankind, eliminates individuals for the sake of the species, sacrifices the "parts" for the sake of the "whole." The suprahuman force of Nature or History has its own beginning and its own end, so that it can be hindered only by the new beginning and the individual end which the life of each man actually is.

Positive laws in constitutional government are designed to erect boundaries and establish channels of communication between men whose community is continually endangered by the new men born into it. With each new birth, a new beginning is born into the world, a new world has potentially come into being. The stability of the laws corresponds to the constant motion of all human affairs, a motion which can never end as long as men are born and die. The laws hedge in each new beginning and at the same time assure its freedom of movement, the potentiality of something entirely new and unpredictable; the boundaries of positive laws are for the political existence of man what memory is for his historical existence: they guarantee the pre-existence of a common world, the reality of some continuity which transcends the individual life span of each generation, absorbs all new origins and is nourished by them.

Total terror is so easily mistaken for a symptom of tyrannical government because totalitarian government in its initial stages must behave like a tyranny and raze the boundaries of man-made law. But total terror leaves no arbitrary lawlessness behind it and does not rage for the sake of some arbitrary will or for the sake of despotic power of one man against all, least of all for the sake of a war of all against all. It substitutes for the boundaries and channels of communication between individual men a band of iron which holds them so tightly together that it is as though their plurality had disappeared into One Man of gigantic dimensions. To abolish the fences of laws between men—as tyranny does—means to take away man's liberties and destroy freedom as a living political reality; for the space between men as it is hedged in by laws, is the living space of freedom. Total terror uses this old instrument of tyranny but destroys at the same time also the lawless, fenceless wilderness of fear and suspicion which tyranny leaves behind. This desert, to be sure, is no longer a living space of freedom, but it still provides some room for the fear-guided movements and suspicion-ridden actions of its inhabitants.

By pressing men against each other, total terror destroys the space between them; compared to the condition within its iron band, even the desert of tyranny, insofar as it is still some kind of space, appears like a guarantee of freedom. Totalitarian government does not just curtail liberties or abolish essential freedoms; nor does it, at least to our limited knowledge, succeed in eradicating the love for freedom from the hearts of man. It destroys the one essential prerequisite of all freedom which is simply the capacity of motion which cannot exist without space.

Total terror, the essence of totalitarian government, exists neither for nor against men. It is supposed to provide the forces of Nature or History with an incomparable instrument to accelerate their movement. This movement, proceeding according to its own law, cannot in the long run be hindered; eventually its force will always prove more powerful than the most powerful forces engendered by the actions and the will of men. But it can be slowed down and is slowed down almost inevitably by the freedom of man, which even totalitarian rulers cannot deny, for this freedom—irrelevant and arbitrary as they may deem it—is identical with the fact that men are being born and that therefore each of them *is* a new beginning, begins, in a sense, the world anew. From the totalitarian point of view, the fact that men are born and die can be only regarded as an annoying interference with higher forces. Terror, therefore, as the obedient servant of natural or historical movement has to eliminate from the process not only freedom in any specific sense, but the very source of freedom which is given with the fact of the birth of man and resides in his capacity to make a new beginning. In the iron band of terror, which destroys the plurality of men and makes out of many the One who unfailingly will act as though he himself were part of the course of History or Nature, a device has been found not only to liberate the historical and natural forces, but to accelerate them to a speed they never would reach if left to themselves. Practically speaking, this means that terror executes on the spot the death sentences which Nature is supposed to have pronounced on races or individuals who are "unfit to live," or History on "dying classes," without waiting for the slower and less efficient processes of Nature or History themselves.

In this concept, where the essence of government itself has become motion, a very old problem of political thought seems to have found a solution similar to the one already noted for the discrepancy between legality and justice. If the essence of government is defined as lawfulness, and if it is understood that laws are the stabilizing forces in the public affairs of men (as indeed it always has been since Plato invoked Zeus, the God of the boundaries, in his *Laws*) then the problem of movement of the body politic and the actions of its citizens arises. Lawfulness sets limitations to actions, but does not inspire them; the greatness, but also the perplexity of laws in free societies is that they only tell what one should not, but never what one should do. The necessary movement of a body politic can never be found in its essence if only because this essence—again since Plato—has always been defined with a view to its permanence. Duration seemed one of the surest yardsticks for the goodness of a government. It is still, for Montesquieu, the supreme proof for the badness of tyranny that only tyrannies are liable to be destroyed from within, to decline by themselves, whereas all other governments are destroyed through exterior circumstances. Therefore what the definition of governments always needed was what Montesquieu called a "principle of action" which, different in each form of government, would inspire government and citizens alike in their public activity and serve as a criterion beyond the merely negative yardstick of lawfulness, for judging all action in public affairs. Such guiding principles and criteria of action are, according to Montesquieu, honor in a monarchy, virtue in a republic and fear in a tyranny.

In a perfect totalitarian government, where all men have become One Man, where all action aims at the acceleration of the movement of Nature or History, where every single act is the execution of a death sentence which Nature or History has already pronounced, that is, under conditions where terror can be completely relied upon to keep the movement in constant motion, no principle of action separate from its essence would be needed at all. Yet as long as totalitarian rule has not conquered the earth and with the iron band of terror made each single man a part of one mankind, terror in its double function as essence of government and principle, not of action, but of motion cannot be fully realized. Just as lawfulness in constitutional government is insufficient to inspire and guide men's actions, so terror in totalitarian government is not sufficient to inspire and guide human behavior.

While under present conditions totalitarian domination still shares with other forms of government the need for a guide for the behavior of its citizens in public affairs, it does not need and could not even use a principle of action strictly speaking, since it will eliminate precisely the capacity of man to act. Under conditions of total terror not even fear can any longer serve as an advisor of how to behave, because terror chooses its victims without reference to individual actions or thoughts, exclusively in accordance with the objective necessity of the natural or historical process. Under totalitarian conditions, fear probably is more widespread than ever before; but fear has lost its practical usefulness when actions guided by it can no longer help to avoid the dangers man fears. The same is true for sympathy or support of the regime; for total terror not only selects its victims according to objective standards; it chooses its executioners with as complete a disregard as possible for the candidate's conviction and sympathies. The consistent elimination of conviction as a motive for action has become a matter of record since the great purges in Soviet Russia and the satellite countries. The aim of totalitarian education has never been to instill convictions but to destroy the capacity to form any. The introduction of purely objective criteria into the selective system of the SS troops was Himmler's great organizational invention; he selected the candidates from photographs according to purely racial criteria. Nature itself decided, not only who was to be eliminated, but also who was to be trained as an executioner.

No guiding principle of behavior, taken itself from the realm of human action, such as virtue, honor, fear, is necessary or can be useful to set into motion a body politic which no longer uses terror as a means of intimidation, but whose essence *is* terror. In its stead, it has introduced an entirely new principle into public affairs that dispenses with human will to action altogether and appeals to the craving need for some insight into the law of movement according to which the terror functions and upon which, therefore, all private destinies depend.

The inhabitants of a totalitarian country are thrown into and caught in the process of Nature or History for the sake of accelerating its movement; as such, they can only be executioners or victims of its inherent law. The process may decide that those who today eliminate races and individuals or the members of dying classes and decadent peoples are tomorrow those who must be sacrificed. What totalitarian rule needs to guide the behavior of its subjects is a *preparation* to fit each of them equally well for the role of executioner and the role of victim. This two-sided preparation, the substitute for a principle of action, is the ideology.

III

Ideologies—isms which to the satisfaction of their adherents can explain everything and every occurrence by deducing it from a single premise—are a very recent phenomenon and, for many decades, this played a negligible role in political life. Only with the wisdom of hindsight can we discover in them certain elements which have made them so disturbingly useful for totalitarian rule. Not before Hitler and Stalin were the great political potentialities of the ideologies discovered.

Ideologies are known for their scientific character: they combine the scientific approach with results of philosophical relevance and pretend to be scientific philosophy. The word "ideology" seems to imply that an idea can become the subject matter of a science just as animals are the subject matter of zoology, and that the suffix *-logy* in ideology, as in zoology, indicates nothing but the *logoi,* the scientific statements made on it. If this were true, an ideology would indeed be a pseudo-science and a pseudo-philosophy, transgressing at the same time the limitations of science and the limitations of philosophy. Deism, for example, would then be the ideology which treats the *idea* of God, with which philosophy is concerned, in the scientific manner of theology for which God is a revealed reality. (A theology which is not based on revelation as a given reality but treats God as an idea would be as mad as a zoology which is no longer sure of the physical, tangible existence of animals.) Yet we know that this is only part of the truth. Deism, though it denies divine revelation, does not simply make "scientific" statements on a God which is only an "idea," but uses the idea of God in order to explain the course of the world. The "ideas" of isms—race in racism, God in deism, and so forth—never form the subject matter of the ideologies and the suffix *-logy* never indicates simply a body of "scientific" statements.

An ideology is quite literally what its name indicates: it is the *logic of an idea.* Its subject matter is history to which the "idea" is applied; the result of this application is not a body of statements about something that *is,* but the unfolding of a *process* which is in constant change. The ideology treats the course of events as though it followed the same "law" as the logical exposition of its "idea." Ideologies pretend to know the mysteries of the whole historical process—the secrets of the past, the intricacies of the present, the uncertainties of the future—because of the logic inherent in their respective ideas.

Ideologies are never interested in the miracle of being. They are historical, concerned with becoming and perishing, with the rise and fall of cultures, even if they try to explain history by some "law of nature." The word "race" in racism does not signify any genuine curiosity about the human races as a field for scientific exploration, but is the "idea" by which the movement of history is explained as one consistent process.

The "idea" of an ideology is neither the eternal essence grasped by the eyes of the mind nor the regulator of reason—as it was from Plato to Kant—but has become an instrument of explanation. To an ideology, history does not appear in the *light* of an idea (which would imply that history is seen *sub specie* of some ideal eternity which itself is beyond historical motion) but as something which can be *calculated* by it. What fits the "idea" into this new role is its own "logic," that is a movement which is the consequence of the "idea" itself and needs no outside factor to set it into motion. Racism is the belief that there is a motion inherent in the very "idea" of race, just as deism is the belief that a motion is inherent in the very notion of God.

The movement of history and the logical process of this notion are supposed to correspond to each other, so that whatever happens, happens according to the logic of one "idea." However, the only possible movement in the realm of logic is the process of deduction from a premise. Dialectical logic, with its process from thesis through antithesis to synthesis which in turn becomes the thesis of the next dialectical movement is not different in principle, once an ideology gets hold of it; the first thesis becomes the premise and its advantage for ideological explanation is that this dialectical device can explain away factual contradictions as stages of one identical, consistent movement.

As soon as logic as a *movement* of thought—and not as a necessary control of thinking—is applied to an idea, this idea is transformed into a *premise*. Ideological world explanations performed this operation long before it become so eminently fruitful for totalitarian reasoning. The purely negative coercion of logic, the prohibition of contradictions, became "productive" so that a whole line of thought could be initiated, and forced upon the mind, by drawing conclusions in the manner of mere argumentation. This argumentative process could be interrupted neither by a new idea (which would have been another premise with a different set of consequences) nor by a new experience. Ideologies always assume that one idea is sufficient to explain everything in the development from the premise, and that no experience can teach anything because everything is comprehended in this consistent process of logical deduction. The danger in exchanging the necessary insecurity of philosophical thought for the total explanation of an ideology and its *Weltanschauung,* is not even so much the risk of falling for some usually vulgar, always uncritical assumption as of exchanging the freedom inherent in man's capacity to think for the straightjacket of logic with which man can force himself almost as violently as he is forced by some outside power.

The transformation of an idea into a premise and the use of the logic of deduction as only demonstration for truth, is certainly only one of the totalitarian elements in ideologies. Another is obviously the claim of all *Weltanschauungen* to offer total explanations of everything, mainly, of course, of past, present and future. And the emancipation from reality this method always implies, since it pretends to know beforehand everything that experience may still have in store, might, psychologically speaking, be even more important. Yet, we insisted on this peculiar logicality of ideologies because the true totalitarian rulers (Hitler and Stalin, not their forerunners) used it more than any other element when they converted ideologies—racism and the premise of the law of nature, or dialectical materialism and the premise of the law of history—into foundation stones for the new totalitarian body politic.

The device both totalitarian rulers used to transform their respective ideologies into weapons with which each of their subjects would force himself into step with the terror movement was deceptively simple and inconspicuous: they took them dead seriously, took pride the one in his supreme gift for "ice cold reasoning" (Hitler) and the other in the "mercilessness of his dialectics," and proceeded to drive ideological implications into extremes of logical consistency which, to the onlooker, looked preposterously "primitive" and absurd: a "dying class" consisted of people condemned to death; races that are "unfit to live" were to be exterminated. Whoever agreed that there are such things as "dying classes" and did not draw the consequence of killing their members, or that the right to live had something to do with race and did not draw the consequence of killing "unfit races," was plainly either stupid or a coward. This stringent logicality as a guide to action permeates the whole structure of totalitarian movements and governments. It is exclusively the work of Hitler and Stalin who, although they did not add a single new thought to the ideas and propaganda slogans of their movements, for this reason alone must be considered ideologists of the greatest importance.

What distinguished these new totalitarian ideologists from their predecessors was that it was no longer primarily the "idea" of the ideology—the struggle of classes and the exploitation of the workers or the struggle of races and the care for Germanic peoples—which appealed to them, but the logical process which could be developed from it. According to Stalin, neither the idea nor the oratory but "the irresistible force of logic thoroughly overpowered (Lenin's) audience." The power, which Marx thought was born when the idea seized the masses, was discovered to reside, not in the idea itself, but in its logical process which "like a mighty tentacle seizes you on all sides as in a vise and from whose grip you are powerless to tear yourself away; you must either surrender or make up your mind to utter defeat." (Stalin's speech of January 28, 1924; quoted from Lenin, *Selected Works*, vol. I, p. 33. Moscow, 1947). Only when the realization of the ideological aims, the classless society or the master race, was at stake, could this force show itself. In the process of realization, the original substance upon which the ideologies based themselves as long as they had to appeal to the masses—the exploitation of the workers or the national aspirations of Germany—is gradually lost, devoured as it were by the process itself: in perfect accordance with "ice cold reasoning" and the "irresistible force of logic," the workers lost under Bolshevik rule even those rights they had been granted under Tsarist oppression and the German people suffered a kind of warfare which did not pay the slightest regard to the minimum requirements for survival of the German nation. It is in the nature of ideological politics —and is not simply a betrayal committed for the sake of self-interest or lust for power—that the real content of the ideology (the working class or the Germanic peoples), which originally had brought about the "idea" (the struggle of classes as the law of history or the struggle of races as the law of nature), is devoured by the logic with which the "idea" is carried out.

The preparation of victims and executioners which totalitarianism requires in place of Montesquieu's principle of action is not the ideology itself—racism or dialectical materialism—but its inherent logicality. The most persuasive argument in this respect, an argument of which Hitler like Stalin was very fond, is: You can't say A without saying B and C and so on, down to the end of the murderous alphabet. Here, the coercive force of logicality seems to have its source; it springs from our fear of contradicting ourselves. To the extent that the Bolshevik purge succeeds in making its victims confess to crimes they never committed, it relies chiefly on this basic fear and argues as follows: We are all agreed on the premise that history is a struggle of classes and on the role of the Party in its conduct. You know therefore that, historically speaking, the Party is always right—in the words of Trotsky: "We can only be right with and by the Party, for history has provided no other way of being in the right." At this historical moment, that is in accordance with the law of History, certain crimes are due to be committed which the Party, knowing the law of History, must punish. For these crimes, the Party needs criminals; it may be that the Party, though knowing the crimes, does not quite know the criminals; more important than to be sure about the criminals is to punish the crimes, because without such punishment, History will not be advanced but may even be hindered in its course. You, therefore, either have committed the crimes or have been called by the Party to play the role of the criminal—in either case, you have objectively become an enemy of the Party. If you do not confess, you cease to help History through the Party, and have become a real enemy. The coercive force of the argument is: if you refuse, you contradict yourself and, through this contradiction, render your whole life meaningless; the A which you said dominates your whole life through the consequences of B and C which it logically engenders.

Totalitarian rulers rely on the compulsion with which we can compel ourselves, for the limited mobilization of people which even they still need; this inner compulsion is the tyranny of logicality against which nothing stands but the great capacity of men to start something new. The tyranny of logicality begins with the mind's submission to logic as a never-ending process, on which man relies in order to engender his thoughts. By this submission, he surrenders his inner freedom as he surrenders his freedom of movement when he bows down to an outward tyranny. Freedom as an inner capacity of man is identical with the capacity to begin, just as freedom as a political reality is identical with a space of movement between men. Over the beginning, no logic, no cogent deduction can have any power, because its chain presupposes, in the form of a premise, the beginning. As terror is needed lest with the birth of each new human being a new beginning arise and raise its voice in the world, so the self-coercive force of logicality is mobilized lest anybody ever start thinking —which as the freest and purest of all human activities is the very opposite of the compulsory process of deduction. Totalitarian government can be safe only to the extent that it can mobilize man's own will power in order to force him into the gigantic movement of History or Nature which supposedly uses mankind as its material and knows neither birth nor death.

The compulsion of total terror on one side, which, with its iron band, presses masses of isolated men together *and* supports them in a world which has become a wilderness for them, and the self-coercive force of logical deduction on the other, which prepares each individual in his lonely isolation against all others, correspond to each other and need each other in order to set the terror-ruled movement into motion and keep it moving. Just as terror, even in its pre-total, merely tyrannical form ruins all relationships between men, so the self-compulsion of ideological thinking ruins all relationships with reality. The preparation has succeeded when people have lost contact with their fellow men as well as the reality around them; for together with these contacts, men lose the capacity of both experience and thought. The ideal subject of totalitarian rule is not the convinced Nazi or the convinced Communist, but people for whom the distinction between fact and fiction (that is, the reality of experience) and the distinction between true and false (that is, the standards of thought) no longer exist.

I V

The question we raised at the start of these considerations and to which we now return is what kind of basic experience in the living-together of men permeates a form of government whose essence is terror and whose principle of action is the logicality of ideological thinking. That such a combination was never used before in the varied forms of political domination is obvious. Still, the basic ex-

235

perience on which it rests must be human and known to men, insofar as even this most "original" of all political bodies has been devised by, and is somehow answering the needs of, men.

It has frequently been observed that terror can rule absolutely only over men who are isolated from each other and that, therefore, one of the primary concerns of all tyrannical government is to bring this isolation about. Isolation may be the beginning of terror; it certainly is its most fertile ground; it always is its result. This isolation is, as it were, pretotalitarian; its hallmark is impotence insofar as power always comes from men acting together, "acting in concert" (Burke); isolated men are powerless by definition.

Isolation and impotence, that is, the fundamental inability to act at all, have always been characteristic of tyrannies. Political contacts between men are severed in tyrannical government and the human capacities for action and power are frustrated. But not all contacts between men are broken and not all human capacities destroyed. The whole sphere of private life with the capacities for experience, fabrication, and thought are left intact. We know that the iron band of total terror leaves no space for such private life and that the self-coercion of totalitarian logic destroys man's capacity for experience and thought just as certainly as his capacity for action.

What we call isolation in the political sphere, is called loneliness in the sphere of social intercourse. Isolation and loneliness are not the same. I can be isolated—that is in a situation in which I cannot act, because there is nobody who will act with me—without being lonely; and I can be lonely—that is in a situation in which I as a person feel myself deserted by all human companionship—without being isolated. Isolation is that impasse into which men are driven when the political sphere of their lives, where they act together in the pursuit of a common concern, is destroyed. Yet isolation, though destructive of power and the capacity for action, not only leaves intact but is required for all so-called productive activities of men. Man insofar as he is *homo faber* tends to isolate himself with his work, that is, to leave temporarily the realm of politics. Fabrication (*poiesis,* the making of things), as distinguished from action (*praxis*) on one hand and sheer labor on the other, is always performed in a certain isolation from common concerns, no matter whether the result is a piece of craftsmanship or of art. In isolation, man remains in contact with the world as the human artifice; only when the most elementary forms of human creativity, which is the capacity to add something of one's own to the common world, are destroyed, does isolation become altogether unbearable. This can happen in a world whose chief values are dictated by labor, that is where all human activities have been transformed into laboring. Under such conditions, only the sheer effort of labor which is the effort to keep alive is left and the relationship with the world as a human artifice is broken. Isolated man who lost his place in the political realm of action is deserted by the world of things as well, if he is no longer recognized as *homo faber* but treated as an *animal laborans* whose necessary "metabolism with nature" is of concern to no one. Isolation then becomes loneliness. Tyranny based on isolation generally leaves the productive capacities of man intact; a tyranny over "laborers," however, as for instance the rule over slaves in antiquity, would automatically be a rule over lonely, not only isolated, men and tend to be totalitarian.

While isolation concerns only the political realm of life, loneliness concerns human life as a whole. Totalitarian government, like all tyrannies, certainly could not exist without destroying the public realm of life, that is, without destroying, by isolating men, their political capacities. But totalitarian domination as a form of government is new in that it is not content with this isolation and destroys private life as well. It bases itself on loneliness, on the experience of not belonging to the world at all, which is among the most radical and desperate experiences of man.

Loneliness, the common ground for terror, the essence of totalitarian government, and for ideology or logicality, the preparation of its executioners and victims, is closely connected with uprootedness and superfluousness which have been the curse of modern masses since the beginning of the industrial revolution and have become acute with the rise of imperialism at the end of the last century and the break-down of political institutions and social traditions in our own time. To be uprooted means to have no place in the world, recognized and guaranteed by others; to be superfluous means not to belong to the world at all. Uprootedness can be the preliminary condition for superfluousness, just as isolation can (but must not) be the preliminary condition for loneliness. Taken in itself, without consideration of its recent historical causes and its new role in politics, loneliness is at the same time contrary to the basic requirements of the human condition *and* one of the fundamental experiences of every human life. Even the experience of the materially and sensually given world depends upon my being in contact with other men, upon our *common* sense which regulates and controls all other senses and without which each of us would be enclosed in his own particularity of sense data which in themselves are unreliable and treacherous. Only because we have common sense, that is, only because not one man, but men in the plural inhabit the earth can we trust our immediate sensual experience. Yet, we have only to remind ourselves that one day we shall have to leave this common world which will go on as before and for whose continuity we are superfluous in order to realize loneliness, the experience of being abandoned by everything and everybody.

Loneliness is not solitude. Solitude requires being alone whereas loneliness shows itself most sharply in company with others. Apart from a few stray remarks—usually framed in a paradoxical mood like Cato's statement (reported by Cicero, *De Re Publica* I, 17): *numquam minus solum esse quam cum solus esset,* "never was he less alone than when he was alone," or never was he less lonely than when he was in solitude—it seems that Epictetus, the emancipated slave philosopher of Greek origin, was the first to distinguish between loneliness and solitude. His discovery, in a way, was accidental, his chief interest being neither solitude nor loneliness, but being alone (*monos*) in the sense of absolute independence. As Epictetus sees it (*Dissertationes,* Book 3, ch. 13) the lonely man (*eremos*) finds himself surrounded by others with whom he cannot establish contact or to whose hostility he is exposed. The solitary man, on the contrary, is alone and therefore "can be together with himself" since men have the capacity of "talking with themselves." In solitude, in other words, I am "by myself," together with my self, and therefore two-in-one, whereas in loneliness I am actually one, deserted by all others. All thinking, strictly speaking, is done in solitude and is a dialogue between me and myself; but this dialogue of the two-in-one does not lose contact with the world of my fellow-men because they are represented in the self with whom I lead the dialogue of thought. The problem of solitude is that this two-in-one needs the others in order to become one again: one unchangeable individual whose identity can never be mistaken for that of any other. For the confirmation of my identity I depend entirely upon other people; and it is the great saving grace of companionship for solitary men that it makes them "whole" again, saves them from the dialogue of thought in which one remains always equivocal, restores the identity which makes them speak with the single voice of one unexchangeable person.

Solitude can become loneliness; this happens when all by myself I am deserted by my own self. Solitary men have always been in danger of loneliness, when they can no longer find the redeeming grace of companionship to save them from duality and equivocality and doubt. Historically, it seems as though this danger became sufficiently great to be noticed by others and recorded by history only in the nineteenth century. It showed itself clearly when philosophers, for whom alone solitude is a way of life and a condition of work, were no longer content with the fact that "philosophy is only for the few" and began to insist that nobody "understands" them. Characteristic in this respect is the anecdote reported from Hegel's deathbed which hardly could have been told of any great philosopher before him: "Nobody has understood me except one; and he also misunderstood." Conversely, there is always the chance that a lonely man finds himself and starts the thinking dialogue of solitude. This seems to have happened to Nietzsche in Sils Maria when he conceived of *Zarathustra*.

In two poems ("Sils Maria" and "Aus hohen Bergen") he tells of the empty expectation and the yearning waiting of the lonely until suddenly *"um Mittag wars, da wurde Eins zu Zwei . ./ Nun feiern wir, vereinten Siegs gewiss,/ das Fest der Feste;/ Freund Zarathustra kam, der Gast der Gäste!"* ("Noon was, when One became Two . . . Certain of united victory we celebrate the feast of feasts; friend Zarathustra came, the guest of guests.")

What makes loneliness so unbearable is the loss of one's own self which can be realized in solitude, but confirmed in its identity only by the trusting and trustworthy company of my equals. In this situation, man loses trust in himself as the partner of his thoughts and that elementary confidence in the world which is necessary to make experiences at all. Self and world, capacity for thought and experience are lost at the same time.

The only capacity of the human mind which needs neither the self nor the other nor the world in order to function safely and which is as independent of experience as it is of thinking is the ability of logical reasoning whose premise is the self-evident. The elementary rules of cogent evidence, the truism that two and two equals four cannot be perverted even under the conditions of absolute loneliness. It is the only reliable "truth" human beings can fall back upon once they have lost the mutual guarantee, the common sense, men need in order to experience and live and know their way in a common world. But this "truth" is empty or rather no truth at all, because it does not reveal anything. (To define consistency as truth as some modern logicians do means to deny the existence of truth.) Under the conditions of loneliness, therefore, the self-evident is no longer just a means of the intellect and begins to be productive, to develop its own lines of "thought." That thought processes characterized by strict self-evident logicality, from which apparently there is no escape, have some connection with loneliness was once noticed by Luther (whose experiences in the phenomena of solitude and loneliness probably were second to no one's and who once dared to say that "there must be a God because man needs one being whom he can trust") in a little-known remark on the Bible text "it is not good that man should be alone": A lonely man, says Luther, "always deduces one thing from the other and thinks everything to the worst." The famous extremism of totalitarian movements, far from having anything to do with true radicalism, consists indeed in this "thinking everything to the worst," in this deducing process which always arrives at the worst possible conclusions.

What prepares men for totalitarian domination in the non-totalitarian world is the fact that loneliness, once a borderline experience usually suffered in certain marginal social conditions like old age, has become an everyday experience of the ever-growing masses of our century. The merciless process into which totalitarianism drives and organizes the masses looks like a suicidal escape from this reality. The "ice-cold reasoning" and the "mighty tentacle" of dialectics which "seizes you as in a vise" appears like a last support in a world where nobody is reliable and nothing can be relied upon. It is the inner coercion whose only content is the strict avoidance of contradictions that seems to confirm a man's identity outside all relationships with others. It fits him into the iron band of terror even when he is alone, and totalitarian domination tries never to leave him alone except in the extreme situation of solitary confinement. By destroying all space between men and pressing men against each other, even the productive potentialities of isolation are annihilated; by teaching and glorifying the logical reasoning of loneliness where man knows that he will be utterly lost if ever he lets go of the first premise from which the whole process is being started, even the slim chances that loneliness may be transformed into solitude and logic into thought are obliterated.

If it is true that tyranny bears the germs of its own destruction because it is based upon powerlessness which is the negation of man's political condition, then, one is tempted to predict the downfall of totalitarian domination without outside interference, because it rests on the one human experience which is the negation of man's social condition. Yet, even if this analogy were valid—and there are reasons to doubt it—it would operate only after the full realization of totalitarian government which is possible only after the conquest of the earth.

Apart from such considerations—which as predictions are of little avail and less consolation—there remains the fact that the crisis of our time and its central experience have brought forth an entirely new form of government which as a potentiality and an ever-present danger is only too likely to stay with us from now on, just as other forms of government which came about at different historical moments and rested on different fundamental experiences have stayed with mankind regardless of temporary defeats—monarchies, and republics, tyrannies, dictatorships and despotism.

But there remains also the truth that every end in history necessarily contains a new beginning; this beginning is the promise, the only "message" which the end can ever produce. Beginning, before it becomes a historical event, is the supreme capacity of man; politically, it is identical with man's freedom. *Initium ut esset homo creatus est*— "that a beginning be made man was created" said Augustine (*Civitas Dei*, Book 12, ch. 20). This beginning is guaranteed by each new birth; it is indeed every man.

TOTALITARIAN RELIGIONS

Waldemar Gurian

[1952]

WE OBSERVE today an astonishing spectacle. Just as during the worst period of the French Revolution, Christianity, and particularly the Catholic Church, is under systematic attack in wide parts of the world, in the Soviet Union, in its European satellites, and in Red China. These countries are under the control of groups which profess an atheistic doctrine. The official doctrines of the Soviet world express the belief that religion will disappear; it permits the application of tactics which strangulate Church life slowly, but successfully. Leading members of the hierarchy have been arrested and sentenced; schools and monasteries have been closed down; religious orders disbanded; missionary work of centuries has been destroyed. All this is accomplished by systematic and carefully planned campaigns. Every means of deception is used. In profoundly Catholic countries like Poland, caution prevails; in others brutal terror is applied. And all measures against Church life are presented, despite the clear atheism of the official doctrine, as measures against reactionaries and political counter-revolutionaries, churchmen are accused of being American agents and allies of imperialism and capitalism.

But it is not only the Communists who have persecuted the Church in our time; the anti-communist Nazi regime also tried to destroy the Church, though this attack was made in the name of another doctrine, a racial philosophy. What both systems, communism and Nazism, have in common is their totalitarian character. This common totalitarianism, of course, does not mean that they must always be friendly to each other; on the contrary, they fought against each other, accusing each other of being barbaric, inhuman, sadistic.

In this article I will not try to present the history of the anti-religious policies of the two totalitarian systems of our time. I will try to show the basis of these policies, the spirit which makes them develop an absolute hostility against Christ and His Church.

The totalitarian movements which have arisen since World War I are fundamentally religious movements. They aim not at changes of political and social institutions, but at the reshaping of the nature

241

of man and society. They claim to have the true and obligatory knowledge about life and its aims. They emphasize that they are based on doctrines which describe and determine totally and completely the existence and activities of men and society. It does not matter whether these doctrines are presented as the exclusively correct expression of a scientific knowledge of society and the laws according to which history develops—as the Marxist Bolshevik variety of totalitarianism does—or they pretend to justify the domination of the master race and express the myth destined to prevail in the twentieth century—as the National Socialist variety asserts. The pretense of having the true doctrine gives to the totalitarian movements their basic character. They are intolerant. They aim at the extirpation of all other doctrines and philosophies. They cannot tolerate any limitation of their claims and their power. Totalitarian movements cannot conceive of realms of life outside and beyond their control; they cannot accept the fact that there are other doctrines or institutions with the right to remain independent, having a dignity and a validity of their own. That they do accept for a time, as long as power considerations demand it, the existence of other groups and other doctrines does not mean that they abandon their aim of absolute domination, of making all other doctrines disappear.

It is a fatal misunderstanding of totalitarian movements to confuse and identify them with authoritarian political regimes. True, authoritarian regimes do not know and accept real democratic institutions and processes, for example, periodical elections based upon universal suffrage which determine the composition of government; they reject constitutional limitations which do not depend upon decisions of the ruler. But they accept (or at least do not reject) an objective traditional social order which is independent of the ruler and the ruling group. Authoritarian regimes do not claim to bring a new faith, an all-embracing doctrine determining the whole of life; though they are non-democratic, opposed to representative government based on universal suffrage, rejecting parties and the political influence of public opinion which expresses itself in free and uncontrolled discussions.

The authoritarian regimes which in their traditional monarchic form became outmoded after the French Revolution, reappear today as reactions against the dissolution of unifying forces and institutions among nations. Nations in our time are often threatened by anarchy, by the deadly strife of parties which put their particular interests above the common good; for the parties have developed into instruments of the egoistic interests of their members or leaders who have forgotten their obligation towards the community as a whole. Authoritarian regimes of today may try, as the absolute monarchies of the Enlightenment did, to control all institutions—including the Church—claiming that the governments know best what the welfare of the community requires. They are surely anti-democratic, rejecting the participation of the people in government by national suffrage; they believe in a system of government exercised from above by a wise man or by a ruling elite. But they are not based upon the belief that the political regime must regulate the whole of life, that everything, including science and cultural activities, is subordinate to the movement which shapes the public power, that the doctrine of this movement is the key to the understanding of history and nature of society as well as of the destiny of man. The authoritarian regimes do not deny the existence of an objective order which is beyond the reach of political power, and they do not claim that political power determines what is the objective order and the truth. The authoritarian regimes express political views not shared by those who accept democracy and who believe that policies ought to be influenced by public opinion and its discussions. But they are not based upon political religions; their political power, unlike totalitarian power, does not determine the whole life of men and society.

Today, of course, it is not always easy to distinguish between totalitarian and authoritarian regimes. The Fascist regime in Mussolini's Italy rose with totalitarian pretensions; Mussolini himself wrote an article about Fascist doctrine. But I agree fully with Hannah Arendt who in *The Origins of Totalitarianism* cited Nazism and Bolshevism as the prototypes of totalitarianism. For Mussolini employed claims about a particular Fascist doctrine for propaganda purposes in order to justify his superiority over the liberal-parliamentary regime of the past. The Fascist doctrine did not prevent him—despite all clashes and conflicts—from coming to terms with the Church. He accepted—true, for pragmatic reasons—the Catholic tradition prevailing in Italy. His rule had an authoritarian character despite totalitarian trimmings; he emphasized—as authoritarians are inclined to do—the power of the state, and therefore the right of the state to control all life and all institutions, including the Church. The Fascist attitude toward the Church brought about a renewal of the traditional conflicts between the Church and a strong state which would try to put the Church under its control, denying her independence in public life. Fascism tried, for example, to control Catholic Action; this attempt caused Pius XI to write the encyclical *Non Abbiamo Bisogno*. But despite its rhetorical boasts—against which the Church took a stand—Italian Fascism did not try seriously to re-

243

place the faith of the Church by a new religion, a political religion making the totalitarian movement the single force dominating all realms of life and giving true meaning to society and men.

What has been said about Italian Fascism must, also, be said about Franco's Spain. Franco's regime is authoritarian, but not totalitarian. It uses fewer totalitarian trimmings than Mussolini did—for it appeals more directly and intensely to Spanish traditions. It opposes liberalism and modern democracy in the name of those traditions, and it tries to emphasize the power of the state, but it does not assert the mission of a movement destined to bring a new faith and to shape the whole of life correspondingly.

The difficulty in making clear the distinction between authoritarian and totalitarian regimes is increased by the tendencies of totalitarian movements to utilize both traditional ideas and conservative-minded groups to bring themselves and their policies into power. A particularly striking example of this tendency was provided by Hitler and his National-Socialism. One of his most efficient propaganda slogans was the claim that he alone was able to crush communism— liberals and democrats were denounced as its allies—and that, therefore, he would preserve and rescue traditional values and religion. He was anti-communist; so his propaganda tried to spread the wrong impression that his movement was pro-Christian. It was overlooked by his conservative admirers that one can fight one error not only in the name of truth, but in the name of other errors. Not only did the party program mention "positive Christianity," but the first proclamation of Hitler, upon his appointment as chancellor, mentioned protection of religion. Likewise, the Bolsheviks, who began as the fiercest opponents and destroyers of all traditional institutions and beliefs and as indefatigable workers for an international atheistic classless society, have learned to press traditional forces into their service. Stalin's Soviet Union proclaims that its policies realize Russian national aspirations; and the state Church of the Tsarist past is again utilized as an instrument of the government and its propaganda. Thus, the strong state whose rulers are not dependent upon elections, parties, and a free public opinion, appears as characteristic of totalitarian regimes; their claim to have an all-embracing doctrine seems to be only an instrument for the erection of a political system where the state concentrates in its hands the maximum of power.

But I think this attempt to interpret totalitarianism only as a particularly ruthless form of authoritarianism and to explain away the importance of the totalitarian doctrine prevents real understanding of the political religions of the twentieth century. These political religions, the various kinds of totalitarianism, aim not only at the establishment of a strong state, but at the complete transformation and control of men and society. The totalitarian state which intervenes in all realms of life is not the end but merely an instrument of the totalitarian movement. The decisive feature of this movement is the acceptance of a doctrine which justifies absolute domination by those who have accepted it—the leaders and members of the totalitarian party. This doctrine does not exclude practical adaptations. The masses are not told the consequences of the doctrine; they must be seduced and tamed by being persuaded (especially before power is achieved) that their needs and demands will be satisfied. In 1917 the Bolsheviks said that they were for peace—the masses, the Russian soldiers, and peasants did not understand that they were really only for the ending of the imperialist wars and for their transformation into revolutionary wars. They told the peasants that all landed estates would be turned over to them. The peasants did not realize that all land, including their own, would be finally put under the control of the state. The Nazis told the middle class businessmen that they would abolish department stores, and end an economic order dominated by the easy gains of interest-takers. The nature of the totalitarian doctrines was but slowly realized. Hitler introduced even the measures against the Jews only step by step. He began with the Concordat in order to deceive the Catholics about his Church policies. The final status promised by the totalitarian doctrine can even become a myth whose realization is beyond human control. Stalin extended the transitional period during which a strong political power would be necessary, and has, consequently, postponed the withering away of the state as an instrument of coercion to the uncontrollable and unpredictable far-distant future.

What matters is not the content of totalitarian doctrine; its function of establishing total domination by the totalitarian leaders and elites is decisive—to use an expression of Hannah Arendt. Totalitarian doctrine justifies a continuous drive for more and more power as well as the dynamism and expansionism without end characteristic of totalitarian regimes; totalitarian doctrine makes totalitarian rulers deal with men and human groups as pure material; for what matters are not human beings and their reality, but the constant proof presented again and again that the doctrine is right, for it determines reality by power exercised in its name; this power that has no limits —it is expanded and demonstrated again and again—becomes an end in itself, for it is proved to be meaningful because it corresponds to the doctrine and therefore justifies the actions of those who realize and interpret it.

Men and groups are not only to obey and to avoid any public opposition—as in authoritarian regimes—but they are forced to be active and enthusiastic supporters. They are forced in such a way

245

that they do not appear to be forced. They are liquidated, thrown away as if they were unnecessary and useless parts of a machine—according to the whims of the rulers, who show by this behavior their limitless all-embracing power. The totalitarian masters shape the world according to their doctrine; any reality not corresponding to the doctrine is wrong, and its existence is rejected if the doctrine demands it. Hannah Arendt illustrates this attitude by mentioning a story which denies that there are other subways besides that of Moscow, for to admit of other subways would be to oppose the claims of Soviet propaganda which the inhabitants of the Soviet Union must accept as reality. The policy of the iron curtain is a consequence of the totalitarian attempt to make the totalitarian world appear as the real world. The authoritarian regime establishes a form of political rule; the totalitarian regime tries to create an artificial world and impose it as reality. This world has to correspond to the demands of the totalitarian doctrine as interpreted by the rulers so that their power is constantly maintained and demonstrated by expansions. A vicious circle characterizes totalitarian rule: the doctrine justifies the absolute domination by such a group as the party—the instrument for the realization of socialism and communism or the racial elite—and the doctrine is proved to be true by the successful absolute domination consisting not only in the establishment of the totalitarian state, but the imposition of an artificial world. God's order is replaced by a man-made order, the artificial order required by the doctrine and created by the power exercised in its name.

Therefore, the conflict between the Church and the totalitarian regimes goes much deeper than the conflicts between the Church and the authoritarian regimes. The latter are conflicts caused by attempts of the secular power to put the spiritual power with its public functions under its control, to determine, for example, appointments of bishops, to control all educational activities of the Church, to restrict the formation of Catholic associations, to supervise or to forbid religious orders, to make the publication of papal and episcopal pronouncements dependent upon permission of the state authorities (the so-called *placet*). The totalitarian regimes take over all methods of the authoritarian state to control and restrict Church activities; they do not admit, of course, any obligation to regard the Church—as modern liberal-democratic regimes do—as an association of citizens in whose internal life the government does not interfere. For all associations ought to be under control of the totalitarian movement; their "coordination" (*Gleichschaltung*) is carried out as one of the most important policies of the totalitarian regime, and only on account of power politics and propagandist considerations is the Church provisionally exempted from this coordination—Hitler concluded a

Concordat not actually to comply with its terms, but to avoid an immediate open conflict with Catholics and to confuse them. The land and other property of the Catholic Church in Poland are not confiscated. In this the regime's hope is to keep the Catholics quiet.

The totalitarian regimes also apply methods and legislative measures which have been used by authoritarian regimes which tried to put the Church under political control, regarding it as an intolerably dangerous competitor of the secular civil authority posing a threat to loyal behavior towards the government or the nation. But this legislation and these measures are not specific in the totalitarian Church policies. The application of these means by totalitarian regimes has as its aim not the restriction and the control of the public activities of the Church but the complete destruction of religion and the Church. The faith of the Church will be replaced by the myth of the twentieth century, the racialist religion of the leaders of the Nazi movement. True, Rosenberg, the authoritative teacher of the Nazi doctrine, maintained that the racial People's Church of the future would tolerate Catholic and Protestant chapels, "positive Christianity," but racialism would determine what could be accepted as "positive" and what must be rejected as "negative Christianity." The Bolshevik anti-religious religion does not use, as the Nazis did, a misleading pseudo-religious terminology. It asserts that its atheism will necessarily triumph and can afford to accept freedom of religion and conscience. The Communists claim that the realization of socialism and communism will destroy the social roots of religious beliefs, which are "opiates" used either by exploiting groups to fool the masses or by the masses themselves as means of self-deception in order to escape from intolerable realities. If men become masters of society through and in socialism and communism, the Bolsheviks as followers of Marxism pretend there will be no need for a God Who has created men and the world—all religious mysteries will evaporate when faced by the reality of the perfect man-made world of the classless society. The totalitarian movements are hostile to the Church not only on account of their policies towards the Church but on account of their basic belief, of the consciously formulated doctrine which, allegedly, is alone able to explain history and to give the right aim to all human activities.

The totalitarian doctrines are not only political ones, they claim to provide the key to the whole universe, to all realms of human life; they deny to the Church any independence in public activities. They are bitterly opposed to her doctrine, to her influence on the souls of men. This doctrine and this influence must be replaced by the totalitarian ones. Here appears the similarity between the totalitarian movements of the twentieth century and the anti-religious ideologies of the French Revolution in the eighteenth century. These ideologies went beyond the original aim of the new French regime to control the Church; they tried to replace its doctrine by new ones corresponding to reason and the true nature of men.

Modern totalitarianism differs from its predecessor in that it creates its doctrines as explanations of the historical processes—they can be realized only in their culmination, not at once, immediately, by proclamations, pressure, and legislative actions. Marx made satirical remarks about the behavior of Bakunin who, during one of his putsches, issued a decree abolishing belief in God; the Soviet regime has always pretended to respect religious feelings, but this of course has not prevented all kinds of persecution of religious groups, whereas atheistic propaganda is favored and supported. Hitler carefully avoided publicizing his hostility to Christianity—the Nazis fought allegedly only against so-called "political" Catholicism and against ministerial intervention in affairs of state. Another distinction is the abandonment of the attempts made, for example, by Robespierre with his introduction of the cult of the Supreme Being to create special new moral-religious cults; some Nazi fanatics did attempt such a creation but the Germanic religion did not work. The modern totalitarian cult is exercised by demonstrations of power and domination by the totalitarian regime and its leaders. Party congresses, May Day processions, incessant adulatory praise of the leaders, constant announcement that a new era has started and that all representatives of old epochs are doomed—these are the cult and the liturgy of the totalitarian movements. The totalitarian movements have their devils, too—not only external enemies but internal traitors, who are constantly unmasked and defeated, purged and liquidated.

Just because the totalitarian movements believe that their doctrine will be victorious and that all reality will be shaped in its image, they are able to apply deceptive tactics. The masses, which are kept in constant motion, must be educated and prepared to understand the goal grasped at the beginning only by the leaders. When the enemy is too strong, complicated maneuvers are necessary. As Lenin put it, it is necessary to retreat one step in order to be able to advance again. The Bolsheviks abandoned their attempts to destroy the prestige of the Orthodox Church or to split it by supporting the faction known as the so-called Living Church which accused the old Church leadership of being reactionary; they soon realized that this policy would not work; but they have continued to expect the disappearance of all religion as a result of their policies—even today when they use the Orthodox Church both as an instrument for their propaganda, and as a means to refute the accusation that anti-religious policies prevail in the Soviet Union. A final objective here is also to weaken the Catholic Church; the Catholics of the Greek rite, the so-called Uniates, recognizing the authority of Rome, have been put under the authority of the Patriarch of Moscow. Groups of priests cooperating with communism are established and favored in order to confuse and split the believers.

The Nazi policies towards the Church at the beginning were more disguised than those of the Bolsheviks. They tried to mislead Christian believers by their opposition to atheistic communism and by concluding a concordat with Rome. They emphasized always that they were fighting only against political Catholicism and the representatives of religion who—by becoming too power-hungry or even allegedly indulging in vices—were in reality betrayers of the faith. In the name of national unity and the necessity of keeping religion pure the Church was eliminated step by step from the exercise of influence on public life. Catholic schools were abolished, Catholic publications had to stop because of a paper shortage which Nazi publications did not experience. Religious orders no longer had a chance to exist; there was no longer any opportunity to recruit seminarians. But all this was done step by step, cautiously. It is characteristic that Goebbels prevented the arrest of Bishop Count Galen (who publicly criticized such Nazi policies as the liquidation of insane and feeble-minded people) in accordance with the principle: "We do not want martyrs." Churchmen were arrested, allegedly, only because they were criminals and enemies of the national unity, the community of the German people.

Peculiar to totalitarian movements is their attempt to change the center of life. The transcendent world is either absolutely denied as in the Bolshevik belief in the inevitable coming of the atheistic classless society, or it is made into an instrument of purely immanent political and social forces as in the Nazi order. Pope Pius XI's encyclical of 1937, *"Mit brennender Sorge,"* gives a classical analysis of this misuse of religious words and concepts for purely secular meaning. The Pope rejects the Nazi talk about God, which makes God a symbol of the power of a race. He rejects the use of sacred words for the purpose of praising the policy and public acts of the Nazi totalitarian movement. He reveals the misuse of the word justice when it is made to express racial feelings, as in the sentence: "Just is what Nordic-Aryan men regard as just."

The fact that a political movement informed and guided by the allegedly just and at the same time true doctrine is put at the center of life makes this doctrine the aim of life. If religion is not openly rejected—and explained away in Marxian fashion as the product of an imperfect society—it is deprived of all dignity and independence by being made a tool of political and social power politics, a collection of myths which strengthen the will to live and die for the totalitarian movement. The politico-social religions compel the swallowing-up of true religion and universal human ethics by arbitrary pseudo-scientific and pseudo-mythical doctrines. These doctrines claim to correspond to and to be reality—because they are backed by groups which, having achieved political power, can make the system of domination established by them appear to be the reality.

The conflict between the Church and totalitarianism is, therefore, not only a conflict of power and influence, but a conflict over the nature of men and society. Totalitarianism will reduce men not merely to cogs in its power machinery but to creatures utilizing all their capacities to celebrate their own enslavement. What is just, what is good, what is beautiful, what is free, is defined by the totalitarian rulers, for they must always be right and competent in all fields according to the doctrine, the obligatory philosophy, pseudo-theology and mythology of history. This must be constantly confirmed by demonstrations of public enthusiasm and by display of unceasing efforts to prove that the totalitarian fiat has no limitations.

The Church thus must appear to the totalitarians as an intolerable challenge. Even if they succeed in depriving it of any independent role in public life, the fact remains that the Church is not based upon the totalitarian faith, the totalitarian doctrine. And the Christian faith is not compatible with an image of man which can regard as the meaning of his life only participation in worldly society based either on economic achievements or on the master race. The Catholic faith does not accept belief in the power of man to create by his own forces a world in which he is absolute master and which is absolutely perfect and self-sufficient. The Catholic faith does not permit an absolute domination over men, one which regards them simply as material for the achievement and demonstration of power and as instruments of an earthly development looked upon as necessary by the totalitarian doctrine.

The totalitarian movements, the pseudo-religious movements and exponents of anti-religious politico-social religions, have arisen in the twentieth century as products of a religious and spiritual crisis. In the modern secularized world, religion—if not deemed superfluous or unimportant—has continued to be widely accepted only as a traditional force linked with familiar social orders. As these orders experienced a crisis the basic secularistic belief became manifest. What matters is economic productivity and right organization; what matters is political power to form and establish a new society. The totalitarian political religions are expressions of secularist thought in a world where the inherited traditional stability and continuity are threatened or have disappeared. They try to establish again a secure world without uncertainties and internal crises by accepting an interpretation of history and society which claims to be absolute truth, which explains all the failures of the past and present and which announces a happy future. This future will come after a merciless fight to the finish. This belief in the future golden age is connected with a belief in the particular mission of a group, the party which formulates and applies the right revolutionary consciousness of the masses or the racial elite which ends misrule by evil and inferior elements. The present is sacrificed to the future and the individual is regarded as material in and for the necessary and, therefore, just development. World and history are explained by natural laws which are known to those who master the doctrine.

Secularism in its totalitarian form becomes a secular religion, putting a human doctrine in the place of Revelation, a visible worldly society in the place of union with God as the aim of life. Not utilitarian calculations but demonstrations of faith in the unlimited power of the doctrine and its representatives really matter. Utilitarian calculations would limit the policies of expansion and the urge to absolute domination. This totalitarian, immanentist faith cannot be met by an optimistic secularism which is not aware of the fundamental crisis of our time or by an apparently religious attitude for which religion is, despite theoretical denials, indissolubly bound to a particular social order. The pseudo-certainty of totalitarianism which establishes by terror and a refined system of pressure a closed pseudo-real world can be opposed only by the true certainty based upon belief in true revelation and by the realization that man is infinitely more than an instrument for life and society in this world, that there are rights and duties of the human person which cannot be sacrificed to a doctrine about political and social development. The conflict between the Church and totalitarianism is, therefore, much more than a conflict between Church and state, for totalitarianism tries to establish a reality in which all human forces and beliefs serve only this world, an earthly society, which is self-sufficient and has no other end than itself. The world leading to God, totalitarianism replaces by a self-sufficient world which, through the effort and struggles of men, makes God appear merely as a superstitious creation of men before they were able to master their life and society or simply as a mythical symbol of the power exercised by their social or racial elites.

MAN AND REVOLUTION

AN AGE OF

REVOLUTIONARY WARS:

AN HISTORICAL PARALLEL

Alfred Cobban

[1951]

THERE is one point on which both sides in the present world conflict are agreed. Each may denounce the leadership of the other side, but neither supposes that a change in leadership would make any difference, because both believe that it is a conflict not of persons or governments, but of principles, or of systems of society. The commonly accepted explanation of the conflict, in short, is that the world is now divided between Communism and Capitalism. At the risk of seeming paradoxical it must be asked what this explanation explains, and whether, in fact, it does anything but provide convenient labels for the opposing forces. The implied assumption that states with differing economic systems must necessarily be hostile to one another is at least unproved, and goes against historical experience. It would be easier to explain the conflict as a religious war, and Communism certainly exhibits many of the features of a militant religion, but can we be quite content to dismiss Communists and capitalists as the Protestants and Catholics of the twentieth century? And if we are, can we find many religious wars in which secular and political interests did not provide as strong or stronger a motive than religion?

Because of the difficulty of accounting for the conflict in purely ideological terms, some students of the contemporary world fall back on the view that all hostilities between states are mere conflicts of power politics. The fact that we normally tend to resent the reduction of the motives of our states to simple Machiavellianism is no disproof of this interpretation. Historians are willing enough to allow the mere rivalries of power politics to account for many of the wars of the past, why not for the present struggle? If this view is accepted, the whole ideological apparatus on both sides must be dismissed as a gigantic smoke-screen, produced for the purpose of concealing the machinations of self-interest. Such an explanation seems to put human capacity for cold-blooded calculation at too high a level. The discussion thus wanders from one extreme to the other indefinitely: neither the ideological explanation, nor the explanation in terms of power politics seems adequate by itself. The purpose of this study is to suggest that there is another line of approach to the problem, which takes us a good deal farther towards understanding the nature of the conflict. It may be suggested that a weakness in contemporary political analysis is the tendency to see each issue on too short a scale, or, sometimes, on none at all. Looking at the major struggles of our day, beginning with the last phase of the First World War, it is not difficult to see that they fall into a single historical category: they are essentially revolutionary wars. Now this is not an entirely new phenomenon, and to understand it we cannot do better than turn back to the history of the greatest of all revolutionary wars of the past.

At the end of the eighteenth century, Europe, as today the world, was split in two by the existence of a great revolutionary state. When the French Revolution burst on an astonished world it came with the promise of liberty and peace. The rulers of the other states of Europe did not exactly welcome it, but they had no intention of interfering in the affairs of France. The government of Great Britain, which was to prove the most enduring enemy of revolutionary France, was profoundly pacific. The Younger Pitt, in his budget speech of 1792, uttered the famous prophecy: "There never was a time in the history of this country, when we might more reasonably expect fifteen years of peace than at the present moment." Why were these hopes of peace disappointed? Why did such a deep-seated opposition develop between Britain and revolutionary France that instead of fifteen years of peace, over twenty years of war followed? If the question is put in more general terms—why was a revolutionary state unable to live at peace with the rest of Europe?—its contemporary relevance will easily be seen.

It is worth pointing out, because the fact is often overlooked, that however much the other powers disliked the revolution, the declarations of war did not come from them: it was France which declared war in turn on Austria, Prussia, England, Holland, Spain. But the question of responsibility for the beginning of the war is not the essential issue. The important question is not even whether there was any factor in the revolution which was likely to lead to war—there are always plenty of causes of war—but whether there was anything which made peace impossible. Those who lived at the time thought there was. The first point that strikes one, in considering the causes of the long continuance, rather than the origins, of the Revolutionary War, is the fear of propaganda. The revolutionaries aimed at establishing direct relations with all peoples over the heads of their governments. In those who sympathized with their principles they had a Fifth Column everywhere. "The genius of the French Revolution marched forth," said Pitt, "the terror and dismay of the world." Its aim was to bring liberty to all nations. But to quote Pitt once again: "They will not accept under the name of Liberty any model of government, but that which is conformable to their own opinions and ideas; and all men must learn from the mouth of their cannon the propagation of their system in every part of the world." While such a combination of ideas and policies prevailed in the Revolution, the other powers saw no security in peace with France.

Even at the time, however, it was realized that revolutionary propaganda by itself was not a sufficient motive for war. The other countries of Europe, if left to themselves, were quite capable of suppressing their own Jacobins without undue difficulty. To Fox's charge that he was making war on opinion Pitt replied: "It is not so. We are not in arms against the opinions of the closet, nor the speculations of the schools. We are at war with *armed* opinions." The power of French armies was what made revolutionary opinions dangerous. Though we must not underestimate the great wave of genuine idealism with which the revolution began, those who controlled the actions of the revolutionary armies were not moved exclusively by idealistic motives. When, early in the revolution, the French Assembly passed a decree repudiating all conquests, it was undoubtedly sincere. But this idealistic frame of mind did not remain undiluted for very long. Revolutionary dynamism was not to be confined within the narrow limits of a single state. The revolutionaries soon learned to rationalize their aggressive instincts, and imagined that they had thereby moralized self-interest.

With the military genius released by the revolution, with the military tactics adapted to make use of the enthusiasm of the early volunteers, and with the solid weight of man-power provided by the *levée en masse,* it was not long before war meant victory. As it went on, annexation followed occupation, and the plebiscites which at first accompanied liberation by the revolutionary armies rapidly came to be omitted as unnecessary formalities. The frontiers of France swelled, satellite states formed excrescences on the new boundaries, and the pretense of liberation wore thinner and thinner. The French armies brought many good things in their train: they brought a more humane and rational legal system, more efficient administration, opportunities for the middle classes. But the conquered countries had to pay a heavy price in government by small pro-French cliques, whose authority rested on French bayonets and the secret police, and in furnishing continual supplies of men and money for the French armies. As early as 1795 the dominant aims of French foreign policy, which can be traced without any disguise in the records of the Quai d'Orsay, were reduced to two: first, to obtain strategic frontiers and a glacis of dependent territories in front of them. These were to protect the gains of France from counter-attack, and to provide a jumping-off ground for further aggression. Secondly, France required economic advantages—money, corn, cattle, clothing, boots—requisitioned by the generals or legally obtained by treaties of peace and friendship. Bonaparte had nothing to teach the Republic in the arts of aggression and confiscation. The Revolution was aggressive abroad even before it became tyrannical at home, and Pitt was right in believing that the only limit on French conquests was the strength of the resistance opposed to them.

Of course, we must not exaggerate the novelty of much of this. Sorel has pointed out that practically every crime in international relations with which the Revolution has been charged could be found in the repertoire of the *ancien régime.* The difference is that the Revolution did on principle what the *ancien régime* had done from lack of principle. What is the explanation? Is it just the normal decline in the idealism of a political movement under the temptations of power? *"Tout commence en mystique,"* wrote Peguy, *"tout finit en politique."* We might believe this to be the explanation, if it were not that the Revolution turned into something which went far beyond the normal aggressions of international politics. It developed into a bid for universal empire and changed war from a limited struggle between governments into an almost unlimited struggle between nations. The French Assembly even passed a decree—not put into practice—that no British or Hanoverian prisoners should be taken. The speeches and propaganda of the revolutionary leaders, denouncing their enemies as nations of cannibals, inhuman beasts of prey and so on, have a very modern ring. Their opponents retaliated in kind and the result was the first draft—admittedly, a very imperfect one—of totalitarian war, war without restriction in its methods and without limit in its ends.

Such a war did not arise merely out of the customary rivalries of power politics, but from the introduction of some new factor. It is suggested here that the new factor was the development of an ardent opposition of ideas. This opposition was one which played so little part in most international conflicts during the nineteenth century that we tend to forget that it ever could be a cause of conflict. International struggles came to be interpreted as simple clashes of material interests, with which principles had nothing to do. More recently the reaction produced by the exaggerated propaganda of the First World

War increased the tendency, particularly among historians, to look with suspicion on the alleged role of ideas, or principles, in the struggles of the past. History, reviewed in this light, became a mere conflict of interests, and the politics of the present a glorified intrigue. In the course of the last thirty years Communists and Nazis have taught us, at a heavy price, that ideas do matter in history. We could have learnt the same lesson more cheaply from a study of the French Revolution, for what was the Revolution?

In what I have to say, I hope I will not be suspected of attempting to sum up a great movement in terms of a single formula. The Revolution was many things. It was an attempt to reform the government of France, a revolt against well-known abuses, a struggle for power between the bourgeoisie and the privileged classes, and much more. But it was also, and this is what concerns us here, the embodiment of a great idea, the idea of the sovereignty of the people, or nation. For a clear statement of the meaning of this principle of popular or national sovereignty there is no need to go farther than to the little abbé who, in 1789, was the oracle of the *tiers état* in France, Sieyès. "The Nation," Sieyès wrote, "exists before all things and is the origin of all things. It is sufficient that its will is manifested for all positive law to vanish before it. In whatever manner a Nation wills, it is sufficient that it does will: all forms are good, and its will is always the supreme law." This was the essence of the revolutionary creed, and this was what turned an ordinary political conflict into a major war of ideas.

The theory of popular sovereignty is different in one particular from every other theory of government. It is a theory according to which those who exercise power, and those over whom it is exercised, are one and the same. The People rules—whom does it rule?—it rules itself. Popular sovereignty, according to its exponents, is self-government, and, therefore, freedom. The argument is plausible. I think it is fair to say that many, asked to define democracy, would define it in some such way, and would refuse to believe that the definition differs from the normal Western conception of democracy. But it *does* differ, and differ fundamentally. Can anyone in his senses really believe that the people actually, concretely, rule this or any other country? Are *we* the government? Do *we*, the people, impose the taxes on ourselves and decide how to spend them? Do *we* pass and carry out the laws on military service, or tariffs, or capital punishment? Do *we* appoint our Secretaries and Ministers, or any of the civil servants who manage our affairs? Of course we do not. What we mean by saying that we are a democracy is not that we *are* the government, but that through the process of election and representation we *control* the government. This is quite a different thing, as Burke saw when he was first confronted with the revolutionary theory. "The people," he said, "are the natural control on authority. But to exercise and to control together is contradictory and impossible." The identification of the government with the people, Burke realized, was the new thing, and in the long run the fatal thing, in revolutionary theory. The Revolution ended many evils and introduced many reforms, but in letting loose this principle on the world, it released a spirit perhaps more potent for evil than even those that it had exorcized.

The idea that the rulers can be identified with the ruled, the government with the people, and that this is the meaning of democracy, was, is, and must be fatal to liberty. That may seem a sweeping statement, but it will hardly seem exaggerated if we consider the implications of the belief that government and people can be one and the same. The identification is, as I have said, impossible; but the mere *belief* in such an identification makes any constitutional device for attempting to control government in the interests of the people unnecessary and irrelevant. A government has only to assert that it is the government of the people to be automatically emancipated from all restraints. Whoever lifts a finger against it, or utters a word of criticism, is an enemy of the people. He is guilty not of *lèse-majesté*, but, in the words of Robespierre, of *lèse-nation* or *lèse-peuple*. Even under the most despotic regimes, at any rate in Western Europe, it was admitted that the individual had rights. Before the new theory of sovereignty those rights faded away like snow in summer. Whatever the government had the power to do, it had the right to do: any crime was permissible: if it was done in the name of the people it was not a crime.

Internally the theory was a justification of tyranny, externally of aggression, for in the conditions of the modern world popular sovereignty inevitably means national sovereignty. It was because he saw this in the French Revolution that Burke opposed it so bitterly. He had no doubt what the theory of popular sovereignty would come to mean in the end, and he lived to see his fears justified. "What now stands as government in France," he wrote, "is struck out at a heat. The will, the wish, the want, the liberty, the toil, the blood of individuals is as nothing. Individuality is left out of their scheme of government. The state is all in all. Everything is referred to the production of force, afterwards everything is trusted to the use of it. It is military in its principle, in its maxims, in its spirit, and in all its movements. The state has dominion and conquest for its sole objects; dominion over minds by proselytism, over bodies by arms." And who exercises this vast power in the name of the people? The common-sense of the Younger Pitt saw the answer as clearly as the more theoretical mind of Burke. "In what is called the government of the multitude," Pitt said, "they are not the many who govern the few, but the few who govern the many. It is a species of tyranny, which adds insult to the wretchedness of its subjects by styling its own arbitrary decrees the voice of the people, and sanctioning its acts of oppression and cruelty under the pretense of the national will."

The justification for this excursus into history will now, I hope, be apparent. Its extraordinary relevance to the problems of our own times hardly needs to be underlined. Change a few of the circumstances and have we not a picture of the division in the world today? Modern revolutionaries, promising peace, have similarly brought about a climate of war, which, like the French revolutionaries, they have attributed to war-mongers abroad. Neighboring states have been swallowed up, or puppet governments established in them. Revolutionary propaganda has created a Fifth Column throughout the world. Wherever, by arms or propaganda, the revolutionary creed has been able to seize power, a government on its own model has been set up. The expansive pressure is continuous, for like the Napoleonic Empire the modern revolutionary state has no principle of limitation within itself. Its dynamism demands a continual forward movement. Held back in one quarter it breaks out in another, for it lives on the political, economic, and psychological conditions of expansion.

The cleavage, moreover, as a century and a half ago, is between opposed conceptions of government, and one as then based on the principle of the sovereignty of the people, which in practice means the government, and the other today recognizing the rights and interests of the individual. In both, government is in the hands of the few, as it always is, but in liberal democracy it is subject to free criticism and periodic control. In popular democracy criticism is ruthlessly suppressed and the machine of government is organized to prevent control over it from being exercised from any quarter outside the government circle. Of course, though I believe both interpretations of democracy to be sincere—attributions of insincerity, such as are usual when two sides to an argument use the same term in contradictory senses, seem to me out of place here—I cannot believe them to be equally valid. The test of political liberty, as much as anything else, is whether the people, if they are dissatisfied with those who rule them, can freely and peacefully cause their government to change its policy, or themselves change their government. The answer, in Soviet Russia as in revolutionary France, is that they cannot. And one reason why they cannot is the operation of the principle of popular sovereignty.

There is a conclusion of great practical importance, it seems to me, to be drawn from this parallel between the consequences of the French and Russian Revolutions. It suggests that a single historic force is at work in both great revolutions of the eighteenth and twentieth centuries. On both sides of the Iron Curtain it has been assumed too easily that the cause of the cleavage is to be sought in the economic theories and practices of Communism. At the beginning of this paper it was suggested that this form of the ideological explanation was unsatisfactory. It is also unnecessary. The example of the French Revolution suggests that the principle of popular or national sovereignty, pushed to the extreme limit, by itself is capable of producing an unbridgeable gap between a state and the rest of the world. Soviet Russia has undoubtedly been to school to Marx and derived much from him. But if what is called Communism in Russia were a faithful expression of the principles of the author of *Das Kapital*, it would be the first time in history that an idea has been translated into an ideology without suffering a radical change. In fact, one of the ironies of the modern world is that in the name of Marx, whose theoretical pattern was fashioned with a view to the ultimate "withering away" of the state, the state should have reached its apogee.

If the argument so far has any validity, it follows that the world is not quite so clearly divided ideologically as we have been apt to think. For all modern states have been influenced by the theories of the French Revolution, and all, to a greater or less degree, assert the principle of national sovereignty and base it on the claim of the government to embody the will of the people. The conflict, therefore, is not one of absolute opposites and there is no law of the excluded middle to apply. Undoubtedly, the state, being, as Marx saw, the embodiment of power, if it has complete sovereignty, tyranny at home and conquest abroad will be unrestrained. The result of freeing the state from control, by pretending that the people can themselves be the government, was shown between 1789 and 1815. The same experiment has been made in our own day, with similar results. Leviathan lives and moves before our eyes, all the more dangerous because in infancy he was called liberty.

I might end at this point, but the resulting impression would be a false one, based on an artificially simplified antithesis. In what has already been said, indeed, there is the implication, which needs to be made explicit, that the cleavage of principle between the Soviet regime and the Western democracies is one of degree, though so great that it has almost become one of kind. If this is the case, there is no reason for supposing that even the inflated sovereignty of the Soviet state is incapable of modification in the course of time. And, meanwhile, whether it leads to open war depends not on ideas but on the balance of opposed forces. France, once her strength had been released from the bonds of the old regime, was by far the greatest of the land powers at the end of the eighteenth century. A long struggle was needed before the combined weight of the other great powers could put an end to her aggression. Today the balance is much more even, and the weight of the United States, behind Britain and Western

Europe, has so far proved adequate to deter Soviet Russia from an open challenge by arms. China, in an earlier phase of revolutionary psychology, is less likely to be deterred, but cannot by herself start a World War unless Russia also comes in.

The present situation is in this respect a novel one. There is even a possibility that we may witness, for the first time, a state based on the totalitarian principle of popular sovereignty working out its destiny to the end without having its career cut short in the battles its aggressions have provoked. The history of revolutionary France offers some guidance here also. Its internal development, even while it was pursuing its foreign conquests with unparalleled success, suggests that a country cannot live permanently in a state of high political fever. Already in 1794 Saint-Just was saying, *"la Révolution est glacée."* The Napoleonic system kept up the urge for conquest, but behind the military and bureaucratic facade the people of France increasingly longed for peace and tranquillity. Corruption and inefficiency were spreading on all sides. Enthusiasm was dying. Propaganda had ceased to exercise its former effect. All the energy had to be supplied from above. The Revolution was dead at its centre long before the fatal disease had spread to the periphery. Will the Revolution in Soviet Russia similarly become ice-bound?

Such a development would not necessarily weaken the impetus to aggression, though it would sooner or later affect the efficiency with which it was pursued. A more important conclusion to be drawn from the operation of the theory of national or popular sovereignty in the international field is that it is a theory which is very difficult to reconcile with any kind of imperial hegemony, as Napoleon found in Spain. The revolutionary Spanish juntas fought bitterly against the French armies and against a reforming French King, Joseph Bonaparte, and in support of a reactionary Church and Monarchy, which stood for everything they hated most, except French rule. The principle of national sovereignty, which the Revolution had done so much to inculcate, proved stronger than all its other principles and in the end defeated them. There are signs of a similar development today. National sovereignty won a decisive victory in Russia when Stalin defeated Trotzky. It was a source of great strength to Russia in war; but it has become a source of weakness in the Russian attempt to create a combination of nations under Soviet leadership. Of that the Jugoslav revolt is the proof.

In the opposed camp, though of course the principle of national sovereignty is not absent, the situation is very different, and in spite of difficulties a voluntary association of nations has gradually been drawing together. The division in the world today is that between the spheres of American and Russian influence. Is it unreasonable to hold that it is marked by the differences between a moderate policy which attempts to influence its allies by persuasion rather than by force, and which leaves them freedom for the manifestation of their own separate sovereignties, and, on the other hand, a policy which effectively destroys all national independence and every expression of it which conflicts in any way with the will of the dominant power?

It is not our purpose here to discuss the relative balance of power, but in the present uneasy impasse moral factors are more important than they might be if there were an obvious preponderance of power on one side. From what has been said, and indeed from the simple facts, one important conclusion emerges. The Soviet imperium, based on the assertion of extreme rights of national sovereignty by the Russian state and the denial of the same rights to its satellites, is founded on a contradiction, which must become increasingly evident as time goes on, just as the same contradiction did in the history of revolutionary and Napoleonic France. On the other hand, the American policy of international cooperation has the virtue of self-consistency. This policy also is not without its historical antecedents. It was the reaction, however slow and reluctant, of old Europe to the Napoleonic domination, and one may see the United States as in this respect an inheritor of the traditional British policy of the Grand Alliance. It is a policy which Sorel described, with reference to Richelieu, as *"la moderation dans la force."* It has proved itself many times in the past, in war and in peace, as against the policy of national hegemony, and will, I believe, do so again.

THE FORMATION

OF THE MARXIAN

REVOLUTIONARY IDEA

Eric Voegelin

[1950]

THE Marxian idea of the great proletarian revolution that will end the pre-history of mankind and inaugurate its true history sprang into public effectiveness with the *Communist Manifesto*. Well known as is the progress of this idea after its formulation and publication in 1848, we know comparatively little about the process of its formation in the preceding decade. The main cause of this unsatisfactory state must be sought in the fact that the materials for a study of the genesis of the idea have been completely available only since 1932. In the meantime, the monographic literature on the subject has clarified many details; but a comprehensive study is still a desideratum.

GNOSTIC REVOLT

The starting point for the independent movement of Marx's thought seems to have been a gnostic position which he inherited from Hegel. Specifically, the Marxian gnosis expressed itself in the conviction that the self-conscious movement of the intellect was the ultimate source of knowledge for an understanding of the universe; faith and the life of the spirit were expressly excluded as independent sources of order in the soul. Moreover, this conviction was from the beginning accompanied by an attitude of revolt against "religion" as a sphere which recognized a *realissimum* beyond human consciousness. This is the position of Marx as it appears in his doctor's dissertation of 1840–41.

In the "Vorrede" of the dissertation Marx attacked the "theologizing intellect" of Plutarch because it dared to criticize a philosopher like Epicurus. Against such presumption Marx defended the "sovereignty" of philosophy. "Philosophy does not make a secret of it. The confession of Prometheus: 'In one word, I hate all the gods,' is its very own confession, its own sentence against all heavenly and earthly gods who refuse to recognize human self-consciousness (*das menschliche Selbstbewusstsein*) as the supreme divinity—by the side of which none other shall be held." Human self-consciousness is the god for the philosopher and "Prometheus is the foremost saint and martyr in the philosophical calendar."

This central theme was elaborated by Marx in a note on the existence of God. Demonstrations of the existence of God are logically worthless, and besides they miss the point. For, all gods, whether Greek or Christian, have really existed insofar as they were a "real force" in the life of man. If gods are imagined as real they will be effective, indeed, in the minds of the believers. Nevertheless, they are subjective ideas, and they are ineffective where the subjective idea is not entertained. "Bring paper-money into a country where the use of paper is unknown, and everybody will laugh about your subjective idea. Come with your gods in a country where other gods are believed, and people will demonstrate to you that you are suffering from imaginations and abstractions." "What a particular country is for particular gods from abroad, that is the country of reason for God on principle; it is a region where He ceases to exist." The implications of the ultimacy of reasonable self-consciousness become clearer through the use to which, in the opinion of Marx, demonstrations of the existence of God can be put. If they cannot demonstrate the existence of God, at least they will demonstrate the existence of human self-consciousness. In fact they are "logical explications" of consciousness. In the ontological proof, for instance, the being that is given in its immediacy as the source of the idea of God, is not God but the self-consciousness. In this sense, all proofs of the existence of God are in fact proofs of his non-existence. Correctly such demonstrations would have to be formulated: "Because nature is badly organized, God must exist," or "Because the world is unreasonable, God must exist." But what can be the meaning of such formulations unless they mean that "God exists for a man for whom the world is unreasonable, and who therefore himself is unreasonable?" Marx summarizes the result of these reflections in the sentence: "Un-reason is the existence of God."

Thus the sovereignty of consciousness and the anti-theistic revolt are present from the beginning. They enter as motives into the reflections of Marx on the philosophical situation that had been created through the system of Hegel. There are systems like the Hegelian and Aristotelian in which philosophy "closes itself into a completed, total world"; they are "nodal points" in philosophy which interrupt advancement in a straight line. Since further perfection of the system is impossible in contemplation, the successors will turn toward a philosophical practice and critique of the age. "It is a psychological law that the theoretical mind, when it has become free in itself, is transformed into practical energy, and as *will* turns against the mundane reality which exists independent of it." The spectacle of such half-contemplation and half-action is not edifying in either the post-Aristotelian or the post-Hegelian *"curriculum vitae"* of philosophy. But while the performance of the epigoni is depressing, the situation as such is inescapable. Once human self-consciousness has become completely "concretized" in a system of this kind, one cannot go back to the unreason of faith. One can only advance beyond the half-hearted epigonic compromise between philosophy and world toward a complete surrender of philosophy and a radical "critique" of the world. "When Athens was threatened by a devastation, Themistocles induced the Athenians to leave the city entirely, and to found a new Athens on the sea, as on a new element." The precise nature of this step apparently had been clear to Marx even earlier than at the time of the dissertation. At least, in the letter to his father, of November 10, 1837, we find indications that an old faith had been shattered and that "new gods" had to be placed on the altar. From idealistic philosophy, Marx had turned (at the age of nineteen) toward "searching the idea in reality itself." "Formerly the gods had lived above the earth, now they have become its center."

THE THESES OF FEUERBACH—
THE NEW MATERALISM

The dissertation shows Marx dissatisfied with the semi-action of the contemporary political intellectuals. He demands a transition from speculative philosophy to a "radical" critique which can be no less than an embodiment of the idea in reality through revolutionary action. This is the core of the Marxian idea. This core itself has been elaborated frequently and voluminously by Marx, and beyond this part of his work stretch the even more voluminous ramifications of detail. In the present context we must restrict ourselves to the analysis of a few documents in which the formulations are most strongly concentrated. We shall first consider the *Theses on Feuerbach,* a document that is of inestimable importance because it allows us to relate the terminology of Marx with traditional philosophical terms.

On the fundamental problem of the conflict between philosophy and the new non-philosophy, *Thesis II* informs us: "The philosophers have only interpreted the world in their various ways; the point, however, is to *change* it." This sentence is the key to the understanding of the aggregate of theses. If the opposition of "interpretation" and "change" were synonymous with the traditional Aristotelian opposition of theory and practice, there would be no point in the antithesis. Philosophers, of course, "interpret" the world; to deprecate this function of the *bios theoretikos* by pointing to the relevance (*es kömmt darauf an*) of changing the world would be senseless, for nobody maintains that contemplation is a substitute for practice, or *vice versa*. Moreover, one cannot "change the world" as one can "interpret the world"; one can only act *within* the world. Through this curious terminology, Marx reveals his intention of transposing into "practice" an attitude toward the world that is possible only in contemplation. The "practice" of Marx can change the "world," because the world is understood as a stream of existence within which the idea, or reason, moves concretely. The *logos* is not an unchangeable order of the soul and the world, to be discovered in contemplative detachment; it is a dialectically moving idea within the world; and we can come to grips with this moving idea only by embedding ourselves through practice into its historically concrete motion.

The "world" is the concrete stream of history; and the life of man is essentially part of the life of mankind in history. Man has no destiny of the soul in the religious sense, apart from the destiny of the social, historical world of mankind. From this position, Marx criticizes Feuerbach because the latter—while dissolving religion psychologically into an illusionary construction of man—still has left standing the nature of individual man as the originator of the illusion. According to Feuerbach, God is an imaginary subject, projected by the mind of man, to which are attributed the highest human values. "The absolute being, the God of man, is the being of man itself." God is "the mirror of man"; into God man has projected "his highest thoughts and his purest feelings"; God, therefore, is "the essence of man." The great turning point of history will come when "man becomes conscious that the only God of man is man himself." "*Homo homini Deus!*" The spectre of God must be laid; and man must take back what he has thrown away by projecting it into a divine, supernatural existence. With all this, Marx is in hearty agreement. He is not satisfied, however, with what he calls Feuerbach's dissolution of "the religious essence into *human* essence" (*Thesis VI*). Such human essence, the "religious mind" in itself is a non-existing abstract (*VI* and *VII*). Feuerbach assumes an "isolated" individual as the creator of the religious illusion. The individual, however, has no "human essence"; in its reality it is "the whole of social relationships" (*VI*). The "religious mind" in itself is a social product; an individual feels religiously because it "belongs to a specific social form" (*VII*). Feuerbach has correctly seen the "fact of religious self-alienation" in the creation of a supernatural divine existence and, in its wake, "the duplication of the world into a religious and a mundane world." He has, indeed, "reduced the religious world to its mundane basis." But he has not seen the most important problem: that there must be a reason why "the mundane basis sets itself against itself, and fixes for itself an independent realm in the clouds." This peculiar process can be explained only through "a schism and self-contradiction within the mundane basis." Feuerbach's analysis does not go far enough for Marx. The contradiction in the mundane basis itself must be "theoretically understood and practically revolutionized" (*Thesis IV*).

With these clarifications of the meaning of practice in mind, we must read a summarizing sentence like: "Social life is essentially *practical*" (*Thesis VIII*). We shall not understand the practice of social life as a basis for a life of meditation in solitude. The attributes mean that all life is social throughout, that it has no dimension of solitude; and that all life is practical throughout, that it has no legitimate dimensions of contemplation in the Aristotelian sense. Hence, "all mysteries that might induce mysticism in theory, will find their rational solution in human practice and in understanding this practice" (*VIII*). In his zeal for closing the stream of existential practice hermetically against all deviations into contemplation, Marx expressly condemns any attempt at producing social change through education. Such an attempt would overlook the fact that the educators must be educated themselves; it would split society into two parts of which one is superior to the rest in a miraculous manner. Circumstances can be changed only through action; and this change and action coincide so that in fact a change of circumstances is a self-transformation; and this self-transformation is the very process that must be understood as "*revolutionary practice*" (*Thesis III*). The idea of a subject of cognition and morals as distinguished from objects of cognitive and moral action must be abolished; the subject itself must be conceived as "objective" (*gegenständlich*) and human activity as "objective activity." Reality, on the other hand, must not be conceived as object for a subject but as "sensuously human activity" (*sinnlich menschliche Tätigkeit*) (*Thesis I*). Thus, in terms of philosophical tradition, revolutionary practice is defined as an existential stream in which the subject is objectified and the object subjectified. This is the position which Marx calls his "new materialism"; it is the position of "human society or social humanity" as distinguished from the position which recognizes the existence of individual man and bourgeois (*bürgerliche*) society (*Theses IX* and *X*).

CRITIQUE OF HEAVEN AND CRITIQUE OF THE EARTH

The Marxian critical practice starts with the critique of religion and it proceeds to the critique of politics and economics. The problem

269

of this systematically second phase was formulated by Marx in his *Kritik der Hegelschen Rechtsphilosophie.* "The critique of religion ends with the insight that man is the highest being for man; this implies the categorical imperative to overthrow all relationships in which man is a humiliated, oppressed, neglected, despised being."

"The critique of religion is the presupposition of all critique." In the illusionary reality of heaven, man "has looked for the superman (*Übermensch*)"; instead he found the reflection of himself. Now he realizes that he himself is the superman; and he will no longer be satisfied with recognizing himself as the "non-man (*Unmensch*)" that he formerly believed himself to be. "Man makes religion, not religion man." "Religion is the self-consciousness and self-feeling of a man who either has not yet gained himself, or who has lost himself again." This man, however, (directed against Feuerbach!) is not an abstract being outside the world. "Man is the world of man," that is, state and society. This social world produces religion "as a perverted consciousness of the world because it is a perverted (*verkehrte*) world." Religion is the "general theory" of a perverted world. It gives "imaginary reality to human essence (*Wesen*) because human essence has no true reality." "The struggle against religion is the struggle against that world, of which religion is the spiritual aroma." Religious misery is the manifestation of real misery, and at the same time a protest against it. Religion is the cry of the oppressed creature—"it is the opium of the people."

The destruction of religion, thus, is the beginning of the revolution, not its end. The "illusionary happiness of the people" must now be replaced by "its real happiness." The "imaginary flowers on the chain" have not been torn off in order that mankind now should wear an "unimaginative chain without consolation"; on the contrary, man should now throw away the chain and break the living flower. Disillusioned man should now regain his reason, and "move around himself as around his real sun." Now that the "beyond of truth" has disappeared, it is "the task of history" to establish "the truth of this world." "The critique of heaven changes into a critique of the earth," the critique of religion and theology into the critique of law and politics.

WESTERN POLITICAL AND GERMAN RADICAL REVOLUTION

Embarking on his critique of law and politics Marx did not criticize actual institutions; rather, he criticized Hegel's *Philosophy of Law.* In justifying this procedure, he made a contribution to the understanding of German politics and of its conflict with Western political culture that even today is well worth reading as a whole. In the present context, however, we must confine ourselves to his principle of interpretation.

Marx observed the time-lag in political development between Germany and the West. The English and French revolutions abolished the *ancien régime* in their areas and established the modern national state as the expression and instrument of bourgeois society (*bürgerliche Gesellschaft*). The revolutions were carried to success by a class, but they were experienced as representative revolutions of the nation. A revolution of this kind cannot be made with success unless certain conditions be fulfilled. That "a *part* of society emancipates itself and obtains *general* rule" is possible only if the revolutionary class can undertake "the general emancipation of society from its particular position." The political emancipation from the feudal regime can be experienced as generally valid only when the new values of economic and educational privileges become accessible to everybody—at least on principle. Since in fact this will hardly ever be the case, "no class of society can play this role without evoking a moment (*ein Moment*) of enthusiasm in itself and in the masses, a moment in which it fraternizes and flows together with society at large, in which it can be taken for society and be experienced and recognized as its *general representative*." "Only in the name of universal rights of society can a particular class vindicate general rule for itself." "Revolutionary energy and spiritual pathos (*Selbstgefühl*)" are not sufficient for obtaining this emancipation. In order to achieve this "coincidence of a national revolution with the emancipation of a particular class" another class must exist which is experienced as the "social sphere of the notorious crime against the whole of society," so that the liberation from this class can appear as the general liberation. The "negative-general" importance of the French nobility and clergy conditioned the "positive-general" importance of the French bourgeoisie as the emancipating class.

In all these respects, the German political development is behind the times. No revolutions have occurred; an anachronistic *ancien régime* continues to exist. And there is no prospect of a revolution in the Western sense, for neither has Germany a class of such "courage and ruthlessness" that it could appear as the "negative representative" of society, nor does it have an estate of sufficient "breadth of the soul" and "revolutionary audacity" that even the momentary identification with the "soul of the people" would be possible. "In Germany the relation between the various spheres of society is not dramatic, it is epic." As a consequence, every sphere of German society "experiences its defeat, before it can celebrate a victory," develops its narrowness before it can unfold its generosity, is involved in its struggle with the lower class when it begins its struggle against the higher class. "The princes are engaged in a struggle against kingship, the bureaucrats against the nobility, the bourgeoisie against them all, while the proletarians already enter into their struggle against the bourgeoisie."

The difference of political development between the Western national states and Germany has important consequences. The Western revolutions are not the end of history. The modern state in its perfection has liberated man insofar as differences of religion and property no longer determine differences of political status for the individual. "The perfect political state is by its nature the generic life of man in opposition to his material life." Nevertheless, the whole structure of "egoistic life" is retained as social life outside the sphere of the state. In the perfect political state man leads a double life: in political community he lives as the generic being, in society he lives as a private individual. The complete liberation through complete socialization of man is not yet achieved. "Political emancipation is a great progress"; nevertheless "it is not the last form of human emancipation"; it is only "the last form of human emancipation *within* the present world order." In Germany, as distinguished from the West, not even political emancipation has been achieved hitherto. But precisely because the German political situation is anachronistic and below serious discussion, German political speculation could abstract from this reality and instead, through Hegel, develop "the idea of the modern state" into its last consequences. "The Germans have *thought* in politics, what the other nations have *done*. Germany was their *theoretical conscience*." The incompleteness of human emancipation through the political state has come to consciousness in German political thought. The question is: can Germany achieve a practice, that is a revolution, *à la hauteur des principes,* lifting it not only "to the *official level* of modern nations, but to the *human height* that will be the next future of these nations?"

In his theory of the opposition between Germany and the Western nations, and in particular in the question just raised, Marx came closest to being a German national thinker. He was seriously concerned about the place of Germany among the nations. He saw the political misery that seemed to cut off all hope for a historical role of importance; but he also saw the splendid intellectual achievement. He felt himself to be a thinker who could draw out the practical consequences of the Hegelian philosophy of the state; but he was gloomy about the German people's power to become the carrier of the ultimate revolution for the liberation of mankind. Germany, he felt, has not scaled "the middle steps of political emancipation together with the modern nations." It has not reached in practice the steps which in theory it has passed. How could the *"salto mortale"* of the "radical revolution" be possible? Another end seems more probable: "One morning, Germany will find herself on the level of European decadence (*Verfall*), before she has ever reached the level of European emancipation." This prophetic vision, however, was rejected by Marx. He did not consider a political revolution in the Western sense a possibility for Germany, but he still believed in the possibility of the radical revolution. "It is not the radical revolution that is a utopian dream for Germany, not the general human emancipation, but rather the partial revolution that is only political." The German emancipation will never be achieved piecemeal by particular classes of society, as in the West, but it can be achieved at one stroke by a class which is part of the bourgeois society and at the same time not part of it, that is by the proletariat.

The proletariat is "an estate which is the dissolution of all estates," "a social sphere which has universal character through its universal suffering"; it has no particular claim because no particular injustice, but injustice as such, is committed against it; it has no historical title, it has nothing but the human title; it is a social sphere "which cannot emancipate itself without emancipating all other spheres of society"; it is "the complete loss of man and, therefore, cannot regain itself without regaining man completely." "The proletariat is the dissolution of society in form of a particular estate." "When the proletariat announces the dissolution of the present order of the world, it only reveals the secret of its existence, for it is in fact the dissolution of this order of the world." The proletariat, thus, will be the material weapon of philosophy, while in philosophy it will find its spiritual weapons. When the lightning of thought has struck into this soil of the people, the emancipation of the German into Man will be accomplished. "The head of this emancipation is philosophy, its heart is the proletariat. Philosophy cannot become reality without abolishing the proletariat, the proletariat cannot abolish itself without realizing philosophy."

This faith in the translation of philosophy into reality through the German proletariat, is supported by a historical reflection on the German Reformation. The faith in a revolution that starts with speculation makes sense in the light of the German past. "Germany's revolutionary past is theoretical, it is the Reformation. At that time it was the *monk*, now it is the *philosopher*, in whose brain the revolution begins." Luther's Reformation was the first step of a German revolution. Luther broke the faith in authority, but he has put the authority of faith in its place. He has liberated man from external religiousness, but he has made religiousness the substance of man. Protestantism, thus, did not bring the true solution, but it certainly revealed the true task, that is, the struggle against the priestly substance of man. "The most radical fact of German history," the Peasant War, broke against the wall of the new Protestant theology. Today, when this theology itself has broken down, the anachronistic, political state will be broken by the new philosophy. These passages show that Marx was perfectly aware of the connection between his own thought and German Protestantism. There is, indeed, an intelligible line of meaning running from Luther's destruction of ecclesiastic authority, through the destruction of dogmatic symbols in the generation of Strauss, Bruno Bauer, and Feuerbach, to the destruction of "all the gods," that is, of all authoritative order in Marx. While it would be incorrect to say that the way of Protestantism leads with any inner necessity from Luther to Hegel and Marx, it is true that Marxism is the final product of disintegration in one branch of German, liberal Protestantism.

EMANCIPATION AND ALIENATION

Emancipation is the general category under which Marx conceives the advancement of man to his complete freedom. "*All* emancipation is *reduction* of the human world, of relationships, to *man himself*." Religious emancipation is the reduction of religion to the religion-making consciousness of man, as accomplished by Feuerbach. "Political emancipation is the reduction of man, on the one hand to a member of bourgeois society, that is, to the *egoistic, independent* individual, on the other hand to the *citizen,* that is to the moral person." This schism of man must be overcome through the next and last step in emancipation. Only when "the real, individual man takes back the abstract citizen," only when he as individual man has become *generic being* (*Gattungswesen*) "in his empirical life, in his individual work, in his individual relationships," only when man "has recognized his '*forces propres*' as *social* forces and organized as such," only when, as a consequence, he "no longer separates social force from himself in the form of *political force*," is human emancipation completed. The overcoming of the state is a historical problem which resembles in its structure the overcoming of religion. "The political constitution was hitherto the *religious sphere,* the *religion* of a people's life, it was the heaven of its generality in opposition to the *earthly existence* of its reality. . . . *Political life* in the modern sense is the *scholasticism* of a people's life."

The course of past history has been the "alienation" of man, the task of future history is his "emancipation." In alienation (or self-alienation) man loses himself to the beyond of religion and social institutions; through emancipation he draws these objectified sectors of his essence back into his existence. We have arrived at the core of the Marxian philosophy of history. The history of emancipation (from religious, through political, to ultimate social emancipation) is the reversal of the process of alienation. In order to arrive at the critical solution, the revolutionary thinker must have a critical understanding of the genesis of the evil. Since contemporary evil has its origin in the relation between man and nature, it can be overcome only through bringing nature under control of man so that freedom beyond nature can unfold. Since the vicissitudes of man's relation with nature are the subject-matter of history, we must trace the history of man from its most primitive beginnings, when man emerges from his animal condition; we must follow it through the various phases in which man becomes ever more deeply involved in the process of production, to the point of complete self-alienation; we must further study the possibilities of emancipation which grow parallel with increasing alienation; and we must, finally, conceive the idea of the revolutionary overthrow of the order of alienation and its replacement by the order of freedom.

SUBSTANCE AND PROCESS OF HISTORY

All critical history must start with certain "presuppositions." They must, however, not be of a dogmatic nature; they must be "real presuppositions," that is, "the real individuals, their actions and material conditions of life." The first presupposition is "the existence of living human individuals" with a bodily organization and a relation to the rest of nature which is conditioned by this organization. Man distinguishes himself from animal as soon as he starts *producing* his means of life; in such production men indirectly produce their material life. Their way of production becomes their way of life (*Lebensweise*).

From this starting point, Marx traces the differentiation of production from sexual reproduction and division of labor on the level of the family, through further differentiation on the tribal and other local levels, to the systems of production and division of labor under the conditions of modern national societies and their interrelation on a world-market. Parallel with this differentiation of production goes the development of ideas in politics, law, morals, religion, and metaphysics in close correlation with the process of material production of life. "Consciousness can never be anything but conscious being (*Bewusstsein, bewusstes Sein*), and the being of man is his real life-process." "Ideologies" have no history of their own; they are a by-product of the material process. "It is not consciousness that determines life; it is life that determines consciousness." With the development of critical history, "philosophy loses its medium of existence." It can be replaced, at best, "by a summary of general results that can be abstracted from the study of the historical development of mankind."

Such abstractions, however, are worthless if they be separated from real history. They must strictly serve the ordering of historical materials—in the manner in which Marx is doing it.

The "material process of production" and its differentiation through division of labor are established as the irreducible substance of history. This process of differentiation contains an inevitable conflict of increasing acerbity, that is, the conflict between the interest of the working individual and the interest of the larger group of individuals who are engaged in production through division of labor and exchange of products. "As soon as labor is divided, a definite, exclusive range of activity is assigned to everybody; this range is imposed on him, he cannot escape it; he is hunter, fisher or herdsman, or critic, and he must remain within his range unless he wants to lose his means of life." While under more primitive technological conditions such dependence on specialized activity is still bearable because even specialization on this level leaves a broad field for diversified human work, the situation becomes disastrous under conditions of industrial production for a world-market. "The fixation of social activity, the consolidation of our own product into an objective power (*sachliche Gewalt*) dominating us, growing out of control, crossing our expectations, destroying our calculations, is one of the principal factors in historical evolution." "The more wealth he produces, and the more his production gains in power and volume, the poorer becomes the worker." "Work does not produce commodities only; it produces itself and the worker as a *commodity*." "The realization of work is its objectivation." "The worker puts his life into the object; but then his life is no longer his but the object's." "What the product of his work is, he is not." "The life that he has given to the object, opposes him as inimical and alien." "The worker becomes the serf of his object." "His work is external to his being." "He does not affirm, he negates himself in his work." "Only outside his work the worker is with himself, in his work he is outside himself." "He is at home when he does not work, and when he works he is not at home."

"Hence his work is not voluntary but compulsory, it is *compulsory labor*. It is not a satisfaction of his wants, but only a means for satisfying wants outside his work." "The result is that the working man can feel himself free only in his animal functions of eating, drinking and procreating, and perhaps in his housing, ornaments, etc., while in his specifically human functions he is only an animal." "Eating, drinking and procreating certainly are genuine human functions, too. But in the abstraction which separates them from the wider range of human activity and makes them ultimate and sole aims, they are beastly (*tierisch*)."

Man is distinguished from animal through the universality of his relation with nature; he does not produce for necessity alone; but can give form to his material existence through science and beauty. This whole range of productive activity which distinguishes human life is degraded to the level of a means of life. The productive, free existence of man "becomes a means for his physical existence." This "alienation" of human productivity is inherent in the division of labor; it has nothing to do with higher or lower wages. A rise in wages would be nothing "but a better compensation of slaves; it would not for the worker and his work reconquer their human destiny and dignity." "Even an equality of income, as demanded by Proudhon, changes only the relation of the worker to his work into that of all men to their work. Society would then become the Capitalist in the abstract." The conditions of existence in modern society have become an accident for the worker over which he has no control and "over which no *social* organization can give him control."

The last sentences might destroy the assumption (which is frequently made) that Marx was impressed by the material misery of the worker in his time, and that with the material improvement of the worker's lot the necessity for the Marxist revolution would disappear. Social reform is *not* a remedy for the evil which Marx has in mind. This evil is the growth of the economic structure of modern society into an "objective power" to which man must submit by threat of starvation. The principal and characteristic features which appear off and on in the descriptions of Marx can be reduced to the following:

1. The separation of the worker from his tools. This characteristic is determined by industrial technology. No man can individually own and operate the tools of modern industrial production. The "factory" or, generally, the "place of work," cannot be the "home."

2. Job dependence. This characteristic has the same determining cause. No man can earn a living in an industrial system unless he finds a job in some "enterprise" which assembles the tools for production and markets the product.

3. Division of labor. No man can produce any whole product. The process of production must be centrally planned, and the single worker is confined to the phase in the process assigned to him. Marx was very much aware of the supreme insult to human dignity which lies in the fact that at the end of his life, when a man summarizes what he has accomplished, he may have to say: All my life I have spent in cooperating in the production of a certain type of Grand Rapids furniture and, thereby, degraded humanity in myself and others.

4. Specialization. This characteristic is intimately connected with the preceding one. Even if the total product is not an insult to human dignity, the productivity of man has no appreciable range for unfold-

ing if his work is confined to a small sector of production on which as a whole he has no influence.

5. Economic interdependence. No man can live a whole life if his existence is permanently threatened, not by natural catastrophes as in the case of a peasant, but by social actions beyond his control— be they new inventions, or the closing of a market through tariff, or miscalculation of management, or change in customers' taste, or a general economic crisis.

SOCIALISTIC MAN

The enumerated characteristics are those of an industrial system of production. Since Marx did not wish to abolish the industrial system, and in particular since he was fully aware that no change in social organization, such as public ownership of the instruments of production, could abolish these evils, the question arises: what precisely did he want to achieve by a communist revolution? This is the crucial point of the Marxian system of thought, and it is the point which ordinarily is neglected. Marx has not said much about it; but he has said enough for making his intentions clear beyond doubt. Wild as it may sound, he wanted to retain the industrial system of production with its inevitable technological differentiation of work, but he wanted to abolish human specialization. Man was supposed to emerge from the revolution as an integrally productive being that by his own will would work one day at a machine, the next day in an office, and the third day as a *litterateur*. A primitive, but unmistakable formulation of the idea occurs among his complaints that division of labor produces such occupational fixations as hunter, fisher, and the like. This evil will be overcome in

> communist society, where nobody has an exclusive range of activity, but everybody can train himself in every branch; where society regulates general production and thereby makes it possible for me to do one thing today and another thing tomorrow, to hunt in the morning, to fish in the afternoon, to be a husbandman in the evening, and to indulge in literary work after supper, as it pleases me, without any necessity for me ever to become a hunter, fisherman, husbandman or critic.

Again, incredible as it may sound, this is the vision which Marx transfers to the situation of the modern industrial system. The revolution in face of "alienation" is necessary in order for men to regain their "self-activity" (*Selbstbetätigung*) as well as to secure their existence. It will assume the form of an "appropriation of the existing totality of productive forces." Under the international division of labor, these forces exist in the form of a universal, world-wide system of interdependence.

The appropriation, therefore, must have a universal character which corresponds to the universality of productive forces and commerce. The appropriation of these forces is in itself nothing but the development of individual faculties in correspondence with the material instruments of production. Hence, the appropriation of a totality of instruments of production is the development of a totality of faculties in the individuals.

In order to achieve a human revolution of this kind, a certain type of individual is needed. Only the proletarians are capable of performing the feat because their individual existence is no longer bound up with a special type of property that would limit the interest of their activity. All former revolutions were limited (*borniert*), because the self-activity of the revolutionary class was limited by its specific kind of private property. The proletarian without property is the fit agent to bring a mass of productive instruments "under each individual," and to "subsume property under all." Moreover, the method of the revolution is determined by the universal character of the industrial system. Only a universal association of proletarians on the world-scale can, through its revolution, break the power of the present economic and social structure; and only such a universal revolution will develop the universal character and the energy that are necessary to execute the appropriation.

Only after this revolution will "self-activity coincide with material life." Only then "are individuals developed into total individuals," "work will have changed into self-activity," and the "hitherto conditioned commerce will have changed into the commerce of individuals as such." Division of labor cannot be abolished by forgetting about it; the "individuals must subsume the objective forces under themselves and thereby abolish (*aufheben*) division of labor. This is impossible without community. Only in community with others does the individual have the means at his disposal to develop his faculties in all directions."

History, thus, is moving toward the appearance of the "total individual," or—in other contexts—of "socialistic man." Man must recover completely from his alienation in order to become the perfectly free and independent being which in essence he is. The "liberation from property" will be the last act of this drama. In a revealing page Marx has formulated the connection between this conception of history and his original revolt against God. A being—he says— "is independent only when it stands on its own feet; and it stands on its own feet only when it owes its existence to nobody but itself." A man who lives by grace of somebody else is dependent—and I live most completely by the grace of somebody else when he "has created my life," when the sources of my life lie outside myself. The belief in creation is the source of the feeling of dependence; and this idea of "creation"—Marx reflects sadly—is rather deep-rooted in the consciousness of man. The idea that nature should be through itself, as well as the idea that man should exist through himself, is "inconceivable to him because it contradicts all tangible experiences (*Handgreiflichkeiten*) of practical life."

Man knows himself as a link in the chain of being, and inevitably he will feel urged to ask where this chain be suspended. Marx has laid his finger on the resistance to the idea of a "superman": as long as man remains aware of his *conditio humana,* as long as he retains his consciousness of his "tangible experience" of dependence, he will not be easily persuaded that through the mystery of revolution he will be transfigured into a self-contained divinity. Moreover, Marx knows that he is not struggling against a "belief" in creation or in any other symbol that might furnish an answer to the question; the resistance rather arises from the experience and from the question itself. The question must not be raised—or his idea is finished. It is the same situation in which Comte found himself when his positivistic restriction of knowledge to the observation of world-immanent regularities ran into the quest for the *arché,* for the origin of being. And Marx resorts in this situation to the same desperate measure as Comte: since from the immanentist position there is no answer to the question, the question itself must be suppressed. Marx issues a dictatorial prohibition against asking such questions—they are "abstractions"; they have "no sense"; stick to the reality of being and becoming! At this critical juncture Marx, like Comte, declares his intellectual bankruptcy by the refusal to answer questions. And then he continues with the ominous definition: "socialistic man" is the man who does not ask such questions.

CRUDE COMMUNISM AND TRUE COMMUNISM

For socialistic man the "whole so-called history of the world" is nothing but the production of man through the work of man. In this process he has under his eyes "the irresistible proof of his birth: of his genesis through himself." The essentiality (*Wesenhaftigkeit*) of man in nature is given to sensual intuition; in the face of this experience the quest for an *alien* being beyond nature and man becomes a practical impossibility. *"Atheism,* as the denial of this non-essentiality (*Unwesentlichkeit*) no longer makes sense, for atheism is a *negation of God* and through this negation posits the *existence of man."* Socialism needs no mediation; its starts right away with the sensuous consciousness of man in nature as true essence. It is the positive self-consciousness of man, not mediated through denial of religion. And in the same manner, "true life" is the positive reality of man, not mediated through abolition of private property, that is, through communism. In the next phase of history, communism will be positive as "negation of the negation,"—"but communism as such is not the aim of human development,—it is not the form of human society." Communism, like atheism, is the counter-idea to a historical state that must be overcome. Marx, like Bakunin, is aware of the danger that lies in facile attempts at giving content to the vision of the future by elaborating a catalogue of concrete demands which can be nothing but negatives of present evils. Communism is not an institutional reform; it is, indeed, a change in the nature of man.

With this danger in view, Marx has distinguished carefully between "crude communism" (*roher Kommunismus*) and "true communism" or socialism. Crude communism is the "positive expression" of abolished private property; it establishes "general private property"; it is only a "generalization and perfection of private property." The domination of property in things is so enormous that crude communism wants to annihilate everything that cannot be owned as private property by everybody. It considers physical, immediate ownership the only purpose of life. It does not abolish the worker's existence but extends it to everybody; it wants to destroy all distinguishing talent by violence, and so on. The nature of this type of communism becomes particularly clear in its idea of a communization of women. "We may say that the idea of a community of women reveals the secret of this crude and thoughtless communism." Woman leaves marriage and enters into general prostitution; the world of wealth leaves private property and enters into general prostitution with the community. Such communism, "in its radical negation of the *personality* of man," is a continuation of the former private property. "The general *envy* which constitutes itself as power is only a hidden form in which *avarice* restores itself and satisfies itself under a different form." Competition under conditions of private property is both envy and desire of levelling turned against the greater private property. The crude communist manifests the perfection of this desire for levelling. The abolition of private property is not a true appropriation; it rather destroys civilization by its return to an unnatural simplicity of poor people who are not beyond private property but have not yet arrived at it. Hence, the community of crude communism is nothing but a community of work and of equality of income paid out by the community as the general capitalist. "Crude communism, thus, is only a manifestation of the rascality (*Niedertracht*) of private property that wants to establish itself as a positive community."

True communism is the return of man to himself as social man "within the whole wealth of human development up to this point." It is a completed humanistic naturalism, "the true solution of the conflict between man and nature." "It is the solved riddle of history and knows itself as the solution." Communist society "is the true resurrection of nature, the realized naturalism of man and the realized humanism of nature."

THE MANIFESTO

The genesis of the idea is substantially completed with its appearance on the world-scene of the *Communist Manifesto* (December 1847– January 1848). As far as the ideas of history, revolution, and communism are concerned, the *Manifesto* contains nothing that is new; on the contrary, it contains considerably less than the result of our preceding analysis, as is inevitable in a document which has no theoretical intentions but merely wants to propagandize. Nevertheless, we must briefly dwell on the formulations, if not on the ideas, for the *Manifesto* is a masterpiece of political rhetoric. After a century, its formulae have neither lost their revolutionary pathos nor their effectiveness on the political scene.

In the Preamble the authors fix the scale of importance for their pronunciamento. Communism is recognized as a force by all European powers. It is a spectre that haunts Europe. The Pope and the Tsar, Metternich and Guizot, French radicals and German policemen have allied themselves in a "Holy Chase" to lay the spectre. Such recognition by the old powers creates an obligation for the communists to clarify their views and to submit them to the public. The new world force enters the lists against the powers of the old world.

The first section of the *Manifesto* develops the historical perspective of communism. "The history of all society up to the present is the history of class struggles." There have always been classes and estates, oppressors and oppressed. Modern society, however, is distinguished from all earlier periods through the simplicity of the pattern. "Our whole society is splitting more and more into two great hostile camps, into two great classes facing each other—Bourgeoisie and Proletariat." The appealing pattern of Manichaean simplicity is set; there are only two forces, good and evil; anybody who is not on the good side, inevitably is on the bad side. The *Manifesto*, then, follows this pattern and deals, first, with the rise of the bourgeoisie and, second, with the proletariat.

The man of the bourgeoisie has risen from the serf of the Middle Ages to become the operator of modern industry and commerce spanning the globe; and as his political instrument he has created the modern representative state. "The bourgeoisie has a most revolutionary role in history." The description of the revolutionary role itself begins with reflections on the bourgeoisie as the destroyer of "all feudal, patriarchal, idyllic relationships." But the derogatory beginnings soon change into a praise of the achievements of the bourgeoisie such as no enlightened progressivist has ever written. The bourgeoisie "has accomplished much greater miracles than Egyptian pyramids, Roman aqueducts and gothic cathedrals." It has made "production and consumption of all countries cosmopolitan"; it has "drawn away the national soil from under the feet of industry"; the old "local and national self-sufficiency and exclusiveness" are replaced by a general interdependence of all nations. And what has been done for material has also been done for intellectual production. "National onesidedness and limitation becomes more and more impossible, and from the many national and local literatures there rises a world literature." Through improvement of communications "even the most barbaric nations are drawn into civilization." All nations must adopt bourgeois methods of production, unless they want to perish. "In one word, it has created a world in its own image." It has created our great cities, and "torn an appreciable part of the population from the idiocy of rural life." "It has made the country-side dependent on the city, the barbaric or half-barbaric countries on the civilized ones, the peasant nations on the bourgeois nations, the Orient on the Occident." "In its class rule of barely a century the bourgeoisie has created more massive and colossal forces of production than all preceding generations together." In brief: we hear the authentic tones of a Condorcet, with the massive pride in the expected complete destruction of all historical civilizations and the transformation of all mankind into a universal bourgeois society.

The splendor of the bourgeoisie, however, is transitory like everything in the world except communism. The bourgeoisie must go and its achievements will be inherited by the successor that has grown under its rule, by the proletariat, "the class of modern workers who live only as long as they can find work." The characterization of proletarian existence contains nothing new. Of interest, however, is the description of the phases in the struggle. "Its struggle against the bourgeoisie begins with its existence." At the beginning we have no more than individual and local struggles against individual and local oppression. With the expansion of industry, the masses of proletarians grow and their common situation becomes more visible to them. Coalitions and associations are formed; local revolts break out. Momentary victories are followed by defeats; the real result is the nationwide coalition and the centralization of the class struggle. The proletariat is on its way toward organization as a class and party. The progressive proletarization of ever larger groups in society throws educated people into the proletariat. And the disintegration of the old society induces small groups of the ruling class to become renegade and to join the revolutionary class which has the future in its hands.

"As formerly a part of the nobility went over to the bourgeoisie, so now a part of the bourgeoisie goes over to the proletariat, and in particular a part of the bourgeois-ideologists who have worked themselves through to an understanding of the historical movement." Thus, we have finally arrived at Marx and Engels themselves, the bourgeois ideologists who can tell the proletarians what the historical process is all about and provide intellectual leadership in their capacity as organizers of the Communist Party.

The second section of the *Manifesto* deals with the relation between proletarians and communists. Here we find a new set of ideas concerning the function of communist leadership in the proletarian struggle against the bourgeoisie. The opening sentences are of particular importance because they contain the principles which later were developed into the idea of communism as the universal church of the proletariat. The section begins humbly enough: "The communists are not a separate party in opposition (*gegenüber*) to other workers' parties." But the next sentence turns this rejection of rivalry into a universalist claim: "They have no interests separate from those of the proletariat as a whole." The implications are far-reaching, for this sentence is neither a statement of fact that would be open to verification, nor is it a program; it is rather the fundamental dogma which declares the spirit of the proletariat as a whole to be residing in the Communist Party. Any programmatic intention is explicitly rejected by the following sentence: "They do not set up principles of their own by which they want to shape the proletarian movement." The communists are not distinguished from other proletarian groups by principles and programs but by the universal level of their practice. "In the various national struggles of proletarians, they emphasize, and put to the fore, the common interests of the proletariat as a whole, independent of nationality"; and: "In the various successive stages through which the struggle between proletariat and bourgeoisie must pass, they always represent the interests of the movement as a whole." Beyond regional and temporal diversification of the struggle, there looms the central leadership of the communists. And, indeed, the next paragraph formulates the vanguard-principle: "In their practice, the communists are the most resolute, ever forward pushing, section in the workers' parties of all countries; in their theory, they have the advantage over the great mass of the proletariat through their insight into conditions, course, and general results of the proletarian movement. In their immediate aims, for the rest, the communists do not differ from other proletarian parties; these aims are: "formation of the proletariat into a class, overthrow of bourgeois rule, conquest of political power through the proletariat."

The remainder of the second section deals with exposition and defense of the ultimate aims of communism. The authors stress the non-programmatic character of these aims. "The theoretical theses of communists are in no way based on ideas or principles that have been invented or discovered by this or that world-reformer (*Weltverbesserer*)." "They are no more than general expressions of actual relationships in a real class struggle, in a historical movement that goes on under our very eyes." Communist theses, thus, must not be misunderstood as programmatic demands for changing an actual state of things; on the contrary, they reveal the actual state of things and suggest that the tendencies, actually inherent in the historical process, are carried to their full realization. Hence, the accusations levelled against communism are unfounded. Their opponents charge the communists with the intention of abolishing private property. The *Manifesto* agrees that this is the substance of communist theory. But what does this abolition mean in face of the fact that the socially relevant property is capitalist property and the great mass of the people has no such property anyway? And if it is taken from those who have it, is that really expropriation? No, for "capital is a collective product and can be set into motion only through the common activity of many members of society, and in last resort only through the common activity of all members of society. Capital, therefore, is not a personal, it is a social power"; and to be a capitalist means "to hold not a purely personal, but social position in production." "If, therefore, capital is converted into communal property, belonging to all members of society, such conversion does not transform personal property into social property. Only the social character of property is transformed. It loses its class character." The so-called expropriation, thus, only transforms an actual situation into a principle of public order. The same type of argument is, then, applied to the charges against abolition of bourgeois marriage, of nationality, of religion and of "eternal truths, like freedom, justice, etc."

The theses of communism lift the march of history into consciousness. They are not a program for interference with an established order; they are an insight into an order that is coming into being, that is growing under the disintegrating order of the old society. The communists and their followers can feel themselves the executors of the law of history. Again we must note the strong touch of Condorcet in this conception of the communists as the directorate of mankind on its march toward the realm of freedom. Nevertheless, history does not march all by itself; the directorate must lend a helping hand. The raw-material for the realization of the aim is present: the proletarians as a class outside society, without property and without nationality ("The workers have no country"). But this material must be shaped through the awakening of class-consciousness, and then the revolution itself must be undertaken. The conquest of power will be a prolonged process; between bourgeois rule and free society, there will be interposed the transitional period of the dictatorship of the proletariat. The first step will be the elevation of the proletariat to the place of the ruling class in democracy. The political domination will then be used "gradually to wrest all capital from the bourgeoisie, to centralize all instruments of production in the hands of the state, that is, the proletariat organized as ruling class, and as rapidly as possible to increase the total productive forces." This can be done only "through despotic interventions in the right of property and bourgeois conditions of production"; such measures may appear as indefensible by economic standards but they are inevitable for the purpose of revolutionizing the whole method of production. In the course of this development, class-differences will disappear, production will be concentrated in the hands of the associated individuals, public power will lose its political character because it is no longer an instrument of class rule, and, finally, the old society will be replaced by "an association in which everybody's free development is the condition of the free development of all." The *Manifesto* ends with the famous call to revolutionary association: "The proletarians have nothing to lose in it but their chains. They have a world to win. Proletarians of all countries unite!"

TACTICS

The *Manifesto* was published in February, 1848. In 1850, when it was clear that the time for a proletarian world-revolution had not yet come, the eschatological excitement of the *Manifesto* subsided and the problems of revolutionary tactics came to the fore. We may conclude this study of the genesis of the Marxian idea with a few passages on tactics from the *Address* to the *Bund der Kommunisten,* of March, 1850.

The immediate problem for communists was no longer the seizure of power in a democratic revolution. The democrats who were capable of winning a revolution were not communists. The immediate problem was the alliance with revolutionary democratic groups wherever they started moving and the ruthless fight against the allies on the morning after the common victory. It was already substantially the situation that we have experienced in the Popular Front politics of the 1930's and the resumption of the fight against democracy after the victory. Marx informs his listeners that "the democratic petty-bourgeois want to conclude the revolution as fast as possible" as soon as they have taken care of their own interests. But it is our interest and our task to make the revolution permanent until all more or less propertied classes are removed from power, until state power is conquered by the proletariat and until the association of proletarians has advanced not only in one country but in all important countries of the world to the point where rivalry between proletarians in different countries has ceased and at least the decisive productive forces are concentrated in their hands. We are not interested in a change in private property but only in its annihilation, not in conciliation of class antagonisms but in the abolition of classes, not in reforms of present society but in the foundation of a new one.

In order to carry on the fight, as far as possible a stabilization of the political situation must be prevented. During the conflict as well as immediately afterward, the proletarians must counteract all attempts at calming down the revolutionary excitement. The democratic parties must be held to their most radical promises and their most terroristic threats. Mob violence should not be prevented or merely tolerated; it should be fostered and organized by the communists in order to compromise the democrats. In the special German case, the communists must oppose any attempt at a federative construction of the constitution. "Under no circumstances must it be tolerated that every village, city, and province can oppose revolutionary activity which must proceed from a center in order to be most effective." When a constitutional settlement is reached at last, the communists must top every legislative reform measure proposed by the democrats, by a more revolutionary demand of their own.

When the petty-bourgeois propose the purchase of railroads and factories the workers must demand that these railroads and factories should be confiscated by the government without compensation because they are the property of reactionaries. When the democrats propose a proportional tax, the workers demand a progressive one; when the democrats propose a moderately progressive one the workers insist on a tax which rises so fast in the upper bracket that big capital will be ruined. When the democrats propose a regulation of the public debt, the workers demand a declaration of public bankruptcy. Hence, the demands of the workers must always be guided by the concessions and measures of the democrats.

The details of the advice will change with the situation. The pattern is clear and well-known to all of us: it is the systematic disruption of society in the hope of creating such disorder that the communist minority can rise to victory.

V

MAN AND SPIRITUAL

PROBLEMS

THE WASTELAND

OF WILLIAM BLAKE

Frank O'Malley

[1947]

I THE TYGERS OF WRATH

THE question is: how can you put a prophet in his place when, by
the very character of prophecy, he is eternally slipping out of place?
William Blake was not an eighteenth century or nineteenth century
mind or a typically modern mind at all. What I mean to say, right at the
start, is that, although well aware of his time and of time altogether, he
was not in tune with the *main* tendencies of his or our own time.
Indeed time was a barrier he was forever crashing against. Blake's talent raved through the world into the fastnessess of the past and dra-
matically confronted the abysses of the future. His age did not confine
him. As a poet he does not seem finally to have had real spiritual or
artistic kinship with any of the rationalist or romantic writers of
England. As a thinker he came to despise the inadequacy of the limited
revolutionary effort of the political rebels of the Romantic Revolution.
Blake's name is not to be seen mounted first with that of Paine or
Godwin, of Rousseau or Voltaire, of Wordsworth or Shelley or Byron
or Keats. With these he has, ultimately, little or nothing in common.
At any rate, his voice and mood and impact are thoroughly different
from the more publicly successful voices of the period of his life, older
and younger generations alike. The seething Blake cannot be
boundaried. He reached back to Swedenborg and Jacob Boehme, to
Milton (whom Blake would have saved from his spectre and rein-
tegrated through love), to Pascal and Dante, to Virgil and Plato and
Homer, to the Old Testament Prophets, especially to Job (Blake could
say: "The Prophets Isaiah and Ezekiel dined with me"). Blake was
himself, in his own way, a prophet rising out of the spiritual under-
world that twists its fibres deep beneath the surface of modern civiliza-

tion. He belongs with all those who lived or will live in the depths under the wasteland and who will judge the wasteland, directly or symbolically. Blake belongs with de Maistre and Kierkegaard, with Novalis and Nietzsche, with Dostoievski, Solovyev and Berdyaev, with Rimbaud and Baudelaire, with Bergson, with Bloy and Bernanos, with Newman, Hopkins, and Patmore, with Melville, Henry Adams, and T. S. Eliot, with Rilke and Kafka, with Joyce, Yeats, and D. H. Lawrence. For these men, too, have surged against the progress of the physical world and sought, in heaven and hell, the meaning and destiny of man-on-earth.

While it may be a good work to examine Blake's consciousness of the local problems of his particular society and of his particular place, finally such examination is merely academic—notably if the study neglects to emphasize or to realize the spiritual depth and power of Blake's record, in his prophecies, of the barrenness of a creation unnourished by love. I think that Mark Schorer, in his *William Blake, the Politics of Vision,* has been most sensible in discussing Blake as "a man of the world" and in showing that Blake was not just "a little boy lost in a lonely fen" as well as in clearly separating Blake from what Schorer chooses to call "the dubious company" of the mystics. But I think that he has been quite deficient in appreciating the spiritual propulsion of Blake which carried him far and away beyond his moment-of-history, and which makes him the most profound and the most prodigious of the English romantics. Both Schorer and Helen C. White (in her important older study of Blake's mysticism) properly deny Blake's claim to be a genuine mystic. At the same time they fail to do justice to the wonder of his capacity for mystery and eternity, and are content, in niggardly spirit, to conclude that Blake's prophecy is a titanic exercise in obscurity that surely fails. Blake's mythological opaqueness is obvious, of course, and is to be admitted (although S. Foster Damon's classic study of Blake's philosophy and symbols reveals that Blake is not such a dark jungle as he seems). Alfred Kazin, in an immodestly and disdainfully intelligent prefatory essay to the Viking Portable Library edition of Blake, likewise fails to point up the spiritual profundity of Blake. While recognizing that Blake's theme was always the defense of "the integral human personality," Kazin has little insight into the intense spiritual drama of Blake's prophecies, the last of which especially are dismissed as lightless and trackless and as requiring, like Joyce's achievement, the almost fanatical devotion of a lifetime. But, as Christopher Dawson has more wisely and sympathetically suggested, "Whoever has the patience and the imagination to follow Blake through his strange visionary world will gain a more direct insight into the process of spiritual change that was taking place under the surface of European consciousness than is to be found in any other writer." [1]

Let it be accepted that Blake was no authentic mystic. Yet he was a religious mind, able, in radiant though involved revelation, to deal with the death of culture. Let it be accepted that he was conscious of the currents of his time. Yet he was not excessively conscious of them (I do not feel that Blake's political awareness was very obtrusive). In any event, he was not locked into them. And one who simply reads the body of his poetry by itself will not find that "the major currents of opinions of his time" were of great importance to his more searching work. John Middleton Murry, who, according to Schorer, was temerarious in boldly entering Blake's mind and in trying to grasp it "from his own page alone," has shown, I believe, more real insight into Blake than is accomplished by what Schorer terms his own "more halting approach" to Blake's genius. I am afraid that the halting approach of the academy can do little for the splendor of Blake's spiritual genius. This kind of genius is too foreign to the minor tensions and traps of conventional scholarship, which are not quite equal to allowing or holding the greatness of a true and valiant soul. The horses of instruction have never made it evident that they are wiser than the tygers of wrath. Their narrowing formulas and frameworks cannot hold Blake's fiery depiction of the infernal evil and darkness that plague modern civilization, nor can they perceive the strange, burning vision that ministers to the sorrow and savagery of the world.

II THE HEART FULL OF FUTURITY

There is to be seen in Blake a juxtaposition of two elements that Nicholas Berdyaev found in himself: "a passionate love of the world above, of the world of the highest, with pity for the lower world, the world of suffering." Blake's mission comes forth from this combination. In his letters (and in his marginalia) the first element is given remarkable emphasis. There, with unfaltering conviction, he describes his task: essentially to liberate man and his world from the nets of rationalism, to achieve freedom from the slavery of matter through "Imagination, which is Spiritual Sensation." Out of a deep pit of melancholy, Blake says, he emerged and his eyes expanded into regions of fire and "like a Sea without shore, continue Expanding." Although he tried to chain his feet to the world of duty and reality, it was a vain endeavor. The passion of his love for the higher world, for the mansions of eternity was too great:

[1] C. Dawson, "William Blake and the Religion of Romanticism," *The Tablet*, 168 (London, Sept. 12, 1936), 336–338. All further Dawson quotations are from this incisive and unpretentious essay, to which I acknowledge a special debt.

the faster I bind, the better is the Ballast, for I, so far from being bound down, take the world with me in my flights, & often it seems lighter than a ball of wool rolled by the wind. Bacon and Newton would prescribe ways of making the world heavier to me, & Pitt would prescribe distress for a medicinal potion; but as none on Earth can give me Mental Distress, & I know that all Distress inflicted by Heaven is a Mercy, a Fig for all Corporeal! [2]

Blake dwells upon the interest which he keeps closest to his heart, an interest that is "more than life or all that seems to make life comfortable without." His interest, he declares, is

the Interest of True Religion & Science [in this context true knowledge and wisdom], & whenever anything appears to affect that Interest (Especially if myself omit any duty to my Station as a Soldier of Christ), It gives me the greatest of torments. I am not ashamed, afraid, or adverse to tell you what Ought to be Told: That I am under the direction of Messengers from Heaven, Daily & Nightly; but the nature of such things is not, as some suppose, without trouble or care. Temptations are on the right hand & left; behind, the sea of time & space roars & follows swiftly; he who keeps not right onward is lost, & if our footsteps slide in clay, how can we do otherwise than fear & tremble?

Blake continues the description of his spiritual state and of the spiritual responsibility of his task:

But if we fear to do the dictates of our Angels, & tremble at the Tasks set before us; if we refuse to do Spiritual Acts because of Natural Fears or Natural Desires! Who can describe the dismal torments of such a state!—I too well remember the Threats I heard!—"If you, who are organized by Divine Providence for spiritual communion, Refuse, & bury your Talent in the Earth, even tho' you should want Natural Bread, Sorrow & Desperation pursues you thro' life, & after death shame and confusion of face to eternity. Everyone in Eternity will leave you, aghast at the Man who was crown'd with glory & honour by his brethren, & betray'd their cause to their enemies. You will be call'd the base Judas who betray'd his Friend!"—Such words would make any stout man tremble, & how then could I be at ease? But I am now no longer in That State, & now go on again with my Task, Fearless, and tho' my path is difficult, I have no fear of stumbling while I keep it.

Reflecting upon his plan to present to "the dwellers upon earth" by means of his prophecies the history of his spiritual suffering, Blake admonishes the children of man for their mockery of the prophet:

Would to God that they would consider it,—that they would consider their Spiritual Life, regardless of that faint Shadow called Natural Life, and that they would Promote Each other's Spiritual labours, each ac-

[2] All quotations from Blake in this essay are from the complete *Poetry and Prose of William Blake*, edited by Geoffrey Keynes (New York: Random House, 1939).

cording to its Rank, & that they would know that Receiving a Prophet as a Prophet is a duty which If omitted is more Severely Avenged than Every Sin and Wickedness beside. It is the Greatest of Crimes to Depress True Art and Science. I know that those who are dead from the Earth, & who mocked and Despised the Meekness of True Art . . . I know that such Mockers are Most Severely Punished in Eternity. . . . The Mocker of Art is the Mocker of Jesus. Let us go on . . . following his Cross: let us take it up daily, Persisting in Spiritual Labours & the use of that Talent which it is Death to Bury, and of that Spirit to which we are called.

The Mocker of Art is the Mocker of Jesus. The Mocker of Art is the Mocker of Vision. Blake abhorred Bacon and Reynolds and Burke, because they mocked inspiration and vision: "Inspiration & Vision was then, & now is, & I hope will always Remain, my Element, my Eternal Dwelling place; how can I hear it Contemned without returning Scorn for Scorn?" For Blake *Art* was the creative means of liberation from the stranglehold of reason and matter. And the action of Imagination was holy, divine. Christ the Savior became in Blake's sight the Creative Imagination. To him the best Christianity was the exercise of the Divine Art of Imagination: "A poet, a Painter, a Musician, an Architect: the Man Or Woman who is not one of these is not a Christian." Blake knew that there existed "a Class of Men whose whole delight is in Destroying." But to be a Christian, one had to be a Creator: "You must leave Fathers & Mothers & Houses & Lands if they stand in the way of Art." If men, Blake declared, remain just and true to their Imagination, they shall have the world of Eternity where they "shall live forever in Jesus Our Lord." Blake's Imagination, as Dawson has pointed out, is "no subjective human faculty; it is the creative and eternal Logos." It rises not out of the world or of man. Blake insisted that the world of Imagination is not the world of the natural man. Rather

it is the divine bosom into which we shall go after the death of the Vegetative body. This World of Imagination is Infinite & Eternal, whereas the world of Generation, or Vegetation, is Finite and Temporal. There exist in that Eternal World the Permanent Realities of Every Thing which we see reflected in this Vegetative Glass of Nature. All things are comprehended in their Eternal Forms in the divine body of the Saviour, the True Vine of Eternity.

From such beliefs it is easy to see why for Blake the mocker of art became the mocker of Jesus. It is likewise easy to see why he set such great store by the extraordinary products of his own Creative Imagination, the Prophetic Books, why he could rejoice and tremble in his own creations, why he could say that his heart was full of futurity. Blake was rapturous in his enthusiasm for the world above, was convinced of the glory and honor of his utterance and of the self-induced divine sanction for and the insuperability of his mission:

> I see the face of my Heavenly Father; he lays his Hand upon my Head & gives a blessing to all my works; why should I be troubled? why should my heart & flesh cry out? I will go on in the Strength of the Lord; through Hell will I sing forth his Praises, that the Dragons of the Deep may praise him, and that those who dwell in darkness & in the Sea Coasts may be gather'd into his Kingdom.

III THE FURNACES OF AFFLICTION

Blake's pity for the world of suffering no less than his special vision is marked throughout his poetry, for at least the *Songs of Experience* onward. He was conscious, like T. S. Eliot, of the wasteland, into which modern civilization was being transformed, of its denial of light and life, love and hope and faith, of its impoverishment of the body through industry and mechanics, of the soul through science, "the Tree of Death." The images, tones, and rhythms of his language become the forms of his lamentation for a lost world, a world without love, which has neglected or perverted the practice of divine arts. The freshness of his enthusiasm for the creativity of the formal revolutionary causes of liberty darkens into portentous voices of anguish. The poet's simple, uncomplicated lyrical pleasure in the innocence of the world is blasted in the furnaces of human affliction. Man has created his world—and it has fallen back into waste and void. And there is darkness again upon the face of the deep.

Like Léon Bloy, Blake had a keen sense of how *money* had dragged into misery the lives of the poor. Money, he charged, is "the life's blood of Poor Families." Money is the curse of the Art ("The Tree of Life") of Christianity, for "Christianity is Art and not Money." He asserted that the real Christian charity cannot be dependent on money, "on Caesar or Empire or Natural Religion." Money is "the Great Satan or Reason." Blake's "sensitiveness to the suffering of the poor," according to Dawson, marked off his religion from "the orthodox Christianity of the age." Dawson further comments that, although Blake's "ideal of creative imagination and spiritual intuition resembles that of the German romantics, his devotion to social justice has more in common with the utopian socialism of Fourier and the St. Simonians." And the prayer of Los from the second book of *Jerusalem* is cited as an indication of Blake's attitude towards "the callous indifference of Church and State" and "the facile optimism of the radicals with their cult of enlightened self-interest."

> And Los prayed and said, "O Divine Saviour, arise
> "Upon the Mountains of Albion as in ancient time! Behold!

"The cities of Albion seek thy face; London groans in pain
"From Hill to Hill, & the Thames laments along the Valleys:
"The little Villages of Middlesex & Surrey hunger & thirst:
"The twenty-eight Cities of Albion stretch their hands to thee
"Because of the Oppressors of Albion in every City & Village.
"They mock at the Labourer's limbs: they mock at his starv'd Children:
"They buy his Daughters that they may have power to sell his Sons:
"They compell the Poor to live upon a crust of bread by soft mild arts:
"They reduce the Man to want, then give with pomp & ceremony:
"The praise of Jehovah is chaunted from lips of hunger & thirst. . . ."

In an earlier poem Blake had expressed his concern over the unholy poverty of "a rich and fruitful land," poverty that, prevailing against all life-giving light and nurture, had created an "eternal winter."

Is this a holy thing to see
In a rich and fruitful land,
Babes reduc'd to misery,
Fed with cold and usurous hand?

Is that trembling cry a song?
Can it be a song of joy?
And so many children poor?
It is a land of poverty!

And their sun does never shine,
And their fields are bleak & bare,
And their ways are fill'd with thorns:
It is eternal winter there.

For where-e'er the sun does shine,
And where-e'er the rain does fall,
Babe can never hunger there,
Nor poverty the mind appall.

All his days Blake seemed to be able to hear the spectres of the dead crying out from the deeps beneath the hills of England and to hear the English cities groaning in their iron furnaces. D. H. Lawrence, it may be noted, considered his own mining countryside of Nottingham and said that the real tragedy of England is "the tragedy of ugliness";

Now though perhaps nobody knew it, it was ugliness which really betrayed the spirit of man in the nineteenth century. The great crime which the moneyed classes and promoters of industry committed in the palmy Victorian days was the condemning of the workers to ugliness, ugliness, ugliness: meanness and formless and ugly surroundings, ugly ideals, ugly religion, ugly hope, ugly love, ugly clothes, ugly furniture, ugly houses, ugly relationship between workers and employers.

Lawrence's words simply reaffirm the much earlier judgment of Hopkins upon the base and bespotted features of the industrial England he observed. British civilization was dirty, Hopkins reflected, and its cities convinced him "of the misery of town life to the poor and more than to the poor, of the misery of the poor in general, of the degradation even of our race, of the hollowness of this century's civilization." But Blake, long before Hopkins or Lawrence, knew this ugliness and baseness. A man-made rationalist and materialist civilization had confined and spoiled and filled with diseases the freshness and loveliness of human and physical nature. It had put its blight upon the action of the mind, upon work, upon patriotism and sacrifice, upon the Church, upon love and marriage:

> I wander thro' each charter'd street,
> Near where the charter'd Thames does flow,
> And mark in every face I meet
> Marks of weakness, marks of woe.
>
> In every cry of every Man,
> In every Infant's cry of fear,
> In every voice, in every ban,
> The mind-forged manacles I hear.
>
> How the Chimney-sweeper's cry
> Every black'ning Church appalls;
> And the hapless Soldier's sigh
> Runs in blood down Palace walls.
>
> But most thro' midnight streets I hear
> How the youthful Harlot's curse
> Blasts the new born Infant's tear,
> And blights with plagues the Marriage hearse.

One is reminded of T. S. Eliot's time-kept London:

> Unreal City,
> Under the brown fog of a winter dawn,
> A crowd flowed over London bridge, so many,
> I had not thought death had undone so many.

But Blake did not need to be localizing the miserable conditions of man in London or in England. In his being there was response to the universal withering of man's personality in the midst of murderous rocks, the shattering and smashing of the unity of man's spiritual, intellectual, imaginative, and emotional energies. In the disruptive life of modern man there was no chance for synthesis, for the closing and healing of wounds. Blake had a deep feeling for the loneliness and lost way of man in the wilds of a progressive civilization, the loneliness of man's endurance of the hard and sterile disintegration of life. In countless passages of the Prophetic Books, he explored the wasteland with an art appropriate to his task, sufficiently successful anyway to dispose of Schorer's arbitrary notion that Blake's art is "one of the great casualties in the history of poetry." Blake expressed such anguish and fear as were aroused over a century later in the soul of T. S. Eliot when he contemplated the triumphant civilization that seemed to him, as to Blake, capable of generating only limitless mediocrity and misery and war. Where money exists, Blake declared, only war can be carried on. In Blake's earlier poems there are images of drouth and death enough, of the lightless, stony dread fallen on the head of the earth, "her locks cover'd with grey despair," of the dream of the child starved in the pathless desert, of the Garden of Love flowerless and filled with briars, graves and tombstones, of the snake vomiting out his poison on the Bread and Wine. But the dolorous clangor of sterility is terrific throughout the Prophetic Books. Blake's land is a land of black storms and dark valleys and dreadful ruins. The poet pictures the couches of the dead in "a land of sorrow and tears where never smile was seen." There is often the fright of smoke and thunder and flaming winds, of plagues crippling the world and cutting off man and beast amidst howling and shuddering and the rattling of hollow bones. The furious terrors fly around everywhere. This is Blake's rats' alley, where the dead men have convulsively lost their bones.

Yet in the figure of Urizen the terrors of the void are concentrated, for Urizen is the real spectre of death, the creator of emptiness. Urizen is the unintegrated reasoning power in man, separated from Imagination and framing laws "to destroy Imagination, the Divine Body." In the Blakean mythology, Urizen is the dark, evil god of restriction, the foe that enslaves vision in its frigid horrors:

> . . . his ten thousands of thunders,
> Rang'd in gloom'd array, stretch out across
> The dread world; & the rolling of wheels,
> As of swelling seas, sound in his clouds,
> In his hills of stor'd snows, in his mountains
> Of hail & ice; voices of terror
> Are heard, like thunders of autumn
> When the cloud blazes over the harvests.

Urizen is "self-closed, all-repelling," occupied in vast, silent but unprolific labors. To break the rivets of iron that repressive Urizen has soldered upon the life of man, Blake created Orc, the force of fire, passion and revolutionary energy that will endure no restraints. The poet likewise offered his proverbs of hell: "The road of excess leads to the palace of wisdom"; "He who desires but acts not breeds pestilence"; "The wrath of the lion is the wisdom of God"; "Exuberance is beauty"; "Sooner murder an infant in its cradle than nurse unacted desires"; "The soul of sweet delight can never be defiled." The chorus of the Song of Liberty is sung: "Let the Priests of the Raven of dawn no longer, in deadly black, with hoarse note curse the sons of joy . . . For everything that lives is holy." All this will appear to be not only anarchic and anti-rationalistic, but also anti-Christian. Blake, however, gradually came to realize that the uncontrolled energies of desire and revolt would breed their own pestilences. So the fierce, bright creativity of the romantic revolutionary spirit darkens into "apocalyptic terror and gloom" out of which emerges at last the tender voice of the Lamb of God.

For the Urizen-Orc myth Blake substituted another: "Albion, the universal Man, and Jerusalem, the divine Vision." Blake's lamentation, of course, is no less loud and the sense of suffering and death persists: the groans of Jerusalem are great and storms beat around Albion. But Jesus, the Good Shepherd, reducing to nothing the other voices and phantom figures of the prophecies, has appeared and the breath of divine amity blows over the world. In the fourth book of *Jerusalem,* the grievous voice of Jerusalem, lost and wandering among precipices of despair, is heard in the darkness of Philisthea:

> "How distant far from Albion! his hills & valleys no more
> Receive the feet of Jerusalem: they have cast me quite away,
> And Albion is himself shrunk to a narrow rock in the midst of the sea!
> The plains of Sussex & Surrey, their hills of flocks and herds
> No more seek to Jerusalem nor to the sound of my Holy-ones.
> The Fifty-two Counties of England are harden'd against me
> As if I was not their Mother; they despise me and cast me out,
> London cover'd the Whole Earth: England encompass'd the Nations,
> And all the Nations of the Earth were seen in the Cities Of Albion."

Jerusalem laments that Albion had formerly given her "the whole Earth to walk up and down, to pour joy upon every mountain, to teach songs to the shepherd and plowman." Italy, France, Spain, Germany, Poland, and the North "found my gates in all their mountains & my curtains in all their vales; the furniture of their houses was the furniture of my chamber." Turkey and Greece sounded their thanksgiving to her and Egypt, Lybia, and Ethopia enquired for Jerusalem. "And thou, America! I once beheld thee, but now behold no more thy golden mountains." Now Jerusalem must grieve that her altars run with blood, that her fires are corrupt, and her innocence become "a cloudy pestilence," rather than "a continual cloud of salvation." Now she has been closed from the nations "in the narrow passages of the valleys of destruction." Now she walks "weeping in pangs of a Mother's torment for her Children":

> "I walk in affliction. I am a worm and no living soul!
> A worm going to eternal torment, rais'd up in a night
> To an eternal night of pain, lost! lost! lost! forever!"

Then Albion is seen lying cold upon his rock, while "the weeds of Death inwrap his hands & feet, blown incessant and wash'd incessant by the for-ever restless sea-waves foaming abroad upon the white Rock" and "England, a Female Shadow, as deadly damps of the Mines of Cornwall & Derbyshire, lays upon his bosom heavy." Overhead, "the famish'd Eagle screams on boney Wings, and around them howls the Wolf of famine." The black ocean heaves and thunders "around the wormy Garments of Albion." There comes, however, a pause, a silence like death:

> Time was Finished! The Breath Divine Breathed over Albion
> Beneath the Furnaces & starry Wheels and in the Immortal Tomb,
> And England, who is Brittannia, awoke from Death on Albion's bosom:
> She awoke pale & cold; she fainted seven times on the Body of Albion.
> "O pitious Sleep, O pitious Dream! O God, O God awake! I have slain
> In Dreams of Chastity & Moral Law: I have murdered Albion!"

The voice of England pierced the cold ear of Albion, who stirred upon his rock as "the Breath Divine went forth upon the morning hills." Painfully opening his eyelids, Albion looked upon England: "Ah! Shall the Dead live again?" England then rejoiced and entered the bosom of Albion. The inferno of Blake is at this point done and Blake's paradiso (insofar as he achieves one) begins.

The progression through Blake's wasteland is similar to that in T. S. Eliot's. At the very end of Eliot's central poem, *The Waste Land,* the thunder, no longer dry and sterile, speaks with the voice of redemption: after the agony in stony places the winds bear life-bringing rains and the poem ends with "the Peace which passeth understanding." Into Blake's wasteland, Jesus finally comes and stands by Albion as "by the lost Sheep that he hath found, & Albion knew that it was the Lord." Albion asks: "Oh Lord, what can I do? My Selfhood cruel marches against thee, deceitful . . . I know it is my Self, O my Divine Creator & Redeemer." Jesus answers: "Fear not Albion: unless I die thou canst not live; but if I die I shall arise again & thou with me. This is Friendship & Brotherhood: without it Man Is Not." And Albion replies: "Cannot Man exist without Mysterious offering of Self for Another? is this Friendship & Brotherhood?" Finally Jesus says:

". . . Wouldest thou love one who never died
For thee, or ever die for one who had not died for thee?
And if God dieth not for Man & giveth not himself
Eternally for Man, Man could not exist; for Man is love
As God is Love: every kindness to another is a little Death
In the Divine Image, nor can Man exist but by Brotherhood."

Universal man, as Jerusalem laments, has spurned her, the Divine Vision, and has selfishly been preoccupied with his own reason and matter. So the spirit is killed in him. He can be saved from this deadly slavery, this negation of and incrustation upon his immortal spirit, by the constant annihilation of the selfhood. Man must surrender his absolute confidence in rational demonstration and have faith in the Savior and in the mercy of redemption through the Savior. Albion must make a great effort to discard Bacon, Locke, and Newton, must be willing "to take off his filthy garments" and then "clothe himself with Imagination."

This final resolution of Blake is, as Dawson comments, "less Christian than it may appear at first sight, for Blake not only assimilates the Saviour to the Creative Imagination and the Prophet to the artist, but asserts the substantial identity of God and Man in terms that seem to exclude any belief in the divine transcendence." Nevertheless, Blake's attitude is fundamentally religious, full of wonder, love and awe. As Blake himself put it: "I speak of Spiritual Things, Not of Natural." He detested the Spectre of the extreme and sterile rational power that had come to haunt and stupefy man, the Spectre that taught experiment and doubt rather than belief and eternal life and symmetry, the Satanic Accuser that, lacking love and sympathy, had laid waste the world. Here was no water but only rock.

IV THE CONQUEROR

The Christianity to which Blake came was life-giving for him and for the decayed and groaning world he had constructed. But it was, naturally a Christianity of his own composition, baffling, gnostic, theosophical, in the mode of St. Martin and Lavater and of the Lutheran mystique of Jacob Boehme. Even at the end he kept his antagonism (based upon his feeling that faith eliminates obligation) towards the dominion of authority and the moral duty imposed by it. Authority remained repressive and fearsome. It is certain, however, that his pantheistic direction and antinomianism did not compel Blake to ignore the implacable presence of evil, its menace to human life and culture, and the importance of the moral struggle against the power of evil. It is also clear that Christianity was no longer the enemy, no longer embodied, as it had in his earlier thought, the calamitous, curbing force in the world of freedom. Christianity now turned the furnaces of affliction into "Fountains of Living Waters flowing from the Humanity Divine." The real enemy of humanity and universal nature, Blake wrote in the Preface to the third book of *Jerusalem,* is the deist, the preacher of natural morality and natural religion:

> Your Religion, O Deists! Deism, is the Worship of the God of this World by the means of what you call Natural Religion and Natural Philosophy, and of Natural Morality or Self-Righteousness, the Selfish Virtues of the Natural Heart. This was the Religion of the Pharisees who murder'd Jesus. Deism is the same & ends in the same.

It is the rationalists and natural religionists who are responsible for the warring and ruin of history, not "the poor Monks & Religious." These profess "the Religion of Jesus, Forgiveness of Sin"—and this religion "can never be the cause of a War." Those who cause war are deists, who "never can be Forgivers of Sin." And Blake concluded: "The Glory of Christianity is To Conquer by Forgiveness. All the Destruction, therefore, in Christian Europe has arisen from Deism, which is Natural Religion."

Whatever Blake's contact, adequately investigated by Schorer, with the currents of his time, he remained essentially "an isolated figure." But he is still a great clue-figure in the spiritual and intellectual history of the modern world. He reveals, in his odd, unclassical, and unorthodox ways, as Dawson notes, "the spiritual conflict which underlies the social changes of the age and which resulted from the insurgence of the spiritual forces that had been repressed by the rationalism and moralism of the Enlightenment." In Dawson's view, this spiritual revolution had a dual realization: first, as "a movement of return to the tradition of historic Christianity" manifested in the Catholic Revival on the Continent and in Newman and the Oxford Movement leading to a renewal of Catholic life and culture in England; secondly, and in contrast, as "a movement of innovation and change" resulting in new religions of humanitarianism, nationalism and liberalism. Yet these two forms are not so contradictory or disparate as they seem. The religious liberalism of Lamennais, for instance, unfolded out of the religious traditionalism of de Maistre and de Bonald. Likewise, a number of the intellectual and social reformers, moving through their new religions, arrived at traditional Christianity. And although religion did not succeed in giving form to modern civilization, it was at least recognized as an indispensable element in the life of modern man. That is why Dawson thinks that "in comparison with the 18th century, the 19th century, especially the first half of it, was a religious age." It seems to me that something of all this, writers like Helen C. White and Alfred Kazin fail to recognize when they intimate, as

Miss White does, that William Blake is not "a prophet for this modern world" or, as Kazin does, that Blake has not yet spoken "to our modern humanity in tones we have learned to prize as our own and our greatest." In his rather extreme and perverse work, *Blake and Modern Thought,* Denis Saurat comprehends at least Blake's relevance and usefulness as a significant "witness of our own mentality."

Blake is not, however, a witness of the prevalent modern mentality, but rather of all those who have, in one shape or another, fought valiantly in the underground of history for the power of the spiritual as opposed to the success of the material which is enough for the surface-dwellers. At the outset of this essay, I listed the names of some modern seers with whom Blake has relationship. I would not limit his relevance to the fairly familiar figures who are often brought into the Blakean universe—Yeats and D. H. Lawrence, for example. Yeats, like Blake, was fascinated by occultism and spiritualism and created in his poetry his own mythological system. Just as Blake managed to encompass, in one phase of his work, the spirit of the French Revolution and the liberalist uprising in the world, so did Yeats draw into his mythology the heroes and events of the Irish Rebellion. As he grew older, Yeats, much like Blake, became more and more dubious about the new tyrants enthroned by a society devoted to commerce, science, and the liberal point-of-view, the new tyrants that spat upon the pride of the people. But Yeats never seems to have gone down very deep into the inferno—and, in any event, was quite fluid in dreaming it out of existence. Likewise, the making of analogues between Blake and D. H. Lawrence is, at first sight anyway, a quite easy thing to do. Blake, however, is not so one-sided or obsessed as Lawrence in urging the mind to come down from its eminence. And Blake does not stop, like Lawrence, with the dark passional, physical powers. Blake comes closer, as Saurat asserts (even though misconceivingly), to a synthesis of the human spirit, a synthesis of "reason, imagination, passion and instinct." Blake comes toward, I am convinced, many minds whom one might, without reflection, separate from him entirely. Blake is an enduring, unconquerable, and universal witness because, despite his faults and confusions, he understood and assailed the evils which upset and will always upset the great, serious, most worthy thinkers and artists of the present and future, those particularly who find it impossible to take it easy and relax when they are braved by the demons of indifference or compromise, of mediocrity or venality in man. And, as S. Foster Damon recognized, the evils damned by Blake "are even stronger now than when he wrote, and at last the world, beholding the errors, searches for solutions."

In this search for solutions to our evils there are a good many contemporary spiritual minds who have a real (even if not too obvious, perhaps) affinity with Blake. I have selected arbitrarily to develop this point some publications of three rather different intellects: Nicholas Berdyaev, the Russian philosopher who lived in exile in Paris; Franz Kafka, the Czech-German writer; and Georges Bernanos, the French Catholic novelist.

Berdyaev, in *Slavery and Freedom,* reveals, like Blake, his kinship with Jacob Boehme and, in general, the characteristic Blakean terror of any destructive tyranny, together with an urgent love of freedom and creativeness. Blake and Berdyaev seem to maintain the same gnostic idea of freedom as coming only when man has been rescued from the cruel grasp of matter. Both have a terrific anxiety to drag modern man out of the snares that seize him. Berdyaev writes: "I discover in myself something elemental and primitive: a reaction against world data; a refusal to accept any sort of objectivity such as the slavery of man; and the opposition of the freedom of the spirit to the compulsion of the world, to violence, and to compliancy." These could readily be the words of Blake. Blake would have understood, too, the large emphasis which Berdyaev puts upon spirit over nature and love over law. Moreover, Berdyaev's strictures upon the "hidden dictatorship" of money in modern society at least echo those of Blake:

> The life of man depends upon money, the most impersonal, the most unqualitative power in the world, and the most readily convertible into everything else alike. It is not directly, by way of physical violence, that a man is deprived of his freedom of conscience, freedom of thought, and freedom of judgment, but he is placed in a position of dependence materially, he finds himself under the threat of death by starvation, and in this way he is deprived of his freedom. Money confers independence; the absence of it places a man in a position of dependence.

And Blake's sensitiveness to the industrialized torture of modern people is repeated in Berdyaev's judgment: "The development of civilization was accompanied by the oppression and exploitation of vast masses of mankind, of the labouring people; and this oppression was held to be justified by the objective values of civilization."

Blake's apocalyptic pessimism is reduced by Berdyaev to this aphorism: "Optimism about the world order is the servitude of man." But the action of the Redeemer (absorbed into gnosticism from Christianity), of Christ suffering for man and striving with man, in opposition to the "falsity and wrong" of the objectivized world order, will bring man freedom from servitude. Blake no less than Berdyaev underlines this idea. When Berdyaev writes that "the slavery of man to nature . . . is slavery to the object world" and that "creativeness is a fight against the object world," one cannot fail to remember Blake's annotations upon Wordsworth:

I see in Wordsworth the Natural Man rising up against the Spiritual Man continually, & then he is No Poet but a Heathen Philosopher at Enmity against all true Poetry or Inspiration. . . . Natural Objects always did & now do weaken, deaden & obliterate Imagination in Me. Wordsworth must know that what he Writes Valuable is Not to be found in Nature.

I think, too, that the beautiful, vast and surging "chaos" of Blake's poetry which gradually brings itself out to a kind of cosmical focus in the figure of Jesus, might carry, as an epigraph, this sentence from Berdyaev: "There is no beauty of cosmos without the background of chaos." That is, without the background of chaos "there is no tragedy, no climax of human creativeness, no Don Quixote, no drama of Shakespeare, no Faust, no novels of Dostoyevsky." And surely no Blake.

The paradox of the essential chaos of our stupefying efficient bureaucratic civilization (with its fixation of mechanical order, its wondrous files and filing systems, its managerial burrows, its inexhaustible forms and guaranteed procedures) imposed itself upon Franz Kafka. Blake and Kafka are at once alike in that each experienced real hardships and enjoyed no great measure of public success during his lifetime. Each had what Edwin Muir—in the introduction to Kafka's collection of stories and reflections titled *The Great Wall of China*— terms "a passion for rightness." But it seems that Kafka, unlike Blake, had "no trace of vanity" about his works. Blake is more humorless in his effort than Kafka, who had at least "a humour of desperation." Yet Kafka is tied to Blake in his fantastic fidelity "to himself and what he thought the right way of conduct." In his art each is able to evoke (Kafka: quietly, almost geometrically; Blake: tumultuously, even harshly) an atmosphere of such dread and doom as to make the writer appear on "the verge of actual madness." But, whereas Kafka moves in his art "towards proportion and clarity," Blake moves decidedly towards greater and greater complexity (yet, I suppose, reaches the more awesome clarity that lies at the heart of complexity).

Kafka's moral and spiritual problem, according to Muir's description, is, in a considerable way, Blake's also: "that of finding one's true vocation . . . and that of acting in accordance with the will of heavenly powers." Kafka, however, grasps the concept of divine authority (although Kafka's God may seem a too darkling and far-removed Jehovah) and its importance for man. Blake, it would seem, exults in his visions of the higher world but very much on his own terms. He has no faith in a personal God, and any idea of authority is intolerable to him. Kafka indicates, in "The Great Wall of China," that he understands, as well as Blake, the human desire to smash restraints: "Human nature can endure no restraint;" Kafka writes, "if it binds itself it soon begins to tear madly at its bonds, until it rends everything asunder, the wall, the bonds and its very self." Yet Kafka can say, emphasizing the need for "humility and meekness," what Blake could never be expected to say (although he does pray to his Savior to pour upon him the spirit of meekness): "We—and here I speak in the name of many people—did not really know ourselves until we had carefully scrutinized the decrees of the high command. . . ." Blake could talk of the direction of messengers from heaven and of the dictates of his angels, but an objectively existing authority remote from his own Imagination could not excite his devotion or gain his obedience.

In their attitude towards progress and science and towards the burdens modern civilization places upon human freedom, there is notable correspondence between Kafka and Blake. Kafka writes, in "Investigations of a Dog":

> Certainly knowledge is progressing, its advance is irresistible, it actually progresses at an accelerating speed, always faster, but what is there to praise in that? It is as if one were to praise someone because with the years he grows older, and in consequence comes nearer and nearer to death with increasing speed. That is a natural and moreover an ugly process, in which I find nothing to praise. I can only see decline everywhere. . . .

And the instinct that invalidates a man's scientific capacity, Kafka suggests, may be the very one that makes him "—perhaps for the sake of science itself but a different science from that of today, an ultimate science—prize freedom higher than everything else." Kafka reflects that the freedom available today may indeed be a "wretched business." But it is still freedom and a possession. Blake would have sympathized with these thoughts, even though his notion of freedom might not have been precisely reconcilable with that of Kafka. And in "Reflections on Sin, Pain, Hope and the True Way," the aphoristic talent of Kafka strikes out in shapes remarkably suggestive of Blake: "There is only a spiritual world; what we call the physical world is the evil in the spiritual one, and what we call evil is only a necessary moment in our endless development;" "The fact that there is only a spiritual world robs us of hope and gives us certainty"; "The spirit only becomes free when it ceases to be a prop"; "We are sinful not merely because we have eaten of the Tree of Knowledge, but also because we have not yet eaten of the Tree of Life"; and "The whole world is full of them [our rationalizations], indeed the whole visible world is perhaps nothing more than the rationalization of a man who wants to find peace for a moment." These, I think, have at least the accent of Blake.

Admittedly, there are great differences in vision and mode of vision between Blake and Kafka. But the ideas and experiences of Kafka, realized in *The Castle, The Trial, Metamorphosis,* and in such a volume as *The Great Wall of China,* are not alien to the being of Blake and are motivated by some likeness of conscience with respect to the chaos of the condition of man and the terror of his life in what Bernanos calls "the vast agglomeration of cities." Blake and Kafka are joined securely in their sight of "the land of snares & traps & wheels & pitfalls & dire mills."

The resemblances between Blake and the formidable French prophet, Georges Bernanos, are numerous and interesting. Of the lineage of Léon Bloy, Bernanos shares with Blake a horror of the merely restrictive and blindly indifferent institutions of education and government. Bernanos, the tyger of wrath, despises the official leaders and teachers of society, the representatives who monstrously break and crush the people or allow them to be broken and exploited. He also shares with Blake an intense sympathy with these poor, weak and oppressed ones of the earth, a savage hostility towards materialist civilization and a passion for liberty. Bernanos sometimes manages nightmarish moments and images of torrid desolation and pain reminiscent of the immense effects, the "gigantic gnawing," of Blake—as in this passage from *Joy* describing a horrible presence of heat:

> It was not so much like the vast universal conflagration of day as an insidious fire over the dry hillside, the quick undulating flame running from one twig to another, like a tiny scarlet tongue. For at certain hours of the day in unusually hot summers, nature instead of relaxing, stretching out under the caress of the sun, seems on the contrary to shrink silently, timidly into herself, with the motionless, stupid resignation of an animal when it feels the mortal bite of its enemy's teeth sinking into its flesh. And indeed that stiff rain of heat pouring out of the mournful sky, that shower of white-hot arrows, the infinite suction of the sun, made one think of vicious bites, millions upon millions of bites, a gigantic gnawing.

In his novels and essays, Bernanos embodies and assails the spiritual dryness, the talent for compromise and meaninglessness, of the twentieth century Christians, in terms as trenchant as those used by Blake to assail the mediocrity of the Christendom of his age. Blake once said that "Englishmen are all intermeasurable by one another; certainly a happy state of agreement, in which I for one do not agree. God keep you and me from the divinity of yes and no too—the yea, nay, creeping Jesus—from supposing up and down to be the same thing. . . ." Today one might extract many passages similar in tone and text from Bernanos' *Plea for Liberty.* The impact of the voice of Bernanos, appealing to the men of France and England, is often like that of Blake, who could cry out: "Rouze up, O Young Men of the New Age! set your forehead against the ignorant Hirelings! For we have Hirelings in the Camp, the Court & the University. . . ."

With Blake, love is a great word. With Bernanos, Love is the last word. But the Love of Bernanos is clearly a transcendent and consuming Love, flowing out of the charity and grace of the real Christ, about whose nature, Bernanos, unlike Blake, has no confusion. Bernanos is utterly concerned about the freedom of free men. But, different from Blake, he seeks for the truest freedom of man in the authoritative life and strength of the Church and in the profundity of its protection of the life of the Spirit. (Bernanos' feud with ecclesiasticism does not alter in any way the firmness of his belief in the ministry of the Church.) Man will escape from slavery by giving himself up to Christ through the Church which is His Body. The resolution of man's suffering and man's hope is to be expected from the Church which alone in the world today preserves the freedom of the person against the monsters. For, as Bernanos says, it has always been the mission of the Church to fulfill God's expectations "that She shape men truly free, a breed of free men peculiarly effective because freedom is for them not only a right, but an obligation, a duty, for which they must render God an accounting." Naturally, Blake could not have delivered himself in this wise. Still, in his later phase, Blake, without the clear faith of Bernanos, would have been sure that the Christian man is the free man. In Blake's system, of course, this man would be "ever expanding in the Bosom of God, the Human Imagination."

The fiction of Bernanos builds great drama—gloomy but always vital—of the inner life and death, the holiness and evil of man against the background of despiritualized civilization. There is a deep warmth —a density of reality—in Bernanos' recreation of the tragic struggle of the soul against evil, a density that the vaporous although piercing forms projected by the imagination of Blake do not attain. For the mysteries that are transmitted to Bernanos out of the authentic living Christian tradition were not received by Blake. And Blake's Satan, the Accuser, is most indefinite when set beside the reality of the Satan, the stench and ferocity of actual evil and actual sin, that Bernanos can summon. With unique power does *Joy* create such reality: the young, saintly innocence of Mademoiselle de Chantal is confronted full force and violated by diabolical evil. It is the cruel and magnificent strife of earth, of this field between the devil and God. Yet a few might be willing to apply to the soul of Blake the words Bernanos used to describe the soul of the protagonist in *Joy*. By extension, Blake "comes and goes . . . breathes and lives with the light, beyond us, beyond our presence." And, although we may not realize it, he "drags our black souls out of the shadows, and the old sins begin to stir, to yawn, to stretch and show their yellow claws . . . tomorrow, day after tomorrow—who knows—some night, this very night perhaps, they will be altogether wide awake."

This discussion of three writers, stirring in the universe that Blake had entered well over a century before, should help to reveal why his thought and action are not just "interesting" and "suggestive," but really animate and abiding in the present age. It ought also to suggest why Blake was troubled as he reflected upon his tremendous task of opening the Eternal Worlds, and why his hand, as he wrote, trembled "exceedingly upon the rock of ages." But Blake was sure of the eternity of his task. "I still & shall to Eternity Embrace Christianity and Adore him who is the Express image of God; but I have travel'd thro' Perils & Darkness not unlike a Champion. I have Conquer'd & shall Go on Conquering. Nothing can withstand the fury of my Course among the Stars of God & in the Abysses of the Accuser." Blake's then was the conviction of the conqueror. And with reason. I do not suppose that Blake could ever actually have said, like Rimbaud, that in his work the victory over matter is won, that "the gnashing of teeth, the hissings of fire, the pestilential sighs are abating." Still, as one of those who set out "thro' Perils & Darkness" at the dawn of our era to be a vindicator of human life against that which perverts it, he came close to a conquest. His fire touched and still touches the quick of the spirit. Once discovered, all thinkers and artists whose wisdom really burns through the skin of time will give heart to us, will forever help us to know and to be. They become in truth the champions of the soul. We cannot help attaching ourselves to them and depending upon them. For they break the chains that freeze our bones, that require us to live as though dying or already dead.

LAMENNAIS

Waldemar Gurian

[1947]

THE history of the Catholic Church includes men who, after brilliant services to the Church, died outside her fold. Best known among them is Tertullian, the apologetic writer of the Early Church; less known is Ochino, the third vicar-general of the Capuchins, whose flight to Calvin's Geneva almost destroyed his order. In the nineteenth century there were two famous representatives of this group. Johann von Doellinger refused, when more than seventy years old, to accept the decision of the Vatican Council about papal infallibility. He passed away in 1890 unreconciled, though he had been distinguished for years as the outstanding German Catholic theologian. Félicité de la Mennais [1] was celebrated as the new Pascal and Bossuet of his time before he became the modern Tertullian by breaking with the Church because Pope Gregory XVI rejected his views on the relations between the Church and the world. As he lay deathly ill, his niece, "Madame de Kertanguy asked him: 'Féli, do you want a priest? Surely, you want a priest?' Lamennais answered: 'No.' The niece repeated: 'I beg of you.' But he said with a stronger voice: 'No. no, no. I wish to be left at peace.'" He was buried without Church services, without priest; no cross marked his grave, which is unknown today, for, according to his wishes, he was buried in a common grave. This end caused his old friend, Madame de Cottu, who, as a young woman, had regained her Catholic faith because of his influence, to exclaim: "The pity of God is without limits."

But despite Lamennais' obstinate rejection of the Catholic Church, his influence has been celebrated as very beneficent not only for French but for the whole of modern Catholicism. He was praised in 1903 by Msgr. Baudrillart, later rector of the Catholic Institute of Paris and Cardinal, as "the man who is at the beginning of the intellectual movements of the French clergy and at the source of all great movements at the end of the nineteenth century." The Catholic historian, Georges Goyau goes even farther in an article published in 1919 in the *Revue des Deux Mondes,* where he states that the papacy of today has

---

[1] After 1837 he signed himself simply Lamennais. Cf. F. Duine, *La Mennais* (1922), p. 213.

311

accepted Lamennais' program. Lamennais himself would today conclude that something had changed since the hour when he too hastily accused Gregory XVI of being the prisoner of Metternich. He would find that the papal pen uses words so dear to him: "rights of peoples," "aspirations of peoples."

As a theologian and philosopher, Lamennais is of little interest. It is astonishing that his philosophical and theological ideas have been taken very seriously. These ideas—as by the way also those of many of his bitter opponents—must be regarded as symptoms of a sad situation in the theological and philosophical studies of his time. Such decadence is openly admitted in Bellamy's authoritative *History of Catholic Theology in the Nineteenth Century*. There were no chairs of biblical studies in seminaries; Gallican books were used, and among French theologians Cartesianism was all-powerful. Nobody today would dream of defending Lamennais' common sense system which makes the testimony of mankind's universal reason, expressed in tradition and guarded by the Church, the source of certitude, or of accepting the Cartesian arguments and semi-Gallican theories of his opponents. But Lamennais remains, despite the limits of his thought, a central figure of French and modern Catholicism. He developed a new approach to modern secularized society for Catholics, though he connected this approach with systematic formulations and views condemned by the Church. He remains interesting and important as a complicated character who reflects the fundamental tendencies of his time and as a man with a tormented soul who could not stand the terrible responsibilities facing him. He failed as a Catholic just because he had won too great a success in the Catholic world, a success which came to him against his expectations and almost against his will.

Lamennais is surely not a great theologian—therefore the comparison with Tertullian is somewhat questionable—and surely not a profound philosopher. He is primarily a great writer able to coin illuminating and impressive sentences and to evoke images which enable us to grasp fundamental politico-social developments and trends. He has a deep feeling for the atmosphere of the period in which he lives, and for psychological changes. He is an analyst of his time who goes beyond the surface of daily events, and he knows how to present their meaning, though his reputation for exact prophecies is not always deserved. He is too much inclined to exaggerations, seeing catastrophe and disaster everywhere. By his admirable pen—though Sainte-Beuve has said: "the good Lamennais is equal to the bad or mediocre Rousseau"—the defense of religion and piety reached those who were not moved by the shallow religious literature of such mediocre religious writers as Msgr. Frayssinous and Msgr. de Boulogne, and who, on the other side, were not inclined to take very seriously the aesthetic apologetics of Chateaubriand's *Génie du Christianisme*. The younger clergy was not satisfied with the somewhat timid and politically submissive attitude of the higher clergy but was tremendously impressed by Lamennais' direct and fearless presentation of Catholic claims as well as by his ardent belief in the mission of the Church for society and humanity.

In the France of the twenties and early thirties, everyone who tried to renew Catholic life had to accept Lamennais' guidance. His famous house in La Chênaie was the spiritual and intellectual capital of French Catholicism. He showed again that Catholic belief was a living force and reality, not merely a venerable tradition out of touch with the present age and its needs. The stimulation which radiated from him continued after he had broken with the Catholic Church and become one of the utopian democratic and socialist ideologues who were characteristic of the reign of Louis Philippe. Lacordaire, the famous preacher and restorer of the Dominicans in France, had been connected with him. Guéranger, the founder of Solesmes, the restorer of the Benedictines and father of the liturgical movement, was among those who asked for his advice and found inspiration in his words. Young Montalembert, the defender of Catholic rights under Louis Philippe, and later, together with Bishop Dupanloup, a central figure of so-called liberal catholicism, had started his public activities under his patronage. Abbé Gerbet, who helped to popularize his system of *sens commun,* condemned in 1834 by the encyclical *Singulari nos,* became, as well as another of Lamennais' most intimate collaborators, Msgr. de Salinis, a respected member of the French hierarchy. The episcopal careers of Msgr. Gerbet and of Msgr. de Salinis show that the Church did forget the aberrations of the Mennaisiens in their youth, if they were willing to accept her decisions.

We are better able to understand Lamennais today than did his contemporaries. To them he appeared either as a holy man without doubts and hesitations and beyond all weaknesses, or as a fantastical believer in his ideas, a ruthless polemicist without pity for his opponents, and an inhuman doctrinaire. After all, there were few who had the opportunity to meet him intimately, to participate in his life at La Chênaie, and even many of those few turned away from him, sometimes bitterly disappointed by his behavior and by his rejection of all compromises. Today we have several volumes of his letters. The effect of these volumes is the same as that made on Sainte-Beuve after he had read the first samples of the epistolary art of the great Breton. Sainte-Beuve had become alienated from Lamennais. His friendship with the French Catholic leader, never very intimate, had ceased when he publicly expressed his disappointment with Lamennais' refusal to conform to his ideas of priestly obedience. (Sainte-Beuve regarded this obedience, not with the eyes of a believer, but with the eyes of an aesthete who is impressed by tragic sacrifices and the self-immolation of others.) But on reading the volumes of Lamennais' correspondence, edited by Forgues, he was forced to remark that we must "love and pity Lamennais."

Lamennais' letters reveal him as a man eternally looking for peace and quiet, but never really able to find it. There is an almost monotonous sequence of outcries and outbursts in many letters. He is always unhappy, longing for death, announcing disasters and catastrophes. The best known are his desperate letters of the period when he, at the age of thirty-four, received Holy Orders. Some biographers, accepting the interpretation developed first by Sainte-Beuve, have seen in this testimony of despair the key to his whole life, a proof that he was a *prêtre malgré lui,* that he had been forced into the priesthood by his saintly but naive brother, Jean, and by his spiritual father, the extremely well-meaning but imprudent Abbé Carron. These letters are really full of dark feelings: "I am unhappy and will remain unhappy," etc. He admits that he accepted the decision made by others, etc. But what do these outcries prove? They are not unique. They can be observed elsewhere. The statement is ascribed to young Lamennais, that boredom (*ennui*) was born in the family. Such complaints continue in Lamennais' correspondence until his death. They are sometimes manifestly overemphasized—Giraud is not wrong in saying that Lamennais was a writer often too fond of extreme statements and exaggerated formulations of his feelings—but they portray an attitude towards the world and human existence which has a basis irrelevant to any particular event such as the reception of Holy Orders.

Lamennais has a profoundly dualistic nature. He is a pure spiritualist for whom life in the world of senses is a martyrdom. His home is not in this world; it is beyond time and space. But on the other hand, he is profoundly interested in this world—he will change it, transform it, spiritualize it, deprive it of everything perishable; during his Catholic period he sought to overcome death, by accepting death as the entrance to eternal life. He is, sometimes, a marvelous lyricist, living in a world of his own, though a little too sentimental and too rhetorical—that is the basis of Sainte-Beuve's comparison of Lamennais at his best with a poor or mediocre Rousseau. He is always seeking affection and the experience of love which can make him forget the evil of existence on this earth. Lamennais made friends very easily, and was as easily disappointed in them, though some friendships lasted through his whole life, sometimes with persons whose views he did not share or who were completely opposed to his development. But besides these relations based on sentiment and affection, there is the longing for something suprapersonal, universal. Lamennais first found satisfaction for this longing in the Church, which he identified with the true social order (the Church's promises of life after death provided consolation for the catastrophes here on earth). Later, when the Church disappointed him, he selected as her substitute humanity, which remains a secularized christianity. After his defection from the Church, which resulted in the loss of his belief in a personal God and in the Divinity of Jesus Christ, Lamennais continued to profess a vague spiritualism. Humanity, united by a kind of natural love and solidarity, is a pale reflex of the *Corpus Christi Mysticum,* and he retained, too, a secularized and deformed belief in the Trinity which caused the general disapproval of his philosophical work of the forties.

Lamennais' fundamental attitude combines escape into a dream world of the future and after life with wild despair about the existing imperfect world, which, contented with itself, is not aware of its own race towards catastrophe, and with a hope in the necessary victory of the good forces. These forces are first represented by the Church, which will become victorious after a period of catastrophes, and whose victory is certain at the end of the world. Then, they are represented by the humanity which does not need the external constraints imposed by tyrannical princes and their ally, the Church of the Popes. Lamennais' spiritualistic dualism permits him to claim that he knows the course of history and of the development of society and on the other hand, to retire from the evil world into idyllic relations with nature and human beings.

Lamennais is at the same time a fantastic doctrinaire—a victim of the logic of his system, which alienates him from reality—and a man who tries to grasp the true meaning, the "beyond" of the events taking place before his eyes. As long as he is a Catholic, he is related to a concrete community and to a world of specific ideas and institutions. But he tries to put this world into the service of his schemes, which, to some extent, correspond to existing situations; he tries to replace the traditional authority by his own authority and to subordinate the Church to his system. He fails in this attempt and cuts himself off from the Church, thus becoming the master as well as the victim of his democratic humanitarian dream world. He appears more and more as a stiff doctrinaire who substitutes rhetorical fanasies for realities. No longer bound by any authority or objective order, he can create systems by his own fiat. In 1848 he opposed even the slightest change in his constitutional project, which appeared to him as the expression of perfect democracy. It does not matter whether these systems correspond to realities or not; the limits between reality and subjectivity disappear. And we see Lamennais end as an obstinate doctrinaire and a disappointed old man who continues to throw his condemnations against the world in which darkness, evil, and tyranny, as well as injustice, triumph. The ideal people of his fancy—humanity—has replaced the paradise of his Catholic period.

It is very fascinating and very useful for the study of the clash between ideas and political ideologies in the first half of the nineteenth century to follow step by step Lamennais' evolution. Only the general stages can be sketched—a full analysis would involve an attempt to picture all of French life, at least from the First Restoration to the first years of the Second Empire. Here his Catholic period will be the center of attention, for the important part of Lamennais' career is over after his public break with the Church. From a unique position he descends to the role of one among many leaders of secondary importance.

Lamennais was born in 1782, the son of a bourgeois family. He was a Breton, with some Irish blood. He apparently was much influenced by this heritage, as is shown by his attractive and strange mixture of obstinacy and superabundance of sentiment. Often he could not make up his mind, but when he had made it up, he adhered to his decisions stubbornly: note his attitude after he was disappointed by Gregory XVI's condemnation. Unlike his older brother, Jean, he was not very practical. He was inclined to trust everybody, as some fantastic business speculations show. The income from his *Reflections on the Imitation of Jesus Christ,* written during his Catholic period and reprinted with the Church imprimatur until our own day, for years formed a large part of the income of the former priest who publicly, in his *Discussions critiques,* admitted the loss of any Christian faith.

There is nothing spectacular about Lamennais' youth. His father and his uncle de Saudrais survived the Revolution by making concessions. They later returned to more conservative religious views; although the uncle who (or whose library full of authors of the eighteenth century) influenced Lamennais, remained an epicurean sceptic, loving his Horace and opposing all fanaticism. When did young Lamennais become a believing Catholic, following the example of his brother Jean who early decided to become a priest? He can be quoted as a living example of Rousseau's educational methods: he himself decided in mature age upon a positive religion. Impressed by Chateaubriand's *Génie* he received his first Holy Communion in 1804, at the age of twenty-two. A period of close collaboration with Abbé Jean followed. He taught mathematics in an ecclesiastical school. Publications demanding an internal renewal of Church life in France and defending papal infallibility and the rights of the Church against a usurping police state were prepared. Despite some praise of Napoleon, the first book was confiscated, and the second appeared only in 1814, after Napoleon's fall. In 1809 Lamennais received minor orders. In 1815 he fled to England during the Hundred Days. There he experienced one of those exalted friendships which are characteristic of him—a friendship with a young Englishman, Moorman. After his return in 1816 he received Holy Orders. He was thirty-four years old. If he were dragged to the altar as some interpreters claim, then he permitted himself to be dragged. The documents of this period show all the characteristics of the older Lamennais: exaltation, lyricism, belief in his own ideas, despair about the absence of happiness, about the experience of the *silence de Dieu* to use the title of a famous study by Abbé Brémond, who has attempted to describe Lamennais' religious type.

As Sainte-Beuve has correctly noted, Lamennais' lack of interest in the great world and in the historic events of the Napoleonic era is surprising. Lamennais apparently was interested exclusively in his small circle. Napoleon was regarded as an oppressor of the Church. The absence of a regular education and theological training is striking, for Lamennais was never in a seminary, as a result of the conditions of his time. In learning, he was more or less a self-made man. His learning is apparently vast, but if one looks closely, not very solid. The mass of quotations does not hide the absence of sure information. Striking is the general absence of political interest, though there are some critical remarks about the attempts of the First Bourbon Restoration to continue the Napoleonic control of all intellectual life.

Only at the end of 1817 did Lamennais become a public figure. He published the first volume of the *Essai sur l'Indifférence,* which he wrote under the greatest pain, complaining continuously about his work. An avalanche of praise started. He was another Bossuet, etc. Even Hegel (surely not an admirer of Catholic theological books) took the work seriously. The volume was directed against the absence of interest in religion, the denial of religion, or the rejection of the important truths of religion, against complacent Deism. Catholic faith as a necessity for social stability was emphasized. An occasional sentence, apparently putting Lamennais' hope in the influence of the government for good and bad, would show that Lamennais expected a re-christianization of post-revolutionary France from the Bourbon regime. But a closer study reveals the fact that Lamennais was centrally concerned with restoring unity between the spiritual and the political world. The spiritual world alone could help, not its use by a secular political regime.

Lamennais did not yet realize the consequences of his traditionalism for which there was no stable order without faith; faith was identified with the original beliefs of the human race. They were based on the first revelation and had been restored by Jesus Christ, and were now preserved by the Church represented by Rome. This approach made Lamennais a member of the traditionalist school whose heads, de Bonald and de Maistre, opposed the natural-divine order to the artificial creations of the revolution. Lamennais was closer to de Maistre, for he was not satisfied with de Bonald's emphasis on the unchangeable natural constitution, more or less identified with a pre-revolutionary society. With de Maistre he was dominated by what I would call the apocalyptic moment: the function of evil—Protestantism with its individualism and the French Revolution—in world history is to prepare a catastrophic and salutary transformation of the Universe. The world must realize deeply the true order or it is damned to catastrophe and disaster, though the end of the world necessarily means the triumph of truth. Father de Lubac is not the first theologian who has called our attention to the serious defects of traditionalism in all forms. He can quote the Jesuit Father Chastel, whose works, written in the fifties, are read today only by a few specialists. Father Chastel points out that for the traditionalists all religious and moral truth is given exclusively by an external and positive revelation. Revelation replaces reason. Father de Lubac condemns with Father Chastel the error of this system, which he regards as incompatible with Catholic doctrine.

De Maistre and de Bonald, it is true, were not directly condemned because their works never became centers of controversies as stormy as those raging around Lamennais, but they suffered from the same basic defects as Lamennais' theories owing to the excusable absence of a real knowledge of Christian philosophy and theological tradition. In order to oppose a rationalism which regarded men and human reason as self-sufficient, they mixed faith and reason. Thus, peculiarly enough, their fideism could be accepted by a pure positivism: de Bonald with his emphasis upon an eternal objective order developing according to an eternal trinitarian rhythm belongs to the ancestors of Comte's positivism, as Father de Lubac emphasizes: the order is simply given to the individual.

Lamennais became the center of theological attacks after he developed his traditionalist system of the *sens commun,* which bases all certainty on the *raison générale* expressed in the tradition organized by the Church, only because he infuriated influential theological schools by condemning Cartesianism (whose individualistic certainty would, he believed, be destroyed by his philosophy) and by attacking Gallicanism, saying that the Pope is the bearer of the universal tradition whereas Gallicanism is an accommodation to particular egoistic political claims. Joseph de Maistre's attack on Gallicanism in his book on *The Pope* became widely known only because of the polemics about Lamennais.

Lamennais' campaign against Cartesianism and Gallicanism alienated him from the supporters of the Restoration. He did not regard religion as a means of protecting the regime—he demanded a truly Catholic state, whereas in *La religion considerée dans ses rapports avec l'ordre politique et social* (1826) he characterized the state of the Bourbons as a secular state in which the Catholic Church becomes only one tolerated opinion among many. And now his ultramontanism took a turn away from the Restoration towards liberty. To the semi-Gallicanism of the politicians and the bishops of the Restoration he opposed the necessity of an alliance between the Church and the development of society towards liberty. He realized that the regime of the Restoration was condemned, that it was dying—the Church ought to drop its alliance with the princes, as he put it publicly in *Des progrès de la révolution et de la guerre contre l'Eglise* (1829). She should ally herself with the aspirations of the peoples to liberty which do not have to be mixed up with a wrong liberalism based upon revolutionary ideas and upon the world of anti-religious enlightenment.

The society of the Restoration disappeared for Lamennais, but the Church remained as the expression of the eternal truth necessary for the realization of true liberty. The Bourbon regime collapsed in 1830, and Lamennais believed then that the hour for the realization of the alliance of God and liberty had arrived. That was the motto of his famous newspaper, *Avenir*. Lamennais had reached the peak of his Catholic career, but the number of his enemies had increased continuously. He had alienated from himself not only the hierarchy who disliked his anti-Gallican campaigns, and influential theologians, who disliked his philosophy of the *sens commun,* though it was only a reaction against their Cartesianism. He had mobilized against himself the Jesuits, whose enemy he became after he discovered that they had issued a secret censure against his philosophy. He proclaimed that their order was outdated despite all its merits, and he founded a congregation of his own, La Congrégation de Saint Pierre, in order to replace the Society of Jesus in the modern age. In addition, he mobilized against himself not only the newly established Orleans regime from which he demanded liberties—liberty of education, particularly—and which he regarded as a materialistic regime of transition, but also all adherents of the ousted Charles X and the conservative forces in Europe, represented by the Austrian Chancellor Metternich, and Tsar Nicholas I.

It was no accident that Lamennais' ideas on the alliance between Church and peoples were particularly popular in Belgium (which broke off its link with the Netherlands in 1830), in Italy, where they operated against Austrian influence and domination, and in Poland, which tried to liberate herself from Russia. Besides Lamennais, Lacordaire and Montalembert were the most important contributors to the *Avenir*.

Abbé Gerbet, Lamennais' confidant and popularizer of the philosophy of *sens commun,* remained in the background. After a brilliant career, financial difficulties forced the *Avenir* to close down. It was Lacordaire who gave the advice to go to Rome in order to obtain the Pope's judgment about the ideas of Lamennais' publication. This voyage had tragic results.

On his way home Lamennais received, in Munich, the Encyclical *Mirari vos* which condemned the ideas of the *Avenir* without mentioning names. Later, Lamennais in his *Affaires de Rome* attempted to describe the circumstances surrounding the condemnation. Longing for human understanding and affection, he complained that the Pope did not use a paternal approach, but acted like a diplomat, despite all his personal kindness. If he had acted like a father, everything would have been settled. He ascribed the condemnation to political intrigues, to the alliance of the Popes with such reactionary forces as Metternich and Tsar Nicholas I. He turned against the Church in answering the question posed by de Maistre in one of his letters to Lamennais: "Will the Church be renewed or will a new religion come?" But his self-justification, his farewell to the Church in the *Affaires de Rome,* is somewhat colored. Not only is the book full of historical errors and omissions, as Father Dudon, S.J., the relentless and competent prosecutor of Lamennais after his death, has conclusively shown, but it ascribes to Lamennais on the way to Rome, feelings and attitudes which he did not have at the time.

What did the Encyclical *Mirari vos* condemn? It regrets the irreligious character of the time and the loss of respect for true religion, but it rejects the belief in unlimited liberties. The demand for separation of Church and State is condemned. Unrestricted liberty of the press, for example, is condemned because it would put error and truth on the same level and permit the publication of most fatal and dangerous opinions, etc. An attitude of systematic disrespect and attack against established governments is rejected. The Pope manifestly trusts princes rather than revolutionaries who oppose religion. Obviously, the work of the *Avenir* and the *Agence générale* created by Lamennais and his friends in order to defend religion in the name of liberty could not be resumed. It is very doubtful that the *Avenir* would have been started again, even if the Pope had remained silent, despite some statements of Lamennais and Montalembert to the contrary. The condemnation which, according to Father Dudon, Lamennais received with the humble remark, "We must submit to the papal judgment" was a severe blow for him. He had, strangely enough, expected that Rome, though not favorable to the ideas of the *Avenir,* would prefer to remain silent. The condemnation was not a hastily accepted measure or the result of the fact that the conservative Pope Gregory XVI disliked Lamennais' ideas, and particularly his embarrassing demand for a public judgment.

Father Dudon has shown that carefully working experts had made a thorough investigation.

Lamennais was profoundly shocked. In the following months he tried to find a way out. He fell back on the distinction between the Pope as the head of the Church and the Pope who expresses opinions on political matters of the moment. For years he had occasionally expressed distrust of the mentality prevailing in Rome and had regarded Rome as a city full of plotters, of a diplomatic worldly spirit. His letters during the peak of his ultra-montane and anti-Gallican campaigns contain such remarks. But this submission was not enough. Rumors began to circulate. Letters were intercepted and brought to the attention of ecclesiastical authorities. Lamennais had created many enemies for himself—French bishops continued to push a censure directed against Lamennais' ideas, though the condemnation of the *Avenir* by the highest authority ought to have been sufficient. Father Dudon criticizes (though with some restraint) this censure organized by Cardinal Archbishop d'Astros. Particularly bitter to Lamennais was the disavowal forced upon his brother, Abbé Jean, in order to rescue his brother's congregation. But all these difficulties could have been overcome, if an internal change had not begun to develop in his soul. It can be assumed that his periods of belief and unbelief followed each other according to daily experiences and moods rather than according to an iron-bound logic. But this internal change started to destroy Lamennais' beliefs. He announced to the surprised Montalembert who, by his uncautious activities and utterances, had contributed much to make the situation more precarious, that he had decided for the coming of a new religion. At the same time he became tired of debating his status, and he signed a satisfactory and apparently unlimited declaration of submission to the encyclical. As he expressed it in a revealing letter to Montalembert: he would have signed everything, even the statement that the Pope is God, etc.

The final public break came with the publication of the *Paroles d'un croyant* (1834). These lyrical praises of the oppressed and enslaved peoples, and dark, rhetorical condemnations of the oppressors created an immense sensation. There may be much noble feeling in this pamphlet, but there is no contact with political realities. It is an outburst in the name of eternal abstract justice without any sense of prudence or of concrete situations. That injustices could be committed even in the name of oppressed peoples does not enter Lamennais' mind. The princes prevent the realization of liberty and justice. If the people become free, justice will necessarily be realized—that is the fundamental attitude hidden behind lyrical exclamations. The Encyclical *Singulari nos* condemned this book as an appeal to revolution—and condemned also Lamennais' philosophy of the *sens commun*.

This time Lamennais did not even try to negotiate about a declaration of submission. He changed from the Catholic world to the democratic world. Among others, Béranger and George Sand became his friends. A few years later the *Discussions critiques* showed the complete collapse of all his Christian beliefs, clearly proving the statements of his *Essai sur l'Indifférence* according to which all beliefs are interconnected. His four volumes on philosophy, it is true, show that he continued to accept a vaguely spiritualistic progressive humanitarianism. The apocalyptic moment has become an immanent one, the catastrophe of the old world is only a station on the necessary way to the self-realization of humanity in a reign of freedom and mutual love. Lamennais' love for the oppressed and disinherited remains moving, but this love is counterbalanced by a bitter, morose doctrinairism which found strange expression in the stiff letters which old Lamennais wrote to his tailor, Dessoliaire, who had become his ardent disciple.

He died supervised by a friend, whom he had appointed in order to let him pass away in "peace," that is, to bar access to the clergy and to pious souls who might try to convert him *in extremis*. In the last years there are only some letters to his old friends, such as, Baron de Vitrolles or the Baronne de Cottu, which recall the idyllic world of the younger Lamennais. The despair has become more accentuated, no longer balanced by hopes in the eternal peace which awaits the pilgrim after he has accomplished his earthly voyage.

It appears that Lamennais' activities in the Catholic world ended as a complete failure. But that is true only so far as Lamennais' person is concerned. His system was not accepted, nor his political program. His principles were condemned. But his fundamental attitude continued to exercise influence even after his complete break with his Catholic past. Lamennais is a tragic figure because he became the victim of his time. He understood that the time of reliance by the Church upon cooperation with the princes and their bureaucratic states was past. But he connected this belief with a humanitarian belief in necessary progress, with a philosophy whose real meaning he did not understand, because progress first appeared to him as the continuous realization of tradition, and the *raison générale* of mankind as the revelation which was perfected in Jesus Christ and continuously transmitted by His Church. But after the Church refused to accept his scheme of progress, tradition, and revelation easily disappeared and pure immanentism triumphed, which permitted subjective constructions and lyric praises and condemnations. The Church of the Popes was then ranked with the princes among the dark forces, and the people assumed the character of an infallible angelic body. Lamennais of the liberal period, 1828–1834, united liberty and the Papacy against the tyrannical princes and other regimes based upon particular egoist interests. After 1834 Lamennais put the Papacy on the side of those evil forces which, perhaps, after some years of apparent triumphs, are bound to produce catastrophes and to disappear.

This system of Lamennais' was an expression of his belief in his particular mission which brought him in conflict with the Papacy. He was the standard-bearer of an ultramontanism fighting against a Gallicanism which was trying to limit the Papal authority in the interest of egoistic and particular power. But in reality he sought to determine the action of that authority in whose name and for whose rights he was acting. This attitude did not bring about a conflict as long as he did not develop a positive program of action, as long as he did not claim to determine the attitude of the Church toward existing regimes. But that changed when he became, in his *Avenir* period, an open fighter for an alliance between God and liberty, for an alliance between the Papacy and the peoples fighting against tyrannical oppression. He did not realize that his policy tried to bind the Church to a political-social system, and thus subordinated her supra-temporal and supra-political mission to a temporal social and political movement in the same way that his opponents, the defenders of the unity between Church and the regimes of the Restoration, had done. That was the crucial issue behind the condemnation.

Lamennais tried to impose his leadership on the Church, and to replace the authority of the Papacy. And he tried to identify this leadership with certain political and social demands. Surely, Pope Gregory XVI overestimated the practical possibilities of cooperation with the princes—he himself later regretted the confidence which he put in Tsar Nicholas I. It may be that the Pope did not always judge the actual political situation correctly, overestimating the Christian character of the conservative regimes and not trying to discover, as the *Avenir* did, the true longing of the masses behind antireligious speakers. But Lamennais created a situation unacceptable to the Papacy; a group of men without authority, Lamennais and his friends, tried to impose its views on the whole Church by mobilizing public opinion. Lamennais himself had always stressed the Papal authority— he had done it also in the *Avenir* with unquestionable sincerity; how could he hope that Papal authority would subordinate itself to his interpretation of history and of the duties of the Church in contemporary society?

But behind the system which was an expression of Lamennais' subjectivist belief in his own universal mission, were elements which continued to exercise a positive influence among Catholics, even after Lamennais' break with the Church. Lamennais helped to develop the methods of modern Catholicism which—without abandoning the claim of belonging to *the* Church which alone is the true Church—takes into account that modern society is not based upon religious unity.

Thus, the defense of the Church depends upon the activity of its members, upon the utilization of individual and social liberties. The latter, where established, served to prevent any oppression of Catholics and Catholic institutions. Freedom of education is directed against a school monopoly in the hands of an indifferent or even anti-religious state. Freedom of opinion gives to Catholics the opportunity to defend and to propagandize their views. Of course, this freedom must be condemned, in accordance with *Mirari Vos,* if it means a complete license, and an expression of the belief that any religion is as good or bad as another, that truth is not superior to error. And the separation of Church and State does not imply an ideal situation, but does make impossible the subordination of the Church to an anti-religious or indifferent State.

Among many Catholics, after Lamennais, there developed a tendency to mistrust protection by governments; they rely upon the Catholic people who can be mobilized for elections or can be organized in groups most useful for the Church, and at the same time demonstrate the importance of the Church for social movements, for attempts to establish a lasting peace, and the like. It may be granted that Pope Gregory XVI did not realize the possibilities of this methodic utilization of a society based upon liberties for all groups, but, on the other hand, it must be stated that Lamennais did not see the difficulties of the transition period in which he proclaimed his program of the alliance between the Church and peoples. Some of these peoples did not fight their oppressors for revolutionary aims—at least that can be said in general of the Poles fighting against Nicholas I—but in other cases the situation was far from clear. The Pope was surely not in a position to declare war with the same ease as the *Avenir* could against Metternich's influence in Italy; the existence of the Papal State, with its anti-Papal movements, had to be taken into account. The revolutionary forces so optimistically judged by the editors of the *Avenir* could not be seen exclusively in a favorable light. The *Avenir* overestimated the chances for truth to win in a free competition between opinions. Many arguments could be used that the negative liberalism, the spirit of pure secularization, which had been condemned by the *Avenir,* was among them the strongest, if not the decisive factor, as Metternich emphasized and Gregory XVI was inclined to believe.

Lamennais' program of an alliance between Pope and an anti-Metternich and an anti-Nicholas Europe was simply a dream, the wonderful dream of a perfectionist not bothered by considerations of prudence—as proved even by the revolutionary groups who took Lamennais seriously only after his break with Rome.

But despite all its utopian perfectionism, Lamennais' program anticipated the possibility of Catholic and Papal influence on world public opinion. The emphasis on universal social and human problems increased the international prestige of the Papacy after Leo XIII had issued the social encyclicals, and Benedict XV had participated in attempts to establish lasting peace.

Some aspects of Lamennais' activities survived among Catholics against his will. He was the man who publicized the belief that passive confidence in traditional institutions and in support by governments was absolutely insufficient. He was the man who helped Catholics to understand the importance of the services to be rendered to the Church by the active masses; he understood the gains to be obtained for the prestige of the Church if its believers participate in the political and social movements of their time and if the Church remains interested in helping the oppressed and exploited and no longer appears as a supporter of social injustice by her alliance with ruling classes. He tried to liberate French Catholics from a purely negative attitude toward the French Revolution, an attitude which often resulted in linking together the Church and a regime of the past. Though Lamennais' own system was based upon the most crude theological errors, he stimulated the revival of Catholic learning and the participation of Catholics in the discussion of actual problems of the age in which they were living. His own solutions were surely far from being satisfactory, but he stimulated others to go their way. Not all of these men turned against Lamennais and his memory, as Lacordaire and Montalembert more or less did. Abbé Guéranger, who never was as close to Lamennais as those two participants of his unfortunate pilgrimage to Rome in 1831–32, abstained from attacking the man who had been a mentor for him at the beginning of his activities.

Despite the fact that even today Lamennais is used as a club by polemicists attempting to discredit Catholic opponents, it has become possible to distinguish between personal tragedy and the merits which he has in the history of modern Catholicism, though these merits have nothing to do with his system and his belief in his own mission. He is the great figure at the beginning of the participation of modern Catholicism in the life of democratic society. He appeals to public opinion and the masses in order to defend and maintain the Church as a living force—no longer trusting a passive traditionalism based upon custom and protection from above by men without understanding of the masses. It is his tragedy that he made his understanding of a change in society and attitude towards government—active consent as more important than simple acceptance—into a system and an attitude that set his mission in opposition to the authority, for the defense and recognition of which he devoted the best years of his life.

BROWNSON'S SEARCH FOR

THE KINGDOM OF GOD:

THE SOCIAL THOUGHT

OF AN AMERICAN RADICAL

M. A. Fitzsimons

[1954]

In 1815 the rulers and political leaders of Europe—men who had known the terror of witnessing the violent destruction of their social and political institutions—finished their work at the Congress of Vienna, work designed to prevent the resurgence of revolutionary threats. State and Church—and on the continent this generally meant the Catholic Church—cooperated in this conservative and reactionary task. The task was doomed, for the vision of a free, equal, and fraternal society throbbed with all the more compelling radiance in the world of privilege and inequality which the Congress of Vienna restored. Later industrial changes propelled the revolutionary tide, and waves of liberalism and socialism beat against the old order, menacing not only the governments of Europe but the Church. To those captivated by the vision of a better or perfect society on earth, conservative Catholic admiration for the past and reverence for tradition and for the order and treasures of the present seemed peculiarly obscurantist, obstinate blindness to the cause of progress.

Orestes Augustus Brownson (1803–1876) presents the interesting spectacle of an American radical—a leader in the very vanguard of the cause of making a heaven on earth—entering the Catholic Church. This conversion, all the more remarkable for taking place in New England, marked the crowning of his search for the Kingdom of God —not his abandonment of the quest, as his critics suggested.

A study of Brownson's social views, then, may illuminate the story of his conversion. Moreover, as a Protestant and social radical, Brownson was in the main stream of American national life—and his early views have a wider historical significance than his work as a Catholic. As a Protestant he occupied a very conspicuous position in a circle which embraced such men as Ralph Waldo Emerson, Henry David Thoreau, and the historian George Bancroft. He shared to the full the American feeling that the mission and destiny of their new country had to be defined. In confronting this necessity Brownson also had to face the problems created by industrialism. Drawing upon the thought of many European thinkers, including some early socialists, Brownson on several occasions evolved a social analysis and criticism, which entitles him to be classed among the forerunners of American socialism.

Brownson, an American of the Americans, experienced the sweep of all the tides of opinion and thought of his age. This tall, sturdy, lonely, and emotional boy knew first the near pioneer world of Vermont and, later, the rural world of northern New York, a land of religious unrest, the cradle of millenary cults and Mormonism. His quick and incisive intelligence was never disciplined, moderated, or jaded by formal education. He had the unquenchable seriousness of the self-educated. His youthful background and readings left him with three enduring interests: religion, philosophy, and social reform. He read avidly Congregationalist, Presbyterian, Universalist, and Deist books, and his religious feelings remained lively but unsupported by any clear and certain faith. The reading of John Locke confirmed him in the dominant sensationalist philosophy of his time and suggested to him that the change of environment was the basis of social reform. The utopian anarchist visions of William Godwin's book, *An Enquiry Concerning Political Justice,* encouraged Brownson to hope for the rapid coming of a free and perfect society on earth with man and nature tamed in civilized felicity. Godwin's questioning of property and other institutions raised in Brownson's mind problems and solutions, which subsequent experience sternly recalled to his attention. The spell that Godwin's book exercised on Brownson may be, at least, suggested by the fact that Brownson's vigorous style is patterned on Godwin's.

Though these three interests in religion, philosophy, and social reform may be distinguished, they cannot easily be separated or disentangled, for they merged to serve one end, the establishment of the Kingdom of God in the United States. The American Union, as he saw it, had the mission of fulfilling man's history by establishing the reign of humanity, not by the exaltation of a part of man's nature but by the fulfillment of man's nature. After man's troubled early history and eighteen hundred years of misunderstanding of Christ's teaching, the new world would climax world history by achieving social justice, brotherhood, in short, Christian democracy.

This was not Brownson's first formulation of his social philosophy. His vision of Christian democracy was a transformation of his earlier, irreligious social philosophy, which he, in less developed fashion, shared with the rationalist socialists, Robert Dale Owen and Frances Wright, who were seeking to guide and control an early labor movement, the Workingmen's Party of New York. At the time, Brownson was abandoning his ministry as a Universalist and was turning to a career as an independent preacher of the gospel of Philanthropy. For him Universalism, belief in universal salvation, meant a rejection of predestination and a stout but vague affirmation of benevolence and enlightenment.

In the *Gospel Advocate,* one of the many papers and journals, which he edited, he affirmed that "all the essentials of true religion" were confined to a belief in the necessity of kindness, honesty, cultivating one's mental powers in order to aid humanity and to open up new opportunities of enjoyment, and the amassing of the material means to those ends. Soon Brownson found even the profession of Universalism a burden. His rationalist friends of *The Free Enquirer,* Owen and Wright, approvingly published his farewell to the Universalists.

> I do not renounce my former beliefs nor do I denounce the denomination to which I was attached. I but say, I am no longer to appear the advocate of any sect, nor of any religious faith. I am too ignorant to preach Universalism or any religious sentiment and I will be too honest to preach that which I do not know. I become an enquirer after truth in the field of knowledge. Bidding adieu to the regions where the religionist must ramble, casting aside the speculations with which he must amuse himself, I wish to be simply an observer of nature for my creed, and a benefactor of my brethren for my religion.

For the moment, as happened often enough in the future, the cause of social democracy wore a secular guise. Brownson would have shouted amen to the sixteenth toast of the Free Enquirers celebrating the birthday of Thomas Paine. "The clergy of the United States, may their usefulness be commensurate with their intelligence, teaching pure and useful morality; may they live to experience that to mend shoes will be more profitable than to patch creeds."

The influence of Fanny Wright persuaded Brownson to join the Workingmen's Party. This party had developed from the resolution of the workers of New York City to defend the ten hour laboring day and to remedy ills which arose from the unequal operation of the laws on different social groups. From the beginning radicals like Robert Dale Owen and others sought to win this movement to the support of their social programs. Owen and Wright were agreed in seeking to perfect the democracy of the American republic. Each had failed in social projects. Fanny Wright had unsuccessfully sought to persuade Americans, by example, to free their slaves. Owen had sponsored at New Harmony, Indiana, a cooperative community, designed to convince the world by contrast "that individuality detracts largely from the sum of human happiness . . . no man forms his own character, either mentally or physically." In 1826, which Owen proclaimed as the first year of mental independence, his *New Harmony Gazette* was in the second year of its efforts to advance the doctrine that environment determined everything and, therefore, education was the sole means of social reform. In 1829–30, Fanny Wright and Owen sought to use the Workingmen's Party to promote a program of free, compulsory public education, which would separate children from their parents, thereby freeing parents for their own individual development and properly moulding the citizens of the perfect future society.

Brownson agreed with this program and for a time promoted it. But he soon dropped out of the Party, probably because he found the restraints of a party as confining as the burden of being a sectarian minister. Later, he observed, correctly enough, that the influence of property-owners and their servants, the professional politicians, had been too strong for the Workingmen. There was, however, a characteristic lack of proportion in his observation, for Tammany Hall and the Democratic Party adopted and carried through some of the reforms demanded by the Workingmen, notably, free public education and the relaxation of the law concerning imprisonment for debt.

Fanny Wright influenced Brownson's social thinking in a number of ways: first of all, she raised new doubts in Brownson's mind about the rights of property; secondly, she and the Workingmen's Party caused him to consider the question of workers' education—she and, for a time, he favored manual training programs which would prepare the workers for industry; finally, she suggested a way of analyzing social conflict in terms of the struggle of classes. Later reading in the works of that most extraordinary school, the Saint-Simonians, confirmed this analysis as well as his search for a religious basis for social reforms.

The years after 1830 are less troubled. Of the change he noted that "his strong tendency to religion, and to religious faith" asserted itself. The occasion appears to have been a sermon of the distinguished Unitarian, Reverend William Ellery Channing. The sermon, "Likeness to God," read to Brownson by a friend, proposed that our knowledge of the perfections of God derives "from our own souls. The divine attributes are first developed in ourselves, and thence transferred to our creator. The idea of God, sublime and awful as it is, is the idea of our own spiritual nature, purified and enlarged to infinity." The sermon filled Brownson with "indescribable delight." Its thought caused

329

him to believe that he was a Christian and to resume his work as a Christian preacher. Soon he moved back to New England to take part as Unitarian minister in Walpole, New Hampshire. But, in spite of his joy in having found God the Father, his "Christianity was pretty much all comprised in two articles, the divinity of humanity, and the brotherhood of the race."

In short, Brownson was looking for the Kingdom of God on earth. He recognized that the fathers of New England had sought to establish a New Jerusalem in the wilderness but he believed that their emphasis had been too exclusively spiritual. Consequently, there had followed a reaction of matter and reason against the spirit. This reaction had taken the form of the philosophy of John Locke, the conservative rationalism of the Unitarians, deism, and infidelity. These movements had been historically necessary but lacked the dynamism which the law of progress required. The stirrings of the age revealed the operation of that law of progress, which would eventually reunite men in one church, the Church of the Future.

In reaching these conclusions Brownson drew heavily upon the Eclectic philosophy of the Frenchman Victor Cousin and his followers. New England had opened to him a wide world of books and ideas. New England, also, offered him the chance to establish a John the Baptist herald-precursor of the Church of the Future.

Actually, the new church developed out of William Ellery Channing's persistent anxiety about the infidelity of large numbers of the Boston workingmen. It was thought that Brownson's association with the Workingmen's Party would prove valuable in this special ministry. At any rate, Brownson seized the opportunity to preserve the laboring class from infidelity and to win it to the Church of the Future.

Writing on "Christianity and Reform" for *The Unitarian* (1834) Brownson said that the desire to raise man's social and moral position to a level comparable with his material achievements constituted an irrepressible demand for reform. Reform presented a critical challenge to religion, for reform only too frequently allied itself with infidelity. The objective of reform is the improvement of the individual. "What the reformer, then, wants is the power to elevate the individual, to quicken in his soul the love of the highest excellence, and to urge him towards perfection with new and stronger impulses." Infidelity has not this power. "Separated from what it often borrows from religion, it will present no motive to action."

The improvement of the individual is the end, but has not been achieved because the clergy and educators have failed to perceive the end of man. Brownson did not look to government action, for he believed that though good laws were important, the moral habits of a people were far more important. Nevertheless, the perfection of the individual cannot be achieved without social reform. "Man has his social side, social faculties, duties, rights, and interests. Leave out these, and his character will want symmetry, fail in completeness." Morality, then, cannot be properly conceived in the exclusive terms of the individual. All creatures have their special nature and by virtue of that "aspire to a special end, which is also their good." "Each one of these different ends is an element of a total ultimate end which embraced them all. This end is that of creation, an end which is identical with universal order." Thus, "our right and duty to seek our own good begins only when our end is presented to us as a fragment of the absolute good."

Brownson had a ready explanation for the crisis of religion. The religious sentiment was a fact and the universality of man's seeking outside of himself a sense of mystery, which, in spurring man beyond the horizons of what he knows, makes him a progressive creature, proved that religion was not the result of trickery but an essential part of man's nature. "The sentiment is lodged in the bottom of the soul, always the same, unalterable, and eternal; the form is variable and transitory." The crisis was caused by the religious institutions, which men erected in order to make regular and permanent their communications with invisible powers. But man's progress outstripped his institutions, which too readily reduced religion to formulas, observances, and priestcraft. Now the Middle Ages had emphasized spirit at the expense of matter. Protestantism, even more one-sided, was a reaction in favor of matter, a mere negation. Its destructive mission had been accomplished. But the age's need for a new social organization, capable of winning love and obedience, could still be satisfied from one of the innumerable undeveloped seeds in Christianity. Christianity, after all, "is little else than the religious sentiment itself." After the turmoil of negation religions could again enter an organic stage in which even a Voltaire would be a believer.

But the crisis is, also, a crisis of maturity. Man's moral feelings have been progressively refined by Christianity. (Brownson acutely saw and argued that scholars charitably read too much nobility into the actions of the past.) Man has passed through the infancy and childhood of the race and the truly human traits have appeared only in his mature age. Thus the contemporary meaning of Christian almsgiving should include "putting moral courage and energy into the poor, that will enable them to elevate themselves to their proper level in the social scale." "Nine-tenths of mankind are so situated, that they have neither the time nor the opportunity of attending to anything but the wants of their animal nature. This is the real evil, and the real work for the reformer is to put into the hand of the whole—not equal wealth—but the means of spiritual cultivation and growth."

Brownson made no concession to conservative fears, for, he argued, that the workingmen only seek justice for all. The lower classes have never been known to make an unjust demand. The terror they inspire by their demands is always in consequence of their justice, and not their injustice.

To Brownson, lack of faith in man was "the most fatal of all infidelities . . . want of faith hardened the soul into selfishness, and made it inefficient for any good." With the faith of a democrat and a Christian Brownson saw a bright future.

> The birth of Jesus was on a glorious morn. Then the Angel of Improvement hovered with joy over the earth, and saw with rapture, as he looked down the stream of time, the all-comprehensive principles then introduced, gradually, but effectively working their way over all opposition, subduing all enemies, surmounting every obstacle, and fully regenerating the whole moral world. He saw wrong's outrages disappearing with ignorance, vice, and crime yielding up their empire, with man rising from the oppressions of a hundred ages, and looking forth, the Image of his Maker, upon a world of beauty. He heard the last note of discord die away in the distance, the tear which the mother sheds for her son slain in battle was wiped from her eye, the sigh which bespoke unrequited affection was suppressed,—man everywhere opened his heart and gave his hand to his brother.

Such are the major outlines of Brownson's social philosophy. It made him a most radical figure among the predominantly rationalist, conservative Unitarians. The Transcendentalists, who rejoiced in their emancipation from the confines of rationalism and Lockean philosophy, did not equal him in incisiveness, vigor, or radicalism. Few of the Transcendentalists had Brownson's knowledge and respect for the real world, including the social world. Dr. William Ellery Channing, more aware of his limitations, confessed that he had been exclusively concerned with individual activity and reform. Moreover, "reform is resistance of rooted corruptions and evils, and my tendency is to turn away from the contemplation of evils. My mind seeks the good, the perfect, the beautiful."

In 1840, Brownson's radicalism developed in the violence of its expression and in the public shock produced by his views. Although he did not evolve any new doctrines in 1840, a number of factors explain the new intensity. The increased impact on the public was caused by the fact that Brownson's acceptance of a federal government office from the Van Buren administration made him a figure useful for partisan politics. In an election campaign the Democratic Party could be called to account for the opinions of the editor of the *Boston Quarterly Review*.

Brownson knew the conditions of the working class, for his pastoral activities were directed to them. Resentfully he watched their sufferings in the years of depression after 1837. While the workers could not evade their obligations, banks, Brownson noted in "A discourse on Lying," were permitted to lie on a large scale by failing to redeem their bank bills.

The money power drew the angriest criticism from him. To a Canadian rebel against Britain, William L. Mackenzie, who had been imprisoned by the United States, Brownson explained that the imprisonment was the work of the commercial interests. The American government in theory was based on the rights of man and founded on justice. In so establishing their government Americans had been original and had acted for themselves. But in managing their affairs Americans followed the ways of the Old World and acted as though the United States had not achieved independence. "The commercial interest of this country is controlled by England, and we can have no controversy with her without arming the whole business part of our community against our government." Understanding this, Britain could arrogantly press its claims to the Oregon and Aroostook regions. Only a war and soon, Brownson thought, could save the republic and its honor.

Following the Eclectic philosophical method Brownson saw the main social and political problem as twofold: on the one hand politics had to be made moral; and, on the other hand, to harmonize in each individual freedom and the moral and social elements of man's nature. As Brownson saw it, man had passed through three stages. As a savage he had been self-contained and unprogressive. When savage man is tamed and his moral feelings emerge, then man is enslaved by the theocracy of priests. But man's heart and feelings, driving him to form families and society, also ends in another tyranny, the modern state.

In history savage individuality was represented by the feudal baron. Social feeling was represented by the Commons. The English Whigs had won this social victory—but the perfect state called for a fusion of individuality, morality and social feelings. England could not achieve this fusion, for there traditions and the interests of merchants and industrialists blocked the path to a moralized politics and the harmonious development of freedom, society and morality. For this development a new country, where most people worked, was necessary. This, then, is the mission of America in Universal Human history: its mission is to "emancipate labor."

The Whig Party, which from its beginning was the party of business and the banks, opposed to Universal Suffrage, the party of demagoguery, could not rise to the dignity of America's mission. The Democratic Party bore the charge of the country's destiny. Its very beginnings as a States' Rights Party was appropriate, for the American continent was too vast to be ruled by a consolidated empire. Such a monster would simply swallow the citizens. The United States must remain a federation so that in their separate states citizens can clearly take an important part in government. Consolidation would mean tyranny or a split into centers, for the sections of America have diverse interests.

Thus, the cause of the Democratic Party was the cause of America's preservation and the fulfillment of her mission. In that it could look for the support of all Americans and the sympathies of the world's oppressed, for whose cause the Party fought. It will not surprise the reader to learn that the preceding sentiments were expressed at a Democratic Party rally. When about the same time Brownson, in reviewing Carlyle's *Chartism,* expressed his opinions on the condition of the laboring classes, he spoke with even less restraint. The English Chartists, he believed, were fighting the abuse of God and man but he had little faith in what he called a John Bull mob. The conspicuous failure of their earlier struggles was attributable to the power of the middle class, who, in struggling against the feudal aristocracy, proclaimed the equality of all men. But the insincerity of this claim is witnessed in middle class Britain's relentless war against the French Revolution, the cause of humanity, and in the oppression of the English poor. Neither education nor emigration could provide a remedy. The sufferings of the poor would only be vindicated by the ways of Providence in a long and bloody war of the poor against the rich.

By an inexplicable turn of conservative logic, the judgment that society manifests little charity and a conflict of class interests is transformed into a charge of inciting class conflict. The former President of the United States, John Quincy Adams, heard a preacher in Quincy speak "with just severity of the application" of the "spirit of hurly-burly innovation" to the solemn duties of the Christian faith. Adams noted in his diary that this spirit of innovation embraced transcendentalism, phrenology, and Brownson and the Marat democrats, each furnishing "some plausible rascality as an ingredient for the bubbling cauldron of religion and politics." Brownson insisted that he could discover no serious difference between the two systems of labor in modern society, slavery and wage labor. In looking at what he found to be a very sad sight—a factory village, he recalled:

> The man who employs them, and for whom they are toiling as so many slaves, is one of our city nabobs, revelling in luxury; or he is a member of our legislature enacting laws to put money in his own pocket; or he is a member of Congress, contending for a high tariff to tax the poor for the benefit of the rich; or in these times he is shedding crocodile tears over the deplorable conditions of the poor laborer, while he docks his wages twenty-five per-cent; building miniature log cabins, shouting Harrison and "hard cider."

The wage system, Brownson argued, deprived the worker of any prospect of being "an independent laborer on his own capital,—on his own farm or in his own shop." The wage system made hollow "that equality between man and man, which God has established between the rights of one and those of another." The menace to this equality, a menace which justified the attack on the Bank of the United States and all other monopolies, caused Brownson to suggest another proposal as a long-range reform—the abolition of hereditary property. This proposal as well as the unusually emphatic repetition of Brownson's belief that the contemporary churches, the priesthood and ministry were the strongest bulwarks of inequality and privilege, won him general notoriety. After all it was an election year when even the opinions of professors may become news—and Brownson was a Democrat.

These opinions complete the development of Brownson's social views before his conversion. The next four years reveal his increasing mistrust of some of his earlier reformism, and a recognition of the necessity of authority and the Church. In this development he came to believe that the Kingdom of God on earth was not at all imminent or likely—except in the Church. His earlier rejection of poverty was in turn rejected and he came to see in poverty an edifying occasion for sanctity.

In 1840 Brownson's position was that "Jesus was a social reformer, that the aim of his mission was to establish the reign of equality on earth, as well as to secure salvation to the soul hereafter." Brownson's own avowed aim was to Christianize democracy and to democratize the Church. This democratic Christian faith and his opposition to monopolies and the extension of the power of the federal government make him akin to those sterling Democrats of New York, the Loco Focos.

The Protestant career of Orestes Brownson sums up a large part of the intellectual history of the nineteenth-century's first forty years. His major objective was to replace the Puritan theocracy with the perfect society, the Kingdom of God on earth. His objective and some of his principles make him an American forerunner of modern socialism. But unlike the socialists he looked to religion to provide the moral inspiration and dynamism necessary for the establishment of the perfect society. It was this search for the religious dynamic of social reform that brought him to the Catholic Church.

His conversion, deriving from a preoccupation with the religious inspiration of social reform, should be particularly instructive to our time. Brownson, himself, had to concern himself with so many pressing apologetic tasks that he did not fully develop the lessons implicit in his conversion. If these lessons had been worked out, the dominant American leftism of the thirties, which Brownson's social viewpoint so much resembled, might have avoided some of its worst blunders. Unfortunately, the task of drawing the lessons still remains to be done.

Brownson is a prophetic figure as a herald of social reform and a true defender of the human person. He warned and fought vigorously against the American materialist temptation, which results in the tyranny of property over man. But, unlike most social reformers, he clearly perceived the danger of tyranny lurking in the reformer's general willingness to use the power of the state. Brownson, then, was a protagonist of religious social reform, and of liberty—and he came to see in the Catholic Church the surest guarantee of American freedom.

NEWMAN AND THE

SPIRITUAL CRISIS

OF THE OCCIDENT

Otto Karrer*

[1947]

NEWMAN'S is perhaps the most illustrious religious mind in the modern Anglo-Saxon world. Exactly half of his long life (1801–1890) was devoted to the Anglican Church, the other half to the Catholic. However clear and unequivocal his conversion, his intellectual position is nevertheless the same in both periods. The sources of his inner life stem from the revelation of the Eternal, which came to him when he was fifteen years old and never left him his whole life long. His philosophical thinking is influenced by English empiricism that involves an attitude of restraint concerning intellectual speculation. It is in conformity with the English love of the concrete, of the individual-personal element and, with due respect to the spirit of tradition, of Christian freedom. And even though Newman's theology is rooted in ancient Christian tradition, his missionary conscience is directed towards the future, towards the spiritual conflicts of the twentieth century. Their unfolding he sensed with astonishing prevision. Just as his sermons and writings are divided almost equally between the two periods of his life (with the exception of perhaps one decade at the height of his career, in which he saw himself doomed almost to inactivity because of tragic misunderstandings), so his life's work has become the common possession of all Christendom, first, in his native land and, then, increasingly in other countries. For what Newman has to say actually concerns the whole Christian world.

Newman started his academic career at Oxford, whose educational and cultural ideal embodied the fusion of faith and science, liberty and law. There the first inroads of the liberal *"Zeitgeist"* had brought

* Translated from the German and edited by Frederick C. Ellert of the University of Massachusetts State College and Alvin S. Ryan of Notre Dame.

forth a counter-movement supported by such outstanding men of intellect as the discerning poet-priest Keble, the dogmatist Pusey, and the historian Froude. The particular talents of all these men were united in their common friend Newman.

The Oxford Movement, under their leadership, aimed at a revival of the spirit of tradition, of ancient Christianity, of the Catholic spirit. Pitted against this was not a specifically English but an occidental phenomenon: religious liberalism, also called rationalism. In Christian antiquity, it was named *gnosis,* enlightenment of the free mind. Since the Reformation, it had given birth to various sects issuing from the principle of private interpretation of the scriptures and culminating in an arbitrary, supra-confessional ethic of the gentleman. The dilemma of this *"Bourgeois-Gentilhomme,"* as the French called him, Pascal had already exposed. Newman characterizes the gentleman as "the creation, not of Christianity, but of civilization," because personal thinking and feeling are more valuable to the intellectual pride of "private judgment" than divine revelation and the guiding authority of Mother Church.

Newman's point of departure in his establishment of the Christian view of life and in his conversations with seekers of any kind, is at first glance exactly as individualistic as the conception of the world of the religious liberalism that was opposed to him: it is conscience as the intimate evidence of God in the personal inner being. Before Newman reached manhood, he experienced, once and for all, a revelation of God, a spiritual image-less realization of the All-seeing and All-holy. The two self-evident and luminous realities in which Newman believed were God and the soul. The faculty by which the soul becomes aware of its exalted counterpart is really the conscience: the inner awareness of that holy law which we obey in order to become something that is not brought into being by the human will. Human self-respect and dignity have one thing in common, namely that human worth stands or falls on fidelity to conscience. Man without God-relationship, to which conscience bears witness, is only a fraction of man, a fragmentary being. So closely are the moral sense and religion connected that "were it not for this voice, speaking so clearly in my conscience and my heart, I should be an atheist, or a pantheist, or a polytheist when I looked into the world." But in addition the external world in the act of contemplating nature and humanity, transmits to the mind, which is fashioned basically by the conscience, the same divine reality that is immanent and transcendent.

And now Newman's significant cognition: just as conscience with its constant human imperfection and with its constant aspiration toward the holy in Christ achieves a clarification of its intuitions and a final definiteness and certainty, so Christ directs us, on His part, to the

Church of Christ as being His embodiment through generations and the organ of the kingdom of God that goes to shape the holy in man. Accordingly, Newman can develop the theme in one of his profoundest sermons: "I am going to assert what some persons, my brethren, those especially whom it most concerns, will not hesitate to call a great paradox; but which, nevertheless, I consider to be most true. . . . It is this: that it is quite as difficult, and quite as easy, to believe that there is a God in heaven, as to believe that the Catholic Church is His oracle and minister on earth." This is not to say the other religions are thereby proclaimed entirely lacking in divine worth. They are, however, so constituted in God's plan of redemption that as partial truths they cry for completeness; they are steps that must be climbed in order to reach the comprehensive One, no matter where one comes from. For all roads converge and all individual and national values have their place, each according to its own essential nature, where they are destined to come to their settlement and to maturity, in the same Mother. It follows that a man will move "by an infallible succession from the rejection of atheism to theism, and from theism to Christianity, and from Christianity to Evangelical Religion, and from there to Catholicity" completely irrespective of his starting point. But he must travel according to the compass of conscience, without breaking with a single value which he possessed up to this time. Inversely, atheism is the direct result, once belief in the revelation of God in Christ, the Son, is abandoned: logically "there is no alternative between Catholicism and Infidelity to the clear thinker."

"The multitude of men indeed are not consistent, logical, or thorough; they obey no law in the course of their religious views. . . ." Their conscience is dim and they "are set down at this or that point in the ascending or descending scale of thought, according as their knowledge of facts, prejudices, education, domestic ties, social position, and opportunities for inquiry determine. . . ." Abandon the divine authority of Christ manifested in the Church, and the way is cleared first to accept any kind of Christianity, next to become a man without a Church, and then to end in pantheism or scepticism or even atheism —"in a dreadful, but inevitable succession." If a person does not see the consequence, then he may attribute this change to pure accident of situation or to the influence of environment.

That is the point at which the theological and philosophical analysis of contemporary society becomes for Newman's penetrating mind a prophecy of subsequent world development. Conscience in the old religious meaning of the word, reverential obedience to the moral judge over us is not the controlling guide in the development of the modern spirit. In the individual and, increasingly, in the community, there is revealed that which Max Picard calls "disconnectedness," "inner emptiness," "nothingness." This being so, almost anything is possible. To be sure, people still do speak of "conscience," but it is as different from the religiously informed conscience as the ape is different from man. It is only a private feeling, a subconscious need, a noble whim. There is no principle that determines from one moment to the next to which thread in the twisted skein one's will is to be joined. A person allows himself to be persuaded into believing (since of course he needs some kind of metaphysics, some kind of total view) that there is no religious truth but only human conceptions of truth in diverse forms. To a superficial world this is the last word on the subject. Accordingly, it makes no difference what one believes. Religion as doctrine is no longer interesting, only the psychology of religion is. Instead of revelation there is simply a religious feeling, which binds no one. "They really do think it is no harm whatever being an atheist, so that you are sincerely so, and do not cut people's throats and pick their pockets." According to this view, Christianity has been a beneficent power capable of sublimating human thinking and feeling somewhat; on a certain cultural level the only thing that is still necessary is an elevated feeling which requires neither definiteness nor obedience. The religion of beauty, the unhampered shaping of the power of imagination, wisdom of life without stern obligation, feeling the divine (which is designated much more preferably by "It" than by "Thou," at first because of a commendable awe at the thought of humanizing divinity, but then lulled to sleep by the dream of the unconscious and rendered impotent in the man's individual self-consciousness), that is "the great deceit which awaits the Age to come."

Only one more step is necessary to push one into complete atheism. After all everything is merely relative. Why then should not atheism have an equal and logical claim in itself? Of course, it would be unwise to say this to everyone. The gentleman still has a secret fear of taking this step, because of the imminent social consequences; moreover, he would like to have consideration as far as possible for the religious feeling of the people.

But the deeper significance is clear; and, therefore, it is possible for Newman to outline the program that religious liberalism was to follow, as though he had been sitting in the secret councils. Let us start first by eliminating religion from public life; for example, putting aside the oath as being too holy. There follows the agreement to omit religious forms in education wherever it is practicable, or, what amounts to the same thing, to educate practically without religion. Let us at the same time try to give validity to endeavors beneficial to all the commonwealth on the basis of utility as the standard of value, to limit religion to inner feeling and thereby to consign it to the transitoriness and caprice of necessity—obviously an undermining process. Enlightenment, philosophy, learning, intellectual enlargement are to be regarded as substitutes for religion. And although it was formally accepted that religion alone with its supersensuous powers was strong enough to discipline the great mass of the people, now it seems that philosophy and politics, solely, are working to solve this problem. A secular education makes clear to any person that order, diligence, temperance are to his own advantage. Justice, benevolence, veracity, together with the practical wisdom of politics, the advantage of business, finance, public hygiene, international law—these ethical principles suffice as the great motivating forces of the vast majority of people. "As to Religion, it is a private luxury."

Newman not only assumed, as early as the 1830's, that the actual spread of this modern heresy was possible, but he actually expected it. For reason, having become merely an obliging servant of latent desires, is ready and able to carry out every order and prove everything. To a generation inclined toward an uninhibited assertion of its desires "there is a general antecedent leaning to the side of unbelief, as the more reasonable and probable . . . so that men believe atheism before they have discovered revelation." "Believe atheism"—that is it. "Faith," according to Newman's philosophy of faith, means essentially to be disposed toward something. The vast majority is disposed toward unbelief, the more so as liberal doctrines have seeped down from the higher classes to the lower. The real danger, therefore, is no longer Protestantism, within which there still are many religious and essentially Catholic people unaware of all their positive piety. On the contrary the danger lies in "our Heresiarchs, . . . the preachers of infidel science, and our infidel literati and philosophers."

The fruits of this religious liberalism were already acknowledged by the younger Newman as destructive to humanity, which was supposedly being elevated to the highest perfection. One had visions of breeding the gentleman. The social virtues, good taste in the things of this life, these are the beginning and end of practical wisdom. But the gentleman will be short-lived; he is the inwardly hollow creation of the liberal world-spirit and the great masses will unmask the lie. For, since he lacks faith he also lacks conscience. There is no such thing as conscience where God is ignored; otherwise it is merely one of man's nobler wishes, which, imposing no obligation, unchains all the passions, especially where they are exploited by powerful men. The future will draw its own conclusions. Writing at the age of seventy, Newman says he "often thought of and repeated the remark" of a dead friend. "He asked *who* are to be the Goths and Vandals who are to destroy modern civilization . . . ?" And answered, "The lowest class which is most numerous, and is infidel, will rise up from the depths of the modern cities, and will be the new scourge of God." A few years later Newman expands this same theme:

> . . . . my apprehensions are not new, but above fifty years standing. I have all that time thought that a time of widespread infidelity was coming, and through all those years the waters have in fact been rising as a deluge. I look for the time, after my life, when only the tops of the mountains will be seen like islands in the waste of waters. I speak principally of the Protestant world—but great actions and successes must be achieved by the Catholic leaders, great wisdom as well as courage must be given them from on high, if Holy Church is to be kept safe from the awful calamity. . . .

The Church has the capacity to resist the disintegration in the realm of the spirit.

> That great institution, then, the Catholic Church, has been set up by Divine Mercy, as a present, visible antagonist, and the only possible antagonist, to sight and sense. . . . Gentlemen, if you feel, as you must feel, the whisper of a law of moral truth within you, and the impulse to believe, be sure there is nothing whatever on earth which can be the sufficient champion of these sovereign authorities of your soul, which can vindicate and preserve them to you, and make you loyal to them, but the Catholic Church. . . . These more important truths, which the natural heart admits in their substance, though it cannot maintain—the being of God, the certainty of future retribution, the claims of the moral law, the reality of sin, the hope of supernatural help of these the Church is in matter of fact the undaunted and the only defender.

To be sure, believing Protestants and others in the world have religion, but because with them private judgment is separated from obligation to the tangible, divine authority of the Church, their community will not be able to maintain the fruitful tension between belief in revealed religion and private judgment. One can, of course, because of weakness, be satisfied with half-truths, but one cannot make a virtue of incompleteness without suffering the serious consequences of the dissolution of the last remnant of one's religious faith. "Catholicism is . . . in the air," for the very reason that here the tension between authority on the one hand and personal thinking and conscience on the other is real, because the opposition which kindles life here is part of a system. Thus Catholicism will not lose the allegiance of the religious person, if it confronts him in a dignified state and with the credentials of moral power. Herein lies of course the critical question for Catholicism itself, both sides of which Newman examines with equal candor, inspired as he was by the highest obligation to God.

One part of his views concerns the separation of Christendom. This schism is painful to all good men. Only irreligious people, according to Newman, could be satisfied with the grievous fact that Christians of honest faith are hostile to one another. That is perhaps "the greatest scandal of Christianity and one of the most grievous reasons why unbelief continues to advance," and grows with every lack of mutual justice or love. "After all, your intention is to win over the others, not repel them," he writes at one time to a controversialist. "Abuse is as great a mistake in controversy as panegyric in biography."

But veiling of antagonisms is out of the question. "Nothing," writes Newman in a letter of 1873, "is more unmeaning, as well as more untrue, than compromises and comprehensions." There are real oppositions—side by side with mere differences of opinion. They come up even among people of the same faith and among Catholic theologians, and consist for the most part in differences of emphasis. The proportion of truth on each side must be acknowledged honestly. "It never could be"—to use the words of a self-quotation in the *Apologia*, from the final stage before his own conversion—"that so large a portion of Christendom should have split off from the communion of Rome, and kept up a protest for 300 years for nothing. To suppose the contrary is most unreal and violates all one's notions of moral probabilities. All aberrations are founded on, and have their life, in some truth or other. . . ."

What Newman refers to is (apart from the historical exaggerations and abuses of the doctrine of indulgences in the popular accounts) the concessions of many national educators and religious pamphlets concerning the popular cult of saints—by no means moderate veneration itself. Such observations caused Newman the greatest anxiety at the time of his union with the Church—and if to one of *his* religious purity, how much more anxiety to a mind clouded by prejudice—until the liturgy of the Church permitted him to discover the great theocentricity of faith and devotion.

His principal anxiety, however, first grew out of his more intimate association with the churchly life itself. From the time of his Anglicanism he was accustomed to respect authority; for him the dignity of the episcopal office was, from an emotional point of view, as elevated as it would be for a thoroughgoing Catholic. But what he missed in the contemporary impress of Catholicism—not in faith, in the idea, but in the realization of Catholicism even through authoritative persons—and what he longed to see brought about for the sake of moral esteem and for the sake of the power of the Church, was the sense of Christian liberty, especially in the intellectual discussion of things in which the Christian is free. Through his letters and diary run complaints against the hindrance to the religious spirit of a preponderance of churchly-political interests and narrow-mindedness in theological opinions, conditions which reached a climax at the time of the decline of the Church-

State and almost paralyzed Newman's own vigor in the prime of his life. We need not here examine minutely the questions that were so acute at that time: one of the principal points was the refusal to permit Catholic students to study at the English universities. The religious laity (and later, also, Leo XIII) expressed their sympathy with the purity of Newman's thinking and his intention. But to the authorities of that day he was a "border-walker," one who skirted the edges of truth, a "dangerous man." He considered it a spiritual necessity for the churchly life itself and for the winning back of the right-minded—as he expressed it in detail in an 1859 *Rambler* article, at which offense was taken—that the laity regain their proper role along side the hierarchy. Certainly, all of Protestantism could not be brought back to Mother Church; rather it would, through the immanent logic of its principle of private judgment, dissolve for the most part into infidelity. But if Catholics prepared the ground as well as they could, then the believing remnant among the separatists would reach the point of beholding the Mother Church once again with the gaze of reverence and even of nostalgia.

Newman did not count upon mass conversions or upon the reconciliation of entire churches. He looked upon such a hope as utopian. But we should be careful, he cautioned, not to attribute the difficulty simply to ill-will. Emotional prejudices are deep-seated. As Newman wrote in November of 1874:

> Sad as it is to witness the ineffectual yearnings after unity on all hands, of which you speak, still it is hopeful also. We may hope that our good God has not put it into the hearts of religious men to wish and pray for unity, without intending in His own time to fulfill the prayer. And since the bar against unity is a conscientious feeling, and a reverence for what each party holds itself to be the truth, and a desire to maintain the Faith, we may humbly hope that in our day, and till He discloses to the hearts of men what the true Faith is, He will, where hearts are honest, take the will for the deed.

And in any case, the first step in the direction towards unity for all religious people is "to live upon the Gospels."

The world on the whole, with its increasingly a-Christian view of life, believes in "Reason" as the measure of the true and right. The optimism of the faith in reason—in vogue since the Age of Enlightenment—possesses something that is captivating to many souls. "I have no intention at all of denying, that truth is the real object of our reason, and that, if it does not attain to truth, either the premise or the process is in fault." But there is little sense in speaking theoretically of "right reason," since we have to deal with reason practically as it works in historical man, that is, man having original sin.

. . . and in this point of view, I do not think I am wrong in saying that its tendency is towards a simple unbelief in matters of religion. No truth, however sacred, can stand against it, in the long run; and hence it is that in the pagan world, when our Lord came, the last traces of the religious knowledge of former times were all but disappearing from those portions of the world in which the intellect had been active and had had a career. And in these latter days, in like manner, outside the Catholic Church things are tending—with far greater rapidity than in that old time from the circumstance of the age—to atheism in one shape or other.

Now certainly, more profound people, even though they were deceived by rationalistic faith, will survive the disillusionments and doubts that were capable of shattering their optimistic rationalism. Apart from the forcible feeling of human insufficiency, it is above all the great human catastrophes that keep admonishing men to reexamine their narrow point of view, that reveal again and again the original error in the tendency toward optimism. But the step that would lead to submission to a spiritual authority is comparable to a leap across an abyss, because of the rationalistic over-estimation of the natural. "If only I could have faith!" many lament. "How amazing that people can actually officiate in the name of God as an authoritative court on religious questions!" It requires only a particle of honesty to acknowledge that the Bible cannot be a book which admits of a thousand interpretations and which is also given only as proof or reference for the living prophecy of later generations. Christ did not give the Scriptures, but the power and dignity of the Apostolic office in His name. And besides, this Apostolic office has in fact proved itself in the course of history, despite the frailty of human incumbents, to be the agent of human dignity and of the most elevated spiritual values. Thus does the authority of the Church, concentrated in the Apostolic Chair, become manifest as "an instrument of Providence," "adapted by the mercy of the Creator, to preserve religion in the world, and to restrain that freedom of thought, which of course in itself is one of the greatest of our natural gifts, and to rescue it from its own suicidal excesses."

But how can people be convinced of the divine authority of the Church? For, once a theoretical insight has been accepted, it is still far different from a "real assent," from a personal inner conversion and surrender. Even the younger Newman realized that it is completely hopeless to try to lead a man to an acknowledgment of the supernatural solely through rational arguments, and the philosophy of faith of Newman, the mature thinker, is founded essentially on this knowledge. Religious truth is not discovered through the intellect alone, nor is the religious attitude engendered by the intellect alone. Christianity, from the beginning, has demanded the whole man, in his deeper self-consciousness; whence arises that sense for the holy which knows more than is comprehended by the intellect. Even the consciousness of the being of God is not a purely intellectual matter, however urgently it tries to justify itself to the reason: faith will insinuate itself only into a spiritually harmonious, and inwardly inclined man who seeks what is holy and loves it, whether it be faith in the Holy and Redeeming God or the legitimate claims of the Church. Insofar as it particularly concerns the latter, it is not merely insufficient for Newman's interpretation but even misleading as far as actual fact is concerned, to insist upon making the Church credible as something divine, holy, by means of cultural apologetics, as its defenders often seem to think. Cultural achievements have nothing whatsoever to do with the Holy, or if so, then most indirectly. What Newman achieves in this respect perhaps seems surprising to some people; but I personally believe that the more one reflects upon it, the more proper it seems. The more it is taken to heart in church apologetics, the more effectually can the Catholic Church be brought close to people even in this period. I even venture to believe that in discourse with educated people no other way is possible.

In the first place, according to his argument as early as in the Oxford University Sermons

> it is indeed by no means clear that Christianity has at any time been of any great spiritual advantage to the world at large. The general temper of mankind, taking man individually, is what it ever was, restless and discontented, or sensual, or unbelieving. In barbarous times, indeed, the influence of the Church was successful in effecting far greater social order and external decency of conduct than are known in heathen countries; and at all times it will abash and check excesses which conscience itself condemns.

Everyone is willing to acknowledge these civilizing accomplishments—but will anyone be converted to faith because of them? The religious element distinctly belongs to a different order. With regard to the cultural values, "Why should they not be referred to that mere advancement of civilization and education of the intellect, which is surely competent to produce them?" Have not, for example, the Greeks or the Chinese, without revealed Christianity, a high mode of life and in many respects a mode of life just as high as the Christian Occident? And are not the customary virtues of human society already improved by intellectual cultivation even without the aid of Christianity?

And even if the comparisons with cultural achievement should signify something positive for the religious dimension (a fact which does not hold unequivocally according to what has just been stated), then, in accordance with Newman's repeated hints, Catholicism would have a difficult time making credible its superiority to Protestantism in this province. For how could Catholic England during Newman's age convince one of its superiority to Anglicanism; or Catholic Southern Europe convince one of its superiority to the Protestant North? And insofar as the Christian West, in comparison with Antiquity, is concerned:

> The state of great cities now is not so very different from what it was of old . . . the highest class in the community and the lowest, are not so different from what they would be respectively without the knowledge of the Gospel . . . And so of its [the world's] pursuits and professions; they are in character what they were, softened or restrained in their worst consequences, but still with the same substantial fruits. Trade is still avaricious . . . physical science is still sceptical as it was when heathen. Lawyers, soldiers, farmers, politicians, courtiers, nay, shame to say, the priesthood, still savour of the old Adam. Christian states move forward upon the same laws as before. . . . Human nature remains what it was, though it has been baptised. . . . The knowledge of the Gospel then has not materially changed more than the surface of things. . . . Nor did it ever promise it would do so.

Certainly the Church has the privilege that other religions do not have, namely, that she will not succumb; ". . . for a time, in the course of single generations, nay, I may say in every age and at all times, it seems to be failing, and its enemies to be prevailing." And what is to be taken to heart even more than this: the very progress of society as promoting the cause of civilization is, practically speaking, harmful to the religious element and is its adversary. Science and technology are prone to consider their world as of supreme value and to exaggerate its importance to the point of making it a substitute for higher objectives. The expansion of power, the conquest of nature, the affluence of culture become the idols. "And the more society grows, the worse the world." It is to be noted that such judgments are equally distributed through Newman's Anglican as well as his Catholic period.

Wherein, then, will lie the significance and power of Christianity in the future? In that which from the beginning it characterized as religious evidence: that it is "the leavening influence" in the world, the ferment in world culture and an enemy of the world's illusion. The Church is the witness and the voice of God's kingdom in the world. "God's Kingdom," that is the Holy, the Sovereignty of God in men who are illuminated by the Divine Spirit, who have acknowledged the purely relative significance—and speaking in complete seriousness, the relative vanity—of all purely human, earthly values, and who love that which is Holy. I cannot, to be sure, detect any unmistakable clue which would make it evident that Newman had before his mind the basic conceptions of Pascal's exposition of the *"Ordres,"* or gradations of values, but since he knew Pascal this is quite probable:

> les grands génies ont leur empire, leur éclat, leur grandeur, leur victoire, leur lustre et n'ont nul besoin des grandeurs charnelles où elles n'ont

pas de rapport. Les Saints ont leur empire, leur éclat, leur victoire, leur lustre et n'ont nul besoin des grandeurs charnelles ou spirituelles où elles n'ont nul rapport. Car elles (ces valeurs charnelles ou spirituelles) n'y ajoutent ni ôtent. Cela est d'un ordre infiniment plus elevé.

The Church is the witness of the Holy in the world. For the religious person that is sufficient, and whoever looks for something different will be sadly mistaken if he supposes the Church is there to help him find it. The Saints are the true products and representatives of the Church. The Saints—now that means not only those canonized, but every Christian person who lives honorably in faith, in the fear of God and with charity toward men. The power, duty, attractiveness of Christianity lie not in what the world possesses, too, and performs perhaps even more skillfully, in organizations, numbers, alliances with political powers and the like—all this has its significance in the political-cultural realm and also somewhat for the confinement of the anti-Christian element in the world at large. If Newman shows a certain discretion in regard to all this, it is to be attributed not merely to his personal spiritual qualities, but rather, according to his own words, because he saw in the prevailing interest in power and opportunism (as much as it is humanly evident) the unconscious and disunited "assimilation by the world and its powers," and therefore a danger to that very thing which is most important to a Christian: the shaping of the religious personality, the sanctification of life.

To be sure, it is always the few who, in the first place, have recognized this, and in the second place, realize it in themselves. Newman speaks frequently of the "chosen few"—not in the Calvinistic sense of a predestination, independent of man, to eternal salvation or damnation, but in the sense of the different stages of maturity, according to which most people remain undeveloped. And, in the third place, these few mature Christians, generally speaking, are capable of having any effect only in a limited space, indeed for the most part only within their more immediate circle, for which reason the meeting up with such persons is by no means a daily blessing.

Now surely it is quite evident, and Newman would be the last to deny it, that the highest level of a Christian gentleman is by no means limited to the realm of the visible Catholic Church. Christian gentlemen appear even in separated Christian communities, and Newman himself was unquestionably one of them, even before he became Catholic. But he became Catholic only when he acknowledged the Church to be the true Mother and the homeland of such gentlemen; all the more so since they were already living on the inheritance of the Church before their conversion, and in everything that sanctified them had for a long time been unconsciously Catholic before they became so in reality for the sake of their conscience.

Wherever this real Christian element, the power that was given by Christ to the Church as a dowry and is administered by the Church, wherever it is felt in its true meaning and becomes effective in religious education, there the many will then partake of it in their own way whenever they encounter such men. Christianity, as Newman expresses it in a glorious sermon, "has been upheld in the world not by a system, not by books, not by argument, nor by temporal power, but by the personal influence of such men as have already been described, who are at once the teachers and the patterns of it; . . ." They live by the Gospel and the Holy Communion of the Altar. It is by no means always those persons in high places (although we do not wish to esteem lightly their potentialities) whose achievements are high; on the contrary, the most enduring effects often, as we know, have issued from very simple persons in humble places. They possess a spiritual kinship with the exalted men and women who preceded them, and with a few friends who are inwardly united with them. They are unaware of their own blessed endowments. They do not attract attention; but it is exactly their simplicity, their humility that is convincing by virtue of its genuineness. The attraction that proceeds from them exercises influence upon the weak, the faint-hearted, the wavering, the inquiring, and kindles sympathy and longing in those who are similarly disposed. "Each receives and transmits the sacred flame. . . ." For their sake one can love Christianity, because they represent Christ in their temperance. "And a few such blessed persons—a few in relation to the vast numbers —will save the world for centuries to come."

At the time when Newman uttered these words and wrote them down (and he often repeated words like these) he was unaware of how vividly, though unconsciously, he had portrayed himself, simply because he was speaking from his heart—and he could by no means speak or write differently. All his life he remained the simple priest and Christian gentleman, nor was this changed in any respect by the distinction bestowed upon him toward the end of his life. It merely intensified the after-effect. At the time when Newman in his seventy-ninth year was lifted by Leo XIII from the shadow under which he had been standing for almost the whole period of his Catholic career, speaking in his allocution in Rome as Cardinal about religious liberalism, he ended with these words: "It is well that we keep very vividly in mind the actual condition of Christianity. But not for one moment need we be fearful. The Church has been too often in seemingly mortal danger for us to be fearful now in face of the severity of trials. We must do our duties in confidence and peace, in the stillness of our hearts, and so we shall behold Divine Salvation."

VI

MAN AND THE

AMERICAN WORLD

ORGANIZED RELIGION

AND THE AMERICAN

CREED

Peter F. Drucker

[1956]

THE unique relationship between religion, the state, and society is perhaps the most fundamental—certainly it is the most distinctive—feature of American religious as well as American political life. It is not only central to any understanding of American institutions. It also constitutes the sharpest difference between American and European institutions, concepts, and traditions.

This country has developed the most thorough-going, if not the only truly secular state. It is also the oldest secular state—even on this Continent. When the First Amendment to the United States Constitution categorically banned any "Establishment of Religion" for the infant Republic, nearly half of the constituent thirteen states still had fully established state churches; and the others either had definitely preferred or supported churches or, at the least, imposed religious disabilities of various kinds on members of minority-denominations.

In Europe—even in those countries where a thorough separation of state and church has been attempted—the old Establishment is still visible everywhere: in government salaries for the clergy, in government subsidies to church schools or foreign missions, or in government salaries to teachers of religious instruction in public schools. Within the traditional boundaries of European Christendom only those countries that have deified the state itself are free from such traces of the old Establishment as would always have been held unconstitutional in this country; and of course those countries have simply "established" the new totalitarian creed as the official state religion.

The United States, however, is also the only country of the West in which society is conceived as being basically a religious society.

353

More than a hundred years ago Tocqueville wrote: "There is no country in the whole world in which the Christian religion retains a greater influence over the souls of men than in America. Religion is the foremost of the institutions of the country." And this is still largely true today.

Organized religion plays a part in our society which is altogether unknown elsewhere. One could not conceive of an English, a German, or a French business corporation going to the priest or minister to find out something about a man considered for an executive job; in this country it is standard procedure. Church membership, except in the very largest cities, is everywhere taken for granted. Social life and community activities center around the churches; the Girl Scouts meet in the basement of the church, the Parent Teachers Association in the parish house and so do the Road Commissioners in small communities. One of the local ministers opens the luncheon meeting of Rotary or the annual drive of the Community Chest.

These, of course, are outward and superficial observances, and perfectly compatible with a completely irreligious life. But at least these outward signs indicate a positive emphasis on the part of American society on religion, on active membership in a church, and on active participation of the church in the life of the community. Indeed, one of the most remarkable features of American life is the speed with which this concept of a religious society is made to embrace new social institutions.

We do not have, to be sure, a "Christian trade union federation" such as is commonplace in Europe. It is a concept alien alike to our tradition of political action and of spiritual life. Yet it is quite wrong to conclude therefrom, as practically every European labor leader has been doing, that our labor movement is "non-religious," perhaps like that of Great Britain. On the contrary this totally non-denominational labor movement may well be much closer to organized religion than the typical European "Christian" union. There exists the closest and most intimate bond between the Catholic Church and some locals of the United Automobile Workers or the United Steel Workers, between Protestant churches and some locals of the Rubber Workers, or between Jewish Congregations and Garment Workers' locals in New York.

The dual relationship, strictest separation between state and church and closest interpenetration of religion and society, has been characteristic of this country from the start of its independence. The same Congress that wrote the principle of separation of state and church into the Constitution in perfectly unambiguous form: "Congress shall make no law respecting an establishment of religion or prohibiting the free exercise thereof," also established as a matter of course chaplains for

354

both its houses. In the first United States legislation regarding the military, the Act of March 3, 1791 ("An Act for raising and adding another regiment to the military establishment of the United States") the same Congress provided expressly for the appointment and pay of a regimental chaplain. Many people know that the famous phrase "a wall of separation between Church and State" was coined by Thomas Jefferson. But few people realize that this phrase is to be found in a letter that Jefferson wrote to a religious group, a group of New England Baptists, a letter which expresses a profound belief in the religious basis of society and concludes with the words: "I reciprocate your kind prayers for the protection and blessing of the common father and creator of man, and tender you for yourselves and your religious association assurances of my high respect and esteem."

But even more important than the co-existence of secular state and religious society is the relationship in which the two are placed in the American creed.

Their co-existence has often been believed to be the result of mere intellectual slovenliness, an unwillingness to be logical, fuzzy thinking, and muddling through. Actually, in this country secular state and religious society have not and cannot be conceived as contradictions; they are necessarily complementary to each other. Again let me quote Tocqueville: "I am certain that the Americans hold religion to be indispensable to the maintenance of republican institutions." It is basic to the American creed that a society can only be religious if religion and the state are radically separated, and that the state can only be free if society is basically a religious society. This belief, however confused its formulation, underlies all American approaches to the political and social treatment of religion and to the social and individual value of religion. By its very nature the sphere of the state has to be an autonomous sphere, a sphere entirely of the "natural reason." But also, by definition, a free society is only possible if based solidly on the religious individual. The one without the other simply makes no sense —nor does the European formulation of an absolute in which both state and society must be either religious or non-religious.

This leads to the basic American concept: the state must neither support nor favor any one religious denomination. That would be "Establishment," if not "prohibition of the free exercise of religion," and strictly forbidden by the First Amendment to the Constitution. But at the same time the state must always sponsor, protect, and favor religious life in general. The United States is indeed a "secular" state as far as any one denomination is concerned. But it is at the same time a "religious" commonwealth as concerns its general belief in the necessity of a truly religious basis of citizenship.

II

This has given rise to two problems; the first, what precisely is "religion"? The second, where to draw the line between the constitutional ban on anything smacking of "Establishment" or of a "prohibition of the free exercise of religion" and the compensatory obligation to support and favor religious life? But only the first question, that of the meaning of the term "religion," have we by now thought through at all.

The key word in the first sentence of the First Amendment to the Constitution is "religion." This was not synonymous with "creeds," "belief," "ideology," or "Weltanschauung" in 1790; nor is it to be taken as synonymous with these words today—as the Supreme Court has emphasized in a whole series of decisions during the last two decades on the Flag Salute, on the exemption from military service of "Ministers of Religion," and on the rights of "Conscientious Objectors." If there ever had been any doubt, the Constitution itself would have dispelled it. It provided separately, in the second sentence of the First Amendment, for the protection of "creeds," "beliefs," "ideologies," or "Weltanschauungen," through forbidding Congress from making any law "abridging the freedom of speech and of the press." It is only "religion" however that is specifically protected in its "exercise"—a protection which, by position in the text and by language, has always been recognized as being both more exalted and stronger than the mere ban on the abridgment of free speech.

And "religion," today as in 1790, clearly means two things. To be a "religion," a creed must be supernatural. It must be based on an acknowledgment of a power above man—Jefferson's "common father and creator of man." To be a religion a creed must be based on divine reason and divine will rather than solely upon natural reason. It must find its sanction not in the human mind, not in morality and ethics, but in an appeal to the supernatural. Otherwise, as the Conscientious Objectors' decisions of the Supreme Court reiterated, it is not a religion but an ideology.

Secondly, a religion must seek its kingdom in the other world. A creed, however infallible it claims to be, is not a religion—as the Constitution and the American tradition understand the term—if it aims at establishing its kingdom in this world. This also means, however, that a religion must acknowledge the existence of a "kingdom of this world," that is, of an autonomous realm of natural reason, an expression of which is the Constitution and the allegiance of American citizenship. It need not approve of this world. Its adherents may be taught to scorn this world and all its works, and refrain from all participation therein—let alone from subservience to it—as Jehovah's Witnesses do. But they must recognize that there is a separate and autonomous realm of this world, however worthless and contemptible it may be. If a creed fails to draw this line between the Kingdom of God and the kingdom of this world and, thereby, denies either, it is not a "religion" as we understand the term.

The dualism between strict separation of church and state and closest communion between religion and society which is at the center of the American creed, makes absolutely no sense, unless we recognize that the claim of the Constitution to the allegiance of the citizen, is based on its claim to be an expression of purely natural reason and of nothing else. Then it follows that the state while indifferent to all religions, must demand complete non-interference in the state from all churches, and must at the same time respect and sponsor religious life. For it is of the essence of natural reason that it recognizes its own limitation and incompleteness, while, at the same time, proclaiming its autonomy.

There are clearly difficulties in this concept. The millennial sect—Jehovah's Witnesses today, the early Mormons a century ago —always comes dangerously close to refusing to accept the autonomy of the kingdom of this world, yet is clearly a "religion" within the common usage of the term. Perhaps even more difficult is the problem presented by church schools of any denomination. The school in this country is part of the body politic: it prepares for our common citizenship and, therefore, pertains to the "kingdom of this world." At the same time, however, the claim—whether of the Catholic Church, of Orthodox Jewry, or of High-Church Episcopalians—that children must be brought up in the faith if they are to live in it as grown-ups, is undoubtedly well founded, and thoroughly in conformity with the American concept of religious life.

But at the same time the American concept of religion is clear enough to make it certain that the totalitarian creeds are not entitled to the protection afforded religion under the First Amendment. It is not the fervency of belief or the claim to infallibility that makes a "religion" in the American meaning of the term, but the nature of the belief and its relationship to the two "kingdoms." The totalitarian creeds do not seek their basis in the supernatural. Their sanction lies in natural reason alone. Their kingdom is exclusively of this world; they neither respect nor accept an autonomous realm of natural reason but aim at swallowing up state and government in an infallible ideology. Whatever protection they are entitled to under the Bill of Rights, it is not under that first and supreme guarantee of freedom of religion on which all our other freedoms rest.

Much less clear is the line between that governmental act which constitutes legitimate, indeed, required protection and furtherance of religious life, and that act which constitutes "establishment of religion" or a "prohibition of its free exercise:" in other words, forbidden interference with religious life or forbidden intervention on behalf of one denomination. One, perhaps the major, reason for our difficulty here is the fact that until recently we had no need to try to find the line. Lately, however, the problem has come up in several forms; and it is a reasonable assumption that it will stay with us.

The way we have handled the problem in the few cases that have come up so far is nothing to be very proud of. The *cause célèbre* is of course the Supreme Court Decision in the McCollum Case. I am convinced that it is a thoroughly untenable decision on ordinary legal grounds alone.

It assumed that the Fourteenth Amendment extended to the several states the entire Bill of Rights including the first half of the first sentence of the First Article which enjoins Congress not to make a law respecting an establishment of religion. This assumption was made, so to speak, subconsciously, for the problem had never come up before. Actually, it is a most dubious assumption. Historically, it is practically certain that the intention of the drafters of the Bill of Rights was to make Establishment of Religion another area exclusively reserved to the States in addition to the areas specifically enumerated in the Constitution itself. For, at the time the Bill of Rights was written, Establishment or Disestablishment was a crucial issue in all thirteen states. Only two, Virginia and Rhode Island, had disestablished. In five states, New Hampshire, Massachusetts, Connecticut, Maryland and South Carolina, a state church was still officially established. The remaining six states had various religious qualifications for full citizenship.

The Supreme Court majority further read the whole sentence "Congress shall make no law respecting an establishment of religion or prohibiting the free exercise thereof" as saying the same thing twice. But this would not only be most unusual in the Constitution which otherwise errs on the side of brevity. It is also certain from all the sources that the sentence was meant to do two distinct and separate things: to make it impossible for the Federal Government to interfere in the fights over Establishment and Disestablishment raging in every one of the thirteen states except Rhode Island; and to make it impossible for the Federal Government to interfere with the citizens' religious freedom.

Finally, the Supreme Court majority which ruled that it was unconstitutional for a school district to grant "released time" for religious instruction because to do so interfered with the religious freedom of an atheist school child, was forced by its own logic to the absurd conclusion contradicting its entire agreement, that the phrase in the Constitution that forbids Congress to make a law respecting an Establishment actually means the very opposite, namely, that the Federal Government controls the question of Establishment anywhere within the States.

The most important point is not the constitutional one, but that the decision missed the basic problem: that the American creed does not just establish a "secular" state but presupposes a religious society. It missed the point that "secular" in the American language does not mean "laic"; it means "non-sectarian." And the basic relationship between religious life and political power cannot, therefore, be founded on a purely negative policy of non-encouragement. It requires a positive policy of impartial encouragement of all religions and of all truly religious life and activity in American society.

III

The fundamental difference between the European concept of the "secular" state which is a concept profoundly hostile to religion, and the American concept of the "secular" state which is based on a religious society and on the furtherance of religion, is, in the last analysis, a difference in origins. The European concept is originally a political concept. Its starting point was the attempt to make possible political stability in a country that had lost its religious unity. It started out with the assumption that religion is a political nuisance and that religious belief is a threat to political unity and stable government. From there the road led to toleration and, finally, to anti-clericalism and to secularism. Nothing is quite so obvious to the European politician, no matter what his political beliefs, as that a "secular" state is not one that is neutral in matters of religion but one that is opposed to religion—at the very least, it frowns on any social influence of religion.

In the American creed, however, the origin of secularism is not political but religious. Its parents were not the politicians of the nation state, but two great religious thinkers, Roger Williams and Jonathan Edwards. The European concept is based on the firm belief in the supremacy of the political. The American concept is grounded in the firm belief in the incomparable value of the religious life—a value not necessarily superior to all others but necessarily of such an entirely different character and nature as to make it unique. The separation of state and church is thus in the American creed primarily a need of religion itself.

This tradition is not a specifically American one. In fact, it traces back through Nicholas of Cusa, Dante, and St. Bonaventura all the way to St. Augustine. It is thus one of the oldest of the religious traditions of the West. But in Europe the tradition—despite its eloquent exposition by Leibnitz and by the great Cardinal, St. Robert Bellarmine —was by and large lost under the impact of Reformation and Counter-Reformation. In this country, however, it became dominant.

Being a religious tradition many of its consequences are religious rather than political and thus lie well outside the scope of this paper. But there are also political consequences. One of them is, for instance, the complete absence of anti-religious or even anti-clerical movements in American history. Indeed, the very forces in society which in Europe led to anti-religious movements, all aiming at eliminating religion as a force in social life, produced in this country specifically religious movements within the churches, the various "liberal" movements which have had as their main purpose the strengthening of the bond between organized religion and society. And the fact that in this country religion never "lost the working masses"—to the point where the American worker may be the real strength of most major religious denominations in this country—is also directly traceable to the unique American tradition of a secular state made possible and kept free by a religious society.

Obviously this tradition does not in itself guarantee either a free state or a religious society. It does not "produce"—let alone automatically—a flourishing religious life (all it tends to produce are flourishing church-membership figures). It certainly does not by itself give certain promise of spiritual well-being or of a spiritual answer to the crisis of our time. But it is a foundation—both for a religious people and for a free political order. As such it is the greatest achievement of the American political spirit, and the one on which all others rest.

THE ORIGINS AND

CHARACTER OF IRISH-

AMERICAN NATIONALISM

Thomas N. Brown

[1956]

One in name and one in fame,
The sea-divided Gael.

Thomas D'Arcy McGee.

THE Irish have always been proud of their ability to assimilate their conquerors, who often, like the Burkes and Geraldines, became *hibernis ipsis hiberniores*. No doubt the charm of Ireland explains this phenomenon as well as the boast of John O'Leary that one had but to live in Ireland six years and he was Ireland's. But why should the immigrant who abandoned the old country and his son who never saw it become in many ways more Irish than the Irish themselves? What was there in the immigrant experience that transformed the indifferent peasant into a fierce and aggressive Irish nationalist? What was the character of this nationalism that shifted the balance of Irish political power, so that in 1885 the London *Times* could say with confidence that "the Irish Question is mainly an Irish-American question?"

Lecky and Froude thought the immigrant's hatred for England derived from their bitter memories of the Famine. And undoubtedly that terrible tragedy added to the immigrant's sense of wrong, determining many of them to achieve freedom for Ireland so that that horror could not be repeated. But the peasantry in Ireland, who had directly borne the Famine, were largely unmoved by the revolutionary movements that excited the immigrant. The peasantry looked back to the days that were gone rather than forward in hopes for an independent Ireland; not until another famine threatened in 1879 did they join the nationalists. The Famine clearances, as one Irishman observed, "had sown dragon's teeth from the Hudson to the Mississippi." If this phenomenon was more apparent here than in the land of the Shannon, it was because of the peculiar experience of the Irish in America.

Over three million Irish came to the United States in the years between 1845, the first year of the Famine, and the death of Charles Stuart Parnell in 1891. The immigrant tide ebbed and flowed according to the push and pull of conditions in Ireland and America. It was at flood in 1851, when more than 221,000 entered and lowest in the depression year of 1877, when less than 15,000 came over. Munster and Connacht suffered the greatest losses, but the North and the rich land of Leinster were stripped as well. The youngest and healthiest of Ireland's laborers and farmers got out; pushed off the land by cattle, they saw that Ireland offered them little and America a great deal. "The wheat pulled up," a friend of Thomas Davis lamented in the dark year of 1847, "and the tares left."

The immigrants landed in America like tired migratory birds. Prisoners of their own poverty, they were confined to the cities in which they landed or to those of the interior, on rivers and railways, where work was available. The potato culture of Ireland had not prepared them for the hard ways of the frontier farm, nor given them the skills to work the land the Yankees left behind. Gregariousness led later immigrants to adhere to the pattern of urban settlement. In 1890, when the number of Irish-born in the United States was highest, less than 15 per cent were engaged in agriculture; the remainder were bunched in the great cities, with 190,418 in New York, 71,441 in Boston and 70,028 in Chicago.

Everywhere the Irish performed the crude labor of the factory, construction gang, and mine; the women, when fortunate, worked as servants in homes of the wealthy. The Irish were the "hewers of wood and the drawers of water," as they had been at home. In many ways life in the New World was as harsh as that in the Old. Rents were high, the fear of eviction everpresent, and wages were often only enough for subsistence. The tenements of Boston's Fort Hill, New York's Five Points, and Chicago's Bridgeport were as unhealthy as the wretched huts of Ireland. By the 1890's, many sons and grandsons of immigrants had risen into the ranks of the middle class. But the recent arrival and his family perpetuated the tradition that a great portion of America's poor be of Irish blood.

The Irish were the exploited and proscribed poor; used but not accepted by the Protestant majority. And economic exploitation was a harder irony to bear in America because it occurred within the forms of civil and religious liberty. Moreover, America taught the Irish that poverty was not a necessary condition of existence. The squalor of Ireland infuriated Irish-Americans as it never had the peasant Irish. And their own poverty they laid upon the conscience of England.

The Irish were also the most homesick of all immigrants; their songs and poems, equalling in pathos those of the Negro, became a part of America's folk literature. The very isolation of their lives in Ireland intensified the anguish felt when separated from old scenes and faces. To quiet the pangs of loneliness and to meet the problems of American life the immigrants grouped together. Despite the suspicions of nativists, who believed them divisive, the organizations formed were natural and healthy, reflecting the pluralism of American society and the divisions within the Irish-American community, for Irish societies expressed class as well as group consciousness. The wealthier Irish in Boston could join the Charitable Irish Society, those in New York and Philadelphia the Friendly Sons of St. Patrick, while the corner saloon and the neighborhood clubs served for the poor. Many early Irish militia companies were recruited exclusively from workers of particular skilled trades; and among the most effective organizations were those dedicated exclusively to the economic welfare of their members.

But loneliness also evoked in the immigrant mind an image of Ireland that cut through the divisions natural to the immigrants in America. Batt O'Connor, an immigrant bricklayer, whom a St. Patrick's Day parade in Providence, Rhode Island, helped convert to revolutionary nationalism, said that "to leave Ireland does not make one love Ireland more, but it does make one aware of the strength of that love." Since his arrival in 1893, O'Connor had been lonely in America: "I would try to recall the smell of the turf, and I would think of the streams in which I went fishing, and the places where I found a bird's nest. . . ." Ballybeyond could not easily be recaptured, but longing for it brought Irishmen together and from their meeting came a new awareness of love for Ireland: "I walked in that procession [the Providence Parade] and in the emotion I felt, walking as one of that vast crowd of Irish emigrants celebrating our national festival, I awoke to the full consciousness of my love for my country."

Irish-American nationalism was thus in part a symptom of the immigrant's homesickness; the immigrant agitator was not a swindler or filibusterer, but "that much more unreasonable animal, a dreamer." Nevertheless, the immigrant's nationalism was too fierce an enthusiasm to derive simply from the passivity of a nostalgia for the Old Country. Indeed, it was the ruling passion for many of the second and third generation who knew only America. Like the almost mythic Captain William Mackey Lomasney, who was born in Ohio and blown to bits by his own dynamite under London Bridge in 1883, the fiercest nationalists were often the sons of immigrants.

Patrick Ford, who was born in Galway in 1837 and came to America when he was eight, during the first year of the Famine, is a reliable witness of the experiences that made him the most influential American advocate of Irish freedom in the second half of the nineteenth century. To a reporter from the *Pall Mall Gazette,* he admitted that as a youth in Boston he knew nothing of Ireland. "I might as well have been born in Boston. . . . I brought nothing with me from Ireland—nothing tangible to make me what I am." Young Patrick Ford walked the streets of Boston during the years when the Know-Nothings controlled the state of Massachusetts and anti-Irish feeling was strong everywhere. Day after day he sought work only to see the signs reading "no Irish need apply" that were the insulting barriers which separated the Irish from the American community.

> I was seeking in this way for some months . . . finding constantly that the fact that I was Irish and a Catholic against me. I was not yet awake about Ireland, but I began to think early, to read whatever I could lay hands on . . . and to think over what I had read.

Under the pressure of Know-Nothingism, young Ford came to the conclusion that he was the victim of the "conditions of poverty and enslavement" which gripped the land of his birth; and decided that "it was necessary for everyone of Irish blood to do all in his power to change that state of things."

The Know-Nothing movement made the immigrant aware that he was despised and that the lines separating him from the Protestant Ascendancy (his term) were more sharply drawn than in Ireland, where generations of personal relationships had blurred them over. The battle lines were first clearly drawn during the 1840's when the Irish had achieved sufficient political power to threaten institutions long cherished by the Protestant majority, as in New York and Philadelphia, or to frustrate hopes for social reform, as in Boston. In the conflict which raged during the 1840's and 1850's the composition of the immigrant community was shaped. Many of the Protestant Irish joined the Know-Nothings, as did some non-Irish Catholics. But the latter were engulfed by the immigrant wave and Catholic and Irish became identified. The passive Church of the gentle Bishop Cheverus gave way to the militant Church of Archbishop Hughes. When Orestes Brownson, anxious to preserve the earlier Anglo-American character of the Catholic Church in America, attempted criticism of the Irish immigrant, he found that for the majority of the hierarchy and for the Catholic press defense of the Irish was the greater imperative. It was natural then for Patrick Ford to see nativism as primarily an expression of hatred for the Irish-Catholic poor and it was not unreasonable for him to conclude that the germ of the immigrant's predicament lay in Ireland.

Irish-American nationalism then had its origins in loneliness, poverty, and prejudice. Compressed into ghettos, the Irish used their numbers and the group consciousness which the ghetto fostered to nourish, as nativists complained, "their foreign feelings and their foreign nationality." Within the Irish-American community old allegiances were reflected in the Kerry villages and Donegal squares found in all the great cities. Nevertheless, the immigrants realized that in a hostile land their Irishness mattered more than their provincial differences. Life in America, said Patrick Ford, lifted the Irishman out of "the littleness of countyism into the broad feeling of nationalism."

Rooted in the immigrant's experience, this nationalism was peculiarly Irish-American, reflecting his compulsive sense of inferiority, his sensitiveness to criticism, and his yearning for respectability. For the immigrants, as their first historian said, paid too high a price "for butcher's meat and glazed shoddy instead of honest frieze," and were badly in need of America's esteem. Stage Irishmen learned to their surprise that jokes which evoked laughter in Dublin drew hisses in New York. Dion Boucicault, the prolific Irish playwright, had his play the *Shaughraun,* based on a popular Irish folk tale, mobbed in Boston. The stage Irishman was too much like the stereotype believed in by nativists and indeed was often too close to the truth of the immigrant situation to be accepted by the sensitive. Michael Davitt, the most compelling Irishman of his generation, reveals in a speech, given before a large audience at Cooper Union in 1880, how the soft spot in immigrant psychology served the interests of Irish nationalism:

> You want to be honored among the elements that constitute this nation, as a people not coming from a paupered land; and in order that no sneers be cast on you when you stand for any position . . . you want to be regarded with the respect due you, that you may be thus looked on, aid us in Ireland to remove the stain of degradation from your birth and the Irish race here in America will get the respect you deserve.

This appeal was a commonplace of Irish nationalist oratory and immigrant responsiveness to it involved the United States in the latter half of the nineteenth century in many an embarrassing situation abroad and often snarled domestic politics in the thicket of Anglo-Irish relations. A United States court in 1856 warned the Irish Emigrant Aid Society of Cincinnati, a revolutionary body led by Michael Doheny, the Forty Eighter, that there "can be no such thing as a divided allegiance." In the years before the Irish-American community was moulded under the impact of Know-Nothingism there had not been such a problem. The Irishman, whether Catholic or Protestant, was not then cut off from the main stream of American life.

When the United Irishman, Thomas Addis Emmet, came to the United States in 1803, he found that his "principles and his sufferings" opened the most fashionable doors in New York to him. His career and that of his friend and fellow rebel, Dr. William Mac-Neven, were brilliant and happy; and like those of other prominent Irishmen of the period were essentially American, not Irish-American. The poor, ragged immigrants of post-Famine years were men of another sort. Neither their principles nor their proletarian character commended them to America. They could not reply to sneers about their foreign birth with an answer like Emmet's to William Pinkney "that he was Mr. Pinkney's equal in birth, in rank and in connexions." Unlike Emmet and MacNeven, outstanding Irishmen in the latter half of the century, whether businessmen like William Onahan, or politicians like Patrick Collins, depended for their influence upon the ability to exploit the sentiments of the Irish-American community.

It is true that the Irish in America always revealed some interest in the affairs of their native land; but in the early years of the nineteenth century this did not distinguish them from native Americans. In the 1840's the increase of evangelical fervor to spread democracy must have brought many Americans into the branches of O'Connell's Repeal society, which were organized in Richmond, Savannah, and elsewhere where the Irish population was slight. Those who tried to persuade James Gordon Bennett to join the Repeal society of New York assured him that the "great movement of Repeal in Ireland . . . was only the beginning of a grand revolutionary drama, that soon would be able to subvert the monarchies and aristocracies of England, France and all western Europe. . . ." Most of the delegates to the Repeal convention which met in New York City in the fall of 1843 had Irish names, but many did not. That Robert Tyler, the son of the President, headed the Convention was perhaps less important than the fact that Richard Johnson and Lewis Cass, as well as the Whigs, Horace Greeley and William Seward were among those who thought action to restore self-government to Ireland was a legitimate interest of a citizen of the United States; and this at a time when denouncing the immigrant paid greater political dividends than twisting the lion's tail.

From the collapse of the Repeal agitation, however, until Parnell and Gladstone joined hands in 1886 responsible native Americans generally refused to participate in American societies designed to further Irish freedom. Their reluctance was not due, as one English propagandist suggested, to loss of sympathy as a result of experience with the troublesome Irish, but rather to changes in character and orientation of Irish-American national societies. However much American supporters of Repeal may have been entranced by the possibility of democratic revolutions going off like fused dynamite throughout Europe, they had preferred to dwell on its peaceful aspects and constitutional purposes. But after the arrival of the Forty Eighters Irish national societies here, no matter how euphemistically named and ostensibly peaceful their purposes, were controlled in varying degrees by revolutionists. As John Mitchel discovered, Americans, despite their sympathy, were disinclined to embarrass their own country by backing revolution in Ireland.

A more important influence in persuading native Americans to remain aloof from Irish societies was the heavy cloud of hate and fear that hung over them, the bitter heritage of the Know-Nothing conflict. When the thunderheads of Civil War lowered in 1861, the immigrants, as Professor Hansen has said, were flung upward to positions in field and factory that they could not have aspired to during the preceding years. Nevertheless, they did not lose their sense of group consciousness. Spokesmen for the Irish remained extremely sensitive to discrimination in the army, and the Draft Riots of 1863 demonstrated that the Irish poor retained their sense of grievance. On that famous occasion at the Rappahanock when Irish soldiers in both blue and gray joined their voices across the battlefield in singing the immigrant lament, "Deep in Canadian Wood," they expressed the powerful emotional ties which held them together in a nation torn by war. Those who did not share in this emotional legacy of Irish-America could only have been uncomfortable in the societies that it produced.

It is true that Irish-American nationalism was as much an affair of the spirit, a state of mind, as it was a matter of birth or religion. One did not have to be Irish to love Cathleen na Houlihan. Nor did one have to be an Irish-American to share in his ideals. What was needed was to feel his special grievance, the injustice of being alien. In England and America Irish nationalism was largely the cause of the poor—those, according to the *Irish World,* who felt "heavily the shame of the disgraced condition to which our race is reduced. . . ." Except in cities like San Francisco, where the Irish bore no social stigma, the wealthier Catholic Irish ("lace-curtain Irish") kept themselves aloof from the organizations of the poor. And the Protestant Irish found it necessary to describe themselves as Scotch-Irish in order that they be distinguished from the peasant poor. On the other hand, Americans like Wendell Phillips and James Redpath, who had ridden the tide of pre-Civil War reform and were marooned when it ebbed, found a natural place as champions of Irish-America in the years of the Great Barbecue.

Nevertheless, Wendell Phillips and James Redpath were exceptions. Americans not of Irish origin only rarely involved themselves in the nationalist affairs of the immigrant in the years preceding the alliance of Parnell with Gladstone. This isolation from the American community intensified the immigrant's problem of divided loyalties. At once more American than the Americans and more Irish than the Irish, the immigrant, in the phrase of the sociologist, Robert Park, was the "marginal man," astride two worlds. The task of his leaders was so to interpret his experience that the tensions created by this ambivalence might be resolved. Loyalty to Ireland had to be reconciled with loyalty to America.

William MacNeven suggested the proper approach to the problem when he stated in his *Pieces of Irish History,* alluding to the American Revolution and Irish resistance to British rule, that "What was tyranny against the American would necessarily be tyranny against the Irish; and the resistance so glorious in one country could not be accounted a crime in the other." He spoke, however, only in defense of the revolutionary enterprises of the United Irishmen. Later leaders were to link the fate of Ireland to America in a broader stream of history. Most significant were the lectures given by Thomas D'Arcy McGee, another Forty-Eighter. Beginning with the possible discovery of America by St. Brendan, according to an interpretation of an old legend, McGee catalogued the names of Irishmen prominent in the colonial and early national periods of America. Lacking the brilliant insights into the situation of the immigrant often found in his other works, the lectures adequately demonstrated that the Irish were not new to America. When told to go home to Ireland if he did not like the treatment received in America, the Irishman could use McGee's facts to answer: "This is our country. We bought it dearly. We like it well and we intend to stay in it." America belonged to the Irish as much as anyone.

McGee did not originate this form of apologetics, but he was the first to give it such wide currency. Later enthusiasts, stirred by the possibilities of the argument, ransacked libraries for more information and gave their imagination freer rein. William R. Grace and Honest John Kelly embellished the lectures of McGee to the delight of audiences in the 1880's. In a later series of lectures McGee had said that at the dawn of American history there were three Catholic figures: a lady, a sailor and a monk. His successors would have it that there was also an Irishman; as indeed they insisted there was at every important turn in America's development. St. Brendan, in their opinion, was the undoubted discoverer of the New World; and the glory of the Irish was further enhanced by the knowledge that an Irishman accompanied the admiral of the Ocean Sea on his first voyage. This latter information proved, according to the Boston *Pilot,* "that the Irish is no bastard or corrupt stock, but one of the seminal races of the earth. . . ." And as befitted such a race its soldiers were virtually responsible for winning the American Revolution against a vicious horde of English and German Protestants; and its blood was to be found in the veins of innumerable famous Americans, even in the nativist veins of Samuel Morse.

In his compulsive love for Ireland the immigrant was only intensifying his Americanism, for Ireland struggled for democracy. "The cause of America in 1776 is the cause of Ireland in 1876." England was the enemy of both and in a curious way continued to oppress America. Not only was the corrupt Irishman of America's cities a direct product of English rule, but the money he sent home to Ireland was a tax levied upon America. The United States in the 1880's, said James Redpath, voicing the argument of many, in this way suffered the very injustice of taxation without representation that had sparked the American Revolution.

This glorious confusion of fact with fancy was neither descriptive of the immigrants' true situation, nor of their ambitions. They had not simply dedicated themselves as American democrats to the spread of that faith in Ireland, where indeed it was held at a discount by many nationalists. But McGee's system of apologetics did help to bridge over one gap which yawned beneath the immigrants as "marginal men," giving them a dramatic sense of participation in the greatness of America, while ignoring the massive squalor under which they lived. And this must have nourished egos suffering from painful feelings of inferiority.

The immigrants, of course, realized that they did not voice influential American opinion; that the Irish national struggle did not join Ireland and America, but rather the discontented and depressed of both countries. Armed with this insight, they employed another argument—one closely entwined with that from history but even more imaginative and grand—that derived from their view of themselves as Celts. The sea-divided Gaels were bound together by the ties of race; and these all men must respect. The trans-Atlantic allegiance worked to the benefit of America, for one of the Celt's special missions was to protect the Declaration of Independence against "derogation by the Anglo-Saxon Ascendancy." The struggle for human freedom, which bound the destinies of Ireland and America was in truth an aspect of the epic struggle of the Celt against the Saxon.

Modern awareness of the Celt is not much older than the publication in 1765 of MacPherson's *Ossian,* which made the melancholy Celt of the young Scot's imagination a familiar figure to the reading public of Goethe's Europe. MacPherson's "translations" began a long literary war over the question of their authenticity and, as a by-product, another over the character of the ancient Celts, stimulating Irish antiquarians to defend as well as to discover their country's past. This work was carried on largely under the patronage of the Ascendancy and did not dispose the antiquarian toward hostility to England. Charlotte Brooke, whose *Reliques of Irish Poetry* served to refute many of the Celt's detractors, presented her study in the hope that it would improve Anglo-Irish relations.

But Celtic studies pursued by members of the middle class, anxious as many were for reform, did stimulate antagonism to the Saxon. Charlotte Elizabeth Phelan, interested in using Gaelic as an instrument of Protestant proselytizing, confessed that her studies converted her from being a "dangerous Orangewoman" into "something like a rebel." Some ten years later Thomas Davis deliberately fostered this tendency with his writings in the *Nation*. Then for the first time the Celtic past became a factor in modern Irish politics. Though Gavan Duffy believed that Davis had succeeded only in making converts to antiquarianism, his pseudonym "The Celt" became one of the important symbols of militant Irish nationalism in the last half of the nineteenth century. A symbol that soon found employment in America.

The Know-Nothing conflict had generated self-consciousness among native Americans, leading them to explore their Anglo-Saxon origins and to assert the moral superiority of that race over "the untaught and wretched Celt." In the years following the Civil War the arrogance of the Anglo-Saxon myth-makers increased as Darwinian thought appeared to give scientific validity to their claims. In response, the Irish, emboldened by their increasing economic and political status, elaborated a Celtic interpretation of history. Lacking historians and publicists of the caliber of Edward Augustus Freeman, James Anthony Froude, or even Goldwyn Smith, second only to Froude in denigrating the Celt, the Irish were forced to rely upon the standard works of Irish apologetics, and the scholarly if difficult studies of Eugene O'Curry, John O'Donovan, and W. K. Sullivan. They drew also upon such eccentric enthusiasts as Martin O'Brennan, who believed the language of the Celts had been the speech of the Garden of Eden. The backhanded compliments of Matthew Arnold and the findings of Zeuss and other continental philologists were available to them in that disorganized collection of other men's ideas which Father Ulick Bourke, of St. Jarlath's College, Connacht, published as *The Aryan Origins of the Gaelic Race and Language* (1876).

The American Celts had little use for the dreamy ineffectual race of Arnold's *Study of Celtic Literature*. The virtues they found in their race were typically American. Not magic but the ability to assimilate and fuse together disparate racial groups they believed to be the special genius of the Gael, whose ancient society erred only in being too democratic. Though they agreed with Arnold that the Celt was less materialistic than the Saxon, they generally claimed for their race the very achievements that Freeman and his American counterpart, Herbert Baxter Adams reserved for the Germanic peoples. The origins of democratic institutions, which these historians traced back to the "tun" of the dark German forests, the philo-celts found on the sunny slopes of Tara. Representative government, trial by jury, popular education were found to be among the gifts tendered the modern world by the Celts of Ireland.

The American Irish were aware that they were insisting upon Celtic particularism at a time when philologists were asserting a common Aryan origin for Saxon and Celt. There was a certain embarrassment also in the fact that some of the most ancient Gaelic names belonged to members of the anti-nationalist Irish gentry, while Celtic partisans bore names obviously Saxon or Norman in origin. Nevertheless, the Celtic myth served as a useful defensive weapon at a time when prevailing American opinion had it that America in its people and institutions was essentially Anglo-Saxon. So long as this view prevailed the Irish were prepared to claim America for the Celts; to insist that the foundations of America rested on the Blarney stone, not on Plymouth Rock.

Defenders of the Celt organized Philo-Celtic societies throughout America for the revival of the Irish language, which had some influence upon the language revival in Ireland, preceding by four years the foundation in 1876 of the Dublin Society for the Preservation of the Irish Language. In 1873 the first of the Philo-Celtic societies was begun in Boston. By 1878 there were five societies in New York and in the following year branch societies were in existence in over thirteen American and Canadian cities, from Boston to San Francisco. And the study of Gaelic was reported to be a favorite recreation among soldiers in the forts of the frontier.

Father Ulick Bourke was impressed by the phenomenon of immigrants in America learning there the language they had the "misfortune not to have learned at home." But these were few. In America as in Ireland the mass of the Irish were ashamed of or had no use for the old tongue. Even the Philo-Celtic clubs as it turned out were less interested in the language than they were in disproving Froude's statement, made during his lecture tour in 1870, that the "Irish as a nation have done nothing which posterity will not be anxious to forget." When T. O'Neill Russell of the Dublin language society came to the United States in 1878, he found the Irish-American press indifferent and even opposed to his efforts to revive the language. The *Irish World,* whose enthusiasm for Gaelic had influenced Dubliners as well as immigrants, warned the hopeful Russell that it had taken up the language movement in 1871 only to prove to "educated dunces" that Ireland had a glorious literature in her native language. The Land League soon proved more exciting than Irish grammar, robbing the Philo-Celtic societies of members and their quarrels over whether

Roman or Irish type should be used further weakened these organizations.

Ten years after its founding the Boston Philo-Celtic society reframed its constitution in order that new members might join without committing themselves to the labor of studying Gaelic. The society continued to insist, however, that the "cultivation of the Irish or Celtic language and the publication of Irish or Celtic literature," was the only way to "vindicate the character of the Irish as a race, from the foul slanders heaped upon them for centuries by English or Anglo-Saxon writers. . . ."

The American Irish used the symbol of the Celt, as had Davis, to disarm their detractors and to give their people hope by giving them pride in the past. But they used it also to provide Irishmen, no matter how far removed in time and place from Ireland, with a rationale for nationalist action and to justify such action before their critics. They bent history to their will, but better scholars in the camp of the enemy were as guilty with less reason.

The principal instrument of instruction in Celticism and in the dogmas of nationalism was the Irish-American press. Newspapers in Ireland were largely irrelevant to the fixed life of the peasantry, but to the uprooted Irish of America they were almost a necessity. The paper brought the news of home, of ship sailings and arrivals; it offered correspondence columns to locate lost relatives and others to locate jobs. It taught the peasant the customs and manners of bourgeois America, and was his champion in a hostile society. All newspapers devoted to the immigrant taught some brand of nationalism, if for no other reason than that it aided circulation. It was to the newspapers that the immigrant turned when in his newly awakened consciousness he sought knowledge of the Irish and of Ireland.

Not until the 1840's was the newspaper assured a stable place in immigrant culture. Catholic newspapers, fed by the increasing anti-Irish feeling of the 1830's, served the immigrant, but efforts to establish purely secular Irish newspapers had failed. The immigrant flood of the 1840's, especially that after the Famine, provided the Irish press with readers and the Know-Nothing movement gave it a cause. The defeat of Young Ireland at Ballingarry made writers available. Thomas D'Arcy McGee, John Mitchel, T. F. Meagher, Michael Doheny, and John O'Mahony were among those who tried their hand at teaching nationalism by means of the immigrant press in the 1850's. Mitchel's *Citizen,* begun in New York in 1854, boasted a circulation of 50,000 within a few months.

The identification of Irish with Catholic, with Archbishop Hughes the exalted defender of both, was simple enough to maintain during the years when the Liberator strode the boards. But the advent of

Young Ireland introduced new factors. To Archbishop Hughes, as to his friend Cardinal Cullen, the young refugees reeked with the smell of Mazzini. "Political confectioners," Hughes called them in his best style, "who seal up the poison of their infidelity in sugar plums of flattery to popular prejudices. . . . They are not of those Irishmen who have preserved the nationality and honor of their country by preserving their faith in the midst of persecution." Aroused by McGee's "strong doses of patriotism," administered in his *Nation* and later by Mitchel's attack upon the temporal claims of the Papacy, the Archbishop verbally smashed the *Nation* and then John Mitchel's *Citizen* and helped to drive their editors out of New York.

That Irish nationalism was not to be identified with Catholicism was apparent in the varying ways cleric and nationalist approached the Celtic myth. For the priest, Irish history was a religious drama, a long martyrdom of a people naturally Christian that was permitted by God in order to spread His Word. Aware of the pleasant irony that the immigrant Irish were carrying Catholicism everywhere throughout the English speaking world, churchmen saw in that tattered figure an arm of the Lord and in the Famine which sent him forth the mysterious "logic of God." Nationalists furiously rejected this fatalism; and argued persuasively that Catholic England had been as destructive of the liberties of the Irish as was Protestant England. Daniel O'Connell, of course, was the hero of the Catholic Celtophile. Nationalists remembered his surrender at Clontarf and believed his political doctrines had corrupted the Irish people. Nationalists were also convinced that clerics thought of Ireland as a pawn that could be sacrificed whenever the diplomacy of restoring England to the Faith demanded.

When John Mitchel was attacked, as he said, by "Archbishop Philo-Veritas," on the one hand and by a "true-blue Orangeman" on the other, he defined by implication the road nationalists in America would have to travel. Similar though it was to that followed by their brethren in Ireland, it had fewer stones. The American Irish, having acquired the aggressiveness of their new country, were less submissive to the clergy than the Irish at home. Moreover, with the decline of Know-Nothingism the clergy lost their place as spokesmen for the Irish in public affairs. Even in the 1850's the most popular historical defense of the immigrant was not that of Archbishop Hughes, but those lectures of his enemy, Thomas D'Arcy McGee. The Archbishop's personal influence remained until his death, but shortly afterwards the fire-like spread of Fenianism demonstrated how weak was the control of the priest in Irish affairs. And no churchman in after years was able to wield the power of Archbishop Hughes.

Politicians, reformers, and nationalists took over the leadership of the depressed Irish, guiding them often into uncharted waters, too murky and dangerous for the Church. Opposition to those excursions by the hierarchy, however wise and foresighted, gave verisimilitude to the charge of some that the Church blocked the path of the Irish poor. Few nationalists, however, wanted a break with the Church. They understood its influence in Ireland and the faith of the Irish in America. And the majority of the American hierarchy in the last half of the century, fearing to weaken that faith by unwise opposition and often themselves in sympathy with Irish aspirations, were more cautious than their counterparts in Ireland in challenging the nationalists. Sharing to some extent each other's faith, but responsive to different allegiances, the churchman and the nationalist lived in a state of uneasy tension.

The decline of clerical influence in secular affairs and the development of a national body of readers (most major Irish papers had national circulations) rendered the press independent of the local bishop. New York was the chief center of Irish-American publishing in the 1880's, with five weeklies designed for Irish consumption; but every important center of Irish population supported at least one newspaper. The *Irish World,* founded in 1870 by the messianic Patrick Ford, driven to advocate almost every kind of social radicalism during the bad times after 1873, fought many battles with the clergy and was barred from at least two dioceses, but it remained during the 1870's and 1880's the most popular Irish-American paper in the country. Having for readers the same class whom Joseph Pulitzer would try to reach in the next decade, the *Irish World* anticipated the techniques of Yellow Journalism. Sensational headlines and drawings (tearful Erin crouching in terror over her unstrung harp under the bloodied whip of John Bull) enlivened the front page. Ford specialized in collecting money for Irish causes and the thrill of seeing one's name in print as a contributor perhaps aided circulation.

But Ford was also a serious moral reformer. The abolition of slavery, temperance, social reform, Irish national freedom had at one time or another commanded his energies. Like William Lloyd Garrison, on whose *Liberator* he had learned the printer's trade, he was rigidly righteous and his language was thick with the Old Testament. His paper, studded with complex speculations on subjects ranging from usury to theology, was witness to the earnestness of himself and his readers. He also possessed a deep capacity for self-deception and the *Irish World* was able to shift from radical, even revolutionary criticism of capitalism in 1878 to the advocacy of Harrison ten years later without losing its sense of moral rectitude.

Next in influence to the *Irish World* during the Parnellite period was the Boston *Pilot,* whose shrewd realism, under the brilliant editorship of John Boyle O'Reilly, was in sharp contrast to the quarrelsome evangelicism of Ford's paper. A man of fine literary gifts and great personal charm, O'Reilly was disposed by character and experience towards moderation. Born in Ireland in 1844 and at the age of twenty-two sentenced to imprisonment for participating in the Fenian conspiracy, the *Pilot* editor very early knew the limitations of revolutionary organizations. Though he remained the confidant of the revolutionaries and was prepared to support their projects, his own energies were expended in ways more in keeping with his talents. Ten years after a romantic escape from an Australian prison colony, O'Reilly was firmly established as owner and editor of the *Pilot,* oldest and most respected of immigrant papers, and as a fully accredited member of Boston's literary community.

More than anyone else, O'Reilly understood the function of the leader in an immigrant group. Each week the *Pilot* taught the displaced peasants the disciplines of toleration and fair play necessary in a multi-racial society, thereby earning the applause of Brahmin Boston. But he was also the champion of the Irish whenever they were (or thought they were) under attack. And he never hesitated to use their considerable political power in the interests of Irish-America. The ambiguity of O'Reilly's public behavior (often denying by action what he affirmed in editorials, novels, and poems) and his limitations as a liberal reformer derived from his role as immigrant leader. For the advance of Irish-America depended upon the solidarity of its members and the impregnability of its fortress. If pursuit of reform divided the immigrant community, the effort was abandoned and the divisions were denied. The *Pilot* was ever alert to assaults from without and always insisted that all was serene within the fortress.

In his concern for the New Ireland O'Reilly did not forget the old. "We can do more good by our Americanism than by our Irishism," he said, believing that in this way American public opinion might be transformed into a powerful moral force that would pressure England to grant Irish demands. This Yankee version of O'Connell's strategy was not, of course, original with the editor of the *Pilot,* nor practiced exclusively by him. But more than anyone else O'Reilly kept constantly in mind that Ireland had to plead her cause in the market place of America; and grateful Irishmen in later years ascribed the policy to him.

If Patrick Ford was essentially the American reformer, not really Irish at all, then John Devoy, editor and founder of the *Irish Nation* from 1881 until it failed in 1886, was preeminently the political refugee abroad; the Irish revolutionary virtually untouched by American experience. Imprisoned as a Fenian in 1867, he came to America upon his release three years later; and against the advice of his friend John Boyle O'Reilly stepped immediately into the turbulent waters of Irish revolutionary politics in New York City. Until his death in 1928 he was the chief guardian of Cathleen na Houlihan in America, protecting her from the radicalism of the Fords and the compromises of the O'Reillys. Though not unaware of the urgency of the need for social reform in Ireland, Devoy would not permit it to slow the quest for national freedom. But in his hands the work of preparing a revolution lost its romance and became a grubby business. It was a principle of John O'Leary's that there were some things a man must not do to save his country. Unencumbered by O'Leary's temperament, Devoy used every strategy and weapon available to him. Perhaps because it was too purely Irish, like its editor, the *Irish Nation* never attained great popularity, but because it represented the considered opinions of a formidable body of revolutionists its influence was not to be measured by circulation.

That the Irish-American press met the needs of the immigrants' peculiar situation was demonstrated by its survival and growth even during the depression years of the 1870's. In the Celtic myth and the promise of nationalism the press gave heroic meaning to the experience of the uprooted. But the immigrants were heirs of O'Connell, as well as of Thomas Davis, and too utilitarian to permit their dreams to become an obsession. While Ireland year by year became more luxuriously green in their memories, they turned to the techniques of organization which Daniel O'Connell had taught them. Collective action, they believed, would win Irish national freedom and thus the respect of Americans; and would also advance their material interests in this country. "We need," said the *Irish Nation,* "a permanent organization of the Irish race in America that will not alone look to the needs of Ireland, but to the defense of Irish interests here."

Many organizations were designed to uplift the Irish. The Catholic Total Abstinence Union professed to accomplish this by the cult of sobriety. Its banner, according to the "hymn" of the Union would fly over a "nation freed from bondage and a race redeemed from shame." The Irish Catholic Benevolent Union, the Ancient Order of Hibernians, and the Irish sections within the Knights of Labor had similar ambitions. All of these subscribed to the dogmas of nationalism and possessed a stability and wealth that the more volatile nationalist organization could not ordinarily command. But their very immersion in the practical problems of the immigrant narrowed their membership and, by stirring up the dusts of class and sectional division, inhibited their capacity for leadership of the Irish-American community.

Inevitably, the Abstinence Union had a limited appeal; when it included mutual aid among its attractions, it met competition from other benevolent organizations and the liquor interests were always powerful enemies. The Hibernians had been discredited in the 1870's by their connections with the labor terrorism of the Molly Maguires in Pennsylvania. The founders of the I.C.B.U. hoped for a grand alliance of Irishmen, but in trying to lure the immigrant from labor unions, the organization bucked a too powerful tide.

Perhaps the most grandiose plan conceived for the salvation of the immigrant was that of the Irish Catholic Colonization Society of America (1878–1891), a bold effort to relocate the slum dwellers on the prairies of the West. It had some success when, as in the colonizing work of Archbishop Ireland of Minnesota, it operated in aid of the normal pattern of land settlement, helping those who already had the money, skills, and desire for farming the West. But the larger hopes of breaking the grip of the cities upon the Irish poor were not fulfilled. Vested interests were opposed, and the mass of the Irish were apathetic, preferring with most Americans of these years the bright lights of the cities. Ironically, during the disappointing life of the Colonization society, the immigrants, nationally organized in the Land League, contributed hundreds of thousands of dollars to make the peasant of Ireland proprietor of the land he worked. "Our people," lamented one enthusiast for colonization, "would be more willing to give five dollars a day to buy a faded green flag with a tarnished sunburst than one dollar for an acre of land." Only by transcending their situation in America, only by fixing on goals sufficiently removed from their American anxieties, could Irish-Americans achieve the solidarity that was their dream. This was the special function of the Irish nationalist organization, of which the first significant one was the Fenian Brotherhood.

A struggling revolutionary body, when begun in 1858, like so many others in that decade, the Brotherhood's membership increased enormously under the stimulus of the Civil War. The name Fenian derived from the Fianna, that ancient warrior band whose exploits under Fionn MacCumhail make up the second cycle of Irish mythology, and is testimony to the lonely romanticism of John O'Mahoney, Young Ireland exile and founder of the organization in America. The sister organization in Ireland, led by that artful conspirator, James Stephens, preferred the less mystical name of the Irish Revolutionary Brotherhood. Though the Irish body was insignificant compared to the American, Stephens insisted upon running both as a dictator until O'Mahoney, responsive to conditions in America, refashioned his group along democratic lines. Anxious to conform to American neutrality laws, as well as to demands here for democratic procedures, and fearing also clerical condemnation as a secret society, the Fenians, in their first national convention in 1863, made the "Head Center" an elective official providing him with a cabinet, also elected by the assembly delegates. They affirmed that the society was neither illegal, nor secret, and, convinced that a war between England and the United States, which would effect their "deliverance," was imminent, they made clear the American nature of their concerns: "We say our deliverance, for the privilege of living among a free people . . . but makes us feel the more keenly the suffering and degradations of our old land."

War, however, did not come and members of the Brotherhood, anxious to precipitate action, forced further reorganization upon O'Mahoney. At the Philadelphia Convention in 1865, with six hundred delegates present, the office of Head Center was abolished and that of a President to be elected by the General Congress of the Fenian Brotherhood was substituted. Congress, made up of a Senate and House of Delegates, was invested with all legislative powers. Members of the individual Fenian circles throughout the country elected the Delegates who, in turn, in Congress assembled, elected members to the more august assemblage of the Senate. Power to originate all money bills was given to the Senate and theirs too was the responsibility to approve all cabinet appointments. The President of that body was also Vice-President of the Brotherhood. With the Constitution of the United States as a model, and the procedure of its Congress as an ideal, the Fenians, as one of them later wrote, formed "a distinct Republic within the American Republic." From their capitol in the old Moffat mansion (opposite Union Square, New York City), which flew the Fenian flag of the harp and sunburst, they raised an army, issued letters of marque and reprisal, negotiated with the United States, and otherwise conducted themselves as an important power.

Having separated their governmental powers in approved American fashion, the Fenians then fell into the bickering between the legislative and executive branches which the system fosters. A few months after the Philadelphia convention, the Senate deposed O'Mahoney as President for exceeding his constitutional authority, thus displaying the same yeasty arrogance that set the Senate of the United States in this same year plotting against Andrew Johnson. O'Mahoney, however, refused to retire as chief of the Fenians and organized his own body that did away with the elaborate paraphernalia of government fabricated at Philadelphia. "Cut and hack the rotten branches around you without pity," O'Mahoney was advised by Stephens, who, like many other Irish revolutionists, disliked the Americanization of the movement by the Senate wing. Nevertheless that body, led by William R. Roberts, a wealthy New York dry goods merchant, of consummate ability in composing flamboyant denunciations of the British Empire, was the more popular of the two among the Irish in America. The abortive raid which it organized against Canada in 1867 was, from an Irish point of view, absolutely mad, but it did reflect the hopes of many American expansionists in the years following the Civil War. The Roberts faction, according to one of its critics, was more interested in annexing Canada to the United States than in winning Irish freedom.

The Brotherhood, however, never conquered, and ran its course without an inch of soil over which to exercise sovereignty. It remained, as the *Freeman's Journal* liked to point out, "a mental Republic," existing precariously in the dangerous spiritual gulf that the Civil War had opened up between Great Britain and the United States. The abortive expedition of the O'Mahoney faction against the island of Campo Bello, then in dispute between the two countries, nicely illustrated how the Fenians exploited the tensions between Jonathan and John Bull. But the Fenians were in turn exploited by the United States; both the administrations of Johnson and Grant used them as a threat to extort better terms from Great Britain in settling disputes arising out of the war. And politicians of all parties and factions, in the scramble for power that developed during Reconstruction years, used the Fenians cynically and were so used by them. Determined, as they said at the Chicago convention in 1863, to wipe out "the foul stigma which attaches to our name," and aware of the dangers to that hope involved in participation in purely American affairs, the Fenians resolved to exclude from their deliberations any discussions of politics. But these were not easy to shut out. When Fenianism swept into the East in 1864, shrewd politicians like young Patrick Collins joined up; and from then on Fenians were too frequently aspirants for public office. The failure of the final raid upon Canada in 1870 was traced to the reluctance of the Senate to commit the Brotherhood to battle out of fear of destroying its political power.

Shattered into splinter groups by sectional as well as political antagonisms, their enthusiasm dissipated in the monotony of repeated failure, the Fenians had already lost their hold upon Irish-America when Grant informed his cabinet in May, 1870, that he would no longer permit Fenians the luxury of the "organization of a Government within the United States." The Brotherhood never had more than 45,000 active members and for most of its existence much fewer than that, but it had the moral support of vastly greater numbers. Over 100,000 persons gathered at the picnic grounds in Jones Woods, New York City, in March, 1866 to attend a Fenian rally, despite the intense opposition of Archbishop McCloskey. The wealthier Irish disliked the movement because it maintained the Irish as "a distinct nationality in the midst of the American population." But mass support came from the urban poor, who felt no scruples over the institutionalizing of the fact of alienation that was so manifest in their lives.

The Fenian movement reveals Irish-American nationalism in its finest flowering and full ambiguity. Rooted in the hard life of the immigrant, not in his Irish origins, nor in his religion, creator of its own sustaining myths, this peculiar nationalism sought to found its own "government" within the United States. Irish nationalism was its unifying cement and the establishment of Irish freedom ostensibly its purpose. But in fact Irish-American nationalism was directed toward American not Irish ends. A free Ireland would reflect glory on the Fenians, but of more immediate and practical value was use of the Brotherhood as an American pressure group. Herein lies the explanation for the curious frailty of the bellicose Fenian Brotherhood and the organizations which succeeded it. So long as they remained close to the warming sun of Irish nationalism they thrived; but when by the very law of their being they came into contact with the divisive realities of American life they inevitably disintegrated.

However strange their behavior, the Fenians left their mark on history. English policy in Ireland, complained a member of the House of Commons during the Fenian terror, has formed "a new Irish nation on the other side of the Atlantic, recast in the mould of Democracy, watching for an opportunity to strike a blow at the heart of the Empire." The military character of the Fenian threat stemmed from the experience of the Civil War. The more telling blows England would next receive would derive from the radical social thought engendered in Irish-America by the depression of the 1870's.

ORIGINS OF CATHOLIC

SOCIAL REFORM

IN THE UNITED STATES:

IDEOLOGICAL ASPECTS

Aaron I. Abell

[1949]

REPRESENTED by a small, pioneering religious group in the Anglo-American colonies, the Catholic faith was not transplanted in conspicuous degree to the United States until the nineteenth century. Mainly through immigration the Catholic population in the United States rose from a mere 50,000 in 1800 to more than twelve millions a century later. Though many believed that countless Catholics were lost in the transition process—the question has been endlessly debated—few denied the preëminent success of the Catholic Church in handling immigrants. Its swelling membership steadily augmented its influence on most phases of American life, including the social movements which played so large and significant a part in the nation's development during the nineteenth century.

In the earlier decades, Catholics as a group lent social movements little or no support. As chiefly immigrants in rising cities, Catholics stood to gain many material benefits from the pre-Civil War humanitarian crusade. They generally opposed the movement on the ground that it was tied up with the nativist agitation of the period. The descendants of colonial Catholics, a group influential and fairly numerous, also opposed reform. Living mostly in the southern and border states, these older Catholics often shared the animosity of their sections against Yankee uplift.

American Catholics were at all times influenced by the drift of Catholic thought and action in Europe. For the most part, European

Catholics were very conservative, resisting the advance of popular government and viewing the labor movement as a communist insurrection encouraged by anti-Christian liberals, Freemasons, and other designing men bent for their own profit on the overthrow of society. In the United States the clergy warmly approved their country's free political institutions, but in common with their fellow-ecclesiastics abroad they opposed militant social reform until late in the 1880's. They did not approve Catholic participation in the chief instruments of reform, namely, secular associations. The clergy feared that the worldly atmosphere and secretive methods of these bodies would wean Catholics away from the Church. Moreover, they looked upon most reform organizations as conspiracies against law and order. As for workingmen's associations, the opinion of James Roosevelt Bayley, Archbishop of Baltimore, was for a time widely shared by his fellow-Catholics. In 1874 he endorsed the recently founded Irish Catholic Benevolent Union because it "extends itself and exerts a proper influence guarding . . . from what is worse than secret societies—that is, the miserable associations called labor organizations. Their idea is Communistic," he believed, "and no Catholic with any idea of the spirit of his religion will encourage them." He was sure that labor unions had done more harm than good. It was no longer a question "of opposition to capital, but to government itself."

Yet, at the time these words were spoken, the clergy and laity were in the midst of a nation-wide crusade to improve the lot of the Catholic poor. Church councils and the religious press made clear during the 1860's and 1870's that the Church had become a predominantly urban institution and that cities threatened a large part of the Catholic body with physical and moral ruin. The colonizers, that is, those who continuously urged Irish Catholics to settle on the remaining frontier, also laid bare the evils to which Catholics in cities were exposed. It was not that many had abandoned the faith, wrote a distinguished leader, Bishop John Lancaster Spalding of Peoria; "our losses are chiefly to be sought for," he believed, "in the almost incredible infant mortality, in the high death rate among the immigrants themselves and in the fact that large numbers of them have not married at all." In the days before public health had made much headway the fear that Catholics were in danger of physical extermination was a real one and prompted far-reaching social efforts, notably in behalf of neglected children and the victims of the drink plague. Some congregations followed in the footsteps of the New York priests, F. H. Farrelly and Edward McGlynn, whose parishes provided for almost every need—moral and physical as well as spiritual. Since, however, the task was too heavy for ordinary congregations, Catholics over wide areas pooled their resources, founding great protectories and industrial schools and, through temperance societies and other associations, setting up many recreational centers to counteract the lure of the saloon and the gambling den.

These efforts won a helping hand from the Catholic societies which in those years were taking on national form: the German Catholic Central Society in 1855, the Society of St. Vincent de Paul in 1860, the Irish Catholic Benevolent Union in 1869, the Catholic Total Abstinence Union in 1872, and the Catholic Young Men's National Union in 1875. Besides promoting the special interests for which they were severally founded, these organizations, construing their work broadly, helped immigrants and the urban poor to make many difficult social adjustments and aided the Church to launch and support an ever-growing number of charitable institutions. Support also came from less obvious sources, for example, from Isaac T. Hecker, the ex-Transcendentalist, and his fellow priests in the Congregation of St. Paul the Apostle. Although founded, it was said, to "convert Mr. Emerson and his friends," the Paulists achieved their most striking success in those earlier years in the social field. Their journal, the *Catholic World,* first issued in 1865, occupied a foremost place in the renaissance of Catholic charities during the ensuing years.

As the welfare crusade gathered momentum it won favor with many Protestants, especially those devoted to theological or social liberalism. These persons were now willing to defend the Catholic Church against persecution on condition that it hold fast to its moral and reformatory work. This proffered alliance was eagerly accepted by many of the newer bishops—among them James Cardinal Gibbons of Baltimore, John J. Keane of Richmond, John Lancaster Spalding of Peoria, and John Ireland of St. Paul. These men, with growing approval of clergy and laity, insisted on the compatibility of the Catholic Church with modern civilization, that is, with late nineteenth century social liberalism, especially in its American form.

Thus motivated, these Catholics were in a position to bring the Church into co-operative relations with all the significant social movements of the later nineteenth century. First of all, they clarified the Church's attitude on the salient aspects of the labor questions, namely trade unionism and the right of the state to regulate private property in the public interest. The growing number of Catholics who after 1880 seriously investigated economic conditions concluded that social injustice as well as evil men caused industrial upheaval and conflict. Rather than being "miserable associations," effective trade unions now seemed necessary and harmless organizations for "praiseworthy" ends. This view, as is well known, became official when in 1886 all but two of the American archbishops acquiesced in the successful effort of Cardinal Gibbons to secure a suspension of Rome's decision against the Knights of Labor. At the instance of Elzear Alexandre Taschereau,

Archbishop of Quebec, Rome had twice condemned the Order. In his letter to Giovanni Cardinal Simeoni, Prefect of the Congregation of the Propaganda, Gibbons elaborated a superb defense of working-men's associations as necessary and legitimate means to the attainment of a better economic order. Gone now were the old feelings of apprehension and distrust. The Knights of Labor, he insisted, was not a secret society in the sense condemned by the Church; in associating with non-Catholic workingmen, Catholics did not imperil their faith but helped to defeat the machinations of atheists, communists, and anarchists; the bloodshed and violence, though deplorable, were only incidental—in fact, the Knights of Labor prevented far more violence than it provoked. Catholics must participate in secular trade unions, Gibbons pointed out, in order to secure material advantages: "labor is now so organized that without belonging to the organization, it is almost impossible to earn one's living."

Besides trade unionism, many Catholics came to believe that association to secure state intervention in the economic field was a requirement of justice. The bitter controversy provoked by Father McGlynn's support of Henry George's crusade against land monopoly encouraged Catholics to familiarize themselves with the Church's traditional doctrines concerning the public regulation of property. McGlynn and his devoted following insisted that "private property in land" outraged Christian ethics. But his religious superior, Archbishop Michael A. Corrigan, denounced the proposal that the state confiscate economic rent as rank socialism, ordered McGlynn to cease propagating his views, and on his refusal to do so suspended him from his priestly functions for insubordination. Later McGlynn was excommunicated by Rome for not going to Rome to explain his conduct. In the end, however, Corrigan was overruled by the Pope's representative, Archbishop Francesco Satolli, who in 1893 lifted the sentence against McGlynn on the ground that "there is nothing" in his opinions "contrary to the faith and teachings of the Church." McGlynn's views were of little moment in themselves; not many progressive Catholics accepted his entire program, regarding it as doctrinaire and unworkable. The significant thing was that the controversy convinced them that a moderate amount of state intervention was quite legitimate, the principle being the scholastic one that while private property is a natural right its exercise may be regulated by public authority in the common interest. Laws effectively controlling corporate monopolies, eliminating child labor, wiping out rotten tenements, and curtailing the liquor traffic—these illustrated the approved type of state intervention.

The changing attitudes toward trade unionism and related issues convinced Bishop Bernard J. McQuaid of Rochester and many others of like disposition that a dangerous brand of liberalism had invaded the

Church. But persons of more discerning mind esteemed effective measures in behalf of labor to be necessary applications to the present day of the Church's age-old philosophy of justice and charity—an interpretation immensely strengthened by Leo XIII's labor encyclical of 1891. The American Church authorities did not, however, acquiesce in economic reform on grounds entirely or even primarily of justice and charity. They were motivated chiefly by practical considerations of a social and political character. They well knew that workingmen in vast numbers would leave the Church if it ignored their claims to economic justice. But even more they feared a second Know-Nothing persecution if they interfered with the liberty of Catholics to participate in social reform movements. Gibbons made much of this in his letter on the Knights of Labor, warning the Roman authorities that the "accusation of being un-American—that is to say, alien to our national spirit—is the most powerful weapon which the enemies of the Church can employ against her." Considerations such as these defeated the efforts of Archbishop Corrigan to have Henry George's *Progress and Poverty* placed on the Index of Prohibited Books and secured McGlynn's restoration. The charges against McGlynn, "as they are understood by the American people," wrote a Brooklyn priest in 1886, "raise the question of the right of the citizen to express his views on all questions that are non-essential." Cardinal Gibbons explained with his usual insight that the Church's teachings on socialism and private property were not directly involved in the controversy and that the fate of the single tax must rest with the whole people judging its expediency and justice as freely as any other proposed public policy. Or, as the *Catholic Standard* of Philadelphia put it, to forbid Catholics to participate in the discussion and decision would be to acknowledge "the truth of the accusation by our enemies that Catholics are not and cannot be truly loyal to the civil authorities of their country."

Much more than the labor question, non-economic social issues obliged Catholics through liberal action to appease public opinion in the later nineteenth century. The reputation of the Church had been badly damaged by the fact that so many Catholics were personally implicated in notorious evils, notably the lawless liquor traffic and corrupt city politics. By the same process of mental association, non-Catholic Americans in large numbers also blamed the Church for the alleged failings and crimes of immigrants against whom opposition and prejudice dangerously revived during the 1880's. As if to make matters worse, various groups of recent immigrants from continental Europe and French Canada repudiated the Americanization policy which had been largely responsible, the hierarchy believed, for such peace and prosperity as the Church enjoyed in the United States. Under the leadership of Peter Paul Cahensly, the Prussian statesman who headed the St. Raphael's Society for the Protection of Catholic Emigrants, disgruntled foreigners, here and abroad, presented to the Holy See in 1891 the Lucerne Memorial which claimed that sixteen million Catholic immigrants had lost their faith because of the American episcopate's studied negligence, and they demanded bishops and priests of their own nationality to safeguard religion through the perpetuation of foreign customs and speech.

In the view of many Cahenslyites, the United States was not a nation, only a juxtaposition of jarring colonies from abroad. Others admitted that American nationality was a powerful reality but denied the right of Catholics to share in it. By habitually referring to English-speaking Catholics as "Irish," they sought to obscure the fact that the majority of Catholics in the United States were Americans by birth, education, and desire. Not sure that a true American could also be a good Catholic, the Cahenslyites played into the hands of the nativist agitators who, from the opposite angle, preached precisely the same doctrine. Together and unrestrained, the two groups might well have encompassed the Church's ruin. Should the Cahenslyite idea prevail, the rapidly Americanizing immigrant element would soon apostatize and the stream of converts, many won by Father Hecker's assurance that Catholicism confirmed and strengthened American civilization, would dry up at its source.

By isolating Catholics from the great body of American citizens, Cahenslyism would have put an end to Catholic participation in social movements. "The foreign party," Father George Zurcher observed, "is afraid of danger [to faith and morals] in almost any association of non-Catholics." In order to serve the reform cause, as well as for other reasons, the friends of social liberalism swung into action. Under the guidance of Archbishop Ireland, leading laymen assembled two Catholic congresses, one at Baltimore in 1889 and the other at Chicago in 1893. Organized on a non-racial basis, these widely attended congresses thoroughly discussed the relation of the Church to the social and intellectual movements of the day. They explained and reaffirmed the Church's progressive stand on trade unionism and state intervention in industry. Nothing was more earnestly insisted upon "than the compatibility of the patriotic profession with the religious one." With scarcely less emphasis the congresses pointed out that Catholics acting alone could accomplish little in the field of social reform. Therefore, they sanctioned co-operation with non-Catholics "in general philanthropic and reformatory movements" and for shaping "civil legislation for the public weal" in matters affecting child labor, Sunday observance, and the liquor traffic. These resolutions—"Freemasonry resolutions" the Cahenslyites scornfully pronounced them—furthered the liberal purpose of dissociating the Church in the public mind from opposition to the labor movement, "foreignism," and other evils that hindered Catholic progress.

This applied with special force to the liquor traffic and its interference with a Christian observance of the Sunday. Already, in 1884, the Third Plenary Council of Baltimore had condemned the continental Sunday and admonished Catholics "engaged in the sale of liquors to abandon . . . the dangerous traffic and to embrace a more becoming way of making a living." At the Baltimore lay congress the journalist, Manly Tello of Cleveland, in a paper denouncing Sunday opening of saloons, beer-gardens, and theatres, explained that "there is a distinctive American way, and a people has a right to its own individuality." If within Catholic lines, "there are two ways to do a thing, and one is exclusively American, for that very reason," he contended, "that way should be universally adopted." In keeping with this theory of cultural nationalism, the Baltimore congress resolved to "seek alliance with non-Catholics for proper Sunday observance. Without going over to the Judaic Sabbath, we can," the congress affirmed, "bring the masses over to the moderation of the Christian Sunday." To this end, the sale of intoxicating liquors on Sunday should be prohibited by law. The corrupting influence of saloons on politics, and the crime and pauperism resulting from excessive drinking also justified legislative restriction "which we can aid in procuring," the congress further resolved, "by joining our influence with that of the other enemies of intemperance."

A surprisingly large number of Catholics were now ready to act along these lines. In order to convince the country that the admonition of the Third Plenary Council was seriously meant, Bishop John A. Watterson of Columbus, Ohio, withdrew approval in 1894 from all diocesan societies having liquor dealers or saloon keepers among their officers, further decreeing that in the future these persons be denied membership in the societies. On appeal, the ruling was sustained by the Apostolic delegate, Archbishop Satolli, whose action was widely hailed as an official condemnation of the saloon evil by the Catholic Church in the United States. Although no other bishop followed Watterson's example, it carried great moral weight, persuading many of the more timid Catholics to enlist in the ranks of the anti-saloon forces. On their own initiative, most of the Catholic societies, beginning with the Catholic Benevolent Legion and the Society of St. Vincent de Paul, excluded liquor dealers. Likewise, in order to conciliate public opinion, the Benedictines at St. Vincent's Abbey at Beatty, Pennsylvania, finally stopped brewing their long-famous "St. Vincent's Beer." The most dramatic incident occurred in 1895 during the convention in New York of the Catholic Total Abstinence Union. At its mass meeting a Tammany politician, in order to test Catholic sentiment, suggested that after the next election the excise and Sunday closing laws would no longer be enforced. Hissed and booed by the vast audience, he "retired in complete discomfiture." This attitude, reported Godkin's *Nation,* revealed the existence of a great power on the side of law observance and a quiet Sunday. The *Catholic Review* of New York was sure that the episode "will help to relieve the Church from the unjustly inflicted odium on the part of non-Catholic Christians."

Even more important for the future, Catholics also entered into co-operative relations with charity organization societies in leading cities. At its convention of 1895 the Society of St. Vincent de Paul recognized "the importance of co-operating with outside organizations for the general good when such co-operation does not conflict with the rules" governing Catholic charities. Since no conflict actually existed, co-operation was carried forward in the ensuing years to mutual advantage. "The relief of suffering humanity, whatever its creed or race," editorialized the *Catholic World,* "is a platform broad enough for all." The new policy would do more to promote Christian unity than tons of pamphleteering.

Catholic interest in social movements during the later nineteenth century is best understood as one aspect—perhaps the most important aspect—of the process by which a uniquely authoritarian Church accommodated itself to a uniquely free, liberal, and individualistic society. Throughout the century dominant public opinion viewed the growing Church with a latent hostility which at periodic intervals broke out into open persecution. In the hope of disarming opposition, an influential group of clerical and lay leaders urged their fellow-Catholics to affiliate with social movements. They discerned no conflict between Catholicism and liberalism rightly understood. What was being introduced into the Church, they reiterated, was a liberal policy, not a liberal theology. On the other hand, a large number of Catholics, including many not under Cahensly influence, feared that liberalism in one field implied liberalism in all others. Moreover, some of the conservatives wished to maintain not only the Catholic faith but Catholic traditions, the outmoded ones as well as the necessary and useful ones. For this reason they could scarcely visualize the possibility of legitimate change within the Catholic system. They had failed to differentiate the labor movement from socialism and anarchy, and the temperance crusade from an effort to impose a Puritanic moral code. They were also repelled by the patriotic emphasis of the social movement, its exaltation of science, its eagerness to share influence in Church work with the laity and its willingness to co-operate with Protestants.

The conservative opposition softened, however, under the impact of argument and circumstance. The liberal social philosophers, especially Archbishops Ireland and Keane, differentiated the two elements in the Church's constitution—the one essential and divine, the other human and accidental. The first must never change; the second must change in order to keep the Church abreast of the age. "Progress," asserted Ireland, "is the law of God's creation." God had implanted the desire for improvement in the hearts of men. The vast material and scientific progress of the nineteenth century was an essentially divine event—a providential step in the onward march of humanity. The new age had intensified, however, some of the old evils such as pride, thoughtlessness, and indifference to the laws of justice. By a social program the Church was trying to balance material and intellectual progress with a corresponding development of moral and spiritual progress. This was what Ireland and his friends called liberalism—a true liberalism as against a false liberalism which denied the primacy of divine authority in human affairs.

Practice as well as theory seemed to justify the liberal social position. Although anti-Catholic movements continued, the Church's social program had taken the venom out of the latest one—the A.P.A. crusade. As for any tendencies toward heresy in the social movement, that fear was dispelled by Pope Leo XIII's letter on Americanism which, while condemning liberal theological tenets, distinguished American social policy from the heresy. Their suspicions allayed, the conservatives soon capitulated to the reform forces. They now bowed to the inevitable Americanization of the immigrant and conceded that social reform through co-operation with non-Catholics was a legitimate part of the Church's work. At the turn of the century they actually assumed leadership of the movement in one of its important aspects. Thus they launched the drive to federate Catholic societies, the success of which in the early twentieth century put flesh and sinew on firmly-held principles of justice and charity.

The new agitation proved all the more necessary in view of the limitations surrounding the movement in the later nineteenth century. Although Catholics, besides accepting the idea of social reform in the context of Americanization, untiringly reiterated that the battle of Cardinal Gibbons in behalf of the Knights of Labor mainly determined Leo XIII to issue *Rerum novarum,* they did surprisingly little in the way of systematic study and effort to implement that great charter of social justice. Several distinguished clerics, some high in the counsels of the liberal group, refused even to discuss the encyclical, esteeming its teachings to be dangerous and revolutionary or to have no bearing on the happy American scene. Other Catholics, though publicly praising the Pope's document, failed to emphasize its socially transforming purpose. Thus William J. Onahan, reputedly one of the leading lay Catholic liberals in the United States, found in the Leonine teachings a great and comforting "bulwark" of the *status quo.* "An evil spirit seems to have taken possession of the masses—a rage against capital and authority," wrote this Chicago philanthropist and public servant to his friend, Monsignor O'Connell, following the Pullman strike of 1894. "It is the Catholic Church chiefly," he continued, "that will be the bulwark of society and even of governments in trials like the present and Pope Leo has made the attitude of the Church invulnerable at all points."

This philosophy of labor which recalls the earlier conservatism of Archbishop Bayley suggests that Catholic affiliation with social movements in the later nineteenth century stemmed more from a desire to Americanize the attitudes of the Church and her children than from a genuine interest in social justice. Moreover, such undiluted economic reformism as Catholics displayed during the 1880's waned considerably by the century's turn. Catholic public men now loved to quote Mark Hanna's defense of the Catholic Church as "a great conservative force," as if their Church was predestined to be a conservative and not a progressive influence in American society. The waxing strength of industrial and financial capitalism during the closing years of the century, the boundless self-assurance of its leaders and their power, demonstrated on many occasions during the years from 1880 to 1900, to keep labor in leash—these things were accepted by many moulders of Catholic opinion as desirable and permanent features of the social landscape. As for the countless workers in Catholic charity, they continued to be unduly impressed with the more immediate causes of human distress. In 1865 the Society of St. Vincent de Paul had reported to Paris that intemperance "is the source of the misery for at least three-fourths of the families we are called upon to visit and relieve." After three decades a broader outlook was not apparent, the Church's temperance experts stating in 1897 "that four-fifths of the social degeneracy, including pauperism, criminality and insanity, is the direct result of intemperance."

In reality, however, the Church's charity by 1900 was undergoing transformation. Although almsgiving and institutional relief were still openly esteemed and practiced with apostolic fervor, Catholic social work was increasingly mindful of the labor movement and, to a lesser degree, of social science as well. In dealing with the perennial liquor plague, the many reformers who looked to Archbishop Ireland for leadership, while stressing the personal causes of intemperance, correlated their agitation with the labor question. Only a sober working class, they insisted, would have sufficient strength of moral character to defeat oppressive capitalists and thus emancipate the toiling masses. The effort to avert social crisis by reforming individuals greatly expanded not alone temperance work but all Catholic charity. Catholics increasingly realized, however, that without improved labor conditions Christian charity could not fully achieve its ends. Clearly indicative of this broader view was the mass meeting in March, 1897, at Lenox Hall, New York City, under the auspices of the Archdiocesan Union of Temperance Societies. Presided over by Archbishop Corrigan, the convention, with the "social betterment of the masses" as its purpose, discussed not temperance but Leo XIII's great encyclical on the condition of labor, the salient features of which were thoroughly explained and liberally interpreted.

The Lenox Hall gathering may be taken to mark the definite emergence of the integrated conception of Catholic social reform—of a Catholic sociology which in the next generation revolutionized Catholic charity. But the newer trend must not be allowed to obscure the fact that in the later nineteenth century Catholic affiliation with social movements was mainly an aspect of the Americanization policy and, as such, was prompted less by arguments based on justice and charity than by a desire to appease public opinion and to ward off persecution. Though largely negative and superficial to a degree, the movement had much to its credit. It won for all Catholics the right to participate in social reform movements. It dissociated the good name of the Church from the evils and scandals in which so many Catholics were involved. It forged a method which enabled Catholics without danger to faith and morals to co-operate with non-Catholics for great social ends. These developments, adjusting the Church on the social side to American institutions and environment, laid the foundation for the broad and constructive achievements of the twentieth century.

BISHOP JOHN LANCASTER

SPALDING AND THE

CATHOLIC MINORITY

(1877-1908)

Thomas T. McAvoy, C.S.C.

[1950]

ROMAN Catholicism in the United States has produced able leaders among its clergy and laymen during the first decades of the twentieth century, but most of them seem to lack the lustre and verve of the Catholic leaders during the waning decades of the nineteenth century. The lay leadership which produced John Gilmary Shea, William J. Onahan, Henry F. Brownson, Patrick V. Hickey, and Henry Spaunhorst had strong backing from such clergymen as James Cardinal Gibbons, John Ireland, John J. Keane, Bernard McQuaid, and Michael A. Corrigan. But the intellectual leader of American Catholicism during the late nineteenth century was John Lancaster Spalding, Bishop of Peoria,[1] and twentieth-century Catholicism has not produced his counterpart.

Intellectual leadership is not hereditary, yet among the Catholic minority in the United States the most substantial cultural leadership has been furnished by the Anglo-American group of Maryland and Kentucky. Other national and racial strains have intermingled with the original English group and many of this descent have rendered their highest service far from Leonardstown or Bardstown. John Lancaster Spalding, born in Lebanon, Kentucky, in 1840, was a member of this group by both paternal and maternal ancestry. Also, from Kentucky he went back to Maryland to Mt. St. Mary's at Emmitsburg

[1] John Lancaster Spalding (1840–1916) acquired the title of Archbishop when appointed to the titular see of Scythopolis in 1908, but is usually called Bishop to distinguish him from his uncle Archbishop Martin John Spalding of Baltimore.

for some of his education. His later training he received at Louvain in Belgium and in Rome and Germany.

When Spalding returned to Kentucky after the Civil War he soon became a notable leader among the younger clergy of the country. He was a forceful speaker, with a dignified bearing and smooth pleasant countenance. He had read widely in several languages, although his thought was eminently American. There was much of the Yankee Emerson in Spalding's appeal to American Catholics to make the best of their minority share of the country's resources, but where Emerson's thought wanders off into an obscure pantheism, Spalding found in everything proof of a personal God who is above, not part of, the human mind. His language was direct American English with each word weighted with meaning. His style, at least in his later writings, has been described as lapidary and each sentence was a carefully hewn stone—so carefully carved as to distract from the whole of many of his essays. Some of these sentences he never formed into essays, being content to publish them as aphorisms.

Spalding returned to the United States at a time when his native Kentucky was enduring the turmoil of Reconstruction after the Civil War. Of his experiences during the next few years we know little. He acted as theologian to Archbishop Norbert Blanchet of Oregon in the Second Plenary Council of Baltimore in 1866 and was one of three priests chosen to address the bishops in public assemblies. His progressive character was manifested by his volunteering to found the first Negro parish in Louisville in accordance with the decrees of the Council. By his labors and his begging he completed the parish buildings in three years. Upon the death of his uncle, Archbishop Martin John Spalding of Baltimore, Father Isaac Hecker, to whom the Archbishop had left his papers, invited the nephew to come to New York and prepare a biography of his uncle. He accepted the invitation but behind the move was a definite disagreement with the new bishop of Louisville, George William McCloskey, who felt that the Spaldings were trying to exert too much influence in the diocese. The biography is the best written of the earlier American biographies although deficient according to present day standards of critical history.

When Spalding completed the biography he did not return to Louisville but remained as assistant pastor at St. Michael's Church in New York. Undoubtedly this service among the Irish immigrants had an important influence on his later writings and with his Kentucky background gave him active experience among the two chief elements of the American Catholic minority—the rural, frontier, and native American Catholics and the newly arrived and non-English immigrants. Mingled with these experiences in the making of the mind of Spalding were the effects of one of the finest university educations possible in Europe for an American ecclesiastic of the 1860's. Perhaps no one has embodied better the cultural nucleus of American Catholicism. His talents were soon recognized in his election to the newly established see of Peoria in 1876. He was consecrated by John Cardinal McCloskey in New York in May, 1877.

Bishop Spalding remained as bishop of Peoria for more than twenty-five years, until ill health caused him to resign in 1908, and he gave his new diocese an active and progressive administration. He increased the number of the clergy, built churches, schools, academies, and colleges, practicing as well as his means permitted the high ideals he proposed in his lectures and essays. But he did not confine his activities to parochial or diocesan functions. His interests were definitely national in scope and particularly in the field of education. Almost from the start of his episcopate he was a frequent visitor at the nearest Catholic college, Notre Dame, where he read some of his finest essays as commencement orator and where he enjoyed the companionship of Fathers Edward Sorin, Daniel Hudson, John A. Zahm and Thomas E. Walsh. He joined with Archbishop John Ireland and William J. Onahan in the formation of the Irish Catholic Colonization Association, whose aim was to enable the Irish Catholic immigrant to escape the slums of the eastern seaboard and to occupy the new farmlands of Minnesota, Nebraska, and Arkansas. Following in the footsteps of his uncle, Archbishop Martin John Spalding, he became the chief proponent of the establishment of a central Catholic university. He was soon recognized by Catholics and non-Catholics alike as one of the country's leading theorists in the field of education. As one of the more progressive group of bishops in the American hierarchy he was notable for his association with non-Catholics in promoting social welfare, in his denying the need for conflict between science and religion, and for his advocacy of women's rights. Columbia and Western Reserve Universities conferred on him honorary doctorates and President Theodore Roosevelt made him a member of the significant arbitration commission in the anthracite coal strike of 1902.

In his writings and lectures, while definitely conscious of the Catholic minority, he found no real conflict between his loyalty to the Church and his zeal for the social betterment and cultural progress of the whole nation. His field was not theology, but humanistic culture and social problems. He had a definite concept of the role of the Catholic minority in the United States although he seemed to believe that the barriers against Catholicism in the United States were fast falling to the ground. He seemed to believe that Americans were willing to hear the Catholic message if the Catholics themselves would live the full Catholic life.

If ever and everywhere men of exceptional intellectual and moral strength were needed, they are needed by American Catholics, thrown as a minority burdened with many disadvantages, into the midst of the eager self-confident and all prevailing democracy of the new world. Here the church lives and acts in virtue of its own power, neither having nor desiring the support of the state, content to lack the privileges which in other ages resulted from social conditions unlike our own. We could not have these privileges if we would, and could we have them they would hurt, not help us. It is enough that we have the rights which in a free country belong to all alike—freedom to teach, to publish, to organize, to worship.

The Catholic minority, much divided during his episcopal career on nationalistic lines and too much interested in the immediate problems of material welfare, did not pay much attention to his majestic plan and has not fulfilled the role he hoped for it.

Spalding's first national activity as Bishop consisted chiefly in promoting the return of the Catholic slum dwellers to rural life. After a few years in New York he seems to have been repelled by the unhappy conditions of the Catholic immigrants in the slums of the cities along the eastern coast. Some politically-minded Catholics might rejoice at the political influence of the compact immigrant vote in the cities. Spalding thought otherwise. He apologized for the fact that he, who was not Irish, was talking to the Irish on the problem. He seems to have had no national or racial prejudices. He could have added that as a westerner from Kentucky and Illinois he knew of the happier and healthier condition of those Catholic immigrants who owned their own farms and built their own schools in the rural regions of the Middle West. His arguments were very blunt.

. . . The traditional conceit that Protestant nations are superior to the Catholic is kept alive and strengthened by the contrast which exists between Protestants and Catholics in these commercial centres and manufacturing towns. It is, of course, easy enough to explain that the Church is in no way responsible for this; but "things seen are mightier than things heard," and the prejudiced eye accepts the fact that pleases it, and asks for no explanations. . . . Who can travel through New England without being forced to recognize the existence of two distinct and separate peoples there? The one has wealth and social position; the other does the drudgery and hard work. If nothing else had been left for our people to do but to make themselves the slaves and servants of others, we might accept the humiliating experiences in silence; but to congratulate ourselves upon the good there is in it seems to be little less than folly. For myself, I cannot see the jewel in the toad's head. . . .

Spalding in his essay on *The Religion Mission of the Irish People*, published in 1880, frankly advocated "a redistribution of our Catholic population." His condemnation of city life may seem a bit overdrawn, but he had observed during his New York curateship the slum conditions of seventy years ago. He foresaw, with far better vision than some other Catholic clergymen, that there was little hope that these slum dwellers would ever greatly improve their condition—although improved sanitation and communications did effect higher standards later. He was aware that the urban population was a dying population.

> It is constantly asserted that the natural increase of the Catholic immigrants would give us today a population of not less than twelve millions, whereas our numbers do not exceed seven millions. Therefore, it is argued, five millions, or nearly one-half, have fallen from the Church. Nothing could be more fallacious. Comparatively few have abandoned the faith and our losses are chiefly to be sought for in the almost incredible infant mortality among our people, in the high death-rate among the immigrants themselves, and in the fact that large numbers of them have not married at all . . . the fountain-head of the evil, compared with which all other causes of loss are insignificant, was the fatal and never sufficiently to be deplored concentration of the Irish immigrant in the great cities, the factory towns and the mining districts.

To this he added the observation that the Irish by their previous experiences in Ireland had fitted themselves only for rural living.

He blamed much of the sufferings of these urban immigrants on their political activity. "A saint or a sage could barely touch the pitch of American ward politics without defilement; and for the laboring classes they are generally a school of immorality and degradation. . . ." Neither did he think that the newly formed "trades-unions and other societies, the tendency of which in the United States will be more and more in the direction of Communism" would be able permanently to better the condition of the operatives and laborers and secure "the high wages of the past." "If American, or English, or Irish operatives cannot live on wages which will permit American manufacturers to run their business profitably, their places will be taken by Canadian, French, or Belgian workmen. . . . The condition, then, of the Irish Catholics in the commercial centres and factory towns is unfortunate, not merely or chiefly on account of their present misery, but because so long as they remain where they are now there is no hope of a brighter future for them or their children." Spalding later was to say that labor unions, like industrial corporations, had come to stay, but then, in his appeal for settlers in the western colonies, he did not want the immigrant to place too much hope that the unions would be able to change the sadder aspects of urban life. There is essential sincerity in his rejection of the optimism of the immigrant who tried to make his future in the larger cities.

> We have been living on borrowed capital unwisely invested, and there is little risk in asserting that unless vast changes in the territorial distribu-

tion of our population take place, the American Church is today relatively more powerful than she will be twenty-five years or half a century hence. I know this is not the popular view with us, but the question is whether or not it is the true view. We Catholics who speak the English language have grown to feel a kind of impatient resentment even when people tell the truth about us, if it is not altogether pleasant. . . .

In this his first direct appeal to the Catholic minority, Bishop Spalding felt called upon to defend his attempts to rationalize the Catholic position in the United States. "We are living in an age in which the unconscious evolution of society is fast giving place to its conscious development. Wholly different was the era in which the Church presided over the formation of the peoples that have grown to be the modern world." Catholics, Spalding warned, were still waiting for unconscious processes to solve their difficulties and to create a Catholic university. "They do not read aright the signs of the times. A university will no more grow up of itself in our day than will a new language. . . . The tendency of civilization is to increase the self-consciousness both of the individual and of the social body." Spalding pointed for an example to the results accomplished by anti-slavery societies in the United States in eliminating slavery. He did find an increased self-consciousness in the Church in the societies being formed for the propagation of the faith in mission lands, in the spread of Catholic literature, and in the increase in aid for the poor and the young. "It must be confessed, however, that Catholics have not yet fully recognized the significance of the social phase upon which we are entering." He blamed Catholics' "necessary and essential conservatism" for their failure to utilize the opportunities in the country.

There is no part of the world in which there are at present fairer opportunities for Catholics to do a great and lasting work for the Church, for her children, and for the age than here in the United States. . . . The anti-Catholic prejudices which we inherited from England still linger, indeed, in the popular mind, but they are constantly growing weaker in the face of the fact, which is day by day gaining recognition, that Catholics form an integral part of the American people; and there is a common-sense view of the case very generally received, to the effect that, apart from the merits of the controversy about the abuses and tendencies to which the Church is supposed to be committed in the past, we Americans are living in a new world and under new social conditions, and ought not to permit the animosities and quarrels of ages that are gone to enter as a disturbing element into our life.

However different he was in temperament from his friend, Archbishop John Ireland of St. Paul, he agreed with him that Catholics must enter wholeheartedly into the social problems of the day.

397

In discussing the position and future of Catholics in the United States, Spalding did not write as a theologian. In his own diocese as Bishop of Peoria he was concerned with the technical doctrines of Catholic faith and practice, with building churches, and administering the sacraments. His published writings, on the contrary, are so wholly concerned with the problems of the human mind and with natural virtue as to draw occasional criticisms from fellow Catholics that he spoke too much like some of the agnostic writers he quoted so frequently. In his essay on "Agnosticism," however, he rejected the philosophy of these agnostics, showing the futility of their doctrines and the impossibility of real culture without religion. One can only surmise what effects the condemnation of modernism and the revival of Eucharistic devotion in the daily lives of the American people under Pope Pius X would have had on the thoughts and theories of Spalding. They came after his active career. Spalding belongs to the age of Pope Leo XIII, to the early Progressive Era in the United States. He was a "progressive" bishop with John Ireland, James Gibbons, and John J. Keane, and could be said to have held many of the ideas of Ireland, Keane and Hecker which French theologians elaborated into the imaginary heresy of "Americanism" so vigorously attacked by European conservatives at the turn of the century. But aside from these imperfections which he shared with these religious leaders of the day, Spalding remains as the deepest American Catholic thinker, and his pleadings with American Catholics must be weighed not in terms of theological writings, which they were not, but in terms of humanistic, cultural, and social theories, which retain even today a timeliness that is remarkable.

Basic in Spalding's thought was a social mindedness which was quite common among the reformers of the late nineteenth century. He felt that there was enough of this world's goods available to guarantee the removal of the worst social evils of the country. Coupled with this social-mindedness was an optimistic faith in the goodness of democratic Americans closely akin to Emerson's optimism.

> We have become more humane than men have ever been, and accept more fully the duty and the task of extending the domain of justice, of goodness, and of truth. The aim of our civilization is not merely to instruct the ignorant, but to make ignorance impossible; not merely to feed the hungry, but to do away with famine; not merely to visit the captive, but to make captivity the means of his regeneration. . . . While we eagerly strive to control and repress every kind of moral evil, we feel that society itself is responsible for sin and crime, and that social and political conditions and constitutions must change, until the weak and the heavy-laden are protected from the heartlessness of the strong and the fortunate.

Yet Spalding did not have any great faith in political reformers. He spoke contemptuously of the "administrative lie" by which officials denied the existence of evils they did not choose to correct.

> . . . but there is still left in the mass of the people a deep moral earnestness, which, if it can be called into action, may lift the whole nation to higher and purer life. Our two great parties are the principal obstacle in the way of such a movement. It is not possible to arouse the American people thoroughly, except through political agitation, and both of these parties—which have become simply mills to grind the people's corn to make bread for officeholders—oppose the whole weight of their organized power to every honest effort to bring about a moral reformation.

The problems he wanted the new party to solve were chiefly the problems of public education, which he thought should be religious, the liquor evil, woman suffrage, and the licentious and obscene press.

Because he abstained from strictly theological discussions, Bishop Spalding's writings seem often addressed to the American people generally rather than to any Catholic minority but in this can be seen a fundamental tenet in his theory of the role of the Catholic minority. Catholic belief and practice were for him no hindrances to full participation in American citizenship; rather he felt that Catholics would contribute to the perfection of American civilization by their insistence on their Catholic faith. The culture he praised found its perfection in Christ and without religion there could be no real culture. He seems at times very close to the doctrines of several continental apologists of the nineteenth century who found the Christian faith so reasonable as to be demanded by reason independently of the supernatural. His optimism about the future of Catholicism in America was based on his conviction that this reasonableness of the religious and Catholic view of the universe would force acceptance on the newly educated peoples of our democracy. All the universe spoke to him of God and he felt that the more complete man's enjoyment of the things of the mind the nearer would he draw to God and to the attainment of his proper destiny. Most of the published writings of Spalding are discussions of ways and means whereby Americans, and particularly the American Catholics, can attain this cultural ideal.

In his appeals to the Irish in the cities to move out into the new lands of the west and his condemnation of social evils of the city, Spalding seems to be interested chiefly in material welfare but actually he deplored the trend in the United States to decide public questions by materialistic standards. He foresaw the current conflict between capitalism and communism far better than some understand the fact as it has come about today. "So long as our whole national life struggle continues to be carried on around this single point of finance, what hope is there of avoiding fatal conflicts? The rich will worship their god Mammon alone and the poor will plot and scheme to shatter the idol; mechanical contrivances, such as arbitration boards and legislative enactments, will leave the root of the evil untouched. . . . Our politics, our literature, our whole national life, must be more concerned for man than his money." The evil of both Marxist socialism and extreme industrialism with their materialist ideals, he foretold, was that in both cases the liberty and dignity of man would be lost and those cultural ideals which he considered the worthwhile values would be sacrificed. Thus, basically, Spalding found religion essential for human welfare, for the dignity of man, and for the proper understanding of the world in which man lives.

> Now the Christian life, the Christian character, is the most vital social influence, the most enduring social bond. It is this that has made possible what is best in our actual world; it is this that must foster, sustain, and perfect the individual and the family, the Church and the State, if we are to preserve and increase our rich inheritance, and hasten the coming of the kingdom of God in ourselves and in the world around us.

Spalding's strictures on the evils of city life and his praise of rural independence were made with full consciousness that the urbanization of America was permanent.

> On the other hand, industrial progress promotes the formation of vast centres of population, in which life, physical and moral, degenerates, and which consequently are a menace to the highest interests of humanity. . . . But why insist? These populous centres exist and are growing, and they are destined to continue to exist and to grow; and since the law of contrast runs through all things, in them, with all the sin and misery, there is also found the truest wisdom and the most genuine virtue. They furnish opportunity not to the incompetent and the vicious alone, but to the capable, the good, and the loving as well; and it is on these that the salvation of the city depends as it is to them that its development and prosperity are due. . . . The malady from which we suffer is most acute in the municipality, but it is the result of a diathesis. We have all gone astray; we have all believed in gold more than in God, in matter more than in mind. We have all learned to say one thing and do another; to love lies rather than truth; and, like all the sick, we turn from those who could cut deep and administer radical remedies.

To Spalding the solution of the social evils of modern industrialism must be sought on a religious basis.

> After the things of absolute and everlasting import, after God and the soul's immortal destiny, that which most vitally and profoundly concerns awakened minds is the social problem, which touches us as closely as God's

being and our eternal welfare; for only those know Him and love their own souls who strive in all earnestness to found on earth a heavenly kingdom wherein each one shall have opportunity to work and to grow, wherein truth, justice, and love shall prevail.

Spalding claimed that despite the marvelous mechanical and industrial successes "a cry of discontent and distress was raised by the toiling masses. Our political institutions had failed to secure equal opportunities to all." A man who sternly rejects Marxian Socialism as slavery, Spalding condemns with similar severity the owners of great fortunes.

> The money power already dictates in a large measure the policies of our national, State, and municipal legislative bodies. It lies at the root of the all-pervading political corruption. It enables the multi-millionaires and the trusts to make or evade the laws. Justice is interpreted to mean the interests of capital. The rights of industrialism and commercialism are given priority over the rights of man. The money power owns the most potent organs of public opinion. . . . To pay dividends on the over-capitalized stock, the wages of laborers must be kept as low as possible.

Spalding rejected anarchy as the means of social improvement because anarchism "is an insanity whose only issue is crime." Likewise he rejected Marxism.

> As set forth by Marx and its other ablest exponents, it rests on a basis of materialism and atheism, and is the foe, not merely of the fundamental economic institutions, but of the Church and family as well. . . . The evils springing from capitalism and free competition are great, but not so great as those which the domination of a single industrial principle would cause. In a socialistic state the whole people would sink into a mechanical somnolent life, or the gathering discontent would break forth into revolutions which could be quelled only by a military despotism. . . . The radical blunder of socialism lies in thinking that what a civilized race most craves is food and other things which the animal needs and delights in, and not freedom and the wrestling of the soul to give life a fuller spiritual import and value.

But Spalding was not unaware of the factors that were tempting the workers to Socialism.

> Though we cannot accept the fundamental principles of Socialism and Collectivism as true, and though we are persuaded that society cannot successfully be established upon them as a basis there are none the less bonds of sympathy between us and the Socialists. The desire, which in the case of many of them is doubtless earnest and sincere, to come to the relief of the poor, to find some means by which their lot may be less miserable, springs from a divine impulse. It is Christian and human and the anti-religious spirit of modern Socialism comes from an unphilosophic and unhistoric view of the forces which create civilization and give promise of

a better future. . . . Those who lose faith and hope and love, lose patience too; and it is futile to preach the sacredness of wealth to the poor when their miserable lives are the sad witnesses to the immortality of the means by which it is acquired.

Most of Spalding's writings, however, were not directed against the evils of modern society. He devoted his talents rather to the propagation of the Christian doctrine that the body is more important than the raiment, the mind more important than the body, and the soul more important than the mind.

> A decent physical existence for those who labor for employers should be considered a first charge on business; and their wages should be sufficient to make it possible for them to found a family under conditions compatible with right human life, and favorable, therefore, to mental, moral, and religious improvement. . . . The living wage is a postulate of justice, but man does not live on bread alone. We may not exclude religion from ethics, nor ethics from economics.

Once man could be assured the goods necessary to attain the full dignity of a human being Spalding wanted those higher faculties of mind and heart developed in that great process he called education. This education begins in the home and in the family. His chief strictures against industrialism condemned its tendency to destroy the home. The school was merely a continuation of the process that began in the home and without which the school was destined to failure.

> Education is furtherance of life. It is a quickening, strengthening and purifying of the original sources of human power; it is an unfolding of man's endowments; a striving of the impulses which enable him to become more perfect in his physical, intellectual, aesthetic, moral and religious nature. He is the most complex of beings. He is not a body nor a soul, not a mind nor a heart, not an imagination nor a conscience, but all these in organic union and communion.

Information alone he did not regard as education. Education must include likewise the use of that information to attain the real dignity of man. In this, despite his plea for the things of the mind, he places the higher good in the action of the will, particularly in a life of love of the good, especially in the love of one's neighbor and of God. "Knowledge is not power; but a vigorous, alert, and inquiring mind is power. Vital energy lies not in knowing, but in doing; not in the pages of a book, but in thinkers and workers." Neither can sound education exclude religion any more than true culture can be attained without religion.

> If the chief end of education is virtue; if conduct is three-fourths of life; if character is indispensable, while knowledge is only useful,— then it follows that religion—which, more than any other vital influence,

has power to create virtue, to inspire conduct, and to mould character—should enter into all the processes of education. . . . The denominational system of popular education is the right system. The secular system is a wrong system.

Spalding's attitude on the parochial schools was one of common sense, at a time before the majority of the American people had lost their reverence for religion through non-religious education.

Education for Spalding continued throughout life and the State and the Church were in this sense also schools; but he was especially interested in formal education. He praised the dignity of the teacher.

> It is the teacher's business to exalt the mind and the imagination, to confirm the will and the conscience, to purify and ennoble the heart. It is his mission to open new worlds to eyes he trains to see, to ears he trains to hear, to break down the confining walls of ignorance and indifference, and to lead his disciples forth into the light and joy of freedom and truth.

Convinced of the necessity of religious education and of the dignity of the teacher, Spalding logically argued for the erection of Catholic normal schools wherein the Sisters and Brothers who devoted their life to the work of Catholic education could receive special training for their work. To his interest in this training is given the major credit for the establishment of the Catholic Sisters' College at the Catholic University of America.

But a normal college was not enough if Catholic education in the United States was to be complete. Neither would theological seminaries, nor technical schools, nor undergraduate colleges furnish the necessary leadership in intellectual matters or give to the Catholic ideal in education an intelligent voice in contemporary America. John Lancaster Spalding, while not the first to argue for a central Catholic university, became one of the most active proponents and probably the chief planner of the ideal Catholic university for the United States. His words of warning to the bishops assembled for the Third Plenary Council of Baltimore in 1884 constitute a harsh commentary on the cultural deficiencies of the Catholic minority since that day.

> But if we are to be intellectually the equal of others, we must have with them equal advantages of education, and so long as we look rather to the multiplying of schools and seminaries than to the creation of a real university, our progress will be slow and uncertain, because a university is the great ordinary means to the best cultivation of the mind. The fact that the growth of the Church here, like that of the country itself, is chiefly external, a growth in wealth and numbers, makes it the more necessary that we bring the most strenuous efforts to improve the gift of the soul. . . . Without this [a Catholic university] we can have no hope of entering as a determining force into the living controversies of the age; without this it must be an accident if we are represented at all in the liter-

ature of the country; without this we shall lack a point of union to gather up, harmonize and intensify our scattered forces; without this our bishops must remain separated and continue to work in random ways; . . . without this we shall vainly hope for such treatment of religious questions and their relations to the issues and needs of the day, as shall arrest public opinion and induce Catholics themselves to take at least some little notice of the writings of Catholics; without this in the struggles for reform and contests for rights we shall lack the wisdom of best counsel and the courage which skillful leaders inspire.

Spalding's warnings in 1884 were far more prophetic than he himself could have understood because he was confident that his ideal of a Catholic university would be established. As the foundation of his university, he proposed first a school of high theological studies, because it would be easier to establish and require less expense than a foundation in the arts or sciences and in the hope that around this, as around a similar theological school of Paris in the Middle Ages, a full university could develop. This theological school was not to be a seminary where clerics received the technical training for their vocation but a university school of theology where chosen clergy would be sent by the bishops of the country for continued study. They would not only perfect themselves to become leaders in their own dioceses and communities but would offer to the Catholics in the United States an authoritative center where solutions could be found for national problems in the field of religious knowledge and practice. Eventually Spalding hoped this university would become a center likewise of higher study in philosophy, in the arts, and in science.

> Certainly a true university will be the home of ancient wisdom and of new learning; it will teach the best that is known, and encourage research; it will stimulate thought, refine taste, and awaken the love of excellence; it will be at once a scientific institute, a school of culture, and a training ground for the business of life; it will educate the minds that give direction to the age; it will be a nursery of ideas, a centre of influence.

Thus his ideal university, above the undergraduate colleges of the day and apart from the technical and vocational schools, would consist of scholars training other scholars in all the branches of human knowledge and at the same time giving enlightened solutions to the problems of the day.

Spalding's plan for the Catholic minority in the United States might have built the missing bridge between this minority and the non-Catholic majority which he and the other "progressive" bishops felt was drawing near to Catholicism at the end of the nineteenth century. He recognized better than most American educators of his day—Catholic and non-Catholic alike—that the great social problems of the United States were common to both groups. Those problems were chiefly the checking alike of the materialistic tendencies of great industrial corporations and the communistic tendencies of labor organizations, the elimination of dishonesty in public office, and the spread of true humanism through religious denominational education. For the Catholic minority, relatively poorer in this world's goods and deprived in its immigrant groups by persecution and political oppression of the advantages of higher culture, he advocated a seeking of a humbler but more independent livelihood in rural America, the perfection of the parochial school and religious academies and colleges, and finally the creation of a real Catholic university capable of defining the Catholic position on the highest levels.

Perhaps Spalding was premature in his hopes. The immigrants, for the most part, remained in the cities to become witnesses of the truth of his prophecies. The reaction to the condemnation of modernism and the insistence upon Roman training for the specially qualified clerics aided the reaction against the University established in Washington. Many bishops undoubtedly felt that they could not spare their best clergymen to form this ideal "High School of Theology," about which he hoped to build a university. The European scholars whom the first rectors of the Catholic University of America gathered for the first faculties did not always enter fully into the American educational problem and soon split the faculty and the hierarchy over problems of European national origin. Financial support was never offered in the amount necessary if the University was to carry out the high ideals of Spalding. Perhaps the idea of one central university was impractical among a group of nearly twenty millions of Catholics of all national origins, spread over a large part of a continent; but his ideal university remains the highest ideal in American higher education and was a fitting apex to the whole social teaching of Spalding. Monsignor John A. Ryan was to credit Spalding with some of his own high Christian social ideals. Spalding's educational ideals have yet to receive an interpreter in recent years.

John Lancaster Spalding retired from his diocese in 1908 because of ill health and spent the remaining eight years in comparative retirement. It is to be regretted that his poor health and advanced age prevented him from adjusting his theories to the great dogmatic and sacramental reforms instituted by Pope Pius X. From the vantage point of later developments there are two important defects in his theories which he held in common with many Catholic theorists of his day. Lacking Thomistic clarity common to recent scholastic theology, he failed to insist upon the clear distinction between the natural and the supernatural, and he did not include in his education the great sacramental force of the Eucharist which has become again such an integral part of Catholic education. There was no inherent conflict between his ideal of Catholic humanism and the practical, sacramental Catholicism of the present day. His social ideals were essentially the same as those of the late Monsignors John A. Ryan and William Kerby. His notion of the proper development of the Catholic minority and especially his concept of the nature and work of a truly Catholic university are essentially solid and need to be revived. Had his plans been accepted, the Catholic answer to the great social problems of the age would be more clearly defined in American literature and Catholic higher education would be far better equipped to withstand the materialistic pragmatism which is eating away at the very essence of true humanism in American life.

THE UNIVERSITY OF

CHICAGO AND THE

WORLD, 1929-1951

John U. Nef

[1951]

"The policies of Mr. R. M. Hutchins, the president of Chicago University, are exciting much controversy in the United States. . . . He has severely criticized the superficiality of higher learning . . . , and has espoused the teaching of classical and medieval philosophy as an antidote. In conversation he has a masterful personality. He combines earnestness with joy of combat. His criticisms of the cultural limitations of scientists are shrewd and provoking and demonstrate unanswerably that educational changes are necessary."—*The Manchester Guardian,* May 31, 1938.

In April 1929 the trustees of the University of Chicago, in the midst of an unprecedented boom on the stock exchange, chose Robert Maynard Hutchins, the thirty-year-old dean of the Yale Law School, to be the University's fifth president. During the twenty-two years that followed, Hutchins made an impression upon the organization and the life of the young University of a kind such as his sponsors for the office and the newspaper public, which enjoyed the spectacle of a youthful rising star, hardly expected. He made this impression as a student, a thinker, and a teacher. He made it not, as the times prompted him to do, by trying to keep the University abreast of the morning newspaper, which is dead the next day, but by trying to raise it toward the philosophical heights of Aristotle and the poetic heights of Homer, whose ideas and words are as fresh now as more than two millennia ago. The career of the University during these twenty-two years is inseparably linked with his career, and the most important aspect of both has been their relation to the hopes and destinies of human beings everywhere on this planet. In 1938 the late Marcel Moye, a French professor of finance and financial history, who had

407

taken Doctor's degrees also in medicine and letters, wrote to me that a reading of Hutchins' *Higher Learning in America* had drawn his interest as a scholar and educator for the first time across the Atlantic.

We are not suggesting that the University of Chicago, as it stands in 1951, is the creation of one man, either in its strength or in its weakness. Like all institutions, it is a mixture of both, and Hutchins would be the last to claim a monopoly of the strength or to deny a large share of responsibility for the weakness. But the great significance of his administration lies in a new element of strength which he introduced. The rich world of our time is poor and hungry for the traditional values of Christianity and humanism. He encouraged the reaffirmation of these values and their renewal in fresh forms.

CHICAGO BEFORE 1929

My father was a member of the first faculty of the University of Chicago; he was head of the department of chemistry until his death in 1915. I grew up as a part of the University community and I joined the faculty a year before Hutchins became president. So I remember the place before his time.

The University began with all the enthusiasm and promise characteristic of Chicago at the juncture of the nineteenth and twentieth centuries. That was the Chicago of Jane Addams, with her settlement for the needy at Hull House (a model for the new settlements which were started in other American cities), and her leadership of the women's movement for international peace. It was the Chicago of Martin Ryerson and Charles Hutchinson, who placed their large fortunes and their time at the disposal of science, as represented in the University of Chicago, and of art, as represented in the Art Institute, which they helped to make one of the distinguished museums of the world. Something of the largeness of outlook, the universality and the generosity of such persons as these, was part of the spirit of the young University. John D. Rockefeller's millions, given entirely without restriction on their use, and William Rainey Harper's genius for selecting men did the rest.

There is a story of a visit which Harper paid to Clark University in 1892, before the doors of the University of Chicago opened. G. Stanley Hall, president of Clark and a force in education in his own right, had gathered a remarkable faculty in the natural sciences. Calling on Hall, and knowing that Clark had appointed more men than it was able to pay decently or even at all, Harper hit on the ruse of asking his colleague which scientific members of the Clark faculty were best suited for Chicago. Somewhat over-eagerly, Hall supplied him with a list, which Harper gravely examined. After taking his leave, Harper invited to Chicago only men who were *not* on Hall's list.

Among these were Michaelson, Whitman, Jordan, Frank R. Lillie, and my father, John U. Nef. Within a year or two, Harper had assembled a faculty which could be compared favorably with any in the United States and which was hardly inferior to that of Harvard in the time of William James. As Hutchins remarked when he first became president, such a faculty will make a great university even if it has to assemble "under a tent."

As time went on the University became less and less of a tent. The chemistry department, for example, moved out of a small flat in a house of flats on 53rd Street, nearly a mile from the campus, into a specially constructed edifice which then seemed ample, but which is now supplemented by a still larger one. Buildings engaged an attention that was not always given to men. Getting and spending, assembling large numbers of undergraduates in what had been first thought of as a great institute for graduate study and research, setting up correspondence schools and extension lectures—these activities became more and more a preoccupation of the University of Chicago. It was everywhere in the United States an age of activity. No wonder that little thought should have been given to long-range purpose, when so many felt that growth and change by themselves would solve not only material, but moral and intellectual problems. Nowhere were prominent men disposed to re-examine the motives which were driving our society along with the societies of Europe. On the occasion of the twentieth anniversary in 1912 members of the original faculty were asked how Chicago had appeared to them at the beginning in 1892. My father was quoted as saying: "I remember wondering whether Chicago would become a great university devoted to research and thought or simply another educational institution of which there were already so many."

If one had tried to give an objective answer to this question in 1928, a year before Hutchins came, the answer would not have been reassuring. Plenty of research was going on in many lines, but there was nothing approaching a common purpose behind the research. Scholars were enlisted only in the search for new facts or theories concerning their increasingly narrow special subjects. They lacked the sense of a mission greater than themselves, a mission such as enlists the artist devoted to the service of truth and beauty, such as enlists the moralist who seeks the good, a mission capable of lifting a man out of himself so that his work becomes a part of the life stream of our race. The University of Chicago was far larger and more wealthy in 1928 than in its first years, but it was not richer in great conversations, in reading and creative ideas such as can arouse in some students and young scholars a sense of calling beyond that which comes from solving intellectual problems or satisfying a learned curiosity. By the time Hutchins came, relations between students and faculty had lost some of the intimacy that had characterized them in the early years of the University. The somewhat cynical impudence with which a few popular teachers treated subjects which called for seriousness and art, their crude use of slang, were no substitute for the genuine enthusiasm for creative discovery. That was manifested only by a few specialists and most of these were regarded by the students as inaccessible. It was a time when individualism as a value was pushed to an extreme in the United States, and it was not perhaps surprising that teachers sometimes felt free to indulge in undisciplined self-expression. One professor of English, who had retired just before Hutchins came, took pleasure in remembering that his two courses in literature had been generally known among his students as "Love-one" and "Love-two."

The late Shailer Mathews, long dean of the Divinity School, when put on the witness stand in 1930 or thereabouts, in a case brought against the faculty club for the payment of taxes, was confronted with a list of books purchased for the club library. They were thrillers of a light and lurid sort. The State contended that a club which purchased such books could hardly claim exemption from taxes as part of an educational enterprise. The best way Dean Mathews could meet the charge was by observing: "Professors don't read books; they write books."

The chief assets of the University of Chicago were the men of reputation in various fields who belonged to its faculty. These were the days when college alumni all over the country attached immense importance to the all-American football teams selected by the late Walter Camp. Each college vied with the others to get as many men as possible onto the three of Camp's elevens. It came to be assumed that the scholarly standing of the leading universities might be measured in a similar way. I seem to remember that the late Charles Eliot once selected an all-star faculty. So it became a favorite pastime to add up the names on the faculty belonging to "starred men of science" or appearing in *Who's Who*. The number was then compared with the numbers at other leading universities. Chicago came off usually in first, second, or third place. On the basis of these scorings, it was impressed upon the young members of the faculty that they belonged to what was probably the greatest University in the country, if not in the world. Such an assertion jibed with the banner under which the leading Chicago newspaper sailed into its public each day, "the world's greatest newspaper."

These claims had a hollow ring. The criteria and the tempo of sport and sporting journalism had invaded the realm of scholarship and thought, where they had even less relevance than had the criteria and the tempo of business administration, about whose disquieting influence on scholarship Thorstein Veblen had recently written. The great problems in the world of knowledge were how to combine specialties, how to work toward at least some measure of unity, and how to regain for the work of the mind a relevance to human existence as a whole. About these problems one heard next to nothing. I found the University of Chicago a most agreeable place. My colleagues were friendly and generous. The students were polite and receptive. As a native of Chicago I accepted the ugliness and the dirt of the huge city, and liked the companionship with people I had known as a child. But when I used to hear President Hutchins, as was frequent in those early days of his career at Chicago, defining a university as "a community of scholars," I concluded that he was talking about some distant place, as far from the realities of the world of abundance where we lived as was Heaven for the atheists, whose view of the universe, empty of any destiny for humanity, was the accepted view of most of the faculty.

The remarkable change that occurred in the twenty-two years that followed Hutchins' arrival, can be simply stated. When some Europeans now tell me that I belong to the greatest University in the United States, I am still much surprised; I tremble to think what other universities may be like; but the words no longer seem empty. I shall try to explain why.

HUTCHINS' SELF-EDUCATION AND RESEARCH

Few persons realized in the nineteen-twenties, few persons realize now, how almost infinite are the opportunities open to an American university president when it comes to occupying his waking hours, even if he can get on with little sleep, or how restricted are his opportunities for occupying these hours in ways relevant to the intellectual life, with which traditionally universities are concerned. In his essay on the administrator in *The Works of the Mind,* published in 1947 by the Committee on Social Thought, under the editorship of Robert B. Heywood, Hutchins explained that a university president cannot confine himself to a single constituency as some politicians can. The students, the faculty, the alumni and the trustees all clamor for his attention, and the services that each group expects of him, though they differ, have all one thing in common. They are lacking in the finer qualities of intellectual exercise. The president has, for example, the obligation to shake hands with, and hand out diplomas to, every member of the graduating class, to take a leading role as actor in the faculty theatricals, to occupy a box at football games even when the thermometer descends below freezing, to sit at the speakers' table at dinners for visiting businessmen, ambassadors and Hollywood film stars. Since universities are always short of funds, he can easily spend most of his energy going about from business office to business office with a tin cup for donations. He can as easily spend most of his energy on problems of business administration connected with the commencement reunions, the erection of buildings, or such weighty matters as whether facilities shall be installed in the university bookshop for dispensing bottles of Coca-Cola.

Even if he goes in for what can be classified as "educational activities," the university president has it open to him to adopt purely bookkeeping methods. A. Lawrence Lowell was one of the more distinguished American university presidents of the last fifty years. Yet the late Professor Edwin F. Gay, of Harvard, told me that early in Lowell's administration he received a letter from his new chief pointing out that the grades Gay gave in his courses in economic history were above the average for the university as a whole. The president asked him to mark more severely. It emerged from the correspondence that one of Lowell's first acts on becoming president was to conduct a survey of the grades given in every course in the university. Gay countered by putting his assistant to work doing research on the same documents from another point of view. He was able to show that the students who took his courses in economic history had, on the average, higher grades than the average student!

From Hutchins' published work, we know that he was struck, when he took over the direction of the University of Chicago, by the inadequacy of the education he had received in school and at college. As he explained in some of his early speeches to undergraduates, when he had been in their place, he had wondered what possible relation could exist between the facts which the professors gave out in their lectures or which appeared in the textbooks they recommended, and his own existence as a human being. After a respectable record at various elementary and secondary schools, at Oberlin, at the college of Yale University and in the Yale Law School, he found himself uneducated.

The entirely unorthodox idea came to him that, as a man to whom had been confided one of the major educational posts in the country, he should begin by trying to get an education. It required no objective tests, no advice from modern social scientists, no consultations with psychoanalysts, for Hutchins to grasp the age-old principle that the most promising method of learning is to teach. He decided to leave undone a vast number of things that university presidents can do, but which brought about results that frequently added up to nothing more than President Lowell's inquiry into the grades awarded at Harvard college. The young philosopher Mortimer Adler pointed out to him that the reading of most university presidents was confined to the pages of the daily papers. So, in Adler's company, he set about to educate himself, with the help of some books that have endured, and with twenty to thirty under-graduates as fellow students, selected from each incoming class for their promise. Thus was started in 1930 a four-year course in great books at Chicago.

During the first ten years of his presidency, Hutchins' study turned his mind in directions, and his researches produced results, that startled him. They were to startle the faculty even more. The subject of inquiry was the most original and powerful thought, and the greatest writing, of the Christian past and of classical antiquity. The books, the essays, the plays, and the poetry were concerned with the nature of man's destiny, and so with the meaning of human life both for individuals and for societies. Since these problems of meaning and destiny remain fundamentally the same, and since the search for human happiness, for the good life, has always a strong appeal for a sensitive mind not corrupted by the notion that values are only relative, Hutchins found himself examining present-day individuals and societies, and the teaching and scholarship of present-day faculties, in the light of what he read.

What he read differed profoundly in purpose and in character from the books and articles which were being written and read by the scholars of the age. Nearly all the writers to whom Hutchins turned were convinced that immutable values exist concerning the ultimate problems confronting man and society. This led Hutchins to recognize the need for relating the new material provided by modern research to these values. It led him also to consider the values afresh in relation to authentic new material.

The great books of classical antiquity, of the Middle Ages and of early modern times, were almost invariably concerned with the whole problem of human experience. Consequently, unlike most of the research done by recent scholars, the study of a part was not pursued in isolation, but in relation to the other major parts. There was, finally, another decisive difference between the authorities Hutchins studied and those which commanded the attention of most modern scholars. The great authors he sought as masters wrote with a seriousness of purpose, and most of them with a clarity, an imaginative wit, and an elegance that was missing in contemporary work. The older works possessed, in consequence, a permanence that almost all contemporary writers, who were not denied it by an inadequate endowment of talents, denied themselves.

The great works of the past provide a scale of values against which Hutchins judged the activities of the age in which he had grown up, and the curricula of the educational system of which he had become a part. The older values, which his penetrating mind understood, led him to question the validity of the prevailing aims and methods of both contemporary scholars and men of action. He found himself in a position that was novel among American university presidents. In their efforts at reform, the others had been able to follow the pragmatist school of philosophers, which had come into the ascendancy with William James and John Dewey. Other reformers had only to follow the "trends," to move with the crowd, and when it came to matters of general interest which lay outside their special competence, the great majority of every faculty proved to be members of the crowd.

As Hutchins educated himself, he began to doubt whether the directions in which industrial society was moving were the right directions. In a commencement address of 1931, he remarked that *The New Atlantis,* Francis Bacon's three hundred-year-old dream, of a paradise of material abundance created with the help of scientific knowledge, had been realized. The New Atlantis was an ideal state, he told the graduating class, and quickly added:

> Do you feel as if you were living in one. . . . People are dying in equal misery in Chicago and in China . . . one-half the world is starving to obtain the goods the other half is starving to dispose of, and we see no way of bringing them together. . . . Though we know more about political institutions than we ever did, and though thousands of students graduate every year filled with this information, we can hardly say that all our public officers are more honest or effective than Bacon was. . . . Few of those who remain in office seem to qualify for intellectual eminence.

Hutchins found disturbing the widespread uncertainty concerning the goals for which men work that he encountered everywhere, and not least in education. "Hail confusion," seemed, he said, to be the only principle on which educators could approach agreement.

How were these results of Hutchins' researches related to his position? In addition to the academy for graduate study and research that had been in the beginning its *raison d'être,* the University of Chicago now operated many varieties of educational enterprise, reaching all the way from a kindergarten and an elementary school to a school of law and a school of medicine. Almost everything was to be found except a faculty of dentistry and a faculty of engineering. Therefore it became Hutchins' intellectual problem to consider the reform of every aspect of education and even of research in the industrialized nation and the industrialized world of which the University of Chicago was a part.

While Hutchins adopted as axiomatic the popular American view that all children and young people were entitled to an education, he suggested that it was no less important that they should get a better education, or at least that something should be done to prevent a further decline in the quality of the education that most young persons were getting. The increasingly prevalent practice, in so-called "progressive schools," of substituting self-expression for sober routine and drill; the equally prevalent practice of prolonging the years devoted to education at all levels, so that the American might remain a child almost until he reached the age of second childhood; the notion that education in the colleges should be practical in its nature, and should include schools for hairdressers and dancers; all such practices and notions became the target of his speeches.

In order to gain a wider audience for his criticism, he began to publish articles in popular magazines. Perhaps the most telling was a series that appeared in the old *Saturday Evening Post,* at a time when it may still have had the largest single audience in the United States.

In his first year out of college, as a master in English and History in the Lake Placid preparatory school, Hutchins had acquired a habit of clear and forceful writing and speech, lightened by the charm of apt anecdote. During his later years of self-education, his writing, at its best, is marked by a terse inevitability, combined with a just sense of ethical and intellectual values, and with a moral integrity personal to him. This distinguishes his essays and lectures from other comparable American writing of the period and gives them a claim to endure.

He had more to say than merely to criticize, brilliant though his criticism was becoming. What his mind sought, above all, was construction. There was much of the scholar about him, and he acquired a strong sympathy for scholarship, which made him feel on occasions that his was a *vocation manquée.* There were times when, if his generosity had not led him to acquire heavy financial obligations, he would have willingly exchanged the presidency for a professorship. Not long after the articles in the *Saturday Evening Post,* he published two carefully worked out essays on the political thought of Edmund Burke, which satisfied the most rigorous canons of scholarly composition. The first appeared in the *Thomist* volume of essays in honor of Jacques Maritain (New York: Sheed and Ward, January, 1943), for whose thought and career Hutchins felt much sympathy. The second appeared in the REVIEW OF POLITICS (Vol. V (April, 1943), pp. 139–155). There was a striking contrast between the almost complete silence which greeted these articles, and the numerous manifestations of interest arising from those in the *Post.* Hutchins was not a little surprised to discover how small is the audience accessible to the modern scholar. The episode revealed to him a further weakness in modern university work: the absense of a general public.

In *The Higher Learning in America,* published in 1936, he attempted to sketch a plan for a university capable of serving mankind in what was destined to be, as was becoming increasingly plain, one of the most critical periods in its long history. Without unifying principles for all studies, he suggested, a university is likely to become a mere collection of experts offering special knowledge, some of which (particularly that in the natural sciences) is useful, some of which is antiquarian, and some of which (like most of such work as home economics—with research into the most effective ways of washing dishes) more properly belongs under the head of housekeeping. The American university was attempting to teach many practical things that are best learned in the school of doing. This attempt got in the way of making the university effective in its proper sphere— the sphere of creative thought, of ideas.

How could unifying principles be found, which would help a university to become "a community of scholars"? Hutchins suggested that the study of metaphysics, concerned as it properly is with *being* in the most universal sense, might contribute to the discovery of the principles.

Metaphysics transcends natural science, concerned as natural science is with material phenomena, and so can lead us more readily to the examination of those things which are of importance to men everywhere and always, the things of the soul. Metaphysics can bring men, therefore, to the subjects concerning which unity of outlook is worth-while; it can help men toward wisdom, as science, concerned with the more particular, can not. But can it *prove* what is universally wise?

The way that question is answered depends on man's view of the nature of proof. During the past four centuries this view has undergone a profound change among the peoples of European origin. What was once considered rational came at the beginning of the twentieth century close to being treated as irrational. According to the great sixteenth-century English theologian, Richard Hooker, "reason" is the process by which "man attaineth unto the knowledge of things that are and are not sensible." That is the only way, for example, by which we reach the Aristotelian conclusion that actions such as adultery, theft, and murder "are always sinful." In the modern meaning of "reason," there is no possible way of *proving* such a proposition. It is only by experiment or observation, it is only when verification by the senses makes agreement possible, that men now reach what they consider rational conclusions. Therefore "reason" has become the process of attaining knowledge of things "that are sensible."

By championing the study of metaphysics as a means of helping scholars to find unifying principles, Hutchins seemed to be flying in the face of modern science. Societies of learned men brought up, as ours are, under the dominance of scientific procedures as the only firm means of reaching truth, cannot be persuaded that conclusions in the realm of metaphysics, where the final appeal cannot be to the controlled experiment or to observation, can ever be convincing, or, if convincing, can have any relevance to practical life. Yet at the very time Hutchins was educating himself in the traditions and the traditional knowledge which was treated in most academic circles as obsolete, such great scientists as Sherrington, Whittaker, and Whitehead, from their own researches in physiology, astronomy, and mathematics, were revealing the limitations of modern scientific knowledge. Their work, as Hutchins learned, makes it necessary for us to reconsider the view that reason in the older sense has exhausted its possibilities. For a time he thought that the study of metaphysics might at least help to prove what is universally wise. I am not sure that he has abandoned this view or that it ought to be abandoned.

In *The Higher Learning in America,* Hutchins distinguished sharply between metaphysics and theology, between reason and faith. Such a distinction was perfectly feasible in the tradition of Christian thought, with its classical pagan antecedents. But the modern change in the view of what is rational had blurred the difference between natural reason and belief based on Christian Revelation. Both were separated from science even by those who treated science as unimportant in comparison to wisdom. Thus we find the notable Spanish philosopher and man of letters, Miguel de Unamuno, who was once rector of the University of Salamanca, suggesting in 1906 that what distinguishes wisdom from science is precisely the absence of any possibility of proof. The consequence of this position was to identify wisdom and faith, to make all judgments that are not susceptible to positive determination matters of belief. Unamuno quoted with enthusiastic agreement some lines by Lord Tennyson:

> "For nothing worthy proving can be proven
> Nor yet disproven, wherefore thou be wise,
> Cleave ever to the sunnier side of doubt,
> And cling to Faith beyond the forms of Faith."

The Christian writers whom Hutchins read did not take that position, as the words we have quoted from Hooker show, but they accepted it as axiomatic that man's natural reason went beyond faith

417

only in the sense that it was possible by natural reason to discover truths "that are not sensible" beyond those revealed by God. Christian believers, who were Hutchins' contemporaries, were eager to point out to him that religion was even more essential than metaphysics to the discovery of the unifying principles that are lacking in modern learning.

Whether he sought for a sense of dedication in university work by means of metaphysics or of "Faith," Hutchins was bound to alarm the faculties. In metaphysics, most of the faculty men sniffed what they knew little or nothing about at first hand, but regarded as the crude and sterile reasoning of the mediaeval logician. In religion, most of them sniffed the odor of the Inquisition. In whichever direction Hutchins' researches seemed to be carrying him, he stirred up a hornets' nest.

THE CRISIS

So it came about that Hutchins' self-education brought on a crisis in the faculty. If the intellectual issues were not clear, this was hardly Hutchins' fault. The tentative conclusions toward which his learning led him, got mixed up in other minds than his own with a series of practical reforms, some of which he had been advocating ever since he became president.

An acute phase in the controversy began with the circulation in February, 1938, of a mimeographed pamphlet drawn up by a small committee of the University chapter of the American Association of University Professors. This body is the nearest approach in the higher learning to a labor union. Unlike the learned associations, which include only special groups of scholars, it is open to all members of university faculties, and it has, on occasion, taken a helpful stand in many parts of the United States on behalf of academic freedom. "Report of the Committee on Academic Tenure," the pamphlet was entitled. It was bound with another, called "Report of the Committee on the Organization of Departments."

Neither of the committees professed to do more than offer suggestions. But some implications of their suggestions were tendentious, and it was confidently expected that the subjects would be taken up by the faculties, and particularly by the senate, the chief faculty governing body. The main implication was that the president was setting about to become a dictator and to impose his views on the University. Neither committee explained what these views were, but it was generally assumed that what were involved were his philosophical aims, as expressed in *The Higher Learning in America* and other published essays. Lurking in the background were more occult and mysterious religious ideas that he was suspected of having.

There was whispered that he had a secret plan, in which "Dr. Adler" was of course the kingpin and spiritual guide, to make Chicago's modern Baptist academy a kind of "medieval monastery." It was suggested that the method Hutchins would employ in accomplishing these ends would be to stuff the faculty with appointees who agreed with him.

The Report of the Committee on Academic Tenure concluded:

> In a period of transition an element of the faculty which is relatively strong in both conviction and personality may contribute to healthy expression of dissent. But if these are replaced by key appointees sympathetic to the presidential program . . . there will be a tendency to convert the whole University into an instrument of presidential policy, accompanied by a decline not only in a sense of faculty responsibility, but in freedom of opinion and freeness of speech. If that time comes, although the program may be advanced, the university will decline. It is inherent in the situation.

It was the intention of both reports to bring about a reduction in the administrative powers of the president. To anyone looking with knowledge and objectivity at the situation in the higher learning, the plan attributed to Hutchins was nothing more than what Bentham once called "nonsense on stilts." Where in the country, or for that matter abroad, was Hutchins to find accredited scholars to appoint who shared his actual philosophical position, let alone the positions fancifully, but freely, attributed to him? The personal appointments he had made, and particularly the temporary appointments in 1936–37 of two educational reformers previously with the University of Virginia, Stringfellow Barr and Scott Buchanan, had caused a considerable outcry among the faculty. But they had not brought men who were in anything approaching deep sympathy with Hutchins' philosophical position. In any event the president's powers, and particularly his powers over appointments, were already small. To reduce them further would have deprived the University of a remarkably shrewd judge. While Hutchins had undoubtedly made (who in his position has not?) some mistakes in appointments, he had shown through some years a remarkable talent for selecting gifted and intelligent men independent of their personal views, and for exercising an overall judgment concerning the general qualifications of candidates, which departments, committed above all to covering specialties, have often lacked. Moreover Hutchins had already revealed himself as exceedingly reluctant to exercise such powers as he possessed. "Hutchins likes to have authority, but I have never known any man who hates so much to use it," such was the considered and penetrating opinion expressed by a leading scholar in the social sciences, devoted to statistics and positivism and to the use of the scientific method outside the realm of the natural sciences, a use which Hutchins' studies had led him to question.

The decision of the alarmist element in the faculty, after the circulation of the two reports, to bring a motion in the senate for a committee to investigate the administration of the University aroused strong opposition from a minority. One older man, who had been with the University before Hutchins came, and who has now gone to his rest, brought me a speech which he proposed to make on the occasion of the motion. Fortunately I was able to dissuade him, as his remarks would only have fanned passions which were already inflamed. But he left me a copy of his remarks, and as I look at them now, some fourteen years afterward, they seem to me to represent a sound point of view, which never obtained expression in any of the governing bodies during Hutchins' term of office.

> Ever since 1930, I have watched with growing concern the misguided and sometimes malicious campaign of obstruction carried on here at the expense of the president of the University. The weapons used have sometimes been of a sort that I had supposed would be unknown among scholars, presumably trained in the examination and sifting of evidence— political manoeuvring, the spread of unfounded rumors, the misrepresentation of the ideas and objectives of the president, in spite of the fact that most of these ideas and objectives have been clearly expressed in print. This campaign has culminated in this motion. The time has come when I must speak out against the medieval witch-hunting of one of the most distinguished men his generation of Americans has produced. . . .
>
> The policies of Mr. Hutchins have, I believe, done much for the university during the ten years he has been its leader. They would have done much more if they had been carried out and supported by the faculty. From reading Mr. Hutchins' writings, I think that the constructive work he can do, if the faculty will cooperate, has only begun, that it is likely to continue for some decades.
>
> In the light of ten years' experience, does not the real danger to the future of research in this university lie in the movement to diminish the president's statutory powers? In the light of ten years' experience, is it not evident that the danger to freedom of thought and expression comes not from the president, but from the persons who wish to curb the president's freedom of thought and expression? No one in this country has done more for freedom of speech in universities than he. I need only refer to the history of the Walgreen investigation and its sequel. When we are told, in one of the reports recently issued by the Chicago chapter of the A. A. U. P., that the president is threatening what the report calls "freedom of opinion and freeness of speech," the most charitable interpretation we can reach is that, for the authors of the report, words have lost their meaning, that they have learned from the current debates in international politics to call white, black and black, white.
>
> It will be well if you vote with the real issue in mind. By defeating

this motion, you have a chance to show your confidence in President Hutchins and his leadership. Let none of you who vote for it let yourselves be fooled into thinking you are supporters of the president, that you are voting for freedom of speech, for the future of research or for the advancement of the creative life. I have heard several members of this faculty protest their loyalty to the president. If he were threatened in any way, they have told me, they would rush to his support. This afternoon they have a chance to show that their words are not empty.

Our late friend was perhaps better freed from the ordeal of delivering such a speech. It would have damaged Hutchins to have made it appear that the passage of the motion would amount to a vote of no-confidence, for the faculty had already determined to pass the motion. In politics, we are told, few votes are changed by speeches, and politics is not absent from the affairs of universities.

PERSUASION AND REFORM

I have quoted at some length the remarks which my late colleague had proposed to make, because they provide a key to the last, and from the practical point of view the most constructive, phase of Hutchins' association with the University of Chicago. Hutchins' experience with faculty opposition during his first ten years as president produced an effect upon his subtle personality. To a degree that is very rare, he combines a remarkable capacity for serious thought with an equally remarkable capacity and desire for action. The methods of action, of which he was becoming a master, were much more in keeping with the outlook of the faculty, and with the past practice of the country, than were the tentative conclusions about the purpose of a university toward which his study and thought had led him.

What Americans traditionally admire in their administrators is the ability to get things done. Too often it matters too little what the things are, whether they ought to be done at all. But there were many specific things in connection with American education which Hutchins had become convinced ought to be done and to which the faculty was by no means generally opposed. The price of getting most or even some of them done was threefold. First, Hutchins had to build up outside the University an enthusiasm for himself as a leader and for the University of Chicago as an institution uniquely devoted to the kind of educational pioneering which raises nostalgic feelings among a nation founded and developed by "pioneers." Second, he had to gain the instinctive support of at least a substantial minority of the faculty. Finally, he had to separate each of the realizable reforms from the others, to separate them above all from what people were inclined to call his "educational philosophy," and

421

then to present them, one by one, for action in the most favorable light, at the most favorable time and to the most favorably disposed of his constituencies. In that way, he could on occasion convert the minority of the faculty, whose instinctive support he was gaining, into a temporary majority.

Such strategy and tactics, while almost invariably necessary under democratic processes to effective reforms of any kind, were not congenial to the serious thinker and writer that Hutchins had become. Yet, as *The Manchester Guardian* remarked in 1938, Hutchins "had demonstrated unanswerably that educational changes are necessary." Had he not the duty to make the changes which could be made? Ought he not to pay the price necessary to make them? The overwhelming majority of his colleagues suggested to him that on the basic and fundamental issues of educational philosophy he was wrong, not right. A university was better off without a common purpose, a faculty without a sense of mission, such as he sought for it. Better for scholars to remain confused on general principles than to take seriously the rational processes that had guided thinkers from Aristotle to Hooker. These suggestions hardly convinced Hutchins, for he found that his critics had little that was rational to offer by way of argument. But he became convinced that he could not convince them. The late Henry Schultz, whose skill in mathematical economics masked a considerable talent for faculty politics, and who apparently fancied himself at one time the appropriate mediator between president and faculty, remarked: "if Hutchins tries to reform scholarship, he will be beaten." Another active graduate teacher said: "I will support him in his reform of the college, but he better not touch the graduate school!"

It is my impression that during the early years of Hutchins' presidency, where the faculty was concerned he took little pains over politics. This was partly because of his genuine respect for the scholar and thinker, whose calling he put above other callings. But, by 1938, it had become only too plain that the faculty had not used the same restraint in greeting the realizable policies of reform that he brought forward.

Conditions therefore obliged Hutchins to give much more attention than before to the effects his words and activities might have on the faculty. He had here advantages over his opponents. The character of the *grand seigneur* was a natural part of his being, at a time when the qualities of the *grand seigneur* were bound to impress sensitive persons in a university community. His own sensitive nature enabled him, with persons for whom he felt any sympathy, to get inside his interlocutor and to appeal to the best the interlocutor had to offer. In an interview he knew how to forget himself; how to listen and to encourage. Visitors left him fired with an enthusiasm which enabled him to carry them along, sometimes even on points with which they disagreed. He was incapable of stooping to a courtship with persons who were his out and out opponents or whose character he distrusted, but he could court most effectively many whose philosophical outlook was different from his. This is illustrated by his relations with the late Charles H. Judd, an ardent believer in progressive education, who had succeeded John Dewey in 1909 as head of the School of Education. Hutchins was drawn to Judd as a man, and this is what he had to say at a dinner in a neighboring city, on the occasion of Judd's retirement:

> I have journeyed from Chicago for only one reason, to pay my tribute to one of my closest friends, to whom I owe my own general education, such knowledge of public education as I have, and indeed such common sense as I still possess. From the moment almost nine years ago when I first met Mr. Judd he has given me instruction in private and support in public. He has been responsible for every intelligent move I have ever made. When I have made unintelligent ones, it has been because he has been out of town. His departure is the greatest personal and official blow I have sustained. This will be obvious from the remarks I propose to make this evening. This is almost the first speech I have ever delivered without showing it to your guest of honor first.

These particular remarks were obviously not political. Judd was leaving the University, where he had never been a popular figure with the elements among whom Hutchins needed to win votes. Hutchins was paying a debt of affection and gratitude. The words reveal the spontaneous warmth of his generous personality. They also disclose the manner in which he could approach, with a more practical purpose, visitors, colleagues and subordinates. It is little wonder that, for persons who are neither crooks, machines, nor pedants, he could be irresistible.

ATTEMPTS AT REALIZATION

It is a commonplace that human beings think of their ills and take their blessings for granted. Not the least of the blessings possessed by the University of Chicago during the twenty-two years of Hutchins' administration has been its freedom from all trace of persecutions of race or of opinion. This is in no small measure a result of Hutchins' position, from which he never deviated and which on occasions he maintained fearlessly under attack, that the only questions that matter in a university are serious questions of education and scholarship. No secret endorsement ever came from him of the methods not uncommon in American educational institutions of establishing quotas for Jews or for colored people. He made freedom of thought and freedom of speech something more than an idle boast, both by his practice and his words. The security of the professor in the University of Chicago is complete at this moment of his leavetaking. Under Hutchins a request for the resignation of a member of the faculty for expressing an unpopular opinion became a request for the president's own resignation, as in the case of Robert Morss Lovett, a stimulating professor of English who was always getting mixed up with what were often called in the twenties and thirties "progressive and social movements." The principle inherent in such a stand as Hutchins took on that occasion became an accepted part of University policy. Faced with challenges from without, the University of Chicago was put in a position to meet as a single unit —in which the wishes of trustees, central administration, faculty and students were merged—every attack on the liberty for which our nation at its best has stood since the time of Jefferson. Hutchins' words during the latest investigation by the Illinois legislature, that this investigation itself is "unAmerican, undemocratic and unnecessary," reveal the firmness of the American foundation on which he built.

Of the deeper meaning of free speech for scholarship, he spoke in terms which gave his pronouncements on academic freedom a moving and a timeless validity. "Socrates used to say that the one thing he knew positively was that we were under a duty to inquire," Hutchins told a radio audience in 1935, when he raised the question, *What is a University?*

> Inquiry involves still, as it did with Socrates, the discussion of all important problems and of all points of view. You will even find Socrates discussing communism in the *Republic* of Plato. The charge upon which Socrates was executed was the same that is now often hurled at our own educators: he was accused of corrupting the youth. The scholars of America are attempting in their humble way to follow the profession of Socrates. Some people talk as though they would like to visit upon them the fate which Socrates suffered. Such people should be reminded that the Athenians missed Socrates when he was gone.

Many other external difficulties, besides bigotry and persecution, beset those who attempt, in their humble way, to follow the profession of Socrates. What was needed to clear away these other difficulties was not a heroic defense of the professor's calling, but a general house-cleaning within the university which would rid the calling of irrelevancies, red tape, and trivial pursuits, for a good many of which the faculties themselves have to bear a large share of responsibility. With patience and persistence Hutchins proceeded to slough off one impediment after another.

Not the least of the impediments was competitive football. This semi-professional game opens the college year during the pleasantest season which our North American climate presents. It arouses among the students and even their teachers an atmosphere of excitement irrelevant to any scholarly purposes for which they have assembled after the summer holidays. This atmosphere persists beyond the end of the football season in late November. The heroes of the football games remain heroes in their classrooms until practice starts in the spring in preparation for the following autumn. Of all the extra-curricular activities which tend to convert some of our educational institutions into playgrounds and country clubs, with just enough routine book work and lecture attendance to whet young people's appetite for the good time which is looked upon as the main reason for going to college, competitive football looms largest. In persuading the trustees, by unanimous vote, to abolish it in 1939, Hutchins undermined the citadel of college triviality. Gone are the crowds that used to surge up and down the streets which approached the athletic field, to create a blood-tingling excitement in the young and a depression in the few old who cared for the values of the mind. The nearest approach to crowds of football size occurs only when a great architect, Frank Lloyd Wright, or a great but modest and quiet man of letters, T. S. Eliot, delivers a lecture under the auspices of the Committee on Social Thought.

The notion that undergraduate study and even study for the higher degrees are matters of bookkeeping is perhaps even more of a handicap than football to the life of the mind. Compulsory attendance at classes, class meetings every weekday through the entire academic year, a system of credits determined by the number of courses passed—these are devices for keeping the faculty employed, the students busy and for providing a means of scoring to determine when a student is ready to receive a degree. None of these outward emblems of good behavior has much to do with the reading, the thought, the discussion, the experiment, the investigation and the composition for which a great university exists. Under Hutchins' influence the central administration at Chicago ceased to endorse these conventional requirements. Compulsory attendance, with the obligation on professors to call the roll and report absences, went at the beginning of the Hutchins' regime. Other entrenched bookkeeping practices proved to be weeds much harder to eradicate. As one professor remarked, the real problem for the faculty was "how to get back to the old system under the new plan." Professors showed no lack of ingenuity in solving this problem. When a higher scale of salaries was adopted in 1943, subject to the provision that all outside earnings must be turned over to the University, many professed to see nothing in the reform but a cruel desire to starve the faculty.

When course credits were abolished and general examinations were made the basis for granting degrees, so that a student had the opportunity, if brilliant, to complete his work much more rapidly than the average student, professors continued to judge candidates largely on the basis of their course records. It was noised abroad among the students that those who had not a satisfactory record of course credits with high grades could hardly expect to pass the general examinations. I well remember the concern of an older man with an established position on the faculty of a small college, who was granted leave of absence to take his Doctor's degree in one of the units of the University of Chicago which had gone farthest in adopting the Hutchins' reforms. He wanted to devote himself to graduate research and had worked out an excellent plan which would engage all his time, but he was continually haunted by the fear that unless he took for credit what had once been the required number of courses, he would never get his degree.

The tenacity with which in many departments the faculty clung to the right to give a large number of courses and to meet their classes continuously through the year, the claims put forward by many professors that they were doing what the Hutchins' administration wanted by occupying themselves fully with the externals of course requirements, were droll features of the past twenty-two years. I have it on the authority of the late Dr. Frank Lillie, who as dean of the division of the biological sciences was present, that when Hutchins first proposed to the faculty committee on policy that formal meetings with classes be reduced by one-third—with "reading periods" of three or four weeks three times a year—a leading spokesman complained that the president was trying to interfere with the research of the faculty. Some professors pointed out that they would have to rewrite their lectures to fit into the shorter periods. Others professed alarm over the danger that the students might go on vacation!

No calamities occurred when any of these reforms were actually put through, unless it was the inflation which reduced the purchasing power of professors' salaries all over the country. The attendance at interesting classes has been at least as large as when a roll was called. The serious written work done by students has improved in quality when a genuine opportunity has been provided for constructive composition. Young instructors have completed valuable books that they had been waiting to write for years, in those sections of the University where the most was made of the opportunities provided by Hutchins' administration. While the old bookkeeping methods linger on in many units of instruction, it is now much more easily possible than it was for a student or a professor, if he has the

426

inclination and the talent, to devote himself wholeheartedly to the life of the intellect and the imagination and to the improvement of his works.

How is such an inclination for the creative life to be awakened? How is such talent to be nourished? These questions lead us to consider the positive sides of Hutchins' efforts at reform. They also lead us to examine the difficulties in the way of the attainment of the hopes he has aroused that a great university might contribute to a "moral, intellectual and spiritual revolution" among mankind, when the industrialized world seems to be rushing toward the kind of destructive explosion which Henry Adams, with what were then regarded as unduly gloomy forebodings, predicted a half century ago.

Not long after Hutchins' arrival at Chicago the College adopted, with his encouragement, a plan (which has been widely copied in this country) to substitute for the elective system a series of broad general courses in the physical and the biological sciences, in the humanities and the social sciences. As Hutchins pursued his own researches during his first ten years at Chicago, he became more and more dissatisfied with the College curriculum—particularly with the inconsequential nature of the books (mainly the latest textbooks) assigned for reading, and with the flimsy content of many of the lectures. He also became convinced that, where the students were concerned, college work began and ended too late. The coming of the Second World War played into his hands in this matter of age. All over the country what were called "acceleration programs" were introduced, in order to enable more young men and women to complete their college work before they entered the services. By a very narrow margin in the University of Chicago senate, a motion was carried in 1942 making it possible for undergraduates to enter a new "four-year college" at an age when they would normally become juniors in high school, and for all eligible students to receive the Bachelor's degree at the end of what is in the United States the sophomore year of college.

Meanwhile, in 1937, the direction of St. John's College at Annapolis was confided to Stringfellow Barr and Scott Buchanan. Independently of their association with Hutchins, both these men were strongly committed to a complete reform of the American college curriculum, involving the abolition of textbook reading, the substitution of great books, many of which were those used by Hutchins and Adler in their small seminar at Chicago. They were also determined to lay a far greater emphasis than was common on the seminar method of instruction, in which the college student becomes an active participant. Thus a curriculum of the general kind Hutchins advocated was adopted at St. John's.

Beginning in 1940 Hutchins and Adler embarked on a program to extend their own curriculum and teaching methods. The extension has assumed considerable dimensions. It has taken two directions. The first development was in the College of the University of Chicago. Under the able leadership of the dean, Dr. Clarence Faust, a new curriculum was introduced at the time the four-year program of study was set up in 1942. As a result the content of the courses, so far as reading matter is concerned, is of a better quality. Textbooks have largely disappeared. Discussions have increased. Attempts have been made, by means of seminars, to relate, interpret and integrate the subject matter of the natural sciences, the humanities and the social sciences.

The other direction taken by the reading program in great books is adult education. An attempt is being made to offer men and women in the United States the type of education that Hutchins offered himself. For the first time during the academic year 1940–41 a number of classes, modeled on the Hutchins-Adler class, were opened to the public. A year or two later, several of the trustees of the University of Chicago asked Hutchins and Adler to conduct a bi-weekly class for a small group of citizens. This group continues to meet; it has become something of a city institution. At about the same time, through the enterprise of William Benton, now United States senator, the University of Chicago entered into a special relationship with the *Encyclopedia Britannica,* of which Benton, while still vice-president of the University, became chairman of the board. The *Encyclopedia Britannica* set about to help popularize the "great books" by a venture in publishing. An independent corporation, *The Great Books Foundation,* was started, with Hutchins as chairman. Under its auspices, classes in reading and discussion were organized all over the country. It is estimated that at present there are some 35,000 participants. Since the inception of the program in 1947, there have been over 100,000 members.

Hutchins' voice had been raised more and more frequently on behalf of peace, at a time when the world embarked on total war. On the occasion of the German defeat he was the first prominent American to hold out his hand, and to advocate the treatment of the late enemy with the magnanimity and dignity which is in the best tradition of the Western spirit. He inaugurated a regular exchange of professors with the University of Frankfurt. He took a leading part in the organization of the Goethe Festival at Aspen, Colorado in 1949, to commemorate the two hundredth anniversary of the master's birth. It was the object of the assembly to stress the international character of the work of the mind and the spirit, to put this work in its rightful place above the national rivalries and the violence of this age of world wars.

During the Second World War he accepted an invitation to form a Committee on the Freedom of the Press. Behind the inquiry which this Committee conducted and the report which it published lay a profound concern over the way in which leading elements in the American press have ignored their intellectual and moral responsibilities in the effort to increase their circulation. The international anarchy of our time, and the decay of standards—intellectual, moral, and artistic—can be traced in part to this irresponsibility. The Hutchins Committee performed an immense service by calling attention to this evil which, while obvious, is usually accepted as inevitable.

The end of the Second World War, and the unexpectedly explosive nature of its conclusion, led one of the members of the University of Chicago faculty, G. A. Borgese, to draw Hutchins into an enterprise for world government. A committee was organized and, through the untiring efforts of Professor Borgese, a constitution was prepared, for a possible world commonwealth. Of all recent documents designed to make possible the creation of a single authority for the government of mankind, it is the most carefully and rationally worked out.

It may be suggested that the hope in this matter of a common humanity rests, however, not with any scheme of organization but with changes in men's hearts. These changes are perhaps impossible, but without them world government is not even a happy dream. It is more likely to be a realization of George Orwell's blueprint of 1984.

If one seeks a universal society of human beings, rather than an empire of slaves or of robots, is not its foundation to be sought in a common sense of a single mission in the interest of the human being, independent of nations, races and classes, but inspired by the Christian message of love and charity? As a members of the University of Chicago faculty, one is led back to some of the speeches Hutchins made in the thirties. Again and again Hutchins emphasized the limitations for the happiness of man, of societies whose *raison d'être* has become the continual multiplication of the volume of material goods. Such a purpose can never unite mankind. It is too empty; the more you have the more you want. It breeds hatred, because no individual or society is likely to be satisfied with its share.

"Getting on," he told the graduating students in 1935,

is the great American aspiration. And here the demoralizing part comes in; the way to get on is to be "safe," to be "sound," to be agreeable, to be inoffensive, to have no views on important matters not sanctioned by the majority, by your superiors, by your group. We are convinced that by knowing the right people, wearing the right clothes, saying the right things, holding the right opinions and thinking the right thoughts we shall all get on; we shall all get on to some motion picture paradise, surrounded by fine cars, refreshing drinks, and admiring ladies . . .

So I am worried about your morals. . . . Believe me, you are closer to the truth now than you will ever be again. . . . Do not let practical men tell you that you should surrender your ideals because they are impractical. Do not be reconciled to dishonesty, indecency, and brutality because gentlemanly ways have been discovered of being dishonest, indecent, and brutal.

Circumstances drew Hutchins more and more into the world whose goals he has continued to question. Circumstances drew him farther and farther from the small seminar room where he formed the "philosophy" which alarmed many of the University of Chicago faculty and some of the public. But he has never repudiated either his "philosophy" or the condition which led him to form it. It is a good philosophy. What is its future in the world? What future has the Hutchins' regime left it in the University of Chicago?

THE FUTURE

Here and there throughout the world a few voices have been raised during the twentieth century, as Hutchins' voice has been raised, to question the adequacy of natural science, of pragmatism, of positivism, of specialized scholarly investigations as means to the attainment of a greater measure of human felicity. It is possible that these voices are misguided. It is possible to hold, with young Professor Charles Morazé, in his recently-published *Essai sur la civilisation d'Occident,* that "it is not the future of science that divides humanity; it is the past, it is history." In any event, a good deal will depend on what kind of science the science of the future will be. We are confronted with abundant evidence of the destructive potentialities of science for human life and for what men have built. We are confronted also with the less obvious destructive potentialities for human personality of the stereotyped and mechanized production and consumption, which relieve men and women of the need for thought and of the capacity for joy. The aims and the methods of science have to be critically examined, and this can be done only with the help of the creative imagination, of the older and more venerable "science" of wisdom, and of the faith to which Lord Tennyson pays tribute in his stanza.

A graduate school or several graduate schools might contribute to this mission of inquiry. If such a school is to serve this purpose, it needs not only freedom in the external sense of freedom from the paraphernalia of the modern university; it needs also freedom to seek for truth in every subject matter and with the help of every method, not excluding the ways of the man of letters and of other artists and the ways of the man of faith. Beyond freedom it has the responsibility of drawing together subject matter that is separate, and of seeking a common purpose.

In his recent inaugural lecture as professor of social and moral science under the Committee on Social Thought, Professor Friedrich Hayek suggested that the influence of thought upon history in the *long run,* after a hundred years or more, can hardly be exaggerated. In writing for a small audience during the early nineteenth century, Stendhal was fond of predicting that he would be read in 1880. Out of the spirit of inquiry which, according to Plato, Socrates personified in his discussions, grew a perennial philosophy that is as fresh today as it was more than two thousand years ago.

It becomes evident, therefore, how overwhelmingly great are the responsibilities of a school which sets out to husband the resources of all the sciences, from the science of man in the humanistic sense, to sociology and chemistry, and the resources of philosophy, art, letters, and religion. These responsibilities could be discharged only if it were the object of such a school to serve the human being everywhere and always.

This is not the place to consider the nature of a better graduate school. The point to make is that the last twenty-two years have made *possible* at the University of Chicago work of this kind. Perhaps Hutchins' greatest service as a leader was the very position which threatened his popularity, his questioning of the nature of current scholarship and of the current purposes of universities. The appointment to the faculty of men of distinction who cut across departmental and divisional lines in their search for truth has provided something of the vision that is needed. Thus Professor Michael Polanyi, one of Hutchins' last appointments, comes to us as a distinguished philosopher after having started life as a doctor, and after having moved into a great academic career with his contributions to the science of chemistry.

It is easy to remark on the conflicting characteristics of the activities Hutchins has helped to set in motion at the University of Chicago. It is easy to suggest that the manner in which they are conducted will interfere with the pursuit of the goal they were intended to serve.

Again and again Hutchins has emphasized the limitations of modern science and of scientific methods as means of meeting "the sickness of an acquisitive society." Yet during his tenure of office, it was mainly the natural sciences that he strengthened. He took the initiative in starting the new institutes in the physical sciences. As

431

a result of his help in the development of such departments as physics, chemistry, geology, and astrophysics, of the medical school and the hospitals (which have been made more than in other universities an integral part of the scientific faculties) the position of the University of Chicago as a center for scientific research has been greatly improved in his time. Those who complain that he did less for other parts of the University, and that, by doing less, he went counter to his principles, should be reminded that the cause for this emphasis on scientific research lies mainly in the temper and the practice. It is not easy to make strong appointments where there is little strength to draw from, and the very weaknesses in the conventional study of the humanities and the social sciences, which Hutchins has rightly stressed, have made it exceedingly difficult to find the men to give a broad base to the reforms of graduate study which are needed. It is better to "starve" departments than to make conventional and bad appointments merely in order to show a large budget outside the natural sciences. This is especially the case if outside the natural sciences new units are established which put a premium on different, more human and more creative work. It is not without significance that one of the most trenchant recent criticisms of the overemphasis now placed on the natural sciences in our universities, and one of the most vigorous pleas for the future concentration of the free mind and imagination on the broader non-scientific pursuits, has come from one of Hutchins' happiest appointees in the natural sciences, from the distinguished metallurgist, Cyril Smith, the director of the new Institute of Metals.

Again we hear much criticism of the "go-getting methods" of the *Encyclopedia Britannica* and the *Great Books Foundation* in their campaigns for selling their wares. We hear also that the new College of the University of Chicago is resorting more and more to the reading of tiny extracts in place of books, to the administration of objective, mechanized examinations in place of serious essay questions which require thought and constructive writing. Some of these practices are indefensible and the methods do much harm. But here also we must not lose sight of what has been accomplished, nor underestimate the difficulties which stood in the way of getting anything helpful done at all. Years ago, when he was advocating the adoption of more serious reading and subject matter in connection with a general education, Hutchins told an audience of teachers:

> The real question is which side are you on? If you believe that the aim
> of general education is to teach students to make money; if you believe
> that the educational system should mirror the chaos of the world; if you
> think that we have nothing to learn from the past; if you think that the
> way to prepare students for life is to put them through little fake experi-
> ences inside or outside the classroom; if you think that education is in-